· 西北大学"双一流"建设项目资助
（Sponsored by First – class Universities and Academic Programs of Northwest University）

· 国家自然科学基金青年科学基金项目（72202176）

· 西北大学国家社科基金项目孵化计划（21XNFH028）

Economic Consequences of Abolishing A+H Share Mandatory Dual Audit System

A Study Based on Cost of Equity and Audit Quality

A+H股双重审计管制取消的经济后果

基于权益成本和审计质量的研究

张 睿◎著

中国经济出版社
CHINA ECONOMIC PUBLISHING HOUSE
北 京

图书在版编目（CIP）数据

A+H股双重审计管制取消的经济后果：基于权益成本和审计质量的研究／张睿著．--北京：中国经济出版社，2023.7

ISBN 978-7-5136-7382-2

Ⅰ.①A… Ⅱ.①张… Ⅲ.①上市公司-财务审计-研究-中国 Ⅳ.①F239.65

中国国家版本馆CIP数据核字（2023）第130062号

责任编辑 贺 静
责任印制 马小宾
封面设计 华子设计

出版发行 中国经济出版社
印 刷 者 北京艾普海德印刷有限公司
经 销 者 各地新华书店
开 本 710mm×1000mm 1/16
印 张 20.25
字 数 321千字
版 次 2023年7月第1版
印 次 2023年7月第1次
定 价 98.00元
广告经营许可证 京西工商广字第8179号

中国经济出版社 **网址** www.economyph.com **社址** 北京市东城区安定门外大街58号 **邮编** 100011
本版图书如存在印装质量问题，请与本社销售中心联系调换（联系电话：010-57512564）

PREFACE

China abolished the mandatory dual audit system for mainland Chinese companies cross-listed in Hong Kong (AH companies) in 2010. At the end of 2018, over 62% of AH companies continued to use the dual audit system. Arguably, the dual audit system contributes to ensuring auditor independence and improving corporate governance. It also helps provide investors accurate and complete financial information and facilitates mainland local audit firms to accumulate international business experience. The impacts of the deregulation of the mandatory dual audit system greatly concern investors (Sun, 2014) [1]. The dual audit system and its change have drawn persistent attention from researchers. A comprehensive investigation on the consequences of the deregulation of the mandatory dual audit system can enhance understanding of the influences of the dual audit system on financial reporting quality, audit quality and investor protection. Such an investigation can also provide important implications for future audit regime arrangements. However, existing studies are limited to investigating the audit-related consequences of this deregulation, with little attention paid to its economic consequences on the capital market. Moreover, studies focusing on the audit-related consequences have not deeply explored, through the empirical process, about a mechanism whose loss is likely to be the main driver of the decreased audit quality following companies' cancelation of the dual audit system. Given these limitations of previous literature, this study investigates the consequences of the deregulation of the mandatory dual audit system on the capital market and audit market.

The main conclusions and innovative work of this study are embodied in three aspects.

First, this study theoretically elaborates and empirically verifies that mandatory dual audit and voluntary dual audit can reduce the cost of equity to different extents, providing empirical evidence for the economic consequences of the deregulation of the mandatory dual audit system on the capital market. Previous studies focus on the audit-related consequences of the deregulation. These studies only compare companies that have the dual audit with those that do not or companies in the regulated period with those in the period after the deregulation. To the contrary, this study classifies dual audits into mandatory dual audit (before the deregulation) and voluntary dual audit (after the deregulation) and analyzes how both separately affect the cost of equity. The theory of commitment effect of complying with mandatory requirements and the theory of signaling effect of making voluntary choices are used as bases. This study derives the cost-of-equity measure from the GLS model (Gebhardt et al., 2001) [2] and effectively controls for the effects of the audited financial information in the empirical process. This study finds that companies have a lower cost of equity when they mandatorily have the dual audit than when they voluntarily use the dual audit; companies voluntarily using the dual audit have a lower cost of equity than companies using only the single audit in the same period. This study also finds that the effects of mandatory dual audit and voluntary dual audit in reducing the cost of equity are greater in companies with higher demand for equity financing and in companies with higher agency costs; the effect of mandatory (voluntary) dual audit in reducing the cost of equity is irreplaceable (substitutable) by alternative voluntary audit mechanisms. The theoretical elaborations and relevant results suggest that the deregulation of the mandatory dual audit system affects investors' perceptions and decisions. Such effects yield significant economic consequences on the capital market. These results not only enrich the research on the dual audit system and that on the cost of equity, but also enhance understanding of the differential albeit important roles that mandatory and voluntary dual audits separately play in the cost of equity. Furthermore, these results serve as new references for regulators and policy-makers to learn about the influences of the mandatory dual audit system on investor protection. To a certain extent, these results imply why a majority of AH companies persist using the dual audit system even years after the abolition of the mandatory requirement. The results warn regulators to cautiously reassess the costs and consequences of the deregulation of the mandatory dual audit system.

Second, this study verifies that the loss of the positive spillover effect from Hong Kong-based auditors is the main driver of the declining audit quality of companies canceling the dual audit. Although previous studies discuss the audit-related consequences of the deregulation of the mandatory dual audit system, they lack thorough analysis and verification of a mechanism that possibly drives the audit quality change under this policy change. This study measures audit quality by abnormal accruals, quantifies the spillover effect, and uses the analyses of changes. This study finds that companies keeping the dual audit system have higher audit quality when they are subject to a more positive spillover effect from Hong Kong-based auditors. This study also finds that after companies cancel the dual audit system, there is a positive association between the loss of the positive spillover effect from Hong Kong-based auditors and the decrease in audit quality. These findings provide initial evidence confirming that the positive spillover effect from Hong Kong-based auditors helps ensure the higher audit quality of companies keeping the dual audit, whereas the loss of this effect is primarily responsible for the decline in the audit quality of companies canceling the dual audit. Compared with previous studies, the analyses of this study effectively rule out the potential impacts of cross-listing, accounting standards convergence, auditors' shared reputational concern, and unobserved confounding factors. These analyses help to reach rigorous and robust conclusions. Extending the research on the dual audit system and that on audit quality, the results of this study contribute to further understanding of the indispensable role played by the positive spillover effect from Hong Kong-based auditors in the dual audit regime. Furthermore, these results confirm practitioners' concern on the likely damage to audit quality when companies cancel the dual audit and accept the single audits performed by mainland-based auditors. The results caution regulators and mainland local audit firms that becoming truly big and strong is a long and arduous task for local audit firms.

Third, this study develops a measurement method to directly and effectively capture the spillover effect from Hong Kong-based auditors in the dual audit process. Owing to its unobservability, this effect is limited to a description by previous studies, which restricts researchers to deeply exploring the audit-quality issues in the dual audit setting from this perspective. According to relevant rules and previous studies, this study assumes that the stricter H-share audits of a company are likely to have a positive spillover effect on the company's A-share audits by helping prevent earnings management in its A-share financial statements. Accordingly, a closer gap (shorter distance) between a company's H-share and A-share audit quality represents a larger constraint effect of the H-share audits performed by its Hong Kong-based auditor on the A-share audits performed by its mainland-based auditor, that is, a more effective positive spillover effect from the Hong Kong-based auditor. Following this rationale and from the perspective of earnings management, this study creates a proxy for the spillover effect based on the calculation of the distance between the H-share's and A-share's absolute abnormal accruals of a company keeping the dual audit. Compared with previous studies, this study intuitively presents the spillover effect from Hong Kong- to mainland-based auditors through the dual audit process by constructing a novel measure. This study takes an initial step toward relevant empirical work. It promotes the development of research on the dual audit system and that on audit quality.

前　言

我国于2010年取消了对A+H股公司的双重审计管制，然而截至2018年年底，依然有超过62%的A+H股公司继续采用双重审计。双重审计在保持审计师独立性、提升公司治理水平、保证投资者获取准确完整的会计信息、帮助本土会计师事务所积累经验等方面功不可没。双重审计管制取消会造成哪些影响，也是投资者十分关心的话题。与此同时，双重审计制度及其变迁也受到学术界广泛而持续的关注。对相关经济后果进行全面、深入的研究，有助于理解双重审计制度对财务报告质量、审计质量、投资者保护等的影响，为我国今后的审计制度安排提供重要启示。然而，现有文献基本局限于研究双重审计管制取消导致的审计方面的后果，没有充分关注该政策变化可能对资本市场造成的影响；此外，在现存关于双重审计管制取消的审计后果的研究中，缺乏对导致公司放弃双重审计后审计质量下降的内在机制的深入探索。基于此，本书旨在从资本市场和审计市场两方面探究双重审计管制取消的经济后果。

本书的主要结论及创新性工作体现在以下三个方面：

第一，本书理论解释并实证验证了强制双重审计和自愿双重审计能够不同程度地降低权益成本，为双重审计管制取消的资本市场后果提供了经验证据。以往研究局限于考察双重审计管制取消的审计后果，且多在双重审计管制取消前时段和取消后时段之间，或在双重审计公司和单一审计公司之间进行比较分析。本书则关注这一政策变更可能对资本市场造成的影响，并且将双重审计区分为强制双重审计和自愿双重审计两种形式，基于遵循效应理论和信号效应理论，分别分析二者对权益成本的影响机制；根据GLS模型测算权益成本指标，并在实证分析中有效控制已审财务信息的影响。本书发现，公司在管制取消前强制接受双重审计时的权益成本比在管制取消后自愿采用双重审计时的权益成本要低，而管制取消后自愿采用双重审计的公司的权益成本比仅接受单一审计的公司的权益成本要低。本书还发现，强制双重审计和自愿双重审计对权益成本的抑制作用在股权融资需求更强、代理成本更高的公司中更为显著；强制双重审计对权益成本的抑制作用未被其他自愿审计形式削弱，而自愿双重审计对权益成本的抑制作用则会被其他自愿审计形式替代。相关理论分析和实证结论表明，双重审计管制取消影响了投资者的认知和决策，进而对资本市场产生了实质性的经济后果，拓展了关于双重审计的研究和权益成本的文献，还有助于理解公司对于双重审计强制要求的遵循和对于双重审计的自愿选择分别对权益成本所起的作用。同时，这些结论为监管部门了解强制双重审计在投资者保护方面的作用提供了新的参考，也在一定程度上反映出大多数A+H股公司在管制取消多年后依然坚持双重审计的缘由，提醒有关部门对这一政策变更所带来的成本与后果进行审慎评估。

第二，本书深入揭示了香港审计师对内地审计师的积极溢出效应的丧失是导致公司放弃双重审计后审计质量下降的主要内在机制。以往研究虽然探讨了双重审计管制取消的审计后果，但欠缺对该政策变更中驱动审计质量发生变化的内在机制的分析与验证。以异常应计项目衡量审计质量，量化来自香港审计师的溢出效应，采用变化分析的方法，本书发现，来自香港审计师的溢出效应越积极，采用双重审计的公司审计质量越高；公司放弃双重审计后，这一积极溢出效应的丧失与审计质量的下降之间存在显著的正向关系。这些发现提供了新的经验证据，证实了来自香港审计师的积极溢出效应有助于维持较高的审计质量，而这一效应的丧失是公司放弃双重审计后审计质量受损的主要原因。相比前人研究，本书的分析有效排除了交叉上市、会计准则国际趋同、审计师共享同一品牌等因素以及不可观测因素的影响，得出了严谨而稳健的结论。研究结论丰富了双重审计的相关研究和审计质量的相关文献，有助于理解来自香港审计师的积极溢出效应在双重审计制度中所扮演的至关重要的角色。同时，这些研究结论证实了实务界对于审计质量可能因公司放弃双重审计而受损的疑虑，有助于提醒监管部门和会计师事务所注意，实现本土事务所真正做大做强依然任重而道远。

第三，本书建立了一套直接、有效的测度方法，以度量双重审计过程中来自香港审计师的溢出效应。由于这一效应的不可观测性，现有文献对此多限于文字论述，限制了学者们从这一角度出发深入探究双重审计背景下的审计质量问题。结合前人论述和相关规定，本书认为，由香港审计师负责的、更为严格的H股报表审计能够抑制一家公司A股财务报表中的盈余管理，从而对该公司由内地审计师负责的A股报表审计产生积极的溢出效应；一家采用双重审计的公司的A股与H股审计质量之间的差距越小，反映出H报表审计对A股报表审计的约束作用越强，即来自香港审计师的溢出效应越积极。基于此，本书从盈余管理的角度入手，在计算采用双重审计的公司A股和H股报表异常应计项目绝对值之间差距的基础上，形成来自香港审计师的溢出效应的代理变量。相比以往研究，本书通过构建新的变量，较为直观地呈现了香港审计师通过双重审计过程对内地审计师发挥的溢出效应，填补了现有研究在实证工作方面的缺失，有助于推动双重审计相关文献和审计质量相关研究的发展。

CONTENTS

（简体中文版）目录

1 Introduction

The dual-audit and dual-reporting system (dual audit system) plays an important role in increasing auditor independence, improving corporate governance, and enhancing financial information quality. Accounting and auditing researchers pay constant attention to research topics about this audit system and its change. This study investigates the economic consequences of the deregulation of the mandatory dual audit system on the capital market and audit market. This chapter first introduces the practical and theoretical background of the study. Following, the research questions are put forward with the current situation in practice and the limitations of the existing literature as bases. The potential contributions and practical significance of this research are also elaborated. Finally, this chapter describes the research contents, methods and framework.

1.1 Research Background

1.1.1 Practical Background

1.1.1.1 Emergence and Development of AH Companies

Alongside the deepening of economic globalization, international equity financing has experienced rapid development since the 1980s. Cross-listing, as an important way of international equity financing, has attracted much attention in academia (Stulz, 1999; Lang et al., 2003)[3,4]. With the constant development of China's economy, many mainland companies have been listed on overseas exchanges to raise capital. As a special administrative region of China, Hong Kong has a more internationalized and free capital market with sound regulatory systems than mainland China. Thus, Hong Kong has a good market guarantee for companies to finance. Nevertheless, the Hong Kong market and mainland market are similar to each other in terms of some rules and regulations, which, to an extent, facilitates mainland companies to list in Hong Kong. As a result, the Hong Kong market has become the prevailing choice for mainland companies to list abroad. In 1993, mainland Chinese company Tsingtao Brewery Co. , Ltd. (Stock Code: 600600. SH; 00168. HK) was cross-listed on the A-share market in mainland China and the H-share market in Hong Kong as the first "AH company". ① Since then, a growing number of mainland companies have tried entering the Hong Kong market.

Mainland companies play an important role in the Hong Kong market. According to "Hong Kong Exchanges and Clearing Limited (HKEx) Fact Book 2018", there were 2315 companies listed on the Hong Kong market at the end of 2018. Among them, 1146 were mainland companies, accounting for 49. 50% of the total. The market capitalization (turnover value) of mainland companies was 20193 (15480) billion HKD, accounting for 67. 51% (79. 55%) of the market total (equity turnover). Among the mainland companies listed in Hong Kong, there were 243 H-share companies at the end of 2018, comprising 10. 50% of total companies listed in Hong Kong. The market capitalization of H-share companies made up 19. 98% of the equity total. Accordingly, H-share companies have occupied an important place in the Hong Kong market. The number of AH companies has been increasing constantly since the cross-listing of Tsingtao Brewery. At the end of 2018, 109 companies were cross-listed on the A-share and the H-share markets. Figure 1-1 illustrates the growth of AH companies from 1993 to 2018 on the basis of the data collected from the China Stock Market & Accounting Research (CSMAR) database. Listed in mainland China and Hong Kong and increasing in number, AH companies have incited the interest of many Chinese researchers on institutional environment, institution changes, and relevant accounting and auditing issues (Ke et al. , 2015; Tian et al. , 2017)[5, 6].

---

① A shares refer to the common shares issued by a company registered and listed in mainland China. They are traded by domestic institutions, organizations, or individuals with par values indicated in Renminbi (see https: //baike. baidu. com/item/A%E8%82%A1/86002?fr=aladdin). H shares refer to the shares issued by a company registered in mainland China and listed in Hong Kong. They are traded by overseas investors with par values indicated in Hong Kong dollar. Institutional investors in mainland China can also directly trade H shares (see https: //baike. baidu. com/item/H%E8%82%A1/273519?fr=aladdin#2).

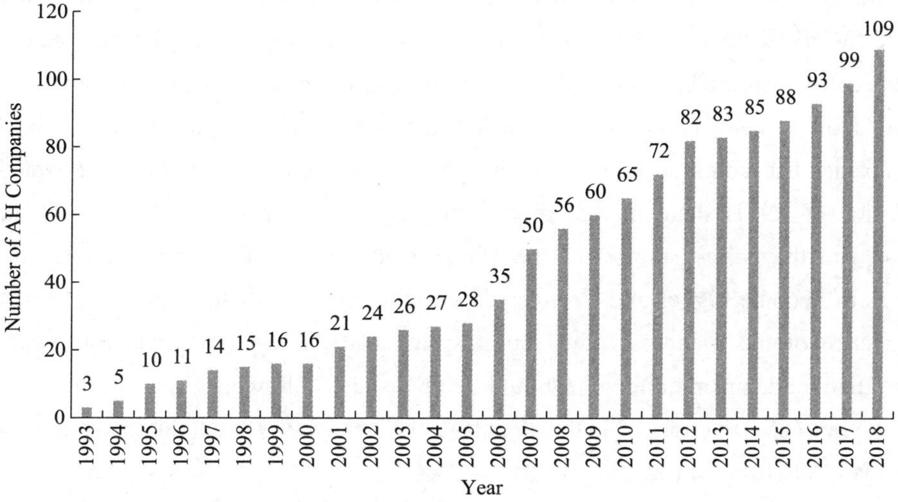

Figure 1-1 Number of AH Companies in 1993-2018

Data source: CSMAR database.

1.1.1.2 Persistent Existence of Dual Audit After Deregulation

Since the establishment of the H-share market in 1993, regulators have imposed the dual audit system on AH companies as a mandatory requirement. In the early 1990s, substantial differences existed between the Chinese Accounting Standards (CAS) and the International Financial Reporting Standards (IFRS) [or the Hong Kong Financial Reporting Standards (HKFRS)]. Thus, the information demands of Chinese and international investors largely differed from each other. In addition, mainland local audit firms were at the initial stage of their development and considered as having relatively low audit quality (MOF, 2009a)[7]. Under this circumstance, an AH company was required to adopt the dual audit system [specifically, hiring a mainland-based auditor to audit and issue an audit report for the A-share financial statements prepared based on the CAS and a Hong Kong-based auditor to audit and issue an audit report for the H-share financial statements prepared based on the IFRS (or HKFRS) each year]. The objective is to improve accounting information credibility and satisfy diversified information demands of Chinese and international investors.

In 2006, mainland China harmonized its accounting standards with the IFRS. The release of the new CAS by the Ministry of Finance (MOF) symbolized the CAS's convergence (equivalence) with the IFRS (HKFRS). Subsequent revisions on the CAS are on the road to achieving continuous and full convergence with the IFRS (MOF, 2010a) [8]. The convergence (and equivalence) of accounting standards between mainland China and Hong Kong, in turn, led regulators to consider that the dual audit system is no longer needed for most AH companies, although AH companies can continue to use the dual audit voluntarily. In addition, the strategic position of the H-share market in the internationalization of mainland local audit firms and the policy support of the Chinese government for mainland local audit firms to become bigger and stronger drove regulators to consider the futility of the existence of the mandatory dual audit system. Taken together, regulators deemed that the mandatory requirement should be abolished. Following a series of efforts by regulators (see Section 3. 1 for details), the mandatory dual audit system was officially abolished in 2010.

Continuing the dual audit system or not has become a voluntary choice for an AH company since the deregulation of the mandatory dual audit system in 2010 (HKEx, 2009) [9]. The company only needs to retain the A-share audits if it considers using the dual audit system unnecessary. Regulators expected most AH companies to follow this policy change and dismiss their Hong Kong-based auditors. However, this expectation was not the case in reality. For example, the news showed that AH companies that canceled the dual audit system were only 10% to 20% of total H-share companies in the initial years after the deregulation of the mandatory dual audit system. This percentage was quite below the original expectation and made some practitioners doubt the achievements of this policy change. ① Figure 1 – 2 illustrates the number and proportion of companies that continue to keep the dual audit system in AH companies from 2010 to 2018 based on the data collected from the CSMAR database. Only 1 firm responded to the abolition of the mandatory dual audit system in the year of the official announcement (i. e., 2010). Despite showing a generally declining trend, the proportion of companies keeping the dual audit system accounted for 62. 39% (68/109) of AH companies even 8 years after the deregulation. This figure, as well as the practical news, suggests that the majority of AH companies persistently use the dual audit system in the absence of the mandatory requirement. The deregulation of the

① See the news reported by Sina Finance in 2011 and 2012 (http://finance. sina. com. cn/stock/hkstock/hkstocknews/20110418/08099706108. shtml; http://finance. sina. com. cn/stock/hkstock/hkstocknews/20121217/130814026393. shtml).

mandatory dual audit system does not mean the disappearance of the dual audit system. The implementation of this policy change is not as successful as regulators originally expected.

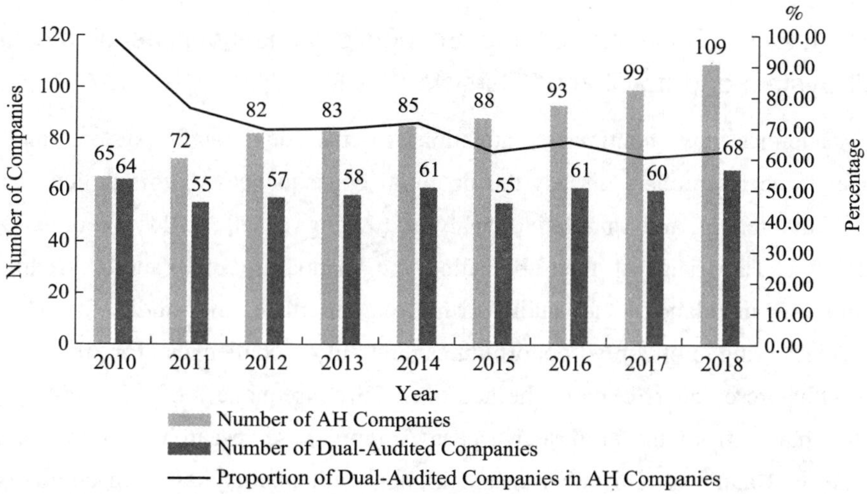

Figure 1-2 Number and Proportion of Dual-Audited Companies in AH Companies After Deregulation of Mandatory Dual Audit System (2010-2018)

Data source: CSMAR database.

The contributions of the dual audit system cannot be denied. These include ensuring auditor independence, improving corporate governance, providing accurate and complete financial information for investors, and accumulating international business experience for mainland local audit firms (Sun, 2014) [1]. Even after the abolition of the mandatory requirement, the dual audit system continues to comprise a large proportion of AH companies. Therefore, the dual audit system has inherent rationality and value for academic research compared with the traditional single audit. In addition, sufficient variation in audit systems adopted by A-share companies (including AH companies) provides me a good opportunity to study issues about the dual audit system, specifically, the economic consequences of the deregulation of the mandatory dual audit system in the Chinese market. Issues such as whether AH companies change their audit systems and whether their audit quality is affected have become investors' major concerns since the deregulation (Sun, 2014) [1]. An in-depth investigation on the economic consequences of the deregulation of the mandatory dual audit system can enhance understanding of the influences of this audit system on financial reporting quality, audit quality and investors' perceptions and decisions. Such an investigation can provide regulators and policy-makers useful references for future audit regime arrangements in China.

1. 1. 2 Theoretical Background

1. 1. 2. 1 Research on the Economic Consequences of the Dual Audit System and Its Change Persists

Academics pay continuous attention to the dual audit system and its change. Some researchers discuss the potential consequences of this policy change through theoretical and qualitative analyses (Zheng et al., 2011; Weng et al., 2012)[10, 11]. They suggest that abolishing the mandatory dual audit system and encouraging mainland local audit firms to undertake the audits of H-share companies bring not only opportunities but also challenges for these audit firms. Other researchers explore the audit-related consequences of this audit system and its change from the empirical aspect. Among these researchers, some suggest that the dual audit system helps ensure higher audit quality based on comparisons among A-share listed companies (including domestic-listed-only A-share companies and AH companies) (Ke et al., 2015; Tian et al., 2017; Lin et al., 2014; Wang, 2014)[5, 6, 12, 13]. Other researchers focus on the effect of this policy change on market share and audit fees (Sun, 2013)[14]. Wang and Xin (2011)[15] show the differences in motivation between Big 4 and non-Big 4 auditors when performing the dual audit. The abolition of the mandatory dual audit system for AH companies in 2010 does not mean that the dual audit system has disappeared since then. Zhong and Zhang (2019)[16] suggest that a deep investigation on this audit system contributes to enhancing understanding of its influences and providing useful references for audit system arrangements in the future.

1. 1. 2. 2 Research on the Cost of Equity Is Constantly Enriched

As a major reflection of investors' expectation and evaluation of risks on their investments (Modigliani and Miller, 1959; Solomon, 1963)[17, 18], researchers have paid considerable attention to the cost of equity for decades. Consequently, theoretical and empirical research on the cost of equity is rich and constantly growing. Some scholars make progress on how to measure the cost of equity through theoretical and model analyses (Gebhardt et al., 2001; Sharpe, 1964; Feltham et al., 1995; Gordon et al., 1997; Claus et al., 2001; Easton, 2004; Ohlson et al., 2005)[2, 19–24]. Other scholars explore the determinants of the cost of equity based on theoretical and empirical studies. The literature reaches a consensus that a strong institutional environment, for example, sound legal system and strong investor protection, lowers the cost of equity (Levitt, 1998; Hail et al., 2005; Himmelberg et al., 2004; Jiang et al., 2008; Xiao et al., 2008; Hong and Chen, 2016)[25-30]. Moreover, the cost of equity can be affected by governmental intervention, and the impact of governmental intervention varies with factors, like ownership property (Xu and Lv, 2007)[31], political connection (Xiao et al., 2010; Zhao et al., 2012)[32, 33], earnings management level (Wang, 2013)[34], and financial ecological environment (Zou and Yang, 2014)[35]. Firm size is another important determinant of the cost of equity, although no uniform conclusion on the direction of the impact has been reached. Some researchers hold that firm size is negatively associated with the cost of equity (Botosan, 1997; Botosan and Plumlee, 2002; Cao et al., 2012)[36-38], whereas other researchers obtain opposite findings (Tian et al., 2003; Ye et al., 2004)[39, 40]. Previous studies suggest that leverage (or debt ratio) also affects the cost of equity, although their conclusions are not totally consistent (Modigliani et al., 1959; Tian et al., 2003; Fama et al., 1992; Richardson et al., 2001; Chen et al., 1999; Tang et al., 2005; Jin, 2008)[17, 39, 41-45]. Researchers also find that book-to-market ratio has a significant impact on the cost of equity. Some scholars show that this impact is positive (Fama et al., 1992; Berk et al., 1999; Cheng et al., 2006; Lei et al., 2014)[41, 46-48], whereas other scholars find it negative (Ye et al., 2004)[40]. Corporate governance is suggested to significantly affect the cost of equity, and scholars draw similar conclusions that strong corporate governance helps reduce the cost of equity (Cheng et al., 2006; Ashbaugh et al., 2004; Huang, 2005; Mazzotta et al., 2014; Jiang, 2009; Jiang et al., 2009; Yan, 2011; Lai et al., 2016; Ke, 2017)[47, 49-56]. Disclosure quality is yet another determinant of the cost of equity suggested by the previous literature. Most studies agree with the negative relationship between disclosure quality and the cost of equity (Richardson et al., 2001; Cheng et al, 2006; Diamond et al., 1991; Mangena et al., 2016; Wang et al., 2004; Zeng et al., 2006; Shen et al., 2010; Li et al., 2016; Zhou et al., 2016)[42, 47, 57-63]. Other studies demonstrate that no significant or even a positive relationship exists (Botosan et al., 2002; Kim, 1993; Yang et al., 2012; Li et al., 2013; Che et al., 2016; Zhang et al., 2017)[37, 64-68]. Accounting conservatism can also affect the cost of equity, with most findings supporting a negative association between them (Easley and O'Hara, 2004; Suijs, 2008; Lafond et al., 2008; Lara et al., 2011; Guay et al., 2018; Wang et al., 2013; Lu et al., 2016; Li et al., 2016; Wang et al., 2016; Ma et al., 2017)[69-78]. Audit quality is suggested to be another important determinant of the cost of equity by previous studies, and high audit quality contributes to reducing the cost of equity (Choi et al., 2014; Houqe et al., 2017; Yu et al., 2008; Wang et al., 2009; Chen et al., 2011; Li et al., 2017; Zhu et al., 2017)[79-85]. The cost of equity is also affected by liquidity. Most researchers find that the cost of equity is lower when stock liquidity is higher (Amihud et al., 1986; Jacoby et al., 2000; Saad et al., 2017; Wang et al., 2012; Yang, 2016)[86-90], whereas a few Chinese researchers have contrary findings (Shen et al., 2005)[91]. In addition, market risk (beta) is suggested as a major factor that determines the cost of equity (Sharpe, 1964; Fama et al., 1973; Ross, 1976)[19, 92, 93]. However, this factor shows different impacts on the cost of equity in the Chinese market in various studies (Shen et al., 2005; Wang, 2013; Wang et al., 2014)[91, 94, 95].

Overall, the cost of equity is closely related to many participants in the capital market as a major concern in companies' financing activities. Previous studies propose a variety of measurements on the cost of equity and a wealth of research on its determinants. I assume that after the deregulation of the mandatory dual audit system, investors may perceive information risk to increase and thereby require higher risk compensation (rate of return) than before. However, existing studies have not yet paid enough attention to the economic consequences of this policy change or this potential important determinant of the cost of equity.

1.1.2.3 Research on Audit Quality Is Popular and Enduring

As an important mechanism to mitigate information asymmetry, alleviate agency conflicts and protect investors, the quality of independent auditing lies at the core of accounting and auditing research (DeFond and Zhang, 2014)[96]. Audit quality has been a hot topic in academia for nearly 40 decades, with a large volume of relevant theoretical and empirical research. Audit quality jointly depends on an auditor's competence and independence (DeFond and Zhang, 2014; DeAngelo, 1981a; Watts and Zimmerman, 1983; Palmrose, 1986; Teoh and Wong, 1993; Lee and Gu, 1998; Francis, 2011; Zhang and Zhang, 1997; Feng, 2002)[96-104]. Similar to the cost of equity, researchers propose various methods to measure audit quality (DeFond and Zhang, 2014)[96]. Prior studies suggest that audit firm size is an important determinant of audit quality. Most researchers suggest a positive relationship between audit firm size and audit quality (DeAngelo, 1981a; Dopuch and Simunic, 1982; Firth and Smith, 1992; DeFond et al., 1999; Wu and Li, 2006; Lin and Wang, 2013; Wu et al., 2015; Lu et al., 2017) [97, 105–111]. Others have different opinions (Wu et al., 2005; Guo, 2011) [112, 113]. Researchers generally find that auditor industry expertise also has a significant positive impact on audit quality (Owhoso et al., 2002; Krishnan, 2003; Liu et al, 2010; Xie and Sun, 2010; Fan et al., 2013) [114–118]. By contrast, others draw opposite conclusions in the Chinese setting (Cai and Xian, 2007) [119]. Additionally, audit firm internal governance is suggested to significantly affect audit quality (Muzatko et al., 2004; Firth et al., 2012; Zhu, 2013; Chen, 2014; Liu and Wang, 2014; Liu et al., 2015; Huang et al., 2017) [120–126]. From the audit client's side, agency conflicts of clients have a significant impact on audit quality, that is, severer agency conflicts drive their demand for higher audit quality (Chow, 1982; Francis and Wilson, 1988; Lennox, 2005a; Blouin et al., 2007; Francis et al., 2009; Guedhami et al., 2009; Wang et al., 2006; Gao and Zhang, 2011; Qi and Han, 2016) [127–135]. Moreover, corporate governance of clients significantly influences audit quality. Many findings support that clients with stronger corporate governance demand higher audit quality (Carcello and Neal, 2000; Beasley and Petroni, 2001; Beasley and Salterio, 2001; Stewart and Kent, 2006; Engel et al., 2010; Cassell et al., 2012; Xiao, 2006; Yu and Liu, 2007; Shen et al., 2009; Pan and Wen, 2017) [136–145]. Nonetheless, a few studies have different findings (Ye et al., 2015) [146]. The relationship between auditors and clients is also suggested to play an important role in determining audit quality. For example, literature suggests that auditor tenure affects audit quality. Some studies note that long auditor tenure helps increase audit quality (Loebbecke et al., 1989; Petty and Cuganesan, 1996; Johnson et al., 2002; Geiger and Raghunandan, 2002; Myers et al., 2003; Litt et al., 2014; Xia et al., 2005; Chen and Xia, 2006; Liu and Tang, 2009) [147–155], whereas other studies argue that long auditor tenure adversely affects audit quality (DeAngelo, 1981b; Shockley, 1981; Arrunada and Cá ndido, 1997; Arel et al., 2005; Carey and Simnett, 2006; Ye et al., 2011; Liu, 2006; Jiang and Li, 2011; Li et al., 2014) [156–164]. Mixed evidence is also found (Yu and Li, 2003; Dong and Zhang, 2010; Shen et al., 2010) [165–167]. Another determinant of audit quality relevant to the relationship between auditors and clients is client importance. Some researchers argue that client importance has an adverse impact on audit quality (DeAngelo, 1981b; Choi et al., 2010; Kanagaretnam et al., 2010;

Hossain et al., 2016; Zhang, 2017; Lu et al., 2012; Cao et al., 2012; Jia and Li, 2015; Xie et al., 2017; Yang and Yang, 2019) [156, 168-176], whereas others hold the contrary viewpoint or find mixed evidence (Stice, 1991; Bonner et al., 1998; Zhang, 1999; Reynolds and Francis, 2000; Gaver and Paterson, 2007; Fung et al., 2016; Fang et al., 2004; Yu et al., 2008; Chen et al., 2010; Liu, 2012; Li and Liu, 2013) [177-187]. In addition, private relationships between auditors and clients are suggested to affect audit quality. In particular, many studies suggest that private relationships, such as employment relationships (Dowdell and Krishnan, 2004; Menon and Williams, 2004; Lennox, 2005b; Wu, 2006; Liu, 2011; Liu and Zhang, 2014; Chen et al., 2015; Wu et al., 2015) [188-195] and social ties (Guan et al., 2016; He et al., 2017) [196, 197], adversely affect audit quality. A few studies draw different conclusions (Geiger et al., 2005; Geiger and North, 2006; Baber et al., 2014; Deng et al., 2017) [198-201]. Scholars also find that external environmental factors affect audit quality, such as institutional environment (Lang et al., 2003; Ke et al., 2015; Tian et al., 2017; Khurana and Raman, 2004; Huijgen and Lubberink, 2005; Choi et al., 2008; Francis and Wang, 2008; Francis et al., 2011; Wang and Tan, 2010; Xin and Wang, 2010) [4-6, 202-208], litigation risk (Feng and Liang, 2010; Zhai and Liao, 2011) [209, 210], regulatory risk (Song and Xiao, 2012; Liu, 2016; Huang and Li, 2016) [211-213], and media coverage (Zhou and Yao, 2015; Zhang et al., 2016; Wu and Li, 2017) [214-216].

Overall, as an enduring hot topic in accounting and auditing research, audit quality has been measured through many proxies from different aspects, such as earnings quality, audit opinion, earnings restatements and audit fees. A variety of studies on its determinants exist, and research on audit quality is ongoing. Specific to the research setting of this study, previous studies assume a mechanism through which the dual audit system ensures high audit quality from the perspective of the institutional environment faced by auditors (Ke et al., 2015) [5]. However, the mechanism remains an abstract description without any measurement or tests on its validation.

1.1.2.4 Limitations of Existing Literature

Taken together, academics pay continuous attention to the consequences of the dual audit system and its change and have obtained enlightening research findings. However, research on this topic may have limitations such as the ones listed below.

(1) The existing research on the mandatory dual audit system for AH companies and its abolition pays attention only to the audit-related consequences, such as audit quality, audit market share and audit fees. Although the mandatory dual audit system was officially abolished in 2010, a remarkable proportion of AH companies choose to use this system after this deregulation, as shown in Figure 1-2. The abolition of the mandatory dual audit system does not mean that the dual audit system has disappeared since 2010. Further investigation on this audit system can explain its influences on financial reporting quality, audit quality and investor protection, and provide useful references for audit system arrangements in the future. Under this circumstance, learning about whether and to what extent the deregulation of the mandatory dual audit system has consequences on the capital market is of academics and practitioners' interest. However, evidence on the capital market-related consequences of this policy change, such as the cost of equity, is limited.

(2) The existing research on the dual audit system for AH companies reaches a consensus that the AH companies using the dual audit have higher audit quality compared with other A-share listed companies that do not use the dual audit (including non-cross-listed A-share companies and some AH companies). Based on this consensus, it can be implied that AH companies potentially experience an audit quality deterioration after they cancel the dual audit system. However, people cannot rule out the possibility that the consistent finding in the existing research is driven by systematic differences between cross-listings and non-cross-listings.

(3) The existing research on the dual audit system for AH companies provides a detailed explanation of the positive spillover effect from Hong Kong- to mainland-based auditors in the dual audit process (Ke et al., 2015)[5]. From the perspective of the institutional environment faced by the engaged auditors, this positive spillover is suggested to serve as an important mechanism by which the dual audit system ensures high audit quality. Nonetheless, this positive spillover effect stays an abstract description. The narratives of this effect have not yet been translated into any valid empirical measure. Whether and to what extent the existence (loss) of this positive spillover affects the audit quality of companies keeping (canceling) the dual audit system remain open questions.

(4) The existing research on the cost of equity puts forward measurements and main determinants of the cost of equity, providing solid foundations for the design of the empirical research on the cost of equity in this study. Nonetheless, while independent auditing is suggested to have a significant impact on the cost of equity by previous literature, it is underexplored whether a change in a particular audit

system, for example, the deregulation of the mandatory dual audit system, can induce any variation in the cost of equity. Based on my research questions in Section 1. 2. 1, I assume that investors may perceive information risk to increase and thereby require higher risk compensation (rate of return) after the deregulation of the mandatory dual audit system. However, previous literature has paid limited attention to this factor that potentially affects the cost of equity in the Chinese capital market.

(5) The existing research on audit quality proposes various measurements and suggests main determinants of audit quality, serving as useful references for the design of the empirical research on audit quality in this study. Nonetheless, specific to the audit quality-related issue investigated in this study, prior studies have largely overlooked how to empirically measure and test the mechanism [as stated in (3)] by which the dual audit system ensures high audit quality from the perspective of the institutional environment.

1. 2 Research Questions and Research Significance

1. 2. 1 Research Questions

Based on the discussions in Section 1. 1, the H-share market acts as an important channel for the mainland Chinese companies to become internationalized, and the number of AH-share cross-listings keeps increasing. In addition, the abolition of the mandatory dual audit system for AH companies does not mean that the dual audit system has disappeared since then. After the deregulation, changes in AH companies' audit systems and in audit quality are of investors' major concern (Sun, 2014) [1]. Academics constantly pay attention to this audit system and its change after the deregulation. A comprehensive investigation on the dual audit system can deepen understanding of this audit system's influences on financial reporting quality, audit quality and investor protection. Such an investigation can provide also helpful references for subsequent audit system arrangements. However, existing studies are limited to investigating the audit-related consequences of this deregulation, with little attention paid to other economic consequences, such as those on the Chinese capital market. Moreover, studies focusing on the audit quality-related issues have not deeply explored, through the empirical process, a mechanism whose existence (loss) may be the main driver of the higher (decreased) audit quality when companies keep (cancel) the dual audit system. Given these potential limitations of the previous literature, this study investigates the economic consequences of the deregulation of the mandatory dual audit system on the capital market and audit market. In particular, this study proposes the following main research questions:

First, in terms of the consequences of the deregulation on the capital market, do companies have a lower cost of equity when they mandatorily have the dual audit before the deregulation than when they voluntarily use the dual audit after the deregulation?

As mentioned in Section 1. 1. 2, existing studies focus mainly on the audit-related consequences of the deregulation of the mandatory dual audit system. However, does this deregulation have effects on the capital market by affecting the cost of equity? In addition, researchers generally compare companies having the dual audit with those not doing so or compare companies in the regulated period with companies in the period after the deregulation. Little research has considered dividing companies having the dual audit into those that are required to use the dual audit before the deregulation and those that choose to use the dual audit after the deregulation. Lacking this consideration, researchers make few comparisons between them or between the latter and companies not having the dual audit in the same period. Do the dual audit in the regulated period and the dual audit after the deregulation have differential impacts on the cost of equity? Rock (2002)[217], Stulz (2009)[218], and Cheng et al. (2013)[219] note that a company's compliance with a mandatory requirement with a powerful enforcement system is regarded by investors as a promise that is made on an ex-ante basis and hard to reverse. As a consequence, investors' concerns on management's self-serving behavior that would damage shareholders' interests can be relieved by such a perceived commitment. This commitment device role of complying with mandatory requirements can reduce agency costs, information asymmetry, and thereby the cost of equity (Monahan, 2006; Hail, 2011)[220, 221]. Based on this argument, compliance with the mandatory dual audit requirement can serve as a mechanism for companies to credibly commit, on an ex-ante basis, to be under the monitoring of two audit firms and disclose two sets of audited financial statements. As a result, companies' compliance with the mandatory dual audit requirement can relieve investors' concerns on management's self-serving behavior. Moreover, it is costly for companies that are required to use the dual audit to breach this requirement, given the powerful enforcement systems, especially those in the Hong Kong market. Contrary to complying with the mandatory dual audit requirement, voluntarily choosing the dual audit after the deregulation is self-serving because this choice allows companies to evaluate the possible consequences before making a dual audit decision. Moreover, for companies choosing to keep the dual audit, whether their use of this audit system will be sustained in the future is questionable because they can freely opt out without any threat of punishment from regulators. Therefore, I expect that the role of complying with the mandatory dual audit requirement in maintaining a lower cost of equity cannot be completely replaced by voluntarily choosing the dual audit. Based on this expectation, this study first investigates the economic consequences of the deregulation on the capital market by analyzing whether the cost of equity for complying with the mandatory dual audit requirement before the deregulation is lower than that for voluntarily choosing the dual audit after the deregulation.

Second, in terms of the consequences of the deregulation on the capital market, do companies that voluntarily choose the dual audit after the deregulation have a lower cost of equity than companies that use only the single audit in the same period?

After investigating the effect of mandatory dual audit relative to voluntary dual audit on the cost of equity, this study then analyzes the effect of voluntary dual audit relative to single audit on the cost of equity. Melumad and Thoman (1990) [222] and Lennox and Pittman (2011) [223] posit that a company can voluntarily incur audit costs to exploit a signaling mechanism in the absence of mandatory audit requirements. Based on this signaling theory, voluntarily choosing the dual audit, which incurs higher audit and disclosure costs than using only the single audit, can convey incremental information about a company's good properties over and above the audited financial information. Such properties include high quality, low risk and profitable prospects. As a result, voluntarily choosing the dual audit can generate a positive signal to distinguish companies doing so from those using only the single audit. This signal can help companies that voluntarily choose the dual audit win investors' preference and raise external equity capital at lower costs. Accordingly, after the deregulation of the mandatory dual audit system, I expect that voluntarily choosing the dual audit is more effective than using only the single audit in reducing the cost of equity. Based on this expectation, this study then investigates the economic consequences of the deregulation on the capital market by analyzing whether the cost of equity for voluntarily choosing the dual audit after the deregulation is lower than that for using only the single audit in the same period.

Third, in terms of the consequences of the deregulation on the audit market, is the audit quality decline following companies' cancelation of the dual audit mainly driven by the loss of a positive spillover effect from Hong Kong- to mainland-based auditors?

After understanding the consequences of the deregulation on the capital market, this study analyzes the consequences on the audit market by focusing on companies canceling the dual audit and their comparison with those keeping the dual audit after the deregulation. As mentioned in Section 1. 1. 2, the existing literature concurs that the audit quality of companies not having the dual audit is lower than that of companies having the dual audit. It can be inferred from this consensus that canceling the dual audit possibly causes an audit quality deterioration for companies. Based on Ke et al. (2015) [5], the loss of a positive spillover effect from Hong Kong- to mainland-based auditors through the dual audit process is likely to be a reasonable explanation for this audit quality deterioration. In particular, the institutional environment in Hong Kong is stronger than that in mainland China, resulting in higher independence and audit quality of Hong Kong-based auditors than that of mainland-based auditors. Moreover, the A-share and H-share financial statements of a company should be substantially consistent with each other according to the rules and regulations. With these situations and requirements, an indirect positive spillover effect may exist from the Hong Kong-based auditor to the mainland-based auditor of a company through the dual process. That is, the exemplary audit work, outcomes, and potential monitoring of the Hong Kong-based auditor can positively influence the mainland-based auditor and make it more difficult for the latter to compromise on audit quality. As a result, audit quality is likely to be guaranteed when companies keep the dual audit, whereas canceling the dual audit is likely to forego the positive spillover effect from Hong Kong-based auditors and impair audit quality. The above elaboration about the potential positive spillover effect from Hong Kong-based auditors in the dual audit process is theoretically comprehensible. However, how should this mechanism be measured empirically? Do companies that keep the dual audit have higher audit quality when they are subject to a more positive spillover effect? Does the loss of this positive spillover effect drive the decline in audit quality of companies that cancel the dual audit? Based on these unresolved issues, this study investigates the economic consequences of the deregulation of the mandatory dual audit system on the audit market by constructing a novel measure of the positive spillover effect from Hong Kong-based auditors and deeply exploring the role that the loss of this effect plays in the audit quality deterioration following companies' cancelation of the dual audit.

1. 2. 2 Research Significance

1. 2. 2. 1 Theoretical Significance

First, this study adds to the literature on the dual audit system by taking into account the economic consequences of the deregulation of the mandatory dual audit system on the Chinese capital market. While previous research focuses on the audit-related consequences of the deregulation of the mandatory dual audit system, this study pays attention to the consequences of this policy change on the capital market and considers the impact of mandatory dual audit and that of voluntary dual audit separately. By investigating their impacts on the cost of equity, this study contributes to developing comprehensive understanding of the economic consequences of the deregulation of the mandatory dual audit system. This study also enriches the perspectives and contents of research on the dual audit system. The results suggest that in addition to the audit-relevant outcomes studied by previous research, the deregulation of the mandatory dual audit system affects investors' perceptions and decisions, and thereby yields significant economic consequences on the Chinese capital market.

Second, this study enriches the literature on the cost of equity by taking the variation in audit systems into consideration as a determinant of the cost of equity in the Chinese setting. While previous studies conclude that financial statements audit contributes to lowering the cost of equity for companies, audit is usually valued for its role in providing independent assurance of financial information reliability (DeFond and Zhang, 2014; Clatworthy and Peel, 2013; Hay and Cordery, 2018)[96, 224, 225]. Limited attention has been paid to whether the variation in audit system affects the cost of equity, regardless of the assurance levels provided by the engaged auditors. With the assurance value of audits effectively controlled in the empirical process, this study compares mandatory dual audit before the deregulation with voluntary dual audit after the deregulation, and it compares the latter with single audit in the same period. By doing so, this study shows the differential effects of mandatory and voluntary dual audits on the cost of equity, thereby broadening the system of determinants of the cost of equity in the Chinese capital market.

Third, this study extends the literature on audit quality by constructing a novel measure to represent a spillover effect from a high-quality auditor (i. e., Hong Kong-based auditor) to a low-quality auditor (i. e., mainland-based auditor) and highlighting the role that this positive spillover plays in audit quality. Previous studies leave a gap between theoretical argument and empirical test in terms of this spillover effect. Although the literature elaborates on this effect, the literature does not present any valid measurement or examination in this regard. To fill this gap, this study takes an initial step toward promoting the empirical work by deriving a measure to capture this spillover effect based on the regulatory rules and Ke et al. 's (2015)[5] argument. Then, this study examines the impact of the existence of the positive spillover effect from Hong Kong-based auditors on the audit quality of companies keeping the dual audit, and it examines the impact of the loss of this positive spillover effect on the audit quality decline of companies canceling the dual audit. By doing so, this study sheds light on an important determinant of audit quality in the Chinese setting.

1.2.2.2 Practical Significance

First, this study provides a new reference for policy-makers and regulators to re-access the costs and consequences of the policy change—the deregulation of the mandatory dual audit system. Overall, this study indicates adverse impacts of this policy change, that is, increasing the cost of equity and decreasing audit quality. The former reflects an increase in investors' suspicions after the deregulation of the mandatory dual audit system about companies' self-serving behavior that may harm their interests. The latter confirms practitioners' concern that companies' audit quality would be impaired if they do not engage Hong Kong-based auditors. The findings suggest that the decision to opt out of the dual audit system is unlikely to help a company achieve cost savings without increasing investors' suspicions or sacrificing audit quality. This study, to a certain degree, demonstrates why few AH companies have responded to regulators' call to cancel the dual audit system, and thus, questions the value of this policy change.

Second, this study serves as an important caution that becoming truly big and strong could be a long and arduous task for mainland local audit firms. Since the reform and opening-up, China's economy develops fast, and scales of companies are expanding constantly. Under this background, the call for bigger and stronger local audit firms becomes louder. In recent years, the Chinese government and Chinese Institute of Certified Public Accountants (CICPA) have made much effort, such as encouraging audit firm mergers, to develop large-scale audit firms. By doing so, regulators are in the hope of bringing up local audit firms with brand reputation. Continuous audit firm mergers during these years have increased the market concentration of the Chinese audit market. So far, a few large mainland local audit firms have earned revenue quite close to that of top international audit firms. However, this growth in revenue is only a result of local audit firms becoming bigger. In other words, it is the increase in business brought about by large audit firms merging small audit firms that leads to the growth in revenue. The market performance of these merged large audit firms is not satisfactory. For example, frequent audit failure cases in recent years have labeled local audit firms as "big but not strong" and "low quality". Consistent with this reality, the findings of this study suggest a significant decline in the A-share audit quality of companies canceling the dual audit system, which is largely driven by the loss of a positive spillover effect from Hong Kong- to mainland-based auditors. Therefore, although regulators have provided considerable policy support for the development of the mainland audit profession, becoming truly high-quality alternatives to top international audit firms could remain a long way to go for mainland local auditors.

1.3 Research Contents, Methods and Framework

1.3.1 Research Contents

Chapter 1 is the introduction of this study. This chapter introduces the practical and theoretical background against which this study is conducted. Moreover, this chapter puts forward research questions and suggests potential research significance based on the practical situations and limitations of prior research. Finally, this chapter briefly states the contents, methods and framework of this research.

Chapter 2 reviews the relevant literature. Centering on the research topic of this study, this chapter reviews existing literature about the dual audit system, the cost of equity and audit quality. It introduces their definitions proposed by previous studies. The main research findings are summarized separately about the consequences of the dual audit system and its change, the determinants of the cost of equity and the determinants of audit quality. Through the literature review, this chapter points out the shortcomings of the existing studies and explores their inspirations for this study.

Chapter 3 introduces the institutional background and conducts the theoretical analysis. First, this chapter provides a detailed introduction of the institutional background—from the establishment to abolition of the mandatory dual audit system for AH companies. Then, it elaborates on the main theories related to this study. Finally, based on the relevant theories and the theoretical analysis of the economic consequences of the deregulation of the mandatory dual audit system on the capital market and audit market, this chapter proposes the theoretical framework of this study.

Chapter 4 investigates the economic consequences of the deregulation of the mandatory dual audit system on the capital market. The objective is to answer the first proposed question of this study. This chapter analyzes the effect of complying with the mandatory dual audit requirement before the deregulation relative to voluntarily choosing the dual audit after the deregulation on the cost of equity. The empirical results in this chapter support the hypotheses about the lower cost of equity for complying with the mandatory dual audit requirement than for voluntarily choosing the dual audit.

Chapter 5 investigates the economic consequences of the deregulation of the mandatory dual audit system on the capital market. The objective is to answer the second proposed question of this study. This chapter analyzes the effect of voluntarily choosing the dual audit after the deregulation relative to using only the single audit in the same period on the cost of equity. The empirical results in this chapter support the hypotheses about the lower cost of equity for voluntarily choosing the dual audit than for using only the single audit.

Chapter 6 investigates the economic consequences of the deregulation of the mandatory dual audit system on the audit market. The objective is to answer the third proposed question of this study. This chapter analyzes the effect of canceling the dual audit relative to keeping the dual audit after the deregulation on audit quality. Furthermore, this chapter deeply explores the role that the loss of a positive spillover effect from Hong Kong- to mainland-based auditors plays in the audit-quality consequences. The empirical results support the hypotheses that keeping the dual audit ensures high audit quality due to the existence of the positive spillover effect from Hong Kong-based auditors, while canceling the dual audit impairs audit quality owing to the loss of this positive spillover. These findings are based on a novel measure constructed in this chapter to represent the spillover effect from Hong Kong-based auditors.

Chapter 7 concludes the study. This chapter presents the main conclusions, policy implications, contributions, and limitations of this study. Based on which, this chapter puts forward potential directions for future research.

1.3.2 Research Methods

This study combinedly uses theoretical analyses and empirical analyses as its research methods. Specifically, based on theoretical analyses, Chapter 2 reviews literature relevant to the dual audit system, the cost of equity and audit quality with a discussion of the shortcomings of the existing studies. Next, through theoretical analyses, Chapter 3 elaborates on the institutional background and related theories, and then constructs the theoretical framework of this study. Su-bsequently, based on the theoretical framework, Chapters 4 to 6 propose the research hypotheses and conduct empirical analyses for hypothesis testing. Finally, Chapter 7 theoretically analyzes and discusses the empirical results, draws main research conclusions, summarizes the contributions, and notes the limitations of this study. The main methods of empirical analyses used in this study are listed below.

Descriptive statistical analysis. This is a basic analysis in the empirical process. In general, the results of this analysis include number of observations, mean value, median value, standard deviation, maximum and minimum for each variable of interest. This analysis helps researchers and readers learn about the general profile and overall distribution of a set of data. In this study, this analysis is used in all chapters involving empirical analyses.

Univariate analysis (mean difference test). This is also a basic analysis in empirical research. It presents the difference (and its significance) in the mean values of each variable of interest between two subgroups of sample. This analysis helps researchers and readers learn about differences in observable characteristics between two subgroups. Moreover, researchers usually can obtain preliminary results consistent or inconsistent with a proposed hypothesis by observing the difference in the mean values of the dependent variable between two subgroups divided based on the values of the independent variable of interest. This analysis is used in all chapters involving empirical analyses in this study.

Multivariate regression analysis [Ordinary Least Squares (OLS) model and Logit model]. This analysis is conducted to examine the relationship of the dependent variable with an independent variable after controlling for the impacts of other independent variables on the dependent variable. In this study, given that all dependent variables in the baseline models shown in Chapters 4 to 6 are continuous variables, the OLS regression analysis is used as the main empirical method for hypothesis testing to examine the relationship of the continuous dependent variable with the independent variable of interest under the condition that the impacts of other factors on the dependent variable are controlled. The Logit model is adopted for cases in which the dependent variable is a dummy variable. In this study, the Logit model is used in the propensity score matching process in Chapter 5 to predict the probability of choosing to use the dual audit for each observation.

Propensity score matching (PSM) analysis. This method is used to deal with potential self-selection bias and impacts of confounding factors. After PSM, the treatment group and control group can usually be tightly matched, facilitating a more accurate and reasonable comparison between them. In this study, the PSM analysis is used in Chapter 5 to rule out the possibility that the difference in the cost of equity between voluntary dual audit and single audit is driven by differences in firm characteristics.

Change analysis. This analysis is used to examine the relationship of a change in the dependent variable with a change in an independent variable after controlling for the impacts of changes in other independent variables. This method can also help address omitted variable issues by differencing out time-invariant factors. In this study, the change analysis is used in Chapter 6 to capture the impact of the loss of the positive spillover effect from Hong Kong-based auditors on the decline in the audit quality of companies canceling the dual audit.

Impact threshold for a confounding variable (ITCV) analysis. This approach is becoming widely used to address endogeneity issues in empirical research by judging to what extent an unobserved confounding variable can turn a statistically significant OLS result into a borderline insignificant one. In this study, the ITCV analysis is used in Chapters 5 and 6 to deal with potential self-selection bias.

1.3.3 Research Framework

Figure 1-3 illustrates the research framework of this study.

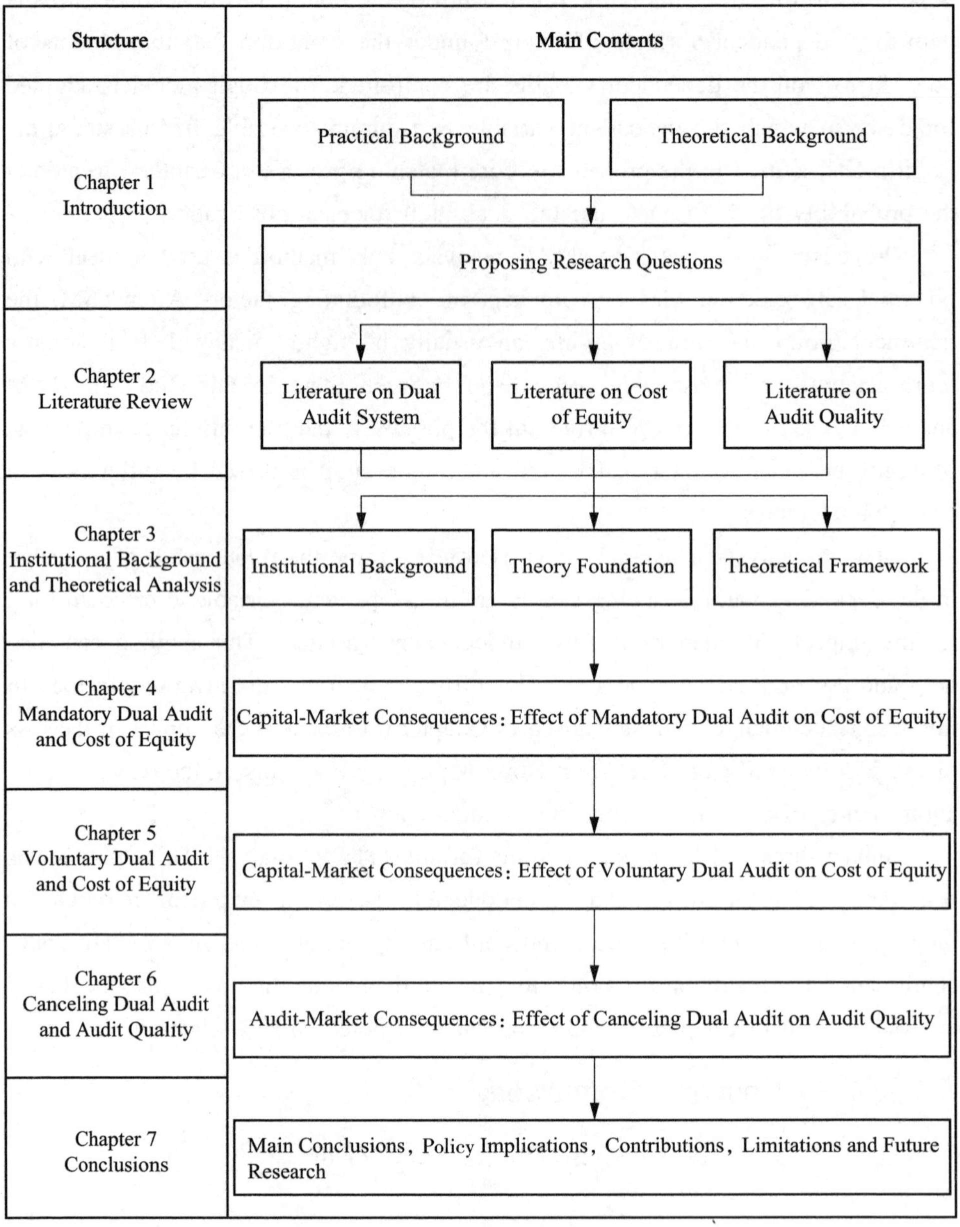

Figure 1-3 Research Framework

2 Literature Review

Undertaking the research questions and contents proposed and stated in Chapter 1, this chapter reviews the literature on the dual audit system, specifically, the definition and consequences of the dual audit system. Then, the literature on the cost of equity, specifically, the definition and determinants of the cost of equity is reviewed. Next, this chapter reviews the literature on audit quality, specifically, the definition and determinants of audit quality. Through reviewing relevant literature, this chapter points out the shortcomings of the existing studies and leads to their inspirations for this study.

2.1 Literature on Dual Audit System

2.1.1 Definition of Dual Audit

Wu (2005) [226] provides a comprehensive study on the dual audit system in China. He holds that a dual audit refers to an audit system where the two engaged audit firms audit a company at the same time and issue separate audit reports in order to produce more reliable audit outcomes.① According to Wu (2005) [226], there are mainly four types of listed companies that should have dual audits: ①A-share listed companies with initial public offering or seasoned equity offering no less than 300 million shares; ②To-be-listed or listed financial companies, including commercial

① A dual audit is different from a joint audit that has been adopted by some European countries. The joint audit is defined as an audit in which audit areas are audited by two or more audit firms. In a joint audit process, the engaged audit firms share audit efforts, cross-check each other's work, and finally issue one single audit report for the areas mutually audited by them (Francis et al., 2009; Ratzinger et al., 2013; Holm and Thinggaard, 2018) [131, 227, 228]. In a dual audit, however, the two engaged auditors audit respective audit areas and issue separate audit reports.

banks, insurance companies and securities companies; ③B-share companies; ④AH companies.

The reasons why this study focuses on the dual audit system for AH companies are as follows. First, A-share listed companies with issuance no less than 300 million shares have a quite small number, and they lack representativeness and universality. Second, owing to particular requirements imposed by the Chinese financial policies on the financial industry and issues left over from history, financial companies are too special to be an object in research on listed companies. Third, although the B-share market thrived in the past, it now has weakened financing function and is marginalized, tending to be merged into the A-share market. As a result, studying the audit systems in that market seems to have little instructive significance to reality. Finally, the financing function of the H-share market becomes increasingly stronger. The H-share market plays an important role in achieving the mainland Chinese companies' internalization; more and more mainland companies have the willingness to be listed in Hong Kong. After the deregulation of the mandatory dual audit system, investors are very concerned about AH companies' audit system change and their audit quality (Sun, 2014)[1]. Therefore, it is of researchers and practitioners' interest to study how the deregulation of the mandatory dual audit system for AH companies affects the cost of equity and audit quality.

Overall, this study focuses on the dual audit system for AH companies. On September 17 1992, the MOF released the "Interim Provisions on Certified Public Accountants (CPA) Providing Services for Pilot Joint-Stock Enterprises". In the same year, the HKEx released the "Listing Rules of the Stock Exchange of Hong Kong Limited". According to these rules and regulations, a dual audit refers to an audit system where an AH company hires a mainland-based audit firm to audit (as per the mainland auditing standards) its A-share financial statements prepared in accordance with the CAS and a Hong Kong-based audit firm to audit [using the international (or Hong Kong) auditing standards] its H-share financial statements prepared according to the IFRS (or HKFRS). Each of the two engaged audit firms releases a separate annual audit report for the same company. This audit system aims at meeting the different information demands of Chinese and international investors.

2. 1. 2 Economic Consequences of Dual Audit System

2. 1. 2. 1 Dual Audit System for AH companies

Given the uniqueness of the dual audit system for the AH-share market, studies on this regime are mainly conducted by Chinese scholars. Some researchers conduct normative analyses. For example, Zheng et al. (2011)[10] analyze the basic pattern and competition status in the H-share audit market. They argue that the deregulation of the mandatory dual audit system for AH companies provides an important opportunity for mainland local audit firms' development and improvement. They propose some strategies of entering the H-share audit market for mainland local auditors. Weng and Huang (2012)[11] list the weaknesses of mainland local audit firms. They also put up with some suggestions to improve mainland local auditors' competitiveness. They point out that although the deregulation of the mandatory dual audit system creates advantageous conditions for local audit firms when competing with others, they still need to become bigger and stronger through their own efforts.

In the empirical aspect, some studies compare audit quality across different groups in the period when the mandatory dual audit system was still in place. The common practice is to compare cross-listed firms with non-cross-listed firms. For example, Lin (2014)[229] and Che (2014)[230] show that AH companies have higher audit quality than non-cross-listings, providing indirect evidence on the role of the dual audit system in maintaining audit quality. Lin et al. (2014)[12] find that China's A-share listed companies that are required to adopt the dual audit system have greater auditor conservatism than those that are not bound by this requirement. In addition, auditor conservatism is highest when the engaged mainland- and Hong Kong-based audit firms belong to different brands. Wang and Xin (2011)[15] compare Big 4 and non-Big 4 auditors under the dual audit system. They find that, in most cases, when an AH firm hires a mainland-based member firm belonging to a Big 4 brand for its A-share audits, it also hires a Hong Kong-based member firm from the same brand for its H-share audits. Thus, any misconduct by one of the audit firms would impair the Big 4's international reputation and the other audit firm would also be adversely affected. Non-Big 4 auditors, however, have no such concerns. Their empirical results show that such a difference in motivation increases the audit quality of AH companies audited by Big 4 auditors compared to that of non-Big 4 auditors' AH clients.

Other empirical studies also involve observations in the period after the deregulation of the mandatory dual audit system. Wang (2014) [13] studies the effect of the dual audit system on audit quality among non-Big 4's audit clients using data from 2001 to 2012. She finds that the audit quality of AH clients is higher than that of clients listed only on the A-share market, suggesting that the dual audit system contributes toward improving audit quality. Focusing on A-share audits conducted by Big 4 auditors in 1995-2012, Ke et al. (2015) [5] find that Big 4 assign more-experienced partners and guarantee higher audit quality for their AH-share clients using the dual audit system than for other A-share clients. They attribute their findings to a potential positive spillover effect from Hong Kong-based auditors through the dual audit system. Using data on A-share firms from 2007 to 2014, Tian et al. (2017) [6] find that mainland-based auditors (including Big 4 and non-Big 4 auditors in mainland China) exert more audit effort and provide higher audit quality for AH firms using the dual audit system than for other A-share firms. Sun (2013) [14] focuses on changes in audit market structure and audit fees after the deregulation of the mandatory dual audit system. Using data on AH firms from 2006 to 2011, she finds that Big 4 auditors still occupy large market share in the mainland audit market. She also finds that after the policy change, audit fees even increase in some firms.

2.1.2.2 Dual Audit System in Other Sectors

Mainland Chinese companies issuing B shares were also bound by the mandatory dual audit system from 2001, the year when the China Securities Regulatory Commission (CSRC) required A-share listed companies who had issued B shares to have overseas audits. ① Before that, they voluntarily adopted the dual audit system. Early studies on the dual audit system for B-share companies mainly focus on the differences between the CAS adopted by the A-share market and the international accounting standards adopted by the B-share market. Based on the A-share and B-share firms, Li (1997) [231] concludes that the main reason why

① In 2001, the CSRC revised the Article 9 of the "Standards for Contents and Format of Information Disclosure by Companies Publicly Issuing Securities No. 2— Annual Report" to "companies that have issued domestic-listed foreign shares (and their derivative securities) and are listed on the stock exchanges shall also have overseas audits". This revision symbolized the implementation of the mandatory dual audit requirement in the B-share market.

accounting standards affect corporate earnings is the differences in accounting system and professional judgement. Chen et al. (2001)[232] use data of B-share companies and find that earnings under the CAS differ from those under the international accounting standards. They suggest that these differences in earnings mainly result from differences in accounting standards. Focusing on the differences between the net income adjusted and audited according to the CAS and the net income adjusted and audited based on the international accounting standards, Jiang (2002)[233] finds that the former is significantly higher than the latter even in 1999 when the CAS is closer to the international accounting standards. This finding implies that mainland auditors have lower independence than overseas auditors.

In 2007, the CSRC officially abolished the mandatory dual audit system for B-share companies. After that, studies mainly focus on testing changes in audit quality and audit fees before and after the abolition of the mandatory dual audit system. Li and Wu (2009)[234] analyze the influence of the abolition of the mandatory dual audit system for B-share companies from two aspects: auditor selection and audit fees. They find that most B-share companies no longer use the dual audit system after the abolition. B-share companies that previously hired a mainland audit firm and an overseas audit firm from different brands have stronger willingness to retain the original mainland auditor. In addition, the audit fee reduction driven by opting out of the dual audit system varies with firm characteristics. Fang (2010)[235] tests market reaction to the abolition of the mandatory dual audit system for B-share companies, and finds that investors do not react to this policy change positively. However, market reaction to firms previously hiring a mainland auditor and an overseas auditor from the same brand is significantly better than that to firms previously hiring two auditors from different brands. He also finds that the audit quality and information environment of firms previously hiring two auditors from different brands become worse after they opt out of the dual audit system. Zhang (2011, 2012)[236, 237] test the effect of this policy change on corporate governance efficiency (represented by earnings management) using sample in 2001–2009. The empirical results show that compared with the A-share market, corporate governance efficiency in the B-share market decreases significantly after the abolition of the mandatory dual audit system, suggesting that the mandatory dual audit system has significant corporate governance benefits. Wang and Liu (2012)[238], however, find that the abolition of the mandatory dual audit system has no significant impact on the audit quality of companies issuing both A shares and B shares (AB companies). After controlling for the impact of new accounting standards, AB companies' audit quality remains higher than that of pure A-share companies. Lin et al. (2014)[12] also find that the abolition of the mandatory dual audit system does not necessarily lead to a decrease in auditor conservatism for AB companies that no longer use this audit system.

As listed in Section 2. 1. 1, A-share listed companies with initial public offering or seasoned equity offering no less than 300 million shares and to-be-listed or listed financial companies also should have dual audits. However, as these two kinds of companies lack representativeness and universality, research on the dual audit systems for them is rather scarce.

2. 2 Literature on Cost of Equity

2. 2. 1 Definition of Cost of Equity

The cost of equity is the price paid by a company to raise capital from shareholders. In other words, it is the necessary rate of return required by shareholders for giving up other investment opportunities (Luo and Zhuo, 2004)[239]. Modigliani and Miller (1959)[17] and Solomon (1963)[18] hold that the cost of equity refers to the rate of return required by investors based on the investment risks they expect to take. In essence, the cost of equity is the discount rate when the future cash flow is discounted to the current value of a company; it reflects investors' expectation and evaluation of a company's future operating risks. As common shareholders, investors are not only the owners of a company's residual income, but also the ultimate bearers of the company's risks. Their required rate of return is a result of weighing between expected benefits and expected risks, and increases with the uncertainty in expected benefits. According to the capital asset pricing model (CAPM), the cost of equity mainly depends on investors' expectation of risks in a company's future cash flow, and it is directly proportional to the firm risk level predicted by investors (Sharpe, 1964)[19]. Lambert et al. (2007)[240] also note that the cost of equity capital is a function of the firm risk level evaluated by investors. Investors take operating risks and information risks into consideration when making decisions, and decide the acceptable rate of return accordingly.

2.2.2 Determinants of Cost of Equity

2.2.2.1 Macro Level Determinants

(1) Institutional Environment

Existing literature generally reaches a consensus that it is easier for a company to reduce the cost of equity in a capital market with sound legal systems and strong investor protection.

Levitt (1998) [25] suggests that high-quality accounting standards in the U. S. benefit a wide participation of investors in the securities market, thereby decreasing the cost of capital while increasing market liquidity. Hail and Leuz (2005) [26] study the impact of difference in institutions on the cost of equity. Based on a sample of listed companies from 40 countries in 1992-2001 and controlling for country level factors, they find that the overall cost of equity of companies listed in a country is lower when the country has more stringent legal systems and supervision on securities. Himmelberg et al. (2004) [27] hold that investors are faced with both systematic risk from the market and unsystematic risk from the company in which they invest. In a poorer investment environment, it is harder for investors to diverse the unsystematic risk, and thereby the cost of equity of listed companies is higher. Chen et al. (2005) [241] suggest that firm-level governance mechanisms significantly constrain the cost of equity. Moreover, this constraining effect is more pronounced when the institutional environment is stronger.

Studies on the relationship between institutional environment and the cost of equity in the Chinese capital market have different emphases while reach similar conclusions. Shen et al. (2005) [91] find that the cost of equity of listed companies decreases with the improvement in legal protection for minority investors. Shen (2007) [242] finds that the cost of equity of cross-listings is lower than that of non-cross-listings, implying that external environment, such as legal supervision, significantly influences the cost of equity of listed companies. Xiao and Shen (2008) [29] find that cross-listings can raise capital at lower costs in the A-share market, suggesting that stringent investor protection systems contribute to reducing listed companies' cost of equity. Through a survey by questionnaires, Jiang et al. (2008) [28] find that investor protection level in the Chinese capital market has a negative association with the cost of equity of listed companies. Wang and Ye

(2011) [243] examine the impact of the new CAS and find that the implementation of the new CAS reduces the overall cost of equity of Chinese listed companies. Hong and Chen (2016) [30] find that companies in regions with stronger legal institutional environment disclose information more promptly and accurately, which mitigates the adverse impact of information asymmetry on investors and decreases the cost of equity.

(2) Governmental Intervention

Unlike markets of developed countries, much governmental intervention exists in the Chinese capital market. As a result, studies on the relationship between governmental intervention and the cost of equity is mainly conducted by Chinese scholars. While they reach a similar conclusion that governmental interv-ention on companies usually reduces their cost of equity, this conclusion varies with different situations. Using the GLS model (Gebhardt et al., 2001) [2] and the OJ model (Ohlson and Juettner, 2005) [24] to estimate the cost of equity, Xu and Lv (2007) [31] explore the impact of the change in governmental intervention on the cost of equity. They find that for state-owned enterprises (SOEs), a reduction in governmental intervention increases firm risk by reducing government's protection for them, while it reduces uncertainty in their business by making their business activities and environment more expectable. These two effects offset each other, leading to no significant impact of the reduction in governmental intervention on SOEs' cost of equity. For non-SOEs that are less protected by government, their cost of equity decreases with the reduction in governmental intervention because less governmental intervention can increase the expectability of their business activities and environment. Xiao and Xia (2010) [32] study the relationships among political connection, governmental intervention and the cost of equity. Their findings indicate that the cost of equity is lower when governmental intervention is stronger, while there is no significant association between political connection and the cost of equity. In companies deeply intervened by government, however, the cost of equity increases with the level of political connection. Zhao and Gao (2012) [33] construct an index to represent the strength of political connection and focus on privately owned listed companies. They find that the effect of political connection on reducing the cost of equity is more pronounced in privately owned listed companies with stronger governmental intervention. Wang (2013) [34] focuses on A-share listed companies with equity financing qualifications in the period of

2005-2007 and uses the residual income model to derive the cost of equity. He finds that companies with higher earnings quality have a lower cost of equity, and this negative association is concentrated in companies without political connection. For companies having strong political connection, governmental intervention reduces the systematic risk and substitutes the role of earnings quality in reducing the cost of equity. Zou and Yang (2014) [35] study Chinese listed companies in 2005 - 2012. They find that many regions in China are less marketized and government dominates in their economic development; enterprise operations and resource allocation are deeply intervened by government. In this financial ecological environment, companies can reduce the cost of equity by establishing political connection with social public departments. Meanwhile, in regions with higher degree of marketization, enterprise operations and resource allocation mainly depend on market mechanism rather than governmental intervention. In this financial ecological environment, companies should focus on sustainably creating firm value, instead of establishing political connection, to lower the cost of equity.

2.2.2.2 Micro Level Determinants

(1) Firm Size

Studies on the impact of firm size on the cost of equity have not reached a uniform conclusion. Overseas scholars generally hold that firm size is negatively associated with the cost of equity, because larger firms have more mature profit models and more stable income than smaller firms. Accordingly, investors may require lower risk premium on larger firms. For instance, Botosan (1997) [36] and Botosan and Plumlee (2002) [37] suggest that a negative association is observed between firm size and the cost of equity. Chinese scholars have different conclusions. For instance, using data from the Shanghai Stock Exchange (SSE) and Shenzhen Stock Exchange (SZSE) in 1999-2000, Tian and Liu (2003) [39] find a higher cost of equity in larger firms. Ye and Lu (2004) [40] find similar results and suggest that the positive association of firm size with the cost of equity is a reflection of a special phenomenon in the Chinese stock market—shareholders are keen to trade the stocks of small firms and thereby tend to undervalue large firms' stocks. Cao et al. (2012) [38], however, suggest that larger firms have a lower cost of equity because the information gap between insiders and external investors is smaller in these firms.

(2) Debt Ratio

Modigliani and Miller (1959)[17] argue that having much debt and high leverage increases a company's financial pressure and the possibility of bankruptcy. As a result, investors would require higher return due to increased investment risks. They suggest that a company's financial risk increases when it relies too much on debt financing and becomes excessively indebted. Therefore, other factors being constant, the cost of equity rises with the increase in leverage. Richardson and Welker's (2001)[42] study based on the Canadian capital market demonstrates that higher-leveraged listed companies usually have a higher cost of equity. Fama and French (1992)[41] also find that the cost equity is higher when companies incur more debt.

Chinese scholars have not drawn consistent conclusions. Chen and Shan (1999)[43] take the year 1997 as the window and find that listed companies' financial leverage does not significantly affect their cost of equity in the short term, while the increase in financial leverage contributes to reducing the cost of equity in the long term. By contrast, Tian and Liu (2003)[39] suggest that there is no significant association of financial leverage with the cost of equity in the long run, whereas the cost of equity increases with financial leverage in the short run. Tang and Liu (2005)[44] develop a theoretical model based on the Chinese capital market and find a positive relationship of financial leverage with the cost of equity. Jin (2008)[45] suggests that stock returns are closely related to stock risks. Investors try to avoid risks and pursue maximized investment profits. If investors have to bear more risks, they would ask for a higher rate of return. One major risk borne by them is the financial risk stemming from a company's usage of leverage. Therefore, the cost of equity increases with financial leverage. However, the analyses of Wang and Zhang (2014)[95] show complicated results suggesting that the relationship of financial leverage with the cost of equity is uncertain.

(3) Book-to-Market Ratio

Overseas researchers consistently hold that book-to-market ratio has a positive impact on the cost of equity. Fama and French (1992)[41] and Berk et al. (1999)[46], for instance, suggest that high book-to-market ratio implies the market's undervaluation of a company's stocks. The company is supposed to have a higher rate of return until its stock price recovers to the normal level. That is, book-to-market ratio is positively associated with the cost of equity. Cheng et al. (2006) [47] also maintain that book-to-market ratio has a significantly positive influence on the cost of equity. Chinese researchers often take book-to-market ratio as a control variable and find different results. Using data from 2000 to 2001 of A-share companies listed on the SSE, Ye and Lu (2004) [40] find that the cost of equity is lower when book-to-market ratio is higher, suggesting that the market overvalues (rather than undervalues) companies with higher book-to-market ratio or these companies have lower firm risk. Lei and Zhou (2014) [48] use a sample of listed firm from 2007 to 2012 and find that book-to-market ratio is positively related to the cost of equity.

(4) Corporate Governance

As an internal monitoring mechanism, corporate governance helps management to make more cautious operating and managing decisions, reducing agency costs. As a result, investors usually require a lower rate of return on companies having stronger corporate governance. In other words, these companies can raise funds at lower costs. Chinese and overseas researchers have similar findings on this determinant. Ashbaugh et al. (2004) [49] divide corporate governance into four dimensions and examine the impact of each dimension on the cost of equity. They suggest a negative association of corporate governance with the cost of equity because good corporate governance reduces agency conflicts and investors' required return on investments. Huang (2005) [50] test the relationship of corporate governance with the cost of equity from the perspective of shareholder rights. They find that in companies with weaker shareholder rights, shareholders are faced with higher investment risks and require a higher cost of equity. Cheng et al. (2006) [47] further find that companies having stronger shareholder rights regimes, more effective board of directors and higher information quality are more likely to obtain equity financing at low costs. Chen et al. (2013) [244] suggest a positive relationship of executive pay disparity with the cost of equity. This relationship is more pronounced when free cash flow agency problems are severer and executive succession plans are more important. Focusing on Italian listed companies, Mazzotta and Veltri (2014) [51] construct a corporate governance quality index based on board independence, board size, internal auditing, nomination/compensation committees and board committee independence. They find a negative association of corporate governance scores with the cost of equity.

Chinese researchers study corporate governance and the cost of equity mainly from the aspects of ownership structure, executive compensation and board characteristics. Kong and Xue (2005)[245] use the ownership of the largest shareholder to measure ownership concentration. In their study, the cost of equity rises with the increase in the largest shareholder's ownership. However, the cost of equity decreases with the increase in the total ownership of the largest five shareholders, implying that listed companies' cost of equity is affected by ownership balance. Focusing on A-share listed companies, Hu and Zhang (2016)[246] find that ownership concentration is positively related to the cost of equity. Xiao (2016)[247] suggests that owing to higher information asymmetry and agency costs, listed companies ultimately controlled by SOEs have a higher cost of equity than those ultimately controlled by non-SOEs. Lei and Zhou (2014)[48] find that equity incentives adopted by listed companies enlarge executive pay disparity, thereby leading to a higher cost of equity. Furthermore, compared with SOEs, the cost of equity of non-SOEs is less likely to be affected by the interaction between executive pay disparity and equity incentives. Zou et al. (2015)[248] find that listed companies adopting equity incentives have a higher cost of equity compared with those not doing so, suggesting that equity incentives drive management to expropriate investors and fail to play the governance role. On the other hand, they suggest that no positive effect is observed between state ownership and equity incentives. They find that reducing state ownership can enhance the role of equity incentives in constraining the cost of equity, and non-SOEs can reduce the cost of equity through using equity incentives in a moderate manner. Li and Dong (2015)[249] explore the effect of executive power and find that an increase in executive power results in an increased cost of equity. They also find that this effect is concentrated in SOEs. Ke (2017)[56] argues that good corporate governance can guarantee firm performance persistence which, in turn, mitigates a company's financing costs. She finds empirical evidence that board independence, separation of CEO and board chairman, and ownership concentration enhance performance persistence, thereby lowering the cost of equity. Based on a sample of listed companies from 2001 to 2004, Jiang (2009)[52] finds that high corporate governance level helps decrease the cost of capital, especially the cost of equity capital. Jiang and Lu (2009)[53] focus on A-share listed companies that have allotment qualifications in four consecutive years. They find that the enhancement of the board governance mechanism contributes to lowering the cost of equity, while the impacts of the ownership structure mechanism, the management compensation mechanism and the controlling rights competition mechanism are uncertain. They also find that the decrease in the cost of equity of listed companies results from the interaction among various governance mechanisms, rather than depends on a single one. Yan (2011) [54] studies the impact of corporate internal governance based on executive pay incentives, board characteristics and ownership concentration. She suggests that companies with better corporate governance can raise funds at lower costs because they have lower investment risks and investors are more likely to obtain high returns from these companies. Lai and Fan (2016) [55] suggest that corporate governance efficiency helps to reduce the cost of equity; affected by corporate governance, there is a U-shaped relationship between investor confidence and the cost of equity.

(5) Disclosure Quality

Overseas studies have not reached consistent conclusions on the relationship of disclosure quality with the cost of equity. Most studies suggest a negative relationship between them, while some literature shows no significant or even a positive relationship. Diamond and Verrecchia (1991) [57] argue that with the enhancement of a company's disclosure quality, its stocks would be preferred by more investors and the cost of equity would be decreased. Handa and Linn (1993) [250] use the arbitrage pricing model to study investors' risk expectation. Their analyses from the perspective of risk compensation suggest that investment risks are higher when stock price is less informative. These stocks are usually required a higher rate of return by rational investors. Richardson and Welker (2001) [42] focus on Canadian listed companies in 1990–1992, and they use the disclosure index released by the Society of Management Accountants of Canada to measure disclosure quality and the GLS model to derive the cost-of-equity measure. They find that disclosure quality has a significantly negative association with the cost of equity. Cheng et al. (2006) [47] focus on 500 listed companies contained in the Stand & Poor's (S & P) Index, and they use the index of transparency and information disclosure released by the S & P in 2002 to measure disclosure quality and the OJ model for estimating the cost of equity. Similarly, they find a negative relationship of disclosure quality with the cost of equity. Mangena et al. (2016) [58] examine the impacts of human capital disclosure and financial information disclosure on the cost of equity. They suggest that human capital disclosure strengthens the negative impact of financial information disclosure on the cost of equity. By contrast, Kim (1993) [64] argues that listed companies are motivated to manipulate earnings. A company may exaggerate its performance by releasing whitewashed financial statements, resulting in severer information asymmetry than that in companies without disclosing relevant information. In other words, this study suggests that disclosing information even increases the cost of equity. Botosan and Plumlee (2002) [37] suggest that one cause of recurrent fluctuations in a listed company's stock price is frequent information disclosure, and too frequent information disclosure increases the cost of equity.

Conclusions drawn by Chinese studies are similar. Wang and Jiang (2004) [59] select A-share companies listed on the SSE, develop an adverse selection model, and use the total number of temporary announcements and quarterly reports in 2002 as the index of voluntary information disclosure. They provide evidence that improving information disclosure level decreases the cost of equity. Li and Liu (2016) [62] further find that marketization process strengthens the effect of voluntary disclosure on reducing the cost of equity. Shen et al. (2010) [61] focus on listed companies in heavy pollution industries and their environmental information disclosure level. Similarly, they find a lower cost of equity when information disclosure level is higher. Zhi and He (2010) [251] use the index of voluntary information disclosure to measure voluntary disclosure quality and financial restatements to measure mandatory disclosure quality. They find that the cost of equity is lower for companies with less frequent financial restatem-ents. Focusing on A-share companies listed in the SZSE and using the residual income model to estimate the cost of equity, Zeng and Lu (2006) [60] find that companies with higher information disclosure quality have a lower cost of equity. Yang et al. 's (2012) [65] study based on the entropy measuring and the extended analysis of the economic timeline suggests that information disclosure quality has no impact on the cost of equity in the current year, while it has a significantly negative impact on the cost of equity in the following first and second years. Zhou and Zhu (2016) [63] study A-share companies listed on the main board of the SZSE and find that improving information disclosure quality helps to increase financing efficiency and reduce the cost of equity. In addition, as a supplement to financial information, non-financial disclosure has attracted increasing attention in academia and practice. Che and Tian (2016) [67] find that companies that do better in corporate social responsibility (CSR) disclosure have a higher cost of equity. These companies bear more social responsibility and incur higher CSR costs. It is likely that their short-term profits decline and investment risks faced by investors increase. Consequently, investors would claim for more risk compensation and raise the cost of equity of these companies. Zhang and Chen (2017) [68] suggest that the effect of CSR disclosure on reducing information asymmetry is jointly affected by companies and market environment. As the quality of CSR reports disclosed by Chinese companies is generally low, information conveyed by these reports fails to reduce firm risks evaluated by investors. Similarly, Li et al. (2013) [66] find that while the release of CSR reports is interpreted as a positive signal by Chinese investors, the quality of these reports are generally too poor to reduce investors' expected firm risks.

(6) Accounting Conservatism

Some researchers find a negative relationship of accounting conservatism with the cost of equity, while others argue that there is no significant association between them. Easley and O'Hara (2004) [69] suggest that accounting conservatism can reduce specific information risk that exists in listed companies and thereby the cost of equity. Guay and Verrecchia (2018) [73] argue that management usually recognize good news in advance while postpone recognizing bad news for the sake of their own interests, which impairs financial reporting quality. Accounting conservatism, by nature, restricts this kind of behavior and helps provide high-quality financial information for investors. Therefore, accounting conservatism can reduce the cost of equity. Suijs (2008) [70] maintains that listed companies' prompt recognition of losses and release of relevant news can diversify risks faced by investors and achieve the goal of lowering equity financing costs. Lafond and Watts (2008) [71] suggest that accounting conservatism can restrict management's discretion on financial information and decrease the cost of equity by mitigating information asymmetry between management and investors. Lara et al. (2011) [72] find that the discount rate adopted by investors when estimating firm value decreases with the increase in accounting conservatism. The decrease in the discount rate, in turn, reduces fluctuations in stock price and eventually the cost of equity. Chan et al. (2009) [252], however, note that the impact of accounting conservatism depends on its type. Specifically, unconditional (ex-ante) accounting conservatism increases the quality of financial reporting. As a result, the cost of equity is decreased. By contrast, conditional (ex post) accounting conservatism impairs the quality of financial reporting, and thus, leads the cost of equity to increase.

Most Chinese studies support a negative impact of accounting conservatism on the cost of equity. Zhang and Wu (2012) [253] find that the cost of equity is lower for companies having higher accounting conservatism. This negative association between accounting conservatism and the cost of equity is weakened by state ownership. Zhang (2012) [254] finds that accounting conservatism helps to constrain the rise of the cost of equity, and this role of accounting conservatism is strengthened by institutional ownership. Based on data in the Chinese capital market, Wang et al. (2013) [74], Lu et al. (2016) [75] and Li et al. (2016) [76] provide consistent evidence that the cost of equity is negatively affected by accounting conservatism. They suggest that accounting conservatism, as an effective information reporting mechanism, plays an important role in increasing firm value. Wang and Xu (2016) [77] find that the effect of accounting conservatism on reducing the cost of equity is more pronounced in companies with stronger financial constraints and when the economy is in a downturn. Ma et al. (2017) [78] study the relationship among carbon information disclosure, accounting conservatism and the cost of equity of A-share listed companies from 2012 to 2015. They find a substitution relationship between accounting conservatism and carbon information disclosure in reducing the cost of equity. Li et al. (2008) [255], however, find that while a negative association lies between accounting conservatism and the cost of equity, this association is not significant enough to reach a convincing conclusion on a negative impact of the former on the latter. Based on a sample of A-share listed companies in 2009 – 2011, Zhang and Yang (2014) [256] also find no significant impact of accounting conservatism on either the cost of equity or the cost of debt.

(7) Audit Quality

Overseas and Chinese researchers reach similar conclusions that improving audit quality helps companies to reduce the cost of equity. Jensen and Meckling (1976) [257] posit that increasing the audit quality of financial reports can alleviate information asymmetry between financial information users and providers and mitigate moral hazard. If a company is not audited by independent auditors and investors lack professional knowledge, it can be difficult for investors to verify and use the information provided by the company. As a result, investors may not be able to make right investment decisions and even give up investing in this company. Francis (2004) [258] suggests that listed companies' cost of equity is largely affected by financial reporting. By improving the audit quality of financial reports, management can increase the use value of information and lower the rate of return required by investors. Khurana and Raman (2004)[202] find that financial reports audited by large audit firms can help reduce the cost of equity. They also point out that this conclusion is suitable for only the U. S. capital market, because the U. S. laws attach much importance to investor protection and audit firms are faced with high litigation risk. In other words, litigation risk enhances the improvement of audit quality. Choi and Lee (2014)[79] find a negative relationship of audit quality (measured by an indicator for Big 4) with the cost of equity. This relationship is more pronounced in companies with severer information asym-metry. Houqe et al. (2017)[80] focus on Indian listed companies and find that companies engaging high-quality auditors have lower earnings management level and cost of equity.

Yu et al. (2008)[81] hold that as an important information intermediary, independent auditing affects companies' cost of equity through two ways. One way is reducing agency costs and affecting investors' expectation on the mean of future cash flow. Affecting investors' expectation on the distribution (variance) of future cash flow is the other way. They find that companies with financial reports audited by Big 8 auditors have a lower cost of equity. Chen et al. (2011)[83] suggest that audit is designed for improving information quality as an external monitoring mechanism. By the aid of audit, less-informed investors can verify the credibility of a company's financial information, leading to a decrease in information risk faced by them. Their empirical findings of a significant impact of audit on reducing the cost of equity support their argument. Li et al. (2017)[84] also suggest that audit plays an essential role in improving financial information validity and mitigating information asymmetry. This role of audit can reduce investors' required rate of return on investments and ultimately affect stock pricing. Wang et al. 's (2009)[82] study on audit and IPO pricing in China supports this argument. Cao et al. (2012)[38] use audit firm size, industry expertise and audit opinion to represent audit quality. They find that high-quality audits contribute to reducing audit clients' cost of equity. This role of high-quality audits is more valuable to small companies. He and Miao (2012)[259] further find that the negative relationship of audit quality with the cost of equity is more pronounced in non-SOEs and in regions with a higher degree of marketization. Based on a sample of A-share listed companies from 2012 to 2015, Liu and Ruan (2017)[260] also find that high-quality audits exert a stronger impact on reducing the cost of equity in small companies and non-SOEs. Zhu and

Li (2017) [85] suggest that audit quality and media coverage are coordinated with and complementary to each other as external monitoring and governance mechanisms. They find that positive coverage strengthens the effect of audit quality on reducing the cost of equity, whereas negative coverage weakens this effect.

(8) Liquidity

Overseas researchers generally hold that the cost of equity is lower for listed companies with higher stock liquidity. Amihud and Mendelson (1986) [86] posit that higher stock liquidity implies that liquidity costs borne by investors are lower. As a result, investors would require a lower necessary rate of return. Brennan et al. (1998) [261] use stock trading volume to measure liquidity and find that stock returns are lower when average trading volume is higher, that is, when stock liquidity is higher. Jacoby et al. (2000) [87] suggest that expected returns on assets are positively related to liquidity costs. Lipson and Mortal (2009) [262] examine the impact of stock liquidity of listed companies on their financing activities. They find that high stock liquidity is contributory to companies' equity financing. Saad and Samet (2017) [88] suggest that when a company has poor stock liquidity, investors tend to require higher liquidity premium owing to increased risk of holding the company's stocks. As a consequence, the company's cost of equity would increase.

Most Chinese studies have similar findings supporting a negative relationship of stock liquidity with the cost of equity, while others find a positive relationship. Lu and Ye (2007) [263] focus on 576 listed companies in 2003 and use stock turnover as the measure of liquidity. They find that liquidity is negatively related to the cost of equity. Wang et al. (2012) [89] analyze the impact of asset liquidity on the cost of capital. They suggest that asset liquidity affects a company's capability to re-allocate its physical assets, its operational flexibility, and thereby the ex-ante cost of capital. A decline in asset liquidity would lead to increased operational risks and consequently a higher rate of return required by investors. Their empirical results provide supportive evidence on a negative association of asset liquidity with the cost of capital in the Chinese capital market. Yang's (2016) [90] theoretical and empirical analyses also indicate that increasing stock liquidity can help listed companies raise equity capital at lower costs. By contrast, Shen et al.'s (2005) [91] study focusing on re-financing listed companies in 1993–2001 demonstrates that the cost of equity of listed companies rises with the increase in stock turnover. They attribute this finding to the unique institutions of the Chinese capital market.

(9) Market Beta

Sharpe (1964) [19] proposes the classical CAPM, which describes how the cost of equity capital forms in an equilibrium market. In the model, beta is the one and only explanatory variable for the cost of equity. This model shows the relationship of risk with the rate of return, that is, a larger value of beta implies higher market risk and is associated with a higher rate of return. Fama and MacBeth (1973) [92] and Blume (1975) [264] also confirm that as a proxy for the systematic risk, beta exerts a significant impact on stock returns. Ross (1976) [93] proposes the arbitrage pricing theory. This theory relaxes the conditions and holds that securities returns are not only affected by the systematic risk (beta), but also a function of other factors. Securities analysis aims to identify these factors and learn about the sensitivity of the rate of return to these factors.

Chinese studies have not reached a uniform conclusion on the association of beta with the cost of equity. Shen et al. (2005) [91] use a sample of re-financing listed companies in 1993 – 2001 and conduct a time series analysis. They find a positive but insignificant relationship of beta with the cost of equity. However, Wang's (2013) [94] empirical results for listed companies in 1999 – 2011 show that the impact of beta on the cost of equity is significant and negative. Focusing on a sample of A-share listed companies in 2000 – 2012 and based on 4 cost-of-equity estimates separately derived from different models, Wang and Zhang (2014) [95] find mixed evidence in terms of the effect of beta on the cost of equity.

2.3 Literature on Audit Quality

2.3.1 Definition of Audit Quality

DeAngelo (1981a) [97] first proposes the definition of audit quality. She defines audit quality to be "the market-assessed joint probability that a given auditor will both detect a breach in the client's accounting system, and report the breach" (DeAngelo, 1981a, p. 186) [97]. This definition is from the perspective of audit risk, and it has become the foundation of future research on audit theory and practice. In DeAngelo's definition, audit quality depends on an auditor's competence, which is the auditor's capability of detecting a breach, and independence, which is the auditor's willingness to provide a fair and objective audit opinion (DeAngelo, 1981a)[97].

Watts and Zimmerman (1983)[98] raise a similar definition that audit quality is the probability that an auditor will discover and uncover a breach in the auditee's financial statements. Palmrose (1986)[99] notes that audit quality is the level of an auditor's assurance that no material misstatement or omission exists in the auditee's financial statements. Teoh and Wong (1993)[100] point out that financial information users cannot directly obtain the true information about a company's earnings. They need to rely on independent auditing to ensure that information disclosed by the company is credible. High audit quality can increase financial information users' credence to the unexpected earnings in the financial statements released by a company. The authors hold that audit quality is a kind of quality that can make the reported earnings more reliable. Lee and Gu (1998)[101] put forward that audit quality is the probability that an auditor colludes with management, and it is significantly affected by auditor independence. Francis (2011)[102] finds that audit quality is reflected by whether an auditor can make an objective judgement on the auditee's financial statements. People cannot judge audit quality through only audit reports; the influence of audit process on audit quality should also be taken into consideration. Accordingly, Francis (2011)[102] proposes a framework of determinants of audit quality, including audit plans, audit procedures, industry expertise, audit firm characteristics and structure of the industry. DeFond and Zhang (2014)[96] define that audit quality refers to the level of an auditor's assurance that the auditee's financial statements is a faithful reflection of its underlying economics. They hold that high audit quality increases financial reporting quality through improving the reliability of the financial statements.

In China, Zhang and Zhang (1997)[103] suggest that audit quality can be disaggregated into the quality of an auditor and the quality of audit process, and it is eventually reflected in the quality of an audit report. They point out that audit quality has the following characteristics: systematic, unified and indistinct. Feng (2002)[104] defines audit quality according to the requirements on the CPA profession. He suggests that audit quality refers to the quality of audit work and outcomes (audit reports), which is determined based on the professionality and sociality standards of the CPA profession.

Overall, while there are various versions of definition of audit quality in academia, most of them agree that an auditor's competence and independence play decisive roles in audit quality.

2. 3. 2 Determinants of Audit Quality

2. 3. 2. 1 Auditor Side Determinants

(1) Audit Firm Size

Academics have not reached a uniform conclusion on whether audit firm size affects audit quality. DeAngelo (1981a) [97] argues that a large audit firm were to lose many potential clients if its reputation was damaged by its poor service quality. Therefore, large audit firms have the motivation to improve audit quality in order to maintain their reputation, resulting in higher independence than small audit firms. Similarly, Dopuch and Simunic (1982) [105] suggest that larger audit firms have higher reputation, and they take initiative to improve audit quality to maintain their revenue and reputation. DeFond et al. (1999) [107] and Firth and Smith (1992) [106] point out that staff in larger audit firms usually have higher professionality, which helps to ensure higher audit quality. Wu and Li (2006) [108] find that in the Chinese audit market, Big 4 have the highest audit quality, and the second tier is the domestic Big 10. The domestic non-Big 10 have the lowest audit quality. Lin and Wang (2013) [109] also find that Big 4's audit clients have significantly lower discretionary accruals than domestic audit firms' audit clients do. Through empirical analysis, Wu et al. (2015) [110] and Lu et al. (2017) [111] draw similar conclusions that audit firm size has a positive association with audit quality. Meanwhile, some researchers have different views; they consider that large audit firm size does not necessarily represent high audit quality. Wu et al. (2005) [112] argue that DeAngelo (1981a) [97] does not take agency costs into consideration. They incorporate the impact of agency costs into their model analysis and find no significant positive relationship of audit firm size with audit quality. Based on a sample of A-share listed companies in 2007 - 2009, Guo (2011) [113] finds no significant difference between Big 4 and non-Big 4 in audit quality. Sun and Zhang (2011) [265] suggest that the positive relationship between audit firm size and audit quality exists only when the reputation mechanism functions well and auditors have a strong awareness of legal risk.

(2) Auditor Industry Expertise

Existing findings about the impact of auditor industry expertise on audit quality are not consistent. Owhoso et al. (2002)[114] indicate that auditors with more expertise and experience are more likely to detect clients' fraudulence. Krishnan (2003)[115] finds that companies are more willing to engage industry-specialized auditors to improve audit quality. In China, Xie and Sun (2010)[117] also demonstrate that industry expertise exerts a positive impact on audit quality, especially in non-SOEs that have stronger motivation to manipulate earnings. Similarly, Fan et al. (2013)[118] find that audit firm industry expertise can constrain companies' earnings management and thereby increase audit quality. However, Cai and Xian (2007)[119] argue that Chinese audit firms generally have low independence and few of them have industry expertise. They suggest that industry expertise cannot improve audit quality in China. Their empirical findings of a negative relationship of audit firm industry expertise with audit quality support their argument. Liu et al. (2010)[116] point out that the inconsistency in conclusions drawn by previous studies is owing to the inappropriate industry-expertise measures adopted by researchers. They suggest that it is more suitable to use industry market share to measure industry expertise in the Chinese audit market. With this measure, they find that industry expertise positively affects audit quality.

(3) Audit Firm Internal Governance

Audit firm internal governance also affects audit quality. Muzatko et al. (2004)[120] find that the 1994 change in the U. S. audit firms' organizational structure from general partnerships to limited liability partnerships leads to a decrease in audit quality. They suggest that this organizational structure change means that the liability borne by audit partners changes from unlimited to limited. This largely reduces the possibility that an audit firm's assets are used to compensate litigation damages and indirectly mitigates the risk that partners suffer losses. As a result, partners are less motivated to carry out intrafirm monitoring, leading to decreased audit quality eventually. In China, along with government supporting mainland local audit firms to "become bigger and stronger", there is a rise of studies on the relationship of audit firm internal governance with audit quality. Firth et al. (2012)[121] focus on the reform that Chinese audit firms were disaffiliated from their governmental parent organizations and became unlimited-liability-partnership or limited-liability audit firms. They find that this disaffiliation reform increases audit firms' uncertainty and exposure to litigation, and thereby makes auditors more conservative and quality-focused in audit work. Chen

(2014)[123] calculates comprehensive internal governance scores based on data from questionnaires and factor analysis. He finds that clients of audit firms with higher internal governance level have lower absolute abnormal accruals, and this relationship is attenuated by state ownership. Zhu (2013)[122] studies the impact of audit firm internal governance based on the change in audit firm organizational form. He suggests that special general partnerships are advantageous over limited liability partnerships in governance and thereby can improve audit quality. Similarly, Liu and Wang (2014)[124] find that the implementation of the policy about changing audit firm organizational structure from limited liability partnerships to special general partnerships systematically increases Chinese audit firms' service quality. Liu et al. (2015)[125] also show that special-general-partnership audit firms have higher audit quality compared with limited-liability-partnership audit firms. Besides, the possibility that an auditor issues a modified audit opinion increases when the audit firm he works in changes from the limited liability partnership form to the special general partnership form. Huang et al. (2017)[126] find that the market also perceive that the change in audit firm organizational structure can improve audit quality.

2. 3. 2. 2 Client Side Determinants

(1) Agency Conflicts

Agency conflicts in audit clients can affect audit quality. Chow (1982)[127] finds that agency costs, represented by firm size, capital structure and ownership, increase the possibility that a company is subject to external auditing and discloses audit reports. Francis and Wilson (1988)[128] find that the U. S. firms having severer agency problems are more likely to engage Big 8 audit firms for auditing. DeFond (1992)[266] draws similar conclusions based on a combination of audit-quality measures and analysis of auditor changes. Blouin et al. (2007)[130] focus on companies that are former clients of Arthur Andersen and demonstrate that those with higher agency conflicts are more likely to switch to a new auditor and demand higher audit quality. Firth (1997)[267] further finds that to guarantee (perceived) auditor independence, companies having more agency concerns are less likely to purchase non-audit services from the engaged auditors. Lennox (2005a)[129] finds a negative association of managerial ownership with audit quality (represented by audit firm size) in unlisted companies with low and high managerial ownership in the U. K.. Focusing on Canadian companies, Khalil et al. (2008)[268] find that companies with large disparity between cash flow rights and control rights demand wider-scope audits and pay higher audit fees. Francis et al. (2009)[131] find that French companies with less concentrated ownership and less family control are more likely to engage Big 4 for audits. Similarly, focusing on privatization cases from 32 countries, Guedhami et al. (2009)[132] find that privatized firms with higher foreign ownership (more diversified shareholders) are more likely to engage Big 4 auditors. However, Barton's (2005)[269] evidence on the defection of Arthur Andersen's clients does not support a significant impact of agency conflicts on companies' demand for audit quality. In China, Wang et al. (2006)[133] find that companies with severer agency conflicts have stronger motivation to choose high-quality audits in order to send a signal and attract potential investors. They further demonstrate that companies' demand for audit quality increases with ownership concentration. Gao and Zhang (2011)[134] find that large audit firms are more likely to be engaged by companies with higher agency costs. Managerial ownership can improve corporate governance and reduce the demand for external audit quality. From the perspective of state ownership, Wang et al. (2008)[270] argue that non-SOEs have severer agency problems than SOEs and thereby are more likely to engage high-quality auditors. The empirical findings confirm their argument. Qi and Han (2016)[135] further find that auditor independence and audit quality of non-SOEs is impaired by abnormal audit fees, whereas that of SOEs is not affected by this factor.

(2) Corporate Governance

Audit clients' corporate governance also influences audit quality. Beasley and Petroni (2001)[137] find that companies with a more independent board of directors are more likely to appoint auditors possessing industry expertise. These companies are also likely to have a more independent audit committee (Beasley et al., 2001)[138]. Stewart and Kent (2006)[139] find that companies having an audit committee, well-functional internal audit and more committee meetings are more likely to pay high audit fees in order to obtain high-quality audit reports. Carcello and Neal (2000)[136] find that a less independent audit committee is associated with a lower possibility of receiving going-concern opinions. Cassell et al. (2012)[141] construct a corporate governance index based on several board characteristics and find that companies having higher corporate governance indexes are more likely to switch from non-Big N to Big N audit firms. Engel et al. (2010)[140] find that firms pay higher audit fees when they have stronger audit committees, implying greater demand for external monitoring. In China, Xiao (2006)[142] shows that auditors provide higher audit quality (represented by audit fees) when issuing audit reports on auditees with stronger corporate governance. Based on the system theory and using the indicator for cross-listing to represent corporate governance system, Yu and Liu (2007)[143] demonstrate that better-governed companies have higher audit quality. Shen et al. (2009)[144] construct a corporate governance index using the principal component factor analysis and find that improving corporate governance contributes to increasing audit quality. Liu et al. (2012)[271] find that auditors are more likely to issue unqualified audit opinions on well-governed clients. Ye et al. (2015)[146] study the impact of corporate governance from the perspective of institutional ownership and supervisory board members. They find a U-shaped relationship of institutional ownership with audit quality whereas a negative relationship of the number of supervisor board members with the latter. Pan and Wen (2017)[145] investigate the impacts of several corporate governance mechanisms, including management compensation, ownership structure and board characteristics. They find that better corporate governance helps improve audit quality for companies having greater information asymmetry.

2. 3. 2. 3 Relationship Between Audit Firm and Audit Client

(1) Auditor Tenure

While auditor tenure is suggested affecting audit quality, previous studies have not reached consistent conclusions on the direction of the impact. Geiger and Raghunandan (2002)[150] hold that with the increase in auditor tenure, information asymmetry between an auditor and a client is reduced, and the auditor becomes more experienced in detecting fraudulence in the client's financial statements. Therefore, audit quality increases with auditor tenure. Loebbecke et al. (1989)[147] find that auditors are less experienced in detecting irregularities in clients' financial statements in the early years of audit engagements. Johnson et al. (2002)[149] find that shorter auditor tenure is related to lower financial reporting quality. Myers et al. (2003)[151] suggest that longer auditor tenure helps auditors to constrain earnings management of their clients more powerfully. Litt et al. (2014)[152] find similar results at audit partner level. Geiger and Raghunandan (2002)[150] show that audit reporting failure occurs more frequently in shorter auditor tenure. Focusing on Australian auditors, Petty and Cuganesan (1996)[148] also indicate higher audit quality in longer auditor tenure. Another explanation for the poor audit quality in the initial engagement years is "low-balling". This refers to a phenomenon that auditors win clients by discounting audit fees at the beginning year of engagements, with the intention that these initial losses can be covered in the subsequent years. Magee and Tseng (1990) [272] suggest that low-balling threatens auditor independence when there is material disagreement among auditors on understanding of accounting standards and judgements. Elitzur and Falk (1996) [273] point out that low-balling impairs audit quality when audit firms underestimate clients' audit costs.

By contrast, in favor of a negative relationship of auditor tenure with audit quality, DeAngelo (1981b) [156] notes that as auditor tenure becomes longer, auditors would pay more attention to obtaining economic benefits from clients, becoming economically dependent on clients. Shockley (1981) [157] suggests that the increase in auditor tenure would bring auditors "learned confidence". This kind of confidence may lead auditors to lose due conservatism, become insensitive to abnormal situations and adopt less rigorous audit procedures, resulting in decreased audit quality (Arrunada and Cándido, 1997) [158]. Using data of Australian companies in 1995, Carey and Simnett (2006) [160] demonstrate that the likelihood that auditors issue modified audit opinions is lower in longer audit partner tenure. Ye et al. (2011) [161] reach similar conclusions after controlling for audit firm tenure. Arel et al. (2005) [159] also note that auditors' familiarity with clients increases with auditor tenure, which makes it more difficult to conduct genuinely independent auditing and thereby impairs audit quality. In addition, some researchers have other findings. For example, Davis et al. (2009) [274] find an inverse U-shaped relationship of auditor tenure with discretionary accruals. Chi et al. (2009) [275] find mixed evidence on mandatory audit partner rotation and (perceived) audit quality.

In China, Xia et al. (2005) [153] and Chen and Xia (2006) [154] indicate a positive relationship between long auditor tenure and audit quality. Shen et al. (2009) [144] present that extending auditor tenure improves audit quality when companies have strong corporate governance. Liu and Tang (2009) [155] demonstrate that audit quality is increased in long audit partner tenure in normal audit engagements where audit partners change along with an audit firm change. Wang and Chen (2010) [276] find that auditors are more likely to issue unqualified opinions in the first 3 years of audit engagements, whereas no significant impairment in audit quality is observed in long auditor tenure. By contrast, Liu (2006)[162] provides evidence that earnings management becomes severer with the increase in auditor tenure. Dong and Zhang (2010)[166] find an inverse U-shaped relationship of auditor tenure with audit quality among Chinese listed companies from 1999 to 2004. However, in companies with high-quality corporate governance, auditor tenure positively influences audit quality. Yu and Li (2003)[165] maintain that it is not easy to conclude whether extending auditor tenure increases or decreases audit quality because there exist both beneficial and harmful factors in long auditor tenure. Shen et al. (2010)[167] consider auditor tenure separately at audit firm level and audit partner level. They find that long audit partner tenure does not impair audit quality (measured by modified opinions), whereas long audit firm tenure reduces audit quality only in audits performed by non-Big 10. However, Jiang and Li (2011)[163] show that as auditor tenure (either at audit firm level or at audit partner level) becomes longer, companies having going concern uncertainty are less likely to receive going concern opinions. That is, long auditor tenure likely impairs audit quality. Li et al. (2014)[164] suggest that long auditor tenure weakens the positive effect of industry expertise on improving audit quality because auditors become more economically dependent on clients as auditor tenure increases. Liu (2011)[192], however, suggests that it is not auditor tenure but the affiliated relationship of auditors with clients that affects audit quality. Huang et al. (2015)[277] find that low-balling impairs audit quality when both audit partners change along with an audit firm change. Zhang et al. (2018)[278] further isolate the impact of audit firm mergers and find similar results. Han and Chen (2009)[279] suggest that mandatory disclosure of audit fees helps constrain the malign competition in the Chinese audit market, thereby alleviating auditor independent issues caused by low-balling.

(2) Client Importance

Arguments and evidence on the impact of client importance on audit quality are mixed. DeAngelo (1981b)[156] points out that it is difficult for audit firms to choose whether to cater to clients or issue objective audit reports due to the bilateral monopoly between auditors and clients. Usually, auditors compromise to their clients, issuing favorable audit reports. She also suggests that audit firms have stronger economic dependence on more important clients in long-term cooperation. Choi et al. (2010)[168] demonstrate that the audit quality of large local offices is higher than that of small local offices within an audit firm because the former are less likely to economically depend on a specific client. Focusing on comparison between large and small audit firms, Chi et al. (2012)[280] find that client importance at audit partner level does not have a negative effect on the audit quality of Big 4 auditors, while this factor impairs the independence of non-Big 4 auditors. Kanagaretnam et al. (2010)[169] focus on banking industry and use loan loss provisions to measure earnings management. They find that the phenomenon that auditors allow clients that pay higher audit fees to have more earnings management exists in small banks. Zhang (2017)[171] draws similar conclusions regarding client importance as a threat to auditor independence in banking industry. Sharma et al. (2011)[281] use a sample of listed companies in New Zealand and find a positive relationship of client importance with earnings management. They also find that stronger audit committees can mitigate the threat of clients to auditor independence and audit quality. Using a sample of Australian companies from 2003 to 2011, Hossain et al. (2016)[170] study the impact of networked clients' importance on audit quality. They find that audit partners have economic dependence on clients that hire the same person as a member of their audit committees. Audit partners compromise to these networked clients by issuing fewer unfavorable opinions and allowing more earnings management.

On the other hand, as larger clients are usually exposed to more intensive scrutiny, auditors are likely to be more conservative when performing audits for them. The objective is to protect reputation and reduce litigation risk. These concerns may offset the threat of economic dependence on clients to audit quality, and even motivate auditors to provide higher-quality services for more important clients (Stice, 1991; Bonner et al., 1998; Zhang, 1999; Reynolds and Francis, 2000)[177-180]. Reynolds and Francis (2000)[180] find that Big 5 audit firms are less likely to issue favorable audit reports to more important clients. Similarly, Craswell et al. (2002)[282] present that fee dependence on clients (either at national level or at local level) does not increase the probability that auditors issue unqualified audit opinions to their clients. Hope and Langli (2010)[283] draw similar conclusions based on a sample of Norwegian private firm. Gaver and Paterson's (2007)[181] study on insurance companies suggests that auditors impose more rigorous oversight on clients that are more important to them by constraining these clients' under-reservation. Using abnormal accruals to measure audit quality, Chung and Kallapur (2003)[284] also find no significant adverse impact of client importance on audit quality. Fung et al. 's (2016)[182] study covers audit firms from 33 countries in 1994 - 2012. They suggest that client importance helps improve audit quality because auditors are concerned more about protecting their reputation than economic dependence on clients.

In China, Lu et al. (2012)[172] use a sample of business groups in 2003-2009 and find that audit firms' economic dependence on important business groups impairs audit quality by reducing the propensity to issue modified audit opinions. Cao et al. 's (2012)[173] study based on sampled firms from 2004 to 2006 also shows that less important clients are more likely to receive unfavorable audit opinions from auditors. Furthermore, this negative relationship of client importance with audit quality becomes insignificant in risky clients. Similarly, Hu and Chen (2014)[285] demonstrate that the adverse impact of client importance on auditors' objective reporting is mitigated by audit risk. Using a sample of listed companies in 2015-2017, Yang and Yang (2019)[176] find that clients more important to auditors are more likely to restate earnings in the future. Furthermore, this negative impact of client importance on audit quality is attenuated by auditors' reputation concerns. Using accounting information comparability to measure information quality, Xie et al. (2017)[175] find that audit firm-level client importance and audit partner-level client importance both negatively affect accounting information quality. Focusing on Chinese concept stocks from 2001 to 2012, Jia and Li (2015)[174] use discretionary accruals and modified audit opinions to represent audit quality. They find that audit firms without economic dependence on clients have higher audit quality than those with economic dependence on clients, and this difference in audit quality increases with client importance. By contrast, Liu (2012)[186] finds that industry-specialized auditors provide high-quality services for only large clients, suggesting that reputation and litigation concerns motivate auditors to provide higher audit quality for more important clients. Other studies indicate mixed relationships. For example, Fang et al. (2004)[183] find inconsis-tent evidence on whether audit revenue from a particular client affects auditors' decision and audit quality using different measures of client importance. Chen et al. (2010)[185] examine the impact of client importance separately at audit office level and audit partner level. They find that client importance (either at audit office level or at audit partner level) is negatively associated with the possibility of issuing modified audit opinions before 2000. When the institutional environment in China becomes stronger (i. e., after 2001), audit partner-level client importance has a positive association with the possibility of issuing modified audit opinions. Based on a sample of listed companies in 2003 – 2006, Yu et al. (2008)[184] observe no significant relationship of client importance with earnings quality before 2006 and in clients of Big 10 auditors, while the relationship becomes significant and positive in 2006 and in clients of non-Big 10. Based on a sample of listed companies in 2007 – 2010, Li and Liu (2013)[187] show that client importance is positively associated with audit quality only in companies with strong corporate governance; for companies with poor governance, there is a negative relationship between them.

(3) Private Relationships

Overseas studies on social ties between auditors and clients started from the release of the Sarbanes-Oxley Act, and the conclusions are inconsistent. Dowdell and Krishnan (2004)[188] argue that companies that hire a former audit partner as the CFO are more likely to evade audit and impose pressure on audit work. Their empirical findings suggest that companies hiring a former audit partner as the CFO have higher earnings management level than those not doing so. Menon and Williams (2004)[189] find that companies whose current CEO or directors are their former audit partners have larger absolute abnormal accruals than other companies, suggesting that this kind of employment relationship impairs auditor independence and audit quality. Similarly, by defining an affiliated company as the company that hires executives previously working for its engaged audit firm, Lennox (2005b)[190] indicates that companies are more likely to receive unqualified audit reports after they become affiliated companies. Ye et al. (2011)[161] find that when audit firms have employment relationships with their clients, audit quality decreases with the increase in auditor tenure. By contrast, Geiger et al. (2005)[198] and Geiger and North (2006)[199] find no significant change in discretionary accruals when companies hire a CFO from their audit firms. Baber et al. (2014)[200] show that companies' earnings response coefficients (ERCs) decrease after they hire former audit engagement members as their employees. Furthermore, discretionary accruals do not increase, implying that the decrease of ERCs is attributed to investor-perceived (rather than real) decline in earnings quality.

In China, Wu's (2006)[191] case study suggests that the audit partner's practices of removing the special treatment label, turning losses into profits and issuing unqualified audit opinions to the client lay the foundation for the future employment relationship of the audit partner with the client. That is to say, auditors may compromise on audit quality before they switch jobs, in order to become employees of their clients. Chen et al. (2015)[194] also find that audit partners increase their tolerance to earnings management of clients that will become their subsequent employers. Similarly, Liu and Zhang (2014)[193] find that auditors increase their tolerance to earnings management of clients whose executives previously worked for the engaged audit firms. Liu (2011)[192] also finds that companies having employment relationships with their auditors are more likely to receive unqualified audit opinions. Wu et al. (2015)[195] test whether auditor independence is affected by the phenomenon that companies hire staff from their engaged audit firms as independent directors, and the results show a negative effect of this factor on auditor independence. By contrast, Deng et al. (2017)[201] find that CFOs who switch their jobs from audit firms to audit clients do not show higher tolerance to earnings management of audit clients they serve. Moreover, companies hiring this kind of CFOs even have higher accounting conserva-tism. Some Chinese studies explore other types of private relationships between auditors and clients. For example, Guan et al. (2016)[196] focus on school ties between audit partners and executives of their clients. They find that companies connected with their auditors through school ties have higher discretionary accruals and higher possibilities of restating earnings and receiving unqualified opinions. These results imply that school ties impair audit quality. He et al. (2017)[197] study social ties between audit partners and their clients' audit committee members, including school ties, teacher-student relationships and employment relationships. They find similar results that audit quality is impaired by these social ties between auditors and their clients.

2. 3. 2. 4 External Environment

External environment also influences audit quality. Lang et al. (2003)[4] find that after non-U. S. companies are cross-listed on the U. S. market, their financial statements compiled and audited under the accounting standards of their home countries show higher quality than those of non-U. S. companies that are not cross-listed in the U. S.. Huijgen and Lubberink (2005)[203] draw similar conclusions against the U. K. market. Both studies imply that strong institutional environment helps to improve audit quality. However, the study of Francis et al. (2011)[206] focusing on private companies suggests that weak institutional environment drives private companies to demand higher audit quality because high-quality audit services can improve investor protection. Choi et al. (2008)[204] separately consider the audit fee variation of high-quality auditors (Big 4) and that of low-quality auditors (non-Big 4) across 15 countries with different institutional environments. They find that Big 4 fee premium declines with the increase in the strictness of institutional environment. This finding suggests that non-Big 4 improve their service quality more than Big 4 do when legal environment becomes stronger, because strong institutions are more costly to low-quality auditors who have higher audit failure rates and expected liability costs. By contrast, Francis and Wang (2008)[205] argue that only high-quality auditors, who have more reputation concerns, would improve their service quality when institutional environment becomes stronger. Their empirical findings based on a sample from different institutional environments and the abnormal accruals measure support their argument. Khurana and Raman (2004)[202] compare Big 4 auditors' clients in the U. S. with their clients in other Anglo-American countries where institutional environments are relatively weaker. They find that the audit quality of Big 4 is higher in the U. S. than in other Anglo-American countries, suggesting that institutional environment influences audit quality through affecting auditors' litigation concerns rather than their reputation concerns.

The institutional environment in mainland China is weaker compared with that in developed countries and regions. Some Chinese researchers exploit the setting of A-share companies cross-listing in Hong Kong to investigate how institutional environment affects audit quality. Based on a combined sample of H-share listed companies and A-share listed companies, Wang and Tan (2010)[207] present that auditors of AH companies are more likely to issue modified audit opinions than auditors of pure A-share companies. Their findings suggest that A-share companies cross-listing on a market with stronger institutional environment improves audit quality. Xin and Wang (2010)[208] demonstrate that cross-listing on a stricter market can restrict company insiders' pursuit of private interests. Consequently, it can constrain the motivation to whitewash financialstatements and increase a company's information quality. Focusing on A-share companies audited by Big 4 audit firms, Ke et al. (2015)[5] suggest that the weaker institutional environment in mainland China (compared with that in Hong Kong) discourages Big 4 from providing higher audit quality. Similarly, Tian et al. (2017)[6] show that compared with other A-share companies, dual-audited AH companies have higher audit quality because their mainland auditors can be indirectly influenced by the stronger institutional environment in Hong Kong. Other researchers focus on the external environment within the Chinese market. Feng and Liang (2010)[209] examine the impact of listed companies' legal events, such as litigations, arbitrations and punishments, on audit opinions. They observe a positive relationship of litigation risk with the possibility of issuing modified opinions, suggesting that Chinese auditors have the willingness to improve audit quality in order to minimize audit risk and litigation risk. Zhai and Liao's (2011)[210] study also suggests that auditors perform more conservatively and provide higher audit quality when they are faced with higher audit and litigation risk brought by auditees with larger discretionary accruals. Measuring regulatory risk by disparity between control rights and cash flow rights of an audit client's ultimate controlling shareholder, Song and Xiao (2012)[211] find that large audit firms provide high-quality services for only audit clients with high regulatory risk. Liu (2016)[212] finds that the inspections of the CICPA improve the overall audit quality in the Chinese audit market, while Huang and Li (2016)[213] find that the interviews of the CICPA have a positive effect on only small audit firms. In addition, media coverage, especially negative media coverage, can form an external monitoring mechanism and help improve auditor conservatism and audit quality (Zhou et al., 2015; Zhang et al., 2016; Wu et al., 2017)[214-216].

2.4 Literature Review and Research Inspiration

2.4.1 Literature Review

Section 2.1 reviews the literature on the dual audit system, from the aspects of its definition and economic consequences. First, studies on the mandatory dual audit system for B-share companies and its abolition are generally earlier. They investigate a variety of consequences, including auditor choices, audit fees, audit quality, market reaction and corporate governance, and find mixed evidence. The domestic-listed-only B-share companies are faced with substantially different institutional environment from the cross-listed AH companies. Thus, generalizing the conclusions from the former to the latter without rigorous analysis is quite hasty.

Second, studies on the mandatory dual audit system for AH companies and its abolition, which is of my interest, focus only on audit-related issues, such as audit quality, fees and market share. Although the mandatory dual audit system for AH companies has been officially abolished by regulators since 2010, a large proportion of AH companies continue to opt for this system. The abolition of the mandatory requirement does not mean the disappearance of the dual audit system. Hence, studying how the deregulation of the mandatory dual audit system for AH companies affects the capital market is of researchers and practitioners' interest. However, evidence on the capital market-related consequences of this policy change is rather limited.

Third, previous literature on the dual audit system for AH companies reaches a consensus that the audit quality of Chinese listed companies not using the dual audit (including pure A-share, AB and some AH companies) is lower than that of AH companies using the dual audit. From this general finding, that the audit quality of AH companies possibly decreases following the cancelation of the dual audit system can be inferred. However, simply based on the comparisons across groups with substantial differences, it is hard to exclude the possibility that the general finding of these studies is driven by systematic differences between AH-share cross-listed and domestic-listed-only companies rather than by variation in audit systems.

Fourth, Ke et al. (2015)[5] provide a detailed explanation of a potential positive spillover effect from Hong Kong- to mainland-based auditors in the dual audit system for the first time in the literature. This explanation helps the audience understand the possible mechanism by which the dual audit system ensures high audit quality from the perspective of the institutional environment faced by the engaged auditors. However, the positive spillover effect proposed by Ke et al. (2015)[5] is limited to a description. The effect has not yet been measured directly. Moreover, it is still unclear whether and to what extent its existence (loss) affects the audit quality of companies keeping (canceling) the dual audit system.

Section 2. 2 reviews the literature on the cost of equity, from the aspects of its definition and determinants. The cost of equity is the price paid by a company to raise capital from shareholders. This topic has been studied by researchers for decades. Rich literature exists with regard to the determinants of the cost of equity. Previous theories and evidence demonstrate that the cost of equity is mainly affected by institutional environment, governmental intervention, firm size, leverage, book-to-market ratio, corporate governance, disclosure quality, accounting conservatism, audit quality, liquidity and market risk. These arguments and findings provide foundations of the design of my research model in the empirical analysis. Meanwhile, one point closely related to my main idea can be drawn from this literature. Specifically, it is generally accepted that independent auditing can affect the cost of equity. However, evidence on whether a change in a particular audit system, for example, the deregulation of the mandatory dual audit system for AH companies, can lead to any difference in the cost of equity is limited.

Section 2. 3 reviews the literature on audit quality, from the aspects of its definition and determinants. While there are various versions of the definition of audit quality, most of them agree that an auditor's competence and independence play decisive roles in audit quality. Audit quality has been explored by academics for nearly 40 years. As a result, a wealth of relevant literature exists. Previous theories and evidence indicate that audit quality is mainly determined by auditor characteristics (including audit firm size, auditor industry expertise and audit firm internal governance), client characteristics (including agency conflicts and corporate governance), relationships between auditors and clients (including auditor tenure, client importance and private relationships) and external environment. These arguments and findings provide foundations of the design of my research model in the empirical analysis. Meanwhile, one point closely related to my main idea can be drawn from this literature. Specifically, Ke et al. (2015) [5] provide an explanation about the mechanism by which the dual audit system ensures high audit quality from the perspective of the institutional environment faced by auditors. However, no one has proposed any direct measurement of this abstract mechanism yet. In addition, whether and to what extent the existence and loss of this mechanism affect audit quality remain open questions.

2. 4. 2 Research Inspiration

The existing literature provides rich theoretical bases and empirical evidence for my research topic, and shows the following research inspirations for me.

First, while the mandatory dual audit system for AH companies was abolished, this audit system does not disappear and academic exploration on this system persists. However, the existing studies focus mainly on the audit-related consequences of the deregulation of the mandatory dual audit system. What about other economic consequences? For example, does this deregulation have effects on the capital market by affecting the cost of equity? In the existing literature, some researchers compare companies having the dual audit with those not doing so. Other researchers compare companies in the regulated period with companies in the period after the deregulation. What about dividing companies having the dual audit into those that are required to use the dual audit before the deregulation and those that choose to use the dual audit after the deregulation and making a comparison between them? What about comparing companies that choose to use the dual audit with those not having the dual audit after the deregulation? That is, do the dual audit in the regulated period and the dual audit after the deregulation have differential impacts on the cost of equity?

Second, as for the consequences of the deregulation of the mandatory dual audit system on the audit market, the previous literature concurs that the audit quality of companies not having the dual audit is lower than that of companies having the dual audit. It can be inferred from this consensus that canceling the dual audit system is likely associated with an audit quality deterioration of AH companies. Ke et al. (2015)[5] provide a notable explanation about the possible mechanism by which the dual audit system ensures high audit quality from the perspective of the institutional environment faced by auditors (i. e., the potential positive spillover effect from Hong Kong- to mainland-based auditors). However, unresolved issues remain. For example, how should this mechanism be measured? Do companies that keep the dual audit system have higher audit quality when they are subject to a more positive spillover effect? Does the loss of this positive spillover effect drive the decline in audit quality of companies that cancel the dual audit system?

To answer the above questions, this study investigates the economic consequences of the deregulation of the mandatory dual audit system on the capital market and audit market. Specifically, this study tests the consequences on the cost of equity by separately comparing (1) companies required to use the dual audit before the deregulation with those choosing to use the dual audit after the deregulation and (2) companies choosing to use the dual audit after the deregulation with those not having the dual audit in the same period. In addition, this study tests the consequences on audit quality by (1) constructing a novel measure of the spillover effect from Hong Kong-based auditors and (2) comparing companies canceling the dual audit with those keeping the dual audit after the deregulation.

2.5 Chapter Summary

Centering on the research topic of this study, this chapter systematically reviews the literature relevant to the definition and consequences of the dual audit system, the definition and determinants of the cost of equity and the definition and determinants of audit quality. Overall, previous studies provide rich theoretical bases and empirical evidence for this study. Meanwhile, shortcomings remain in the existing literature, which leaves interesting unresolved issues for this study to address. This chapter explicitly points out the direction of this study and makes solid literature preparation for the theoretical analysis of the next chapter.

3 Institutional Background and Theoretical Analysis

Following the research questions raised in Chapter 1 and literature reviewed in Chapter 2, this chapter focuses on institutional background and theoretical analysis. First, this chapter introduces the institutional background of the mandatory dual audit system for AH companies from its establishment to abolition. Then, this chapter elaborates on the main theories related to this study. Finally, on the basis of the relevant theories and the theoretical analysis of the consequences of the deregulation of the mandatory dual audit system on the capital market and audit market, this chapter proposes the theoretical framework of this study. Based on this theoretical framework, the next three chapters conduct detailed empirical analyses.

3. 1 Institutional Background

The first AH company, mainland Chinese company Tsingtao Brewery Co. , Ltd. , was cross-listed in 1993. At that time, substantial differences existed between the CAS and IFRS (or HKFRS), and mainland-based audit firms were considered as having relatively low audit quality (MOF, 2009a) [7]. Therefore, the listing rules and regulations in mainland China and Hong Kong compelled an AH company to prepare two sets of annual financial statements. In addition, it was compulsory for theses financial statements to be audited by two separate audit firms. This dual audit requirement is known as the mandatory dual audit system. Specifically, the mandatory dual audit system required an AH company to prepare one set of financial statements in accordance with the CAS (i. e. , the A-share financial statements) and hire a mainland-based audit firm to perform the A-share audits as per the mainland auditing standards. The regulation also required the company to prepare the other set of financial statements according to the IFRS (or HKFRS)

(i. e. , the H-share financial statements) and engage a Hong Kong-based audit firm to perform the H-share audits using the international (or Hong Kong) auditing standards (Wang, 2008) [286]. Each of the two audit firms was required to release a separate annual audit report for the same company.

The institutional foundation of the mandatory dual audit system is the large gaps between mainland China and Hong Kong in terms of accounting and auditing standards. These gaps led to material differences between the audited accounting information of a company's A-share financial statements and that of its H-share financial statements. In addition, the gaps induced diversified information demands from Chinese investors and international investors. For example, an overseas investor may accept only the accounting information prepared according to the IFRS/HKFRS and audited by a Hong Kong-based auditor as per the international/Hong Kong auditing standards. Therefore, an AH company was required to adopt the dual audit system to satisfy the different demands of Chinese and international investors.

The technical foundation of the mandatory dual audit system is to support the audit profession in mainland China. Unlike Hong Kong-based audit firms that have a long history and international reputation, local audit firms in mainland China have been staying low-quality and short of international auditing experience for a long time. To change the disadvantageous position of local auditors, regulators in mainland China required several types of A-share listed firms (including AH companies) to hire a mainland-based audit firm and a Hong Kong-based audit firm for annual auditing. By imposing this requirement, regulators expected that local audit firms can learn from Hong Kong-based audit firms of their relatively mature technical and managerial experience. However, in contrast to regulators' expectations, local audit firms have not achieved much improvement and even lost considerable business to Hong Kong-based auditors during the implementation process. As a result, local auditors are still faced with distrust of investors and discrimination in the market.

The mandatory dual audit system serves as a means to enhance the credibility of accounting information and satisfy diversified information demands from investors in different regions. However, this audit system has disadvantages. For example, the mandatory dual audit system increases the audit and disclosure costs for cross-listed companies (MOF, 2010b) [287]. In addition, such an audit system discourages mainland local audit firms from going abroad because it limits their opportunity to undertake the H-share audits (Zheng et al., 2011) [10].

With economic globalization and China joining the World Trade Organization, the MOF released new accounting standards for enterprises on February 15 2006, containing 1 basic standard and 38 specific standards. The new CAS draws on the IFRS, and, since then, most Chinese accounting policies have been brought in line with the international standards, except for some minor differences in the standards relevant to related-party transaction disclosure, asset impairment loss reversal, and accounting treatment of some government subsidies (Wang et al., 2005) [288]. The new CAS, which took effect on 2007, symbolized the convergence (equivalence) of the CAS with the IFRS (HKFRS) (Kuan et al., 2007) [289]. On May 122006, the China Accounting Standards Committee (CASC) and the Hong Kong Institute of Certified Public Accountants (HKICPA) held a meeting in Hong Kong to discuss the convergence of accounting standards between mainland China and Hong Kong. The declaration they signed later suggests that the CAS and HKFRS have already achieved equivalence; with the development of economic globalization, it has become an inevitable trend for the CAS and HKFRS to be in line with the international practices (CASC and HKICPA, 2007) [290]. Moreover, since the outbreak of the international financial crisis, the Group of 20 and the Financial Stability Board have proposed to create a single set of accounting standards with high quality and global applicability, and they have raised the issue of accounting standards to an unprecedented position (MOF, 2009b) [291]. In this general trend of accounting standards convergence (and equivalence), the trivial differences in accounting and auditing standards shook the institutional foundation of the mandatory dual audit system. Regulators of mainland China and Hong Kong were concerned if it was still necessary to compel an AH company to prepare two sets of financial statements and hire two audit firms for annual audits. Accordingly, regulators took several steps to abolish the requirement and encourage qualified mainland-based audit firms to perform single audits for AH companies.

In December 2007, the CASC and HKICPA signed the *Joint Declaration on the Converged China Accounting Standards for Business Enterprises and Hong Kong Financial Reporting Standards*, stating that "this work will explore, and resolve as soon as possible, acceptance by the regulators of one jurisdiction for the purpose of listing in that jurisdiction, the financial statements of an enterprise of the other jurisdiction that are prepared under the accounting standards of that other jurisdiction and audited by eligible auditing practices in that other jurisdiction applying auditing standards of that other jurisdiction" (CASC and HKICPA, 2007, p. 2) [290]. In August 2009, the HKEx released the *Consultation Paper on Acceptance of Mainland Accounting and Auditing Standards and Mainland Audit Firms for Mainland Incorporated Companies Listed in Hong Kong*, suggesting the acceptance of mainland accounting and auditing standards for AH companies and allowing mainland-based audit firms to audit these companies (HKEx, 2009) [9]. This consultation paper also set out basic principles on approval, registration, monitoring and continuing oversight of mainland-based audit firms. Finally, on December 10, 2010, the HKEx reached an agreement with the CSRC agreeing to accept mainland accounting and auditing standards and mainland-based audit firms for mainland incorporated companies listed in Hong Kong (including AH companies). Specifically, AH company would be allowed to prepare one set of financial statements under the CAS and correspondingly hire a mainland-based audit firm to perform the audits based on the mainland auditing standards. This agreement symbolized the official abolition of the mandatory dual audit system for AH companies. At the same time, regulators approved 12 large mainland-based audit firms to audit AH companies independently for fiscal years ending on December 15, 2010 at the earliest (HKEx, 2010) [292]. The approved mainland-based auditors comprise BDO China Shu Lun Pan CPAs, Pan-China CPAs, BDO Da Hua CPAs, ShineWing CPAs, Ernst & Young Hua Ming CPAs, Crowe Horwath CPAs, Grant Thornton CPAs, PwC Zhong Tian CPAs, Deloitte & Touche Hua Yong CPAs, KPMG Hua Zhen CPAs, RSM China CPAs and Wuyige CPAs.

This final agreement did not prevent a Hong Kong-based audit firm from servicing an AH company (HKEx, 2009) [9], nor did it require those who want to dismiss their Hong Kong-based auditors to do this at the same time. Since the deregulation of the mandatory dual audit system, continuing the dual audit or not has become a voluntary choice for an AH company (HKEx, 2009) [9]. Accordingly, since 2010, some AH companies have stopped using the dual audit system; they dismissed their Hong Kong-based auditors while retained the mainland-based auditors to perform the single audit just like the domestic-listed-only companies do. For example, Tsingtao Brewery Co., Ltd. was the first AH company to cancel the dual audit system; in December 2010, it released a board resolution proposing the dismissal of the Hong Kong-based auditor (PwC CPAs) and retention of the mainland-based auditor (PwC Zhong Tian CPAs). Conversely, others still choose to hire two audit firms from both sides to perform the dual audit. The yearly distribution of the sample presented in Sections 4. 3. 1, 5. 3. 1 and 6. 3. 1 together suggest that there is a variation among the sample firms previously constrained by the mandatory dual audit system in terms of whether to cancel the dual audit system. The majority of them continue to opt for this audit system during the period after the deregulation. Such voluntary demand for the dual audit system cannot be neglected, and seems to be contrast to regulators' view that the value of the dual audit has largely diminished since the convergence of the CAS with the IFRS.

3. 2 Theory Foundation

After introducing the institutional background of the emergence, development and abolition of the mandatory dual audit system for AH companies in Section 3. 1, the main theories related to this study are elaborated in Section 3. 2.

3. 2. 1 Firms' Auditing Demand

Independent auditing refers to public accountants accepting entrustment according to law, independently auditing the financial statements and related information of the auditees and issuing audit opinions (Chen, 1998)[293]. Traditional auditing theories suggest that the separation of asset ownership and asset control is a prerequisite and the foundation of independent auditing. The aim of auditing is to discharge the accountability relationship between principals and agents. Firms demand auditing voluntarily.

3. 2. 1. 1 Economic Root of Auditing Demand

The arrangement of property rights is the economic root of independent auditing. According to the property right economics, if a market is perfect and the contracts are complete and can be effectively implemented, then the impact of each property owner on firm behavior will not be that different. If contracts are incomplete or cannot be effectively implemented, then the impacts of different property owners on firm behavior will be largely different. In this situation, the distribution of property rights will directly affect people's motivation and behavior. Coase (1937)[294] first explains the reason for the existence of enterprises from the perspective of transaction costs. He suggests that if the transaction costs of being engaged in certain business activities in the market are higher than those of being engaged in the same activity inside the enterprise, then choosing the latter way is necessary. Demsetz (1964) [295] suggests that transaction and execution costs determine the distribution of property rights. Competitive forces in the market drive a company to adopt the most effective organization structure to minimize the efficiency loss brought by transaction costs. Alchian and Demsetz (1972) [296] further explain the reason for the existence of enterprises from the angle of organization costs. They think that moral hazard lies in the team-based producing process. Enterprises are an outcome of the metering problem in team production; they exist to reduce the metering costs. Enterprise owners can reduce the metering costs through monitoring because they have rights of cash flow, vote and transfer. Cheung (1983) [297] deepens Coase's (1937) [294] analysis by showing that enterprises are a kind of transaction for factor suppliers to obtain pareto improvement. Factor suppliers with management capability and information advantage trade with capital suppliers to obtain the comparative advantage of labor division. Thus, this event leads to the separation of asset control and asset ownership. The costs of knowledge transmission increase with the dependence on special knowledge, thereby resulting in a greater separation (Jensen et al., 1995) [298]. The separation of asset control and asset ownership induces management opportunism. When no transaction cost exists, management opportunism will not cause efficiency loss if the delimitation of property rights is clear (Coase, 1960) [299]. However, in reality, transaction costs are inevitable; management expropriation can cause efficiency loss and agency costs (Jensen and Meckling, 1976) [257]. Many scholars in the property right economics also explain enterprise ownership structure from the perspective of the relationship of corporate governance with public governance (Coase, 1937; Demsetz, 1964; Cheung, 1983; Coase, 1960; Alchian, 1965) [294, 295, 297, 299, 300]. They highlight the interaction between proper-ty rights and institutional arrangements in determining economic behavior. Instit-utional arrangements, such as traditions, social norms, laws and regulations, play an important role in the development of property structure and governance system in a country. Institutional environment largely determines property arrangements. When a property right owner cannot be strongly protected by the institutions in his country, he may exploit the enforcement of private contracts as an effective substitute for self-protection. A property right owner's purpose, capability and motivation to enforce private contracts are affected by ownership structure. Therefore, ownership structure per se can influence the extent of the enforcement of these contracts. A highly concentrated ownership structure is an effective way of self-protection when the investor protection system is weak. In such an ownership structure, the conflict between controlling shareholders and minor shareholders is severe owing to their different objective functions (Shleifer et al. , 1997; Porta et al. , 1999) [301, 302].

As mentioned in the above paragraph, transaction costs exist in reality, and management opportunism can cause efficiency loss and agency costs. At present, the accrual-based accounting system is used worldwide. In this accounting system, numerous discretionary accruals facilitate managers' opportunistic behavior, such as earnings manipulation. Jensen and Meckling (1976) [257] maintain that in the institutional environment with weak investor protection, to reduce agency costs, investors can protect themselves through the price mechanism when they are aware of any potential risk of insider expropriation. Specifically, they tend to purchase a firm's stocks at a lower price and ask for higher returns. In this case, insiders of a firm have to bear higher issuing costs and take the punishment from investors. Therefore, to avoid these costs and punishment, the insiders are motivated to take measures of self-restriction. By doing so, they wish to show their honesty, diligence and decency to investors. One universally accepted effective measure is to hire an independent third party for auditing (Watts et al. , 1983) [98].

The emergence and development of independent auditing is a necessary consequence of market selection. Based on these economic theories, traditional auditing theories also maintain that independent auditing stems from the separation of asset ownership and asset control. Under the separation of these two rights, information asymmetry lies between principals (asset owners) and agents (asset managers), which can lead to a series of agency issues, such as adverse selection and moral hazard. Owners' interests are very likely to be damaged by these agency problems. To reduce agency costs, owners are motivated to monitor and incentivize management. However, it is costly and inefficient for owners to monitor management by themselves due to lack of specialized knowledge and skills. An independent third party equipped with professionalism (e. g. , an audit firm) can be more capable of this task. To save transaction costs, owners can entrust an audit firm with the responsibility of supervising and judging whether and how management fulfill their fiduciary responsibility. Meanwhile, management are willing to be checked and inspected by an independent third party to prevent owners from adjusting their compensation downward and discharge their fiduciary responsibility. Hence, firms' demand for independent auditing spontaneously arises along with their concerns regarding saving agency costs. Empirical results support the argument that the growing agency conflicts triggered by the separation of asset ownership and asset control generate firms' demand for auditing. For example, Chow (1982)[127] finds that companies having severer agency issues are more inclined to purchase audit services. DeFond (1992)[266] finds that agency costs reduce sharply when audit quality increases.

3. 2. 1. 2 Theories of Auditing Demand

As mentioned before, independent auditing results from institutional arrangements; auditing demand stems from the economic function of auditing. By reducing agency costs, information asymmetry and transaction costs, the ultimate goal of its economic function is to decrease firms' cost of capital and increase resource allocation efficiency. This is the economic value of independent auditing. Then, what are the motivations for a company, as a self-interested economic man, to choose to be audited voluntarily? Three streams of explanations are found according to the existing literature: the monitoring hypothesis, information hypothesis and insurance hypothesis.

(1) Monitoring Hypothesis

Under the monitoring hypothesis, the demand for independent auditing mainly comes from management (agents). An enterprise is made up of a series of contracts (Coase, 1937; Alchian et al., 1972)[294, 296]. A principal-agent contractual relationship exists between enterprise owners and management. A complete contract between owners and management can help owners effectively control agency costs and maximize the interests of both parties. However, the neo-institutional economics suggest that a principal-agent contract is actually incomplete due to bounded rationality, opportunism and specific assets in the relation-ship. The incomplete contract can induce adverse selection and moral hazard. If both parties aim to maximize their own interests and owners cannot monitor management with no cost, then management may not always act in owners' interests. Once the rational owners expect that their own interests are likely to be expropriated through management opportunism, they will protect themselves by adjusting the price paid to management. For example, they may buy the firm's stocks at a larger discount and ask for higher returns. Alternatively, they may cut down management compensation beforehand according to the expected expenses of monitoring by owners themselves. Compared with passively bearing these costs, it is less costly for management to actively seek professional external monitoring mechanisms to show their integrity. Therefore, to assure owners that the activities harming their interests are restricted, management are motivated to make monitoring expenditures (Jensen et al., 1976) [257]. For instance, management would make contractual guarantees to engage a public accountant to audit financial accounts, which can increase financial information credibility, improve investor confidence and reduce agency costs.

(2) Information/Signaling Hypothesis

The information hypothesis is mainly based on the decision-usefulness view of accounting information. In this view, accounting aims to provide useful information for users. This hypothesis addresses accounting information's role in estimating firm value and firm solvency.

Under the information hypothesis, on the one hand, the demand for independent auditing can come from investors. In a general investment decision model, firm value is the discounted future cash flow. Compared with insiders, external investors are at the information disadvantage. Information asymmetry can affect an investor's estimation of the present value of a company's future cash flow, thereby leading to inaccurate valuation and suboptimal investment decisions. As a key information-obtaining channel for external investors, the quality of the financial statements periodically disclosed by a firm remarkably matters. Independent auditing aims to reasonably ensure that no material misstatement exists in a company's financial statements. Thus, independent auditing can help improve accounting information quality, increase investors' trust in the financial statements and mitigate information asymmetry (Beaver et al., 1970) [303]. The third party-audited financial statements can decrease information risk and contribute to enhancing the accuracy of firm valuation. This function, in turn, increases the possibility that an investor makes wise investment decisions and gains benefits. Therefore, investors have the motivation to accept independent auditing.

On the other hand, the demand for independent auditing can come from management. External investors heavily rely on the financial statements disclosed by a firm when making investment decisions. Hence, financial reporting quality has a great impact on their evaluation and decisions. The amount of information provided by all firms being equal, investors are likely to prefer firms with higher information quality and pay them with a higher price. By contrast, investors may stay away from low-quality firms. To attract investors, low-quality firms may disguise themselves as high-quality ones by varnishing or concealing the unfavorable information. This kind of imitation is not much costly and usually can be affordable to low-quality firms. As investors are generally at the information disadvantage, it is hard for them to judge the quality of all financial statements in a certain market by themselves. When investors are aware of the risk that low-quality firms may provide fraudulent information, they tend to treat all financial statements in that market as having average-level audit quality. This treatment can lead to undervaluation for high-quality firms, whereas overvaluation for low-quality ones, and then further cause adverse selection (Fang et al. , 2008) [304] . To avoid being expelled by the "bad money", management in high-quality firms have the motivation to send signals that can convey their advantages to investors. By doing so, they can differentiate themselves from low-quality firms, making investors believe their good characteristics and willing to pay a higher price (Melumad et al. , 1990) [222] . Engaging a third party to perform independent auditing can be an effective signaling mechanism. Because audit service is costly, only firms that have very profitable prospects that can cover the incurred audit costs are capable of making such choices. This sets up a barrier that is hard to overstep for low-quality firms if they want to imitate the same practice. Therefore, regardless of the assurance levels provided by the engaged auditors, a firm's act of being audited can be treated as a useful signal and convey important information. This act can distinguish these high-quality firms from the inferior ones, and send a positive signal about their good characteristics, such as management integrity, low risk and profitable prospects, to the market. Thus, being audited can help these firms win more favor from investors (BarYosef et al. , 1984) [305] .

(3) Insurance Hypothesis

Under the insurance hypothesis, the demand for independent auditing may come from either investors or management. The insurance hypothesis assumes that a firm engages independent auditors to transfer risk (Chow et al. , 1988) [306] . This theory originates in the U. S. and has strong explaining power in that market, wherein audit firms are faced with high litigation risk (Lys et al. , 1994) [307] . The

U. S. Securities Law published in 1933 notes that if investors suffer loss in an investment made based on a firm's audited financial statements and audit failure occurs, then they can claim against management of the firm and the engaged audit firm. In the lawsuit, the audit firm bears the burden of proof. Evidence must be collected to support that the audit firm has fulfilled due diligence. Otherwise, the audit firm shall not be exempted from the compensation liability. Accordingly, hiring an audit firm for financial statements auditing allows a firm's management to share financial reporting responsibility with auditors and transfers part of firm risks caused by business failure to auditors. Moreover, this practice provides some economic security for investors, reducing their investment risks and losses (Dye, 1993; Menon and Williams, 1994; Wallace, 2004) [308-310]. Hence, in a market with a sound legal system and strong investor protection, both management and investors have the demand for independent auditing and its insurance value.

It is interesting why a listed company prefers to choose an audit firm rather than an insurance company to provide insurance. Wallace (1980) [311] suggests four reasons as follows. First, the assurance role of independent auditing has become deeply entrenched in society. Without the involvement of an audit firm, it is hard for management to prove that they have fulfilled due professional care. Second, an audit firm usually trains full-time legal staff and hires defense lawyers to deal with lawsuits. Thus, as a third-party co-defendant, an audit firm can provide solider insurance coverage than an insurance company. Third, when faced with litigations, an audit firm considers both the monetary loss of the out-of-court settlement and the reputational loss brought by the court decision. Conversely, an insurance company focuses on the economic costs and benefits and makes a trade-off between the out-of-court settlement and the court decision mainly based on the monetary loss. Fourth, an audit firm is responsible for its audit engagements and thereby can transfer litigation costs and spread litigation risk to the whole society by increasing audit fees. By contrast, an insurance company is unable to provide insurance for all kinds of investment risks.

3. 2. 1. 3 Summary

Overall, Section 3. 2. 1 suggests that property right arrangement is the economic root of independent auditing. Along with the separation of enterprise ownership and management right, independent auditing emerges as a necessary consequence of market selection to mitigate information asymmetry and agency costs. Three theories mainly explain auditing demand: the monitoring hypothesis, information/signaling hypothesis and insurance hypothesis. These theories indicate that in a mature capital market, market competition, price mechanism, regulations and legal mechanisms interact with each other. In such a market, the economic value of auditing includes improving financial reporting quality, reducing agency costs and information risk, mitigating information asymmetry, decreasing firms' financing costs, optimizing resource allocation, and, ultimately, achieving the goal of investor protection. In the monitoring hypothesis, the demand for independent auditing mainly comes from management. They initiatively hire external auditors to alleviate agency conflicts between owners and management and reduce agency costs. In the information/signaling hypothesis, the demand for independent auditing may arise from either investors or management. The motivation to engage auditors is to mitigate information asymmetry and increase firm value. In the insurance hypothesis, both investors and management have the demand for auditing to provide insurance for them. The key to the monitoring explanation is rational expectations and complete contracts. The key to the information explanation is an efficient market and a perfect price mechanism. The key to the insurance explanation is a stringent litigation mechanism. However, in reality, a market that totally meets the above conditions is unlikely to exist. Therefore, a firm's auditing demand is often a mixture of these three theories.

3. 2. 2 Regulating Independent Auditing

As discussed in Section 3. 2. 1, auditing demand is a kind of market inherent demand. However, national laws worldwide generally require listed firms to be audited mandatorily and disclose audited financial reports in the modern institutional arrangement. This general practice implies that governmental regulation, which serves as an important complementary mechanism to make up for market failure, is necessary for independent auditing to play effectively its part.

3. 2. 2. 1 Theories of Governmental Regulation

The regulation economics provide a theoretical basis for government's involvement in the supervision of the audit market. According to the answers to "Why does a market need to be regulated?", the regulation economics can be classified into the public interest theory and interest group theory. The interest group theory further includes the regulation capture theory and economic regulation theory.

(1) Public Interest Theory

The public interest theory stands on a normative analysis framework. This theory is developed on the basis of the market failure theory and the welfare economics. The public interest theory takes market failure as the driver of governmental regulation. This theory has three basic assumptions. First, the market does not function well on its own and is prone to market failure, such as natural monopoly, externalities and information asymmetry. Second, governmental regulation is a costless and effective response to the public's requirement on efficiency and fairness. Third, government is charitable, all-powerful and all-knowing, and social welfare can be maximized by government. On the one hand, government is assumed to be a "moral person" who considers only public interests and has no private interests. Therefore, it is certain that government pursues public interests selflessly and regards maximizing public interests as the ultimate goal of its action and policies. On the other hand, government is assumed to be a "rational person" who has an order of preferences, impeccable calculating ability and complete information. These characteristics help government to maximize social welfare (Zhang, 2005) [312]. This theory notes that governmental regulation is a means of mitigating or eliminating losses caused by market failure.

(2) Regulation Capture Theory

The regulation capture theory is from an empirical perspective and contrary to the public interest theory. Stigler and Friedland (1962) [313] focus on regulation in the electric power industry and empirically test the effect of regulation on price level, price discrimination and rate of return. They find that governmental regulation fails to achieve the low price expected by the public interest theory, suggesting that regulation is ineffective and the government is possibly captured by the enterprises. This finding arouse people's doubt about the effects of governmental regulation and contributed to the development of the regulation capture theory (Viscusi et al., 2005) [314]. This theory holds that regulators will become increasingly dominated by regulated entities as time goes by. Regulators will gradually cater to regulated entities rather than protect the interests of the public (North, 1990) [315]. Some even argue that the emergence of regulators is an outcome of some interest groups' activities. These groups ask government to provide regulation. By doing so, their objective is to avoid fierce competition and protect their own interests. As a consequence, government will lose efficiency in constraining monopoly power, and regulators will be captured by some industries, becoming their stewards (Stigler, 1971)[316]. In this case, the regulatory activities of regulators will seriously damage resource allocation.

(3) Economic Regulation Theory

The economic regulation theory treats regulation as a commodity whose supply is subject to the demand for it. The study of Stigler (1971)[316] lays the foundation for the economic regulation theory. This theory posits that the supply of regulation aims to maximize the interest groups' benefits. Governmental regulation is a channel through which the interest groups redistribute wealth from other social groups by the aid of the state power. Stigler (1971)[316] suggests that political regimes are assumed to be established and used in a rational way. That is to say, political regimes serve as a proper tool to achieve social members' wishes. Based on this notion, the economic regulation theory is developed and exploited to predict which industries will be regulated and the form of regulation. Unlike the public interest theory and regulation capture theory, this theory has the following assumptions. First, government's primary resource is power, and the interest groups can persuade government to use its power to serve their interests. Second, regulators are an "economic person" who can rationally choose to take the utility-maximizing action. Third, governmental regulation is the product of adapting to the interest groups' need for maximizing their benefits.

3.2.2.2 Governmental Regulation on Independent Auditing

Governmental regulation for the audit market is highly in line with the public interest theory. Audit service has characteristics of "credence goods" and "public goods", which can cause audit market failure. This notion provides a basic premise for regulators' intervention.

As elaborated in Section 2.3.1, audit quality depends on an auditor's competence (i. e., auditor's capability of detecting a breach) and independence (i. e., auditor's willingness to provide a fair and objective audit opinion). Both attributes are unobservable (DeFond et al., 2014; DeAngelo, 1981a)[96,97]. Moreover, audit service consumers (including shareholders, debtholders and other financial statements users) have insufficient information and lack professional knowledge to judge the quality of audit products. In addition, they are unlikely to spend too much money on ensuring audit quality. These factors make estimating the quality of audits difficult for consumers. Accordingly, independent auditing possesses characteristics of "credence goods". ① Specifically, severe information asymmetry lies between the suppliers (auditors) and the consumers (accounting information users) of audit services. Auditors know well about the audit process and have more information about the quality of their services. By contrast, information users cannot judge audit quality even if they have used the audit services and the products (the audited financial statements). This feature brings moral hazard and adverse selection to an audit market. Moral hazard is a phenomenon that auditors may impair audit quality through cutting corners during auditing, compromising with audit clients and losing independence for the sake of their own interests. Adverse selection is a phenomenon of "bad money driving out good money": audit firms with services of high price and quality are likely to be expelled from the market by the majority of low-quality and low-priced audit firms. Without regulation, an audit market can become a "lemon market". In such a market, audit quality likely decreases continuously in general. Once the overall audit quality becomes poor, audit services can no longer provide useful incremental information for customers. Rather, audit services will even mislead accounting information users and exacerbate the information asymmetry between owners and management. As a result, a firm's spontaneous demand for auditing will no longer exist.

Alongside the separation of asset ownership and management right and the development of the modern enterprise system, most enterprise owners are becoming increasingly far from firm operation. This change facilitates management to deviate from shareholders' interests and provide fraudulent information. In addition, in a modern capital market, a listed company's audited accounting information is demanded by not only large shareholders and debtholders but also numerous minority investors and other stakeholders, such as suppliers, customers, government and the public. Auditing has a function of increasing the value of accounting information (Silvoso et al., 1973) [319]. Therefore, countries from all over the world focus on independent auditing as if by prior agreement and legally establish the

① A credence good is a product with quality hard to be determined even after use (Yang, 2008) [317]. This good exists when severe information asymmetry lies between the producers and the customers. Because the producers know well about the producing process of a credence good, they possess more information about its quality. By contrast, the customers cannot judge the quality even after they consume the product (Zhang, 2008) [318].

mandatory demand for audit services when strengthening market regulation. Thus far, the auditing business has developed into a statutory business of a public accountant. As the mandatory demand for auditing requires audit reports to be released along with the audited financial statements, the products of audit services are shared by the public. Excluding certain people from enjoying the products is impossible, and increasing the number of consumers does not increase the costs of production. In this way, audit services possess characteristics of "public goods" and can be regarded as a pure public good paid by enterprise owners. ①

Overall, information asymmetry and externality exist in the audit market, thereby making auditing exhibit characteristics of "credence goods" and "public goods". Accordingly, the optimal allocation of resources cannot be achieved through only the market mechanism which likely leads to market failure. For example, due to the externality of audit services, insiders of a company may purchase low-quality and low-priced audit services for cost saving when they focus mainly on their own interests rather than social welfare. At the information disadvantage, investors and other stakeholders' incapability of precisely judging audit quality facilitates insiders to conduct such opportunistic behavior. Consequently, audit firms would eventually lose the motivation to keep high independence and audit quality. Under this circumstance, it is necessary to call for government to act as a "night watchman" and take corrective measures. Governmental regulation is a complementary institutional arrangement. By making laws and regulations and supervising each party in an auditing relationship, governmental regulation can make up for the deficiencies brought by market failure. Governmental regulation helps improve audit independence and provides an institutional guarantee for audit quality, thereby enhancing the producing of reliable audited accounting information. Therefore, governmental regulation is indispensable to the audit market to develop in a healthy and sustainable way (Barton et al., 2004) [321].

3.2.2.3 Summary

Overall, this section elaborates on the theoretical foundation of market

① "Public goods" is a concept opposite to "private goods". A public good cannot be provided by the private sector through the market mechanism. Rather, this good must be provided by the public sector in a non-market way. A public good is characterized as non-competitive and non-exclusive when consumed by customers. Moreover, a public good has indivisible utility and is technically impossible to exclude any customer from its benefits (Hu, 2001) [320].

regulation and suggests that governmental regulation for the audit market is highly in line with the public interest theory. Due to the unobservability of audit quality and the externality of audit products, completely relying on the market mechanism would lead to market failure. Accordingly, independent auditing cannot function effectively without governmental regulation. Firms' voluntary demand, which is induced by the economic value of independent auditing, had already existed before government made it mandatory (Wallace, 2004; Sunder et al., 1997)[310, 322]. Governmental regulation serves as a complementary mechanism to prevent auditing demand and supply from out of control. The interaction between property right arrangement and governmental regulation determines the structure of supply and demand in an audit market. In China, government regulates the audit market to protect public interests with maintaining social fairness and ensuring the orderly operation of the market as its basic purposes. The Chinese government and regulators play a "night watchman" role in alleviating audit market failure and improving audit quality through their intervention.

3. 2. 3 Auditors' Motivation to Provide High Quality

As mentioned in Section 3. 2. 1, the stakeholders of a company have various demand for independent auditing. However, if suppliers are not capable of independently providing high-quality audit services for companies to select (e. g. , auditing cannot mitigate but even exaggerate information asymmetry, providing no incremental information for investors), then no voluntary demand for auditing will exist. What motivates an audit firm to keep high quality? In today's market economy, an audit firm provides high-quality services to either get rewards or avoid punishment. The former purpose arises from market competition and the price mechanism, whereas the latter stems from regulation and the legal mechanism. Based on these two mechanisms respectively, two theories explain why audit firms keep high independence and quality: the reputation hypothesis and deep pocket hypothesis.

The reputation hypothesis focuses on an audit firm's long-term interests and self-protecting motivation. This theory posits that the lack of independence has an adverse impact on an audit firm's auditing revenue and brand name, which largely exceeds the quasi-rents gained from the clients. Building an audit firm's reputation takes a long time and repeated deals with numerous clients, whereas only one case of audit failure can ruin its reputation, followed by decreased market share. The collapse of the Arthur Andersen is a typical example in this case. Accordingly, an audit firm is motivated to keep independence and provide high quality to establish good reputation, avoid reputational losses and gain long-term benefits (DeAngelo, 1981a; Simunic et al. , 1987) [97, 323] .

The deep pocket hypothesis focuses on litigation risk and relevant costs. According to this hypothesis, an audit firm possesses sufficient wealth and thereby has the ability to compensate. Investors and management transfer risks to auditors by paying audit fees. If audit failure occurs (i. e. , the engaged auditors fail to detect or report the material misstatements in a company's financial statements due to their neglect of duty) and investors suffer investment losses based on their trust in the audited information, then they can sue both management of the company and the engaged auditors. In such cases, auditors will be judged to take the responsibility of compensating investors jointly with management, fulfilling their function of sharing risks (Dye, 1993) [308] . Therefore, auditors have to bear high litigation risk and costs if audit failure takes place. To avoid such punishment, an audit firm has the motivation to keep independence and high quality (Palmrose, 1988; DeFond et al. , 1998) [324, 325] .

3. 2. 4 Commitment Effect of Complying with Mandatory Requirements

In an imperfect capital market, investors are usually much weaker than securities issuers. Successfully suing a company is quite difficult for minority investors who are cheated by the company they have invested in. Therefore, the enforcement by courts cannot always effectively prevent fraud in such a market. In many cases, mandatory policies released by regulators become an efficient institutional option to address market failure (Hay et al. , 1996; Hay et al. , 1998) [326, 327] .

Some scholars are in favor of mandatory requirements stipulated by rules and regulations for their value in mitigating agency conflicts (Mahoney, 1995) [328] . Rock (2002) [217] and Stulz (2009) [218] argue that investors' suspicions about management's self-serving behavior that would damage their interests can be mitigated by a company's compliance with a mandatory requirement with a powerful enforcement system, because investors perceive this act as the company's credible commitment to do something on an ex-ante basis.

Taking mandatory disclosure as an example, Cheng et al. (2013) [219] argue that managers complying with the mandatory disclosure requirement is regarded as making a credible commitment to disclose certain information ex ante in investors' perception. Moreover, the powerful enforcement of regulators enhances the credibility of the commitment by making breaching the mandatory requirement costly (Leuz et al., 2000) [329]. By comparison, voluntary disclosure is self-serving because it allows managers to evaluate the consequences before making a decision on whether to disclose the information (Bushee et al., 2005) [330]. In addition, voluntary disclosure lacks sustainability in the future because companies have the freedom to choose whether to disclose the information without any threat of punishment from regulators. Therefore, mandatory disclosure has a higher potential to mitigate agency costs and information asymmetry than voluntary disclosure. Consistent with their argument, Cheng et al. (2013) [219] find that firms changing from mandatory to voluntary disclosure have increased market illiquidity. They attribute this finding to a loss of the credible commitment effect of complying with the mandatory disclosure requirement.

Hail (2011) [221] suggests that an ex-ante credible commitment in investors' perception has the following characteristics: ① a firm does not know the consequences of the disclosed information beforehand; ② disclosing the information is costly; ③ the market reacts differentially to different disclosure levels. Accordingly, complying with the mandatory disclosure requirement can serve as a mechanism to commit to investors credibly on an ex-ante basis. For example, focusing on the SEC disclosure regulation in the U. S., Rock (2002) [217] suggests that this regulation is implemented along with the powerful enforcement of the U. S. regulators and securities laws, which makes breaching this regulation costly. Hence, firms' mandatory disclosure under the SEC disclosure regulation becomes an ex-ante credible commitment to investors and thereby helps address agency problems effectively. Moreover, the regulation unifies the format and quantity of disclosure and constantly makes adjustment on firms' reporting duties, which are also contributory to solving agency issues.

Information disclosure that provides a credible commitment to investors can mitigate information asymmetry (Stulz, 2009) [218], thereby lowering the cost of equity and increasing market liquidity. For example, Diamond and Verrecchia (1991) [57] find that a company's commitment to a higher disclosure level narrows the informational gap between informed investors and uninformed investors. Consequently, investors tend to believe that companies credibly committing to a higher disclosure level are more likely to trade their stocks at a fair price, resulting in increased market liquidity. Information asymmetry between management and market makers can also be mitigated by a company's commitment to a higher disclosure level (Baiman et al. , 1996; Verrecchia, 1999) [331, 332]. Through this credible commitment mechanism, less information can be extracted from the total net demand by market makers. As a result, market illiquidity is decreased.

Based on the evidence of Lansford et al. (2013) [333] that a disaggregate earnings guidance is possibly an ex-ante choice (instead of an ex post one), voluntary disclosure also likely plays a role of credibly committing (either explicitly or implicitly) to investors (Monahan, 2006) [220]. However, voluntary disclosure cannot perfectly replace mandatory disclosure in this regard. One major reason is that in the absence of mandatory disclosure requirements, reputational concern alone may yield to management's pursuit of possible gains in behaving opportunistically ex post. Therefore, reputational concern alone is not sufficient to motivate management to keep their promise of providing a higher disclosure level (Rock, 2002; Stulz, 2009) [217, 218]. Accordingly, voluntary disclosure is suggested to be not as effective as mandatory disclosure in playing an ex-ante credible commitment role and reducing information asymmetry. Thus, the potential of voluntary disclosure to reduce the cost of equity is weaker than that of mandatory disclosure (Monahan, 2006; Hail, 2011) [220, 221]. In addition, from a dynamic perspective, agency problems would become severer when disclosure changes from mandatory to voluntary. Hope and Thomas (2008) [334] find that to facilitate their pursuit of benefits from empire building, management of a U. S. multinational company tend to reduce the detailed disclosure of the company's earnings in each geographic area when the accounting standards no longer compel these companies to disclose such information. This finding suggests that manag-ement make use of the deregulation from mandatory to voluntary disclosure to conduct opportunistic behavior, such as strategically choosing information to disclose or conceal. By doing so, they aim to gain private benefits with the sacrifice of shareholders' interests, resulting in increased agency conflicts between management and shareholders.

Overall, the argument supporting the role of complying with mandatory requirements in reducing agency costs and information asymmetry has been widely applied to the information disclosure field. Relevant studies generally support the notion that mandatory disclosure has a higher potential in reducing information asymmetry and agency costs than voluntary disclosure by providing an ex-ante commitment of disclosing certain information for investors, which is also costly to breach (Rock, 2002; Stulz, 2009; Cheng et al., 2013; Monahan, 2006; Hail, 2011)[217-221].

Leuz and Wysocki (2008)[335] suggest that the idea of complying with a mandatory regime as a commitment device in reducing agency costs and information asymmetry is not specific to the disclosure regulation. Moreover, this role has been documented in other mandatory regimes, such as legal restrictions on contracts (Aghion et al., 1990)[336]. In auditing research, Chen and Han (2015)[337] find that compared with voluntary internal control audit, mandatory internal control audit can significantly improve investment efficiency for SOEs. The authors attribute this finding to the role of complying with the mandatory internal control audit requirement. That is, complying with the mandatory internal control audit requirement not only forms a potential threat to management by depriving them of the freedom to choose whether to have an internal control audit, but also reduces information asymmetry by conveying a credible commitment to investors on an ex-ante basis.

3. 3 Theoretical Framework

After introducing the institutional background and elaborating on the main theories in Sections 3. 1 and 3. 2, this chapter constructs a theoretical framework of this study, which investigates the economic consequences of the deregulation of the mandatory dual audit system on the capital market and audit market. Figure 3 - 1 shows the framework.

First, based on the commitment effect of complying with mandatory requirements, this study analyzes the consequences of the deregulation on the capital market by examining whether mandatory dual audit before the deregulation leads to a lower cost of equity than voluntary dual audit after the deregulation. As discussed in Section 3. 1, after the deregulation of the mandatory dual audit system in 2010, some AH companies opt out of the dual audit system, dismiss their Hong Kong-based auditors, and retain only the mainland-based auditors to perform the

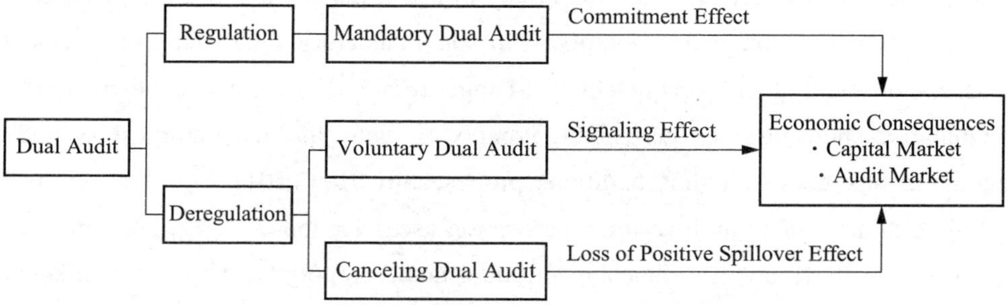

Figure 3-1 Theoretical Framework of This Study

single audit just like the domestic-listed-only companies do. By contrast, other AH companies choose to keep the dual audit system. To study the capital-market consequences of this deregulation, I first focus on the comparison between companies that are required to use the dual audit before the deregulation and those that choose to use the dual audit after the deregulation. As elaborated in Section 3. 2. 4, a company's compliance with a mandatory requirement with a powerful enforcement system is regarded by investors as a promise that is made on an ex-ante basis and hard to reverse. Hence, investors' concerns on management's self-serving behavior that would damage their interests can be relieved by such a perceived commitment (Rock, 2002; Stulz, 2009; Cheng et al. , 2013) [217-219] . This role of complying with mandatory requirements as a commitment device can reduce agency costs, information asymmetry, and thereby the cost of equity (Monahan, 2006; Hail, 2011) [220, 221] . Based on this theory, I argue that compliance with the mandatory dual audit requirement can serve as a mechanism for companies to credibly commit, on an ex-ante basis, to be under the monitoring of two audit firms and disclose two sets of audited financial statements. Consequently, companies' compliance with the mandatory dual audit requirement can alleviate investors' concerns on management's self-serving behavior. By contrast, voluntarily choosing the dual audit allows companies to evaluate the possible consequences before making a dual audit decision and thereby is self-serving. Moreover, due to the powerful enforcement systems, especially those in the Hong Kong market (Ke et al. , 2015) [5] , it is costly for companies that are required to use the dual audit to breach this requirement. As a result, companies' sustainable compliance with this requirement is ensured. However, for companies choosing to keep the dual audit, whether their use of this audit system will be sustained in the future is questionable because they can freely opt out without any threat of punishment from regulators. In addition, whether companies comply with the mandatory dual audit requirement triggers differential market reactions (Fang, 2010)[235]. Taken together, unlike voluntarily choosing the dual audit, complying with the mandatory dual audit requirement satisfies all the conditions proposed by Hail (2011)[221] of an ex-ante credible commitment in investors' perception (see Section 3. 2. 4). Furthermore, compared with voluntarily choosing the dual audit, complying with the mandatory dual audit requirement can enhance the monitoring effect of the two engaged auditors. The reason is that the two auditors mandatorily hired by a company mutually form an ex-ante supervising and controlling mechanism on management's decision-making and implementing process. Therefore, I argue that voluntarily choosing the dual audit after the deregulation cannot fully replace the role of complying with the mandatory dual audit requirement before the deregulation in reducing information asymmetry and mitigating agency costs. Thus, when companies change from complying with the mandatory dual audit requirement to voluntarily choosing the dual audit, their cost of equity possibly increases. Speaking differently, companies may have a lower cost of equity when they mandatorily have dual audit than when they voluntarily use the dual audit.

Second, after investigating the effect of mandatory dual audit relative to voluntary dual audit on the cost of equity, based on the signaling effect of making voluntary audit choices, this study analyzes the consequences of the deregulation on the capital market by examining whether voluntary dual audit after the deregulation leads to a lower cost of equity than single audit in the same period. That is, I second focus on the comparison between companies that choose to use the dual audit after the deregulation and those not having the dual audit (i. e. , using only the single audit) in the same period. According to the signaling theory, high-quality firms would send positive signals to convey their advantages over low-quality ones to investors. They usually take action with additional costs to achieve this purpose (Melumad et al. , 1990; Spence, 1973)[222, 338]. Jensen and Meckling (1976)[257] suggest that firms voluntarily undertake monitoring expenditure to assure external investors that activities harmful to their interests would be restrained. This monitoring expenditure (or bonding cost) refers to contractual guarantees to engage a public accountant to audit financial accounts, contractual limitations on management's decision-making power, and explicit bonding against management's malfeasance. Firms can use the act of engaging auditors to signal their private information to stakeholders with less information (Melumad et al., 1990)[222]. In Melumad and Thoman's (1990)[222] model, audit choice is voluntary, which creates a separating equilibrium. In such an equilibrium, only high-quality firms can have their financial accounts audited. In other words, simulating this act is too costly for low-quality firms. As audit services are expensive, only firms that have very profitable prospects that can cover the incurred audit costs are capable of making such choices. This sets up a barrier that is hard to overstep for low-quality firms if they want to imitate the same practice. Therefore, regardless of the assurance levels provided by the engaged auditors, firms' act of being audited can be treated as a useful signal and convey important information. This act can distinguish these high-quality firms from the inferior ones, and send a positive signal about their good characteristics, such as management integrity, low risk and profitable prospects, to the market. Thus, being audited can help these firms win more preference from investors (BarYosef et al., 1984)[305]. This signaling effect of voluntary audit choices has been documented in many overseas and Chinese studies (Lennox et al., 2011; Dharan, 1992; Ettredge et al., 1994; Haw et al., 2008; Collis, 2010; Collis, 2012; Kausar et al., 2016; Ojala et al., 2016; Hu, 2007; Liu, et al., 2008; Yu, 2008; Zhou, 2010; Jian and Yang, 2012; Han and Zhang, 2013)[223, 339-351]. After the deregulation of the mandatory dual audit system in 2010, some AH companies no longer use the dual audit system in the form of dismissing their Hong Kong-based auditors and retaining only the mainland-based auditors to perform the single audit. Conversely, other AH companies choose to keep the dual audit system. Based on the signaling theory, I argue that after the deregulation, the costly voluntary dual audit choice likely conveys incremental information about a company's good properties beyond the audited financial information. Thus, this choice can create a positive signal that differentiates these firms from those using only the single audit. Accordingly, I argue that firms voluntarily choosing the dual audit likely win more preference from investors and raise external equity capital at lower costs than firms using only the single audit. That is to say, after the deregulation, voluntary dual audit may be associated with a lower cost of equity than single audit.

Third, after understanding the consequences of the deregulation on the capital market, this study analyzes its consequences on the audit market by comparing canceling the dual audit with keeping the dual audit after the deregulation. Specifically, based on a potential positive spillover effect from high- to low-quality auditors through the dual audit process, this study examines whether canceling the dual audit causes a decline in audit quality by foregoing the positive spillover effect from Hong Kong-based auditors. The dual audit conducted by two audit firms complicates the traditional single audit. The two engaged audit firms are supposed to reach a uniform conclusion on whether no material misstatements exist in the auditee's financial statements. Otherwise, financial statements users would question either of the two audit reports, which ultimately leads to the reputational loss of the auditors. In addition, any inconsistent conclusions may provide the basis for investors to initiate lawsuits, which increases the litigation risk faced by the auditors. Therefore, although the two audit firms are not directly involved in each other's work, they feel peer pressure from the other side in the dual audit process (Wang, 2014) [13]. Specific to the dual audit system for AH companies, a common explanation on the audit quality decline after companies cancel the dual audit refers to the loss of a potential positive spillover effect from Hong Kong-based auditors. In other words, the dual audit system can ensure relatively higher audit quality mainly due to the existence of this effect (Ke et al., 2015) [5]. This effect stems from the institutional environment gap, particularly, in the cross-listing setting comprising AH companies. Specifically, the institutional environment in Hong Kong is stronger than that in mainland China in terms of law enforcement, investor protection and media monitoring, among other factors. This stronger institutional environment, in turn, leads to higher independence and audit quality of Hong Kong-based auditors than that of mainland-based auditors. Moreover, according to the rules and regulations of the AH-share market, the two sets of the financial statements of a company, although prepared and audited under different accounting and auditing standards, should be substantially consistent. This implies that the signing off of a company's H-share financial statements by a Hong Kong-based auditor, under the dual audit process, can bring an indirect positive spillover effect from the Hong Kong-based auditor to the mainland-based auditor. The mainland-based auditor is influenced by peer pressure, such as the exemplary audit work and outcomes and the potential monitoring delivered by the Hong Kong-based auditor (Lin et al., 2014) [12]. As a result, it becomes more difficult for the mainland-based auditor to compromise on audit quality, and this attitude guarantees the audit quality of a company keeping the dual audit. However, canceling the dual audit makes it difficult to sustain the positive spillover effect from Hong Kong-based auditors. When the annual audits of AH companies are performed singly by mainland-based auditors, audit quality is likely to be impaired. Therefore, I argue that the loss of the positive spillover effect due to canceling the dual audit by companies may lead to a decline in their audit quality.

Notably, rather than two completely isolated economic consequences, the capital-market consequences and audit-market consequences of the deregulation of the mandatory dual audit system actually have a close inherent relationship with each other, making my study an interconnected whole. As elaborated in Section 2. 2. 2. 2, previous literature generally confirms that audit quality is negatively associated with the cost of equity. Accordingly, to the extent that the association of audit quality with the cost of equity can already have been implied by a wealth of relevant studies, this study does not emphasize testing the relationship between the audit-market consequences and capital-market consequences of the deregulation. Rather, to enhance the potential of this study in making incremental contributions to the literature, the emphasis of my analysis of the capital-market consequences is to shed light on whether and to what extent complying with the mandatory dual audit requirement and voluntarily choosing the dual audit separately affect the cost of equity. These potential effects (if any) are regardless of the assurance levels provided by the engaged auditors, that is, over and above the effects of the audited financial statements (audit quality). Meanwhile, the emphasis of my analysis of the audit-market consequences is to take an initial step toward promoting empirical work on directly measuring the potential positive spillover effect from Hong Kong-based auditors in the dual audit process, and to test whether and to what extent the loss of this positive spillover effect drives the audit quality decline of companies canceling the dual audit.

3. 4 Chapter Summary

This chapter first introduces the institutional background of this study, that is, the mandatory dual audit system for AH companies and its abolition. Then, this chapter elaborates on the main theories related to this study, including theories of firms' auditing demand, regulating independent auditing, auditors' motivation to provide high quality and complying with mandatory requirements. Next, this chapter analyzes the effect of mandatory dual audit on the cost of equity the effect of voluntary dual audit on the cost of equity and the effect of canceling the dual audit on audit quality. Based on these analyses, this chapter finally proposes the theoretical framework of this study. This chapter establishes the theoretical foundation for the empirical analyses in the following chapters. Subsequently, Chapter 4 examines the capital-market consequences of the deregulation of the mandatory dual audit system in the comparison of mandatory dual audit before the deregul-ation with voluntary dual audit after the deregulation. Chapter 5 examines the capital-market consequences of the deregulation of the mandatory dual audit system in the comparison of voluntary dual audit with single audit after the deregulation. Chapter 6 examines the audit-market consequences of the deregulation in the comparison of canceling the dual audit with keeping the dual audit after the deregulation and by deeply exploring the role of a positive spillover effect from Hong Kong-based auditors.

4 Capital-Market Consequences: Effect of Mandatory Dual Audit on Cost of Equity

Based on the theoretical framework proposed in Chapter 3, this chapter analyzes the economic consequences of the deregulation of the mandatory dual audit system on the capital market by examining whether mandatory dual audit before the deregulation has a lower cost of equity than voluntary dual audit after the deregulation.

4.1 Hypothesis Development

Compared with voluntarily choosing the dual audit after the deregulation, I argue that complying with the mandatory dual audit requirement before the deregulation could better mitigate information asymmetry and agency costs. A company's compliance with a mandatory requirement with a powerful enforcement system is regarded by investors as a promise that is made on an ex-ante basis and hard to reverse (Rock, 2002; Stulz, 2009)[217,218]. Investors' concerns on management's self-serving behavior that would damage shareholders' interests can be relieved by such a perceived commitment (Cheng et al., 2013)[219]. Based on this argument, I argue that compliance with the mandatory dual audit requirement can serve as a mechanism for companies to credibly commit, on an ex-ante basis, to be under the monitoring of two audit firms and disclose two sets of audited financial statements. Thus, this perceived commitment can alleviate agency conflicts and information asymmetry between management and investors. Hail (2011)[221] proposes three characteristics of an ex-ante credible commitment in investors' perception (see Section 3.2.4). According to these characteristics, first, when the dual audit system is a mandatory requirement, a company that should comply with this requirement has no freedom to decide whether to follow it. The compliance thus prevents management from evaluating the consequences before making a dual audit decision. By contrast, after the deregulation, in investors' minds, voluntarily choosing the dual audit does not mean that a company credibly commits to be under the monitoring of two audit firms and disclose two sets of audited financial statements on an ex-ante basis. Rather, the company can choose whether to keep the dual audit, based on its expectation on the potential outcomes that this audit system would bring to its own costs and benefits. Second, the dual audit system incurs high audit and disclosure cost burdens on a company. Moreover, when a company complies with the mandatory dual audit requirement, it is also costly for the company to breach this requirement due to the powerful enforcement systems in the two markets (especially in the Hong Kong market) (Ke et al., 2015)[5]. By contrast, when a company has the freedom to choose the dual audit, whether this audit system will be sustained in the future is questionable because the company can freely opt out without any threat of punishment from regulators. Finally, whether to comply with the mandatory dual audit requirement triggers differential market reactions. For example, Fang (2010)[235] shows that investors do not respond positively to the deregulation of the mandatory dual audit system. Overall, complying with the mandatory dual audit requirement possesses all characteristics of an ex-ante credible commitment in investors' perception. Therefore, complying with the mandatory dual audit requirement is likely to have a higher potential than voluntarily choosing the dual audit in reducing agency costs and information asymmetry between management and investors.

In addition, complying with the mandatory dual audit requirement can enhance the monitoring effect of the two engaged auditors. As hiring two auditors is an ex-ante requirement that must be complied with, the two auditors mandatorily hired by a company mutually form an ex-ante supervising and controlling mechanism on management's decision-making and implementing process. By comparison, when the dual audit becomes a voluntary choice, the two engaged auditors tend to show weakened monitoring effect. The reason is that the dual audit can be decided by a company ex post and is adopted only when the company thinks that the benefits of supervision by two auditors outweigh the costs. From this perspective, mandatory dual audit acts as a more powerful potential threat to management's opportunistic behavior than voluntary dual audit.

Overall, I argue that the loss of the role that complying with the mandatory dual audit requirement plays in reducing agency costs and information asymmetry can be costly, and this role cannot be completely replaced by voluntarily choosing the dual audit. If this is the case, then I expect to find a higher cost of equity for voluntary dual audit after the deregulation than for mandatory dual audit before the deregulation. Importantly, I focus on the A-share financial and auditing data of the total sample firms whose A-share financial statements are all audited by mainland-based audit firms. Therefore, the effects of the audited financial information (i. e., audit quality) can be effectively measured and controlled in the empirical process. This practice helps ensure that any change in the cost of equity from mandatory dual audit to voluntary dual audit will be attributed to a loss of the role that complying with the mandatory dual audit requirement plays in reducing agency costs and information asymmetry rather than a change in audit quality.

On the basis of the aforementioned arguments, I formulate the first hypothesis in this study.

Hypothesis 1: Ceteris paribus, companies have a lower cost of equity when they mandatorily have the dual audit than when they voluntarily use the dual audit.

Companies that wish to have a lower cost of equity usually have greater dependence on equity capital. With greater demand for equity financing, these companies have stronger motivation to attract external investors' attention and win their trust (Chen et al., 2019)[352]. This goal may be better achieved through complying with the mandatory dual audit requirement, which has a higher potential in relieving investors' suspicions and concerns than voluntarily choosing the dual audit. That is to say, if complying with the mandatory dual audit requirement can reduce more cost of equity than voluntarily choosing the dual audit, this beneficial effect is likely to be particularly valuable for companies with a greater equity capital need. Speaking differently, the loss of the role that complying with the mandatory dual audit requirement plays in maintaining a lower cost of equity could be more costly for these companies.

Therefore, I formulate the second hypothesis in this study.

Hypothesis 2: Ceteris paribus, the lower cost of equity for mandatory dual audit than voluntary dual audit is more pronounced for companies with higher equity financing demand.

One reason for the necessary existence of mandatory requirements is to solve agency problems (Mahoney, 1995)[328]. A company's compliance with a mandatory requirement with a powerful enforcement system is regarded by investors as a credible commitment made on an ex-ante basis and hard to reverse. Therefore, investors' concerns on management's self-serving behavior can be relieved by such a perceived commitment (Rock, 2002; Stulz, 2009)[217, 218]. Accordingly, if complying with the mandatory dual audit requirement can lower the cost of equity through this mechanism, this beneficial effect is likely more valuable for companies with higher agency costs. In other words, the loss of the role that complying with the mandatory dual audit requirement plays in maintaining a lower cost of equity could be more costly for these companies.

Therefore, I formulate the third hypothesis in this study.

Hypothesis 3: Ceteris paribus, the lower cost of equity for mandatory dual audit than voluntary dual audit is more pronounced for companies with higher agency costs.

Firms can also resort to alternative forms of auditing to reduce information risk. For example, prior research finds that Chinese firms voluntarily purchase audit services for their interim financial statements (Haw et al., 2008)[341]. Chen et al. (2014)[353] show that firms voluntarily hiring auditors to audit their interim reports have lower stock return volatility and lower trading volume, suggesting that the interim report audit significantly reduces information divergence among investors and enhances their confidence. However, as a self-serving choice that is usually made ex post by firms, having an interim report audit is unlikely to completely take the place of the role that complying with the mandatory dual audit requirement plays in reducing the cost of equity. Hence, my fourth hypothesis predicts that the effect of the mandatory dual audit on maintaining a lower cost of equity is irreplaceable by alternative voluntary audit mechanisms, such as the interim report audit.

Therefore, I formulate the fourth hypothesis in this study.

Hypothesis 4: Ceteris paribus, the lower cost of equity for mandatory dual audit than voluntary dual audit is not attenuated by the interim report audit.

4.2 Research Design

4.2.1 Sample and Data

The sample used in this chapter comprises A-share listed companies in China for the period 2007 to 2015. As the new CAS took effect in 2007, I take 2007 as the beginning of my sample period to minimize the confounding impact of accounting standards in this audit-focused study. In addition, this study is conducted against the deregulation of the mandatory dual audit system in 2010. Thus, it seems not very appropriate to include too many years after the deregulation, which may aggravate the unbalance between the periods before and after the deregulation and increase the possibility that confounding factors drive the results. Therefore, I choose 2015, rather than the latest year, to be the end of my sample period.

Although the policy change is mainly experienced by AH companies, I consider that it is important to include domestic-listed-only A-share companies in the total sample in this chapter, instead of focusing exclusively on AH companies. On the one hand, the mainland China market nowadays has attracted increasing attention from international scholars. By conducting the main analyses among a large number of A-share listed companies, I aim to draw conclusions against the background of the mainland China market and generalize my conclusions to offer practical implications for other emerging economies besides China. Therefore, I consider that looking broadly at the entire mainland market and using other A-share companies as a benchmark highlight the contribution of this study and make the study more generalizable than focusing on the much specific AH companies. On the other hand, in the empirical sense, domestic-listed-only A-share companies are unaffected by the deregulation of the mandatory dual audit system and have the same single audit system as the AH companies opting out of the dual audit system do. These features make them serve well as a part of the control group.

After expressing my motivation to include other A-share listed companies apart from AH companies, I start the sample selection procedure of this chapter. All A-share listed firm-year observations with available data on estimating the cost of equity between 2007 and 2015 are obtained from the CSMAR and WIND databases. This yields an initial sample of 11809 firm-year observations. I drop 1207 observations that are in the initial public offering year, since I mainly focus on the costs of re-financing. I then delete 218 observations that were delisted, terminated or under special treatment, because these firms are substantially different from other listed companies regarding financial situation, operating performance, information quality, capital structure, etc. ① I also exclude 313 observations that are in the financial industry, in which the financial indices are not comparable with those in other industries. Since the official abolition of the mandatory dual audit system took place in 2010, to ensure that all the AH sample companies experienced the mandatory dual audit stage, I drop 63 observations that refer to AH companies listing on the A-share market or the H-share market on or after 2010. Finally, I remove 1361 observa tionswith missing financial and auditor information. ② This leaves a final sample of 8647 firm-year observations (2046 firms) for the empirical analyses in this chapter. ③ Table 4 - 1 demonstrates the sample selection process. All continuous variables are winsorized at 0. 01 and 0. 99 to minimize the impact of outliers. ④

Table 4-1 Sample Selection in Chapter 4

Description	Number of Observations
A-share listed observations with available data on estimating the cost of equity during the period of 2007-2015	11809
Less: observations in the initial public offering year	(1207)
Less: observations that were delisted, terminated or under special treatment	(218)
Less: observations in financial industry	(313)
Less: observations that are AH companies listing on the A-share market or the H-share market on or after 2010	(63)
Less: observations with missing financial and auditor data	(1361)
Final Sample used in Chapter 4 (2046 firms)	8647

① According to the Securities Laws in China, a firm that reports losses in 2 consecutive years or more should be labelled with a special treatment sign (ST/ * ST). These firms are subject to a daily price fluctuation limit of 5% and will be terminated from listing if their financial or operating conditions become even worse (e. g. , reporting losses in 4 consecutive years, and reporting negative net assets in 3 consecutive years).

② These observations include 78 observations of non-AH companies that have more than one audit firm recorded for annual auditing, which consist of ①66 A-share observations that have the financial statements of their overseas subsidiaries audited by overseas audit firms, and ②12 AB-share observations that engage different audit firms for their A-share and B-share financial statements audits.

③ For consistency, I use the financial data reported in the A-share market for all the sample companies, including AH companies.

④ Keeping original values or omitting extreme observations from the sample does not change the results.

4.2.2 Measurement of Cost of Equity

Prior research proposes several models to estimate the cost of equity (Gebhardt et al., 2001; Feltham et al., 1995; Gordon et al., 1997; Claus et al., 2001; Easton, 2004; Ohlson et al., 2005)[2, 20-24], while the most commonly used models are the GLS model (Gebhardt et al., 2001)[2], the PEG model (Easton, 2004)[23], the CT model (Claus et al., 2001)[22] and the OJ model (Ohlson et al., 2005)[24]. To select the model that derives the most suitable cost-of-equity measure for the main tests in Chapter 4 and Chapter 5, I follow Botosan and Plumlee (2005)[354] and Mao et al. (2012)[355] and conduct several tests to check the validation of the cost-of-equity measures derived from the four most commonly used models and an average of these four measures. The brief descriptions of the models used to derive these measures are as follows.

Cost-of-Equity Measure Derived from GLS Model:

$$P_t = B_t + \sum_{i=1}^{11} \frac{FROE_{t+i} - COE\_GLS}{(1+COE\_GLS)^i} \times B_{t+i-1} + \frac{FROE_{t+12} - COE\_GLS}{COE\_GLS \times (1+COE\_GLS)^{11}} \times B_{t+11} \tag{4-1}$$

where

P_t = stock price per share at the end of year t.

B_t = book value of equity per share at the beginning of year t.

$FROE_{t+i}$ = forecast return on equity (ROE) for year $t+i$. As the database discloses only the analyst consensus up to year $t+2$, I follow Gebhardt et al. (2001)[2] and Dhaliwal et al. (2006)[356]: for years $t+1$ and $t+2$, $FROE_{t+i}$ is collected from the database; for years $t+3$ to $t+12$, $FROE_{t+i}$ is a linear interpolation to the industry median ROE over the prior 10 years (excluding loss firm-years).

$B_{t+i} = B_{t+i-1} + B_{t+i-1} \times FROE_{t+i} \times (1-k)$. k = expected dividend payout ratio, calculated as the average dividend payout ratio in the prior 3 years.

Cost-of-Equity Measure Derived from OJ Model:

$$COE\_OJ = A + \sqrt{A^2 + \left(\frac{FEPS_{t+1}}{P_t}\right) \times (g - (r_{rf} - 0.03))} \tag{4-2}$$

where

$$A = \frac{1}{2} \times \left((r_{rf} - 0.03) + \frac{DPS_{t+1}}{P_t}\right)$$

$FEPS_{t+1}$ = forecast earnings per share (EPS) for year $t+1$ collected from the database.

P_t = stock price per share at the end of year t.

$g=(STG+LTG)\div 2$. $STG=FEPS_{t+2}\div FEPS_{t+1}-1$. LTG is the average EPS growth rate in the prior 5 years.

r_{rf} = yield on a 10-year Treasury Bond in year t.

$DPS_{t+1}=k\times FEPS_{t+1}$. k = expected dividend payout ratio, calculated as the average dividend payout ratio in the prior 3 years.

Cost-of-Equity Measure Derived from CT Model:

$$P_t = B_t + \sum_{i=1}^{5} \frac{AE_{t+i}}{(1+COE\_CT)^{t+i}} + \frac{AE_{t+5}\times(1+g)}{(COE\_CT-g)\times(1+COE\_CT)^5} \tag{4-3}$$

where

P_t = stock price per share at the end of year t.

B_t = book value of equity per share at the beginning of year t.

$AE_{t+i}=FEPS_{t+i}-COE\_CT\times B_{t+i-1}$. For years $t+1$ and $t+2$, $FEPS_{t+i}$ is collected from the database; for years $t+3$ to $t+5$, $FEPS_{t+i}=FEPS_{t+i-1}+FEPS_{t+i-1}\times LTG$. LTG is the average EPS growth rate in the prior 5 years.

$B_{t+i}=B_{t+i-1}+k\times FEPS_{t+i}$. $k=0.5$ (Claus and Thomas, 2001)[22].

$g=r_{rf}-0.03$. r_{rf} is the yield on a 10-year Treasury Bond in year t.

Cost-of-Equity Measure Derived from PEG Model:

$$COE\_PEG=\sqrt{\frac{FEPS_{t+2}-FEPS_{t+1}}{P_t}} \tag{4-4}$$

where

P_t = stock price per share at the end of year t.

$FEPS_{t+i}$ = forecast EPS for year $t+i$ collected from the database.

Average of Four Individual Cost-of-Equity Measures (Li et al., 2014)[357]:

$$COE\_AVG=\frac{COE\_GLS+COE\_OJ+COE\_CT+COE\_PEG}{4} \tag{4-5}$$

4.2.2.1 Validation Tests of Cost-of-Equity Measures

(1) Descriptive Statistics

Table 4-2 presents the descriptive statistics of the aforementioned five cost-of-equity measures. Among them, $COE\_PEG_{t,i}$ has the largest mean value (14.6%), whereas $COE\_GLS_{t,i}$ has the smallest (6.2%). On average, $COE\_OJ_{t,i}$, $COE\_CT_{t,i}$, and $COE\_AVG_{t,i}$ are similar in magnitude (around 13%).

Table 4-2 Descriptive Statistics of Cost-of-Equity Measures

Variable	N	Mean	Median	Std. Dev	25%	75%
$COE\_GLS_{t,i}$	8647	0.062	0.060	0.025	0.044	0.079
$COE\_OJ_{t,i}$	6861	0.128	0.112	0.074	0.083	0.149
$COE\_CT_{t,i}$	7305	0.129	0.115	0.213	0.059	0.206
$COE\_PEG_{t,i}$	8138	0.146	0.134	0.075	0.099	0.179
$COE\_AVG_{t,i}$	6233	0.131	0.113	0.085	0.081	0.154

Notes: Variable definitions and measurement are reported in Table 4-6.

(2) Correlation Analysis

Table 4-3 reports the univariate Pearson (lower) and Spearman (upper) correlations between the five cost-of-equity measures. All of these measures are highly correlated with one another at the 0.01 level, suggesting that they capture variation in the same underlying construct of the implied cost of equity. Meanwhile, among the Pearson correlations, those between $COE\_GLS_{t,i}$ and the other measures are lower than the remaining Pearson coefficients. A similar situation is observed in the Spearman correlation matrix. These results imply that the variation captured by $COE\_GLS_{t,i}$ is, to a certain degree, different from the variation captured by the other measures.

Table 4-3 Spearman (Upper) and Pearson (Lower) Correlation Coefficients Between Cost-of-Equity Measures

Variable	$COE\_GLS_{t,i}$	$COE\_OJ_{t,i}$	$COE\_CT_{t,i}$	$COE\_PEG_{t,i}$	$COE\_AVG_{t,i}$
$COE\_GLS_{t,i}$	1.000	0.388***	0.301***	0.352***	0.452***
$COE\_OJ_{t,i}$	0.278***	1.000	0.840***	0.523***	0.881***
$COE\_CT_{t,i}$	0.188***	0.770***	1.000	0.594***	0.945***
$COE\_PEG_{t,i}$	0.300***	0.379***	0.452***	1.000	0.727***
$COE\_AVG_{t,i}$	0.292***	0.899***	0.895***	0.548***	1.000

Notes: ***, ** and * represent significance at the 0.01, 0.05 and 0.10 level, respectively, using two-tailed tests; variable definitions and measurement are reported in Table 4-6.

(3) Regressions of Future Realized Return on Cost-of-Equity Measures

I use the buy-and-hold realized return in the following year ($Real_{t+1,i}$) as a proxy for the future realized return. Subsequently, I test the explanatory power of each cost-of-equity measure to the future realized return with a series of univariate regressions (Mao et al., 2012)[355]. Table 4-4 demonstrates the results. All of the five regression models are statistically significant at the 0.01 level. The model of $Real_{t+1,i}$ on $COE\_GLS_{t,i}$ [as shown in Column (1)] and that of $Real_{t+1,i}$ on $COE\_PEG_{t,i}$ [as shown in Column (4)] have the strongest explanatory power (both with Adj. R^2 being 5.9%). The coefficient on each cost-of-equity measure is consistently significant and positive at the 0.01 level across the five regressions. The coefficient on $COE\_GLS_{t,i}$ is the largest [5.944 in Column (1)], followed by that on $COE\_PEG_{t,i}$ [1.974 in Column (4)]. Furthermore, the coefficient difference test (untabulated) shows that the coefficient on $COE\_GLS_{t,i}$ is significantly larger than that on $COE\_PEG_{t,i}$. In summary, these results suggest that $COE\_GLS_{t,i}$ is likely to have stronger power than the alternative measures in explaining the variation in the future realized return in the Chinese capital market.

Table 4-4 Regression Results of Future Realized Return on Cost-of-Equity Measures

Variable	Dependent Variable: $Real_{t+1,i}$				
	(1)	(2)	(3)	(4)	(5)
Intercept	-0.153*** (-8.939)	0.190*** (13.358)	0.198*** (23.842)	-0.070*** (-4.888)	0.115*** (8.521)
$COE\_GLS_{t,i}$	5.944*** (23.283)				
$COE\_OJ_{t,i}$		0.416*** (4.335)			
$COE\_CT_{t,i}$			0.212*** (6.358)		
$COE\_PEG_{t,i}$				1.974*** (22.604)	
$COE\_AVG_{t,i}$					0.970*** (11.195)
N	8634	6851	7292	8125	6223
Adj. R^2	0.059	0.003	0.005	0.059	0.020
F	542.107	18.790	40.423	510.961	125.330

Notes: Columns (1) to (5) separately show the results of regressing future realized return on each cost-of-equity measure; ***, ** and * represent significance at the 0.01, 0.05 and 0.10 level, respectively, using two-tailed tests; *t*-statistics are shown in parentheses; variable definitions and measurement are reported in Table 4-6.

(4) Regressions of Cost-of-Equity Measures on Risk Proxies

In the economic sense, the cost of equity is supposed to have significant associations with risks taken by investors. I take advantage of the following proxies to measure the main risk factors suggested by Botosan and Plumlee (2005) [354] (i. e., market beta, leverage, firm size, growth and information risk): $Beta_{t,i}$ [measured by the unleveraged market beta, that is, market beta divided by (1+ equity ratio)], $DE_{t,i}$(measured by the long-term debt divided by the market value of equity), $LnMV_{t,i}$(measured by the natural log of the market value of equity), $Growth_{t,i}$(measured by average growth in revenues in the prior 3 years) and $Opacity_{t,i}$(equaling 1 for observations rated "C" or "D", and 0 for observations rated "A" or "B" based on the "Rating of Information Transparency for Listed Firms" released by the SZSE). ① Variable definitions are shown in Table 4-6.

Subsequently, I regress the abovementioned five cost-of-equity measures on these risk proxies. The information risk proxy ($Opacity_{t,i}$) has quite a few missing data, which leads to a sharp reduction in the number of observations when including this variable in the models. Considering this issue, I present two sets of results without and with $Opacity_{t,i}$ as an independent variable separately in Panel A and Panel B of Table 4-5.

In Panel A of Table 4-5, Column (1) shows that $COE\_GLS_{t,i}$ is significantly associated with all the risk proxies. Except for $LnMV_{t,i}$, the signs of the coefficients on the other independent variables are all in line with the theoretical expectation. In Column (2), $COE\_OJ_{t,i}$ is significantly associated with only four risk proxies, among which, $Beta_{t,i}$ has a sign contrary to the theoretical expectation. $COE\_OJ_{t,i}$ shows no significant relationship with $LnMV_{t,i}$. In Column (3), $COE\_CT_{t,i}$ is significantly related to only two (i. e., $MB_{t,i}$ and $Growth_{t,i}$) out of the five risk proxies with signs consistent with the theoretical expectation. In Column (4), $COE\_PEG_{t,i}$ is significantly associated with all the risk proxies. The signs of the coefficients on them are generally in line with the theoretical expectation except for $Beta_{t,i}$. Column (5) shows that the significant associations between $COE\_AVG_{t,i}$ and the five risk proxies are similar to those between $COE\_PEG_{t,i}$ and the five risk proxies shown in Column (4).

Panel B of Table 4-5 presents that the additionally introduced information

① Data of the "Rating of Information Transparency for Listed Firms" released by the SZSE is obtained from the CSMAR database.

risk proxy ($Opacity_{t,i}$) is positively related to $COE\_GLS_{t,i}$ and $COE\_CT_{t,i}$, consistent with the theoretical expectation. $Opacity_{t,i}$ shows a negative association with $COE\_OJ_{t,i}$. $COE\_PEG_{t,i}$ and $COE\_AVG_{t,i}$ demonstrate no significant relationship between each of them and $Opacity_{t,i}$.

Moreover, comparing the Adj. R^2 across all the five models in each panel of Table 4-5, I observe that the ones of the models with $COE\_GLS_{t,i}$ as the dependent variable (39.6% in Panel A; 41.1% in Panel B) largely exceed those of the remaining models. This finding implies that these risk factors have stronger explanatory power on $COE\_GLS_{t,i}$ than on the other measures in the Chinese setting.

Table 4-5 Regression Results of Cost-of-Equity Measures on Risk Proxies

Panel A: Regression Results of Cost-of-Equity Measures on Risk Proxies Excluding $Opacity_{t,i}$					
Variable	Dependent Variable: $COE\_GLS_{t,i}$ (1)	Dependent Variable: $COE\_OJ_{t,i}$ (2)	Dependent Variable: $COE\_CT_{t,i}$ (3)	Dependent Variable: $COE\_PEG_{t,i}$ (4)	Dependent Variable: $COE\_AVG_{t,i}$ (5)
Intercept	0.038*** (7.374)	0.142*** (6.599)	0.065 (1.050)	0.474*** (23.978)	0.277*** (10.616)
$Beta_{t,i}$	0.007*** (9.889)	-0.005* (-1.774)	0.005 (0.577)	-0.008*** (-3.066)	-0.007* (-1.884)
$DE_{t,i}$	0.014*** (16.172)	0.041*** (11.491)	-0.013 (-1.291)	0.019*** (5.717)	0.027*** (6.363)
$LnMV_{t,i}$	0.002*** (6.660)	-0.000 (-0.261)	0.003 (1.217)	-0.014*** (-16.118)	-0.006*** (-5.335)
$MB_{t,i}$	-0.005*** (-59.477)	-0.005*** (-14.626)	-0.007*** (-7.387)	-0.003*** (-10.366)	-0.005*** (-11.488)
$Growth_{t,i}$	0.001*** (11.445)	0.008*** (14.457)	0.015*** (10.622)	0.007*** (16.249)	0.012*** (18.354)
N	8647	6861	7305	8138	6233
Adj. R^2	0.396	0.100	0.020	0.082	0.089
F	1134.650	153.265	31.065	145.580	122.914

续表

Panel B: Regression Results of Cost-of-Equity Measures on Risk Proxies Including $Opacity_{t,i}$					
Variable	Dependent Variable: $COE\_GLS_{t,i}$ (1)	Dependent Variable: $COE\_OJ_{t,i}$ (2)	Dependent Variable: $COE\_CT_{t,i}$ (3)	Dependent Variable: $COE\_PEG_{t,i}$ (4)	Dependent Variable: $COE\_AVG_{t,i}$ (5)
Intercept	0. 041 *** (5. 506)	0. 091 *** (3. 227)	-0. 090 (-1. 029)	0. 448 *** (14. 994)	0. 185 *** (5. 112)
$Beta_{t,i}$	0. 005 *** (6. 134)	-0. 008 ** (-2. 457)	-0. 004 (-0. 455)	-0. 006 * (-1. 792)	-0. 008 ** (-2. 125)
$DE_{t,i}$	0. 014 *** (9. 854)	0. 056 *** (10. 378)	-0. 019 (-1. 164)	0. 022 *** (3. 824)	0. 046 *** (6. 651)
$LnMV_{t,i}$	0. 001 *** (4. 275)	0. 002 * (1. 734)	0. 008 ** (2. 020)	-0. 013 *** (-9. 626)	-0. 002 (-1. 302)
$MB_{t,i}$	-0. 005 *** (-47. 320)	-0. 005 *** (-13. 220)	-0. 007 *** (-5. 740)	-0. 004 *** (-9. 503)	-0. 005 *** (-10. 306)
$Growth_{t,i}$	0. 001 *** (9. 842)	0. 008 *** (13. 425)	0. 017 *** (9. 091)	0. 008 *** (13. 585)	0. 013 *** (15. 715)
$Opacity_{t,i}$	0. 002 ** (2. 165)	-0. 011 *** (-2. 917)	0. 055 *** (5. 112)	0. 003 (0. 943)	-0. 002 (-0. 530)
N	4896	4135	4185	4672	3732
Adj. R^2	0. 411	0. 131	0. 031	0. 089	0. 112
F	569. 491	104. 563	23. 439	77. 213	79. 499

Notes: Columns (1) to (5) separately show the results of regressing each cost-of-equity measure on the risk proxies; * * *, * * and * represent significance at the 0. 01, 0. 05 and 0. 10 level, respectively, using two-tailed tests; t-statistics are shown in parentheses; variable definitions and measurement are reported in Table 4-6.

4. 2. 2. 2 Measurement of Cost of Equity Used in This Study

Taking the results of the abovementioned validation tests among the most commonly used cost-of-equity estimates together, I consider that $COE\_GLS_{t,i}$ has relatively better performance and higher reliability in the Chinese capital market than all the other measures. Furthermore, Chen et al. (2011)[83] suggest that the GLS model is the most applicable to the Chinese capital market. Accordingly, I follow Chen et al. (2011)[83] and use $COE\_GLS_{t,i}$ when conducting the main tests in Chapter 4 and Chapter 5. $COE\_OJ_{t,i}$, $GLS\_CT_{t,i}$, $GLS\_PEG_{t,i}$ and $GLS\_AVG_{t,i}$ are used for robustness check in these two chapters.

4. 2. 3 Empirical Model

To empirically test H1 (and the further hypotheses H2 to H4) about the effect of mandatory dual audit relative to voluntary dual audit on the cost of equity, I formulate Eq. (4-6) as follows:

$$COE\_GLS_{t,i} = \alpha_0 + \alpha_1 DUAL_{t,i} + \alpha_2 POST_{t,i} + \alpha_3 DUAL_{t,i} * POST_{t,i} + \alpha_4 AH_{t,i} + \alpha_5 Size_{t,i} + \alpha_6 Beta_{t,i} + \alpha_7 MB_{t,i} + \alpha_8 DE_{t,i} + \alpha_9 Std\_Ret_{t,i} + \alpha_{10} Liq_{t,i} + \alpha_{11} Growth_{t,i} + \alpha_{12} SOE_{t,i} + \alpha_{13} Disp_{t,i} + \alpha_{14} Bias_{t,i} + \alpha_{15} Big4_{t,i} + \varepsilon_{t,i} \quad (4-6)$$

where the dependent variable ($COE\_GLS_{t,i}$) is the cost of equity based on Eq. (4-1), as discussed in Section 4. 2. 2. $DUAL_{t,i}$ is a proxy for dual audits; it equals 1 if a firm uses the dual audit in year t (either mandatorily or voluntarily), and 0 otherwise. $POST_{t,i}$ equals 1 in the period after the deregulation (i. e., 2010-2015), and 0 otherwise. The independent variable of interest is the interaction term of $DUAL_{t,i}$ and $POST_{t,i}$. This interaction captures the incremental effect of voluntarily choosing the dual audit beyond complying with the mandatory dual audit requirement on the cost of equity. As per H1, I expect that companies have a lower cost of equity when they mandatorily have the dual audit than when they voluntarily use the dual audit. Hence, I expect a positive coefficient on $DUAL_{t,i} * POST_{t,i}$ in the regression model.

Notably, Eq. (4-6) is not a difference-in-differences (DiD) design which seems not applicable to my research question. Specifically, as no case complies with the mandatory dual audit requirement (voluntarily chooses the dual audit) after (before) the deregulation in 2010, the comparison between mandatory dual audit and voluntary dual audit is actually a longitudinal comparison between the cases that exist only before the deregulation and the cases that exist only after the deregulation. Consequently, in Eq. (4-6), variable $DUAL_{t,i}$ does not represent the classification between the sample changing from mandatory dual audit to mandatory dual audit and the sample changing from mandatory dual audit to voluntary dual audit in a typical DiD model. Rather, this variable is an indicator for dual audits (comprising both mandatory dual audit and voluntary dual audit). When $POST_{t,i}$ equals 0 (1), $DUAL_{t,i}$ equaling 1 represents the mandatory (voluntary) dual audit cases. The interaction item $DUAL_{t,i} * POST_{t,i}$, which I mainly focus on in this model, captures the incremental effect of voluntary dual audit beyond mandatory dual audit on the cost of equity. ①

As the sample contains both AH companies and domestic-listed-only companies, some may argue that the impacts on the cost of equity are mainly caused by the effects of cross-listing rather than by complying with the mandatory dual audit requirement. To rule out this possibility, I include a control variable, $AH_{t,i}$, in the model. $AH_{t,i}$ equals 1 if the firm is an AH company, and 0 otherwise. If cross-listing on the overseas market lowers the cost of equity, I would expect the coefficient on $AH_{t,i}$ to be negative. On the contrary, Guo and Tang (2008)[358] argue that cross-listing in Hong Kong might not help domestic-listed companies to reduce their cost of capital. Given the mixed evidence, I do not have a prediction on the sign of $AH_{t,i}$.

Following prior studies, I also control for various firm-level characteristics, including size, risk, market-to-book ratio, solvency, stock return volatility, profitability, liquidity and revenue growth, that would influence the cost of equity (Gebhardt et al., 2001; Zeng and Lu, 2006; Chen et al., 2011; Botosan et al., 2005; Dhaliwal et al., 2006; El Ghoul et al., 2011; Mishra, 2014; Lu et al., 2014; Chen et al., 2015; Cao et al., 2017)[2, 60, 83, 354, 356, 359–363]. As large firms are more likely to attract public attention, the information asymmetry between controlling shareholders and external investors and thereby the cost of equity of large firms are expected to be lower than that of small firms (Zeng and Lu, 2006; Chen et al., 2011; El Ghoul et al., 2011)[60, 83, 359]. Hence, I expect a negative sign of $Size_{t,i}$ (which is measured by the natural log of total assets). Following Chen et al. (2011)[83], I include the following control variables: $Beta_{t,i}$ [i. e., market risk, measured by the unleveraged market beta, that is, market beta divided by (1 + equity ratio)], $MB_{t,i}$ (i. e., market-to-book ratio, measured by the market value of equity divided by the book value of equity), $Growth_{t,i}$ (i. e., long-term revenue growth, measured by average growth in revenues in the prior 3 years) and $SOE_{t,i}$ (i. e., an indictor variable that equals 1 if the firm is an SOE, and 0 otherwise). The CAPM suggests a positive relationship of market risk with the cost of equity capital

① By noting this, I admit that this study cannot establish the strongest causal link of complying with the mandatory dual audit requirement and voluntarily choosing the dual audit with the cost of equity. This is a common caveat for studies related to audit choices, as the decision to have audits or not is voluntary. In my setting, this means that firms voluntarily choosing the dual audit probably differ from firms using only the single audit. Nevertheless, I attempt to address such an endogeneity issue with several tests in the following sections[see Column (3) of Table 4-9 and Panel B Column (2) of Table 4-12 for more details].

(Sharpe, 1964; Botosan et al. , 2005) [19, 354] . Investors expect to earn higher returns in the future from firms with lower market-to-book ratio (Fama et al. , 1992; Chen et al. , 2015) [41, 362] . Stocks with higher expected growth are found to have higher volatility, market risk and required returns (Botosan et al. , 2005) [354] . Chen et al. (2011) [83] find that the cost of equity of SOEs is lower than that of non-SOEs. Therefore, I expect the signs of $Beta_{t, i}$ and $Growth_{t, i}$ to be positive while the signs of $MB_{t, i}$ and $SOE_{t, i}$ to be negative.

The following variables are included to control for the impacts of liquidity and solvency on the cost of equity. Long-term solvency ($DE_{t, i}$) refers to the long-term debt divided by the market value of equity. Previous research demonstrates that financial risk increases with the proportion of debt in a firm's capital structure, which increases investors' expected returns (Botosan et al. , 2005; Lu et al. , 2014) [354, 361] . Therefore, I predict that the sign of $DE_{t, i}$ is positive. Stock return volatility ($Std\_Ret_{t, i}$) is measured as the standard deviation of monthly stock returns in the year. Stocks with higher return volatility usually have higher investment risks, and thus, lead to investors' demand for higher returns. This, in turn, increases firms' equity financing costs (Cao et al. , 2017) [363] . Therefore, the sign of $Std\_Ret_{t, i}$ is expected to be positive. Liquidity ($Liq_{t, i}$) is calculated by the sum of daily trading volume divided by the number of trading days in the year. As investors expect lower returns for stocks with higher liquidity (Lu et al. , 2014) [361] , I expect the sign of $Liq_{t, i}$ to be negative.

Furthermore, I include $Disp_{t, i}$ (forecast dispersion, measured by the standard deviation of analyst forecasts for year *t* EPS divided by mean analyst forecasts for year *t* EPS) and $Bias_{t, i}$ (forecast bias, measured as forecast EPS minus reported EPS divided by stock price at the beginning of the year) to control for the two attributes of analyst forecasts. Based on the findings of Botosan and Plumlee (2005) [354] , Dhaliwal et al. (2006) [356] , Hail and Leuz (2006) [364] and Cao et al. (2017) [363] , I expect that the signs of $Disp_{t, i}$ and $Bias_{t, i}$ are positive.

Notably, as mentioned in Section 4. 1, to ensure that any change in the cost of equity from mandatory dual audit to voluntary dual audit will not be attributed to the assurance levels provided by auditors (i. e. , audit quality), I include $Big4_{t, i}$ as a control variable. $Big4_{t, i}$ is an indicator variable that equals 1 if the company engages a Big 4 auditor for the audit, and 0 otherwise. Previous literature mainly supports the argument that the audit quality of Big 4 is higher than that of non-Big 4 owing to larger size, more specialized employees and greater international reputation risk concerns of Big 4 (Ke et al., 2015; DeAngelo, 1981a; Reichelt et al., 2010) [5, 97, 365]. I expect that companies audited by Big 4 auditors have a lower cost of equity, and thus, the coefficient on $Big4_{t,i}$ is expected to be negative (Francis et al., 2008; Cao et al., 2017) [205, 363]. Variable definitions are shown in Table 4-6.

Table 4-6 Variable Definitions in Chapter 4

Variable	Description
Variables in Baseline Model[Eq. (4-6)]	
Dependent Variable	
$COE\_GLS_{t,i}$	Cost of equity estimated following Gebhardt et al. (2001) [2].
Independent Variables of Interest	
$DUAL_{t,i}$	1 the company uses the dual audit, and 0 otherwise.
$POST_{t,i}$	1 if the company is in the period after the deregulation, and 0 otherwise.
Control Variables	
$AH_{t,i}$	1 if the company is an AH company, and 0 otherwise.
$Size_{t,i}$	Natural log of total assets.
$Beta_{t,i}$	Unleveraged beta, calculated as the market beta divided by (1 + equity ratio).
$MB_{t,i}$	The market value of equity divided by the book value of equity.
$DE_{t,i}$	Long-term debt divided by the market value of equity.
$Std\_Ret_{t,i}$	The standard deviation of monthly stock returns in the year.
$Liq_{t,i}$	The sum of daily trading volume divided by the number of trading days in the year.
$Growth_{t,i}$	Average growth in revenues in the prior 3 years.
$SOE_{t,i}$	1 if the company is an SOE, and 0 otherwise.
$Disp_{t,i}$	The standard deviation of analyst forecasts for year t EPS divided by mean analyst forecasts for year t EPS.
$Bias_{t,i}$	Forecast EPS minus reported EPS divided by stock price at the beginning of the year.
$Big4_{t,i}$	1 if the company engages a Big 4 auditor in year t, and 0 otherwise.
Variables in Other Tests	
$COE\_OJ_{t,i}$	Cost of equity estimated following Ohlson and Juettner (2005) [24].

续表

Variable	Description
$COE\_CT_{t,i}$	Cost of equity estimated following Claus and Thomas (2001) [22].
$COE\_PEG_{t,i}$	Cost of equity estimated following Easton (2004) [23].
$COE\_AVG_{t,i}$	The average of $COE\_GLS_{t,i}$, $COE\_OJ_{t,i}$, $COE\_CT_{t,i}$ and $COE\_PEG_{t,i}$.
$Real_{t+1,i}$	The buy-and-hold realized return in year $t+1$.
$LnMV_{t,i}$	Natural log of the market value of equity.
$Opacity_{t,i}$	1 if the company is rated "C" or "D" in year t, and 0 if the company is rated "A" or "B" in year t, based on the "Rating of Information Transparency for Listed Firms" released by the SZSE.
$\mid DACC \mid_{t,i}$	The absolute value of performance-adjusted discretionary accruals for year t (Kothari et al., 2005) [366].
$Restate_{t,i}$	1 if the company announces at least 1 accounting restatement in the year, and 0 otherwise.
$MAO_{t,i}$	1 if the company receives a modified audit opinion, and 0 otherwise.
$Chg\_NtB_{t,i}$	1 if the company switches from a non-Big 4 to a Big 4 auditor, and 0 otherwise.
$Chg\_BtN_{t,i}$	1 if the company switches from a Big 4 to a non-Big 4 auditor, and 0 otherwise.
$Chg\_MtV_{t,i}$	1 if the company switches from mandatory to voluntary dual audit, and 0 otherwise.
$Chg\_MtS_{t,i}$	1 if the company switches from mandatory dual audit to single audit, and 0 otherwise.
$Chg\_VtS_{t,i}$	1 if the company switches from voluntary dual audit to single audit, and 0 otherwise.
$CI_{t,i}$	Convergence index in year t, calculated from Eq. (4-7).

4.3 Empirical Results

4.3.1 Sample Distribution

Table 4-7 reports the sample distribution. Panel A of Table 4-7 shows that the sample firms are distributed across 17 different industries. The manufacturing industry has the largest number of observations (5227 observations), followed by the wholesale and retail trades industry (530 observations), the information transmission, software and information technology services industry (478 observations) and the real estate industry (471 observations).

Table 4-7 Panel B shows a description of distribution by year. Column (1) indicates an increasing yearly trend of the total sample, while Column (2) shows that the annual sample size of the AH sample gradually increases in the first 4 years and remains relatively stable after 2010. Column (3) shows that the annual size of the sample complying with the mandatory dual audit requirement increases in the period before the deregulation (i. e., 2007-2009). Column (4) reports that, after the deregulation (i. e., 2010-2015), the number of companies voluntarily choosing the dual audit shows a generally declining trend, especially from 2010 to 2011. However, even at the end of the sample period (i. e., 2015), companies voluntarily choosing the dual audit still occupy 63.6% (28/44) of the AH sample. This implies that most of the companies in the sample previously bound by the mandatory dual audit requirement consider that the benefits of the dual audit system outweigh its costs and continue to opt for it after the deregulation. Such voluntary demand for the dual audit system cannot be neglected, and seems to be contrast to regulators' view that the value of the dual audit has largely diminished since the convergence of the CAS with the IFRS.

Table 4-7 Sample Distribution in Chapter 4

Panel A: Sample Distribution by Industry	
Industry	Number
Agriculture, Forestry, Husbandry and Fishery	129
Construction	228
Culture, Sports and Entertainment	103
Education	3
Electricity, Heat, Gas and Water Production and Supply	384
Health and Social Work	26
Hotels and Catering Services	47
Information Transmission, Software and Information Technology Services	478
Leasing and Business Services	105
Manufacturing	5227

续表

Panel A: Sample Distribution by Industry	
Industry	Number
Mining	296
Miscellaneous	48
Real Estate	471
Scientific Research and Technical Services	41
Transport, Storage and Post	423
Water Conservancy, Environment and Public Facilities Management	108
Wholesale and Retail Trades	530
Total	8647

Panel B: Sample Distribution by Year				
Year	(1) Number of Total Sample	(2) Number of AH Sample	(3) Number of Mandatory Dual Audit Sample	(4) Number of Voluntary Dual Audit Sample
2007	362	19	19	—
2008	554	27	27	—
2009	768	35	35	—
2010	916	43	—	42
2011	836	41	—	30
2012	1041	42	—	30
2013	1208	42	—	29
2014	1441	42	—	28
2015	1521	44	—	28
Total	8647	335	81	187

Notes: The industry classification is adapted from the "Revised Guidance for Industry Classification of China's Listed Companies" (CSRC, 2012) [367].

4. 3. 2 Descriptive Statistics

The descriptive statistics of the total sample in this chapter are presented in Panel A of Table 4-8. The mean (median) cost of equity ($COE\_GLS_{t,i}$) is 6. 2% (6. 0%), lying in the range of the values estimated by previous studies in the Chinese setting (Chen et al. , 2011; Mao et al. , 2012) [83, 355]. As shown in Table 4-8, 3. 1% of the observations use the dual audit (regardless of mandatorily or voluntarily) ($DUAL_{t,i}$), while 80.5% of the observations are in the period after the deregulation ($POST_{t,i}$). Regarding the control variables, 3.9% of the observations are AH companies ($AH_{t,i}$). The values of other controls are consistent with previous Chinese studies, and the mean values of $Size_{t,i}$, $Beta_{t,i}$, $MB_{t,i}$, $Growth_{t,i}$ and $DE_{t,i}$ suggest that on average, the sample firms are generally large-sized firms in good financial condition and with growth potential. Of the sample firms, 49.4% are SOEs ($SOE_{t,i}$). The mean (median) analyst forecast dispersion ($Disp_{t,i}$) is 0.120 (0.076). The mean (median) analyst forecast bias ($Bias_{t,i}$) is 0.009 (0.005), which is upward but very close to 0. I also find that Big 4 auditors provide audit services for 8.2% of the sample observations ($Big4_{t,i}$).

Table 4-8 Descriptive Statistics and Test of Differences

Panel A: Descriptive Statistics of Total Sample in Chapter 4 (N=8647)					
Variable	Mean	Median	Std. Dev.	25%	75%
$COE\_GLS_{t,i}$	0.062	0.060	0.025	0.044	0.079
$DUAL_{t,i}$	0.031	0.000	0.173	0.000	0.000
$POST_{t,i}$	0.805	1.000	0.396	1.000	1.000
$AH_{t,i}$	0.039	0.000	0.193	0.000	0.000
$Size_{t,i}$	22.353	22.162	1.261	21.430	23.086
$Beta_{t,i}$	0.478	0.442	0.297	0.276	0.647
$MB_{t,i}$	3.799	2.967	2.905	1.884	4.669
$DE_{t,i}$	0.144	0.033	0.269	0.006	0.147
$Std\_Ret_{t,i}$	0.143	0.129	0.063	0.099	0.174
$Liq_{t,i}$	0.027	0.022	0.018	0.013	0.037
$Growth_{t,i}$	1.000	0.577	1.807	0.209	1.117
$SOE_{t,i}$	0.494	0.000	0.500	0.000	1.000
$Disp_{t,i}$	0.120	0.076	0.234	0.032	0.158
$Bias_{t,i}$	0.009	0.005	0.028	-0.001	0.015
$Big4_{t,i}$	0.082	0.000	0.275	0.000	0.000

续表

Panel B: Test of Differences Between Mandatory Dual Audit ($DUAL_{t,i}=1$ and $POST_{t,i}=0$) and Voluntary Dual Audit ($DUAL_{t,i}=1$ and $POST_{t,i}=1$)			
Variable	Mean		Test of Differences
	$DUAL_{t,i}=1$ & $POST_{t,i}=0$ (N=81)	$DUAL_{t,i}=1$ & $POST_{t,i}=1$ (N=187)	t-stat.
$COE\_GLS_{t,i}$	0.056	0.083	−7.283 ***
$Size_{t,i}$	24.285	25.122	−5.584 ***
$Beta_{t,i}$	0.463	0.459	0.101
$MB_{t,i}$	3.348	1.790	4.901 ***
$DE_{t,i}$	0.331	0.603	−4.118 ***
$Std\_Ret_{t,i}$	0.160	0.112	6.513 ***
$Liq_{t,i}$	0.026	0.010	9.910 ***
$Growth_{t,i}$	1.032	0.460	4.350 ***
$SOE_{t,i}$	0.975	0.968	0.325
$Disp_{t,i}$	0.135	0.070	1.374
$Bias_{t,i}$	0.009	0.006	1.157
$Big4_{t,i}$	0.741	0.727	0.228

Notes: ***, ** and * represent significance at the 0.01, 0.05 and 0.10 level, respectively, using two-tailed tests; variable definitions and measurement are reported in Table 4-6.

4.3.3 Univariate Tests

Panel B of Table 4-8 compares the mean values of the dependent variable and control variables between the companies mandatorily having the dual audit (i.e., the sample for which $DUAL_{t,i}=1$ and $POST_{t,i}=0$; $N=81$) and the companies voluntarily using the dual audit (i.e., the sample for which $DUAL_{t,i}=1$ and $POST_{t,i}=1$; $N=187$). The last column reports the t-statistics in the mean difference test. As reported in the panel, the mean cost of equity ($COE\_GLS_{t,i}$) of the companies mandatorily having the dual audit (0.056) is significantly lower than that of the companies voluntarily using the dual audit (0.083). This result shows preliminary support for H1 stating that companies have a lower cost of equity when complying with the mandatory dual audit requirement than when voluntarily choosing the dual audit. In addition, I find that mandatory dual audit is associated with smaller size ($Size_{t,i}$), higher market-to-book ratio ($MB_{t,i}$), greater long-term solvency ($DE_{t,i}$), higher volatility ($Std\_Ret_{t,i}$), higher liquidity ($Liq_{t,i}$) and greater long-term growth ($Growth_{t,i}$).

4. 3. 4 Multivariate Regressions

4. 3. 4. 1 Tests of H1

Table 4-9 presents the findings of the tests of H1 that compares the cost of equity between mandatory dual audit and voluntary dual audit. All the regression models have statistical significance at the 0. 01 level. It is unlikely that the test variables suffer from multicollinearity, given that the variance inflation factor (VIF) for each variable is lower than 10 (unreported) (Kennedy, 2003) [368]. The sample in Column (1) consists of the total 8647 firm-year observations. I observe that the coefficient on $DUAL_{t,i} * POST_{t,i}$ is positive and significant at the 0. 05 level (coefficient = 0. 006, $t = 2.440$). This result suggests that after controlling for the underlying determinants [including audit quality ($Big4_{t,i}$)], voluntarily choosing the dual audit after the deregulation leads to a higher cost of equity than complying with the mandatory dual audit requirement before the deregulation. In terms of economic significance, given that the mean cost of equity of the total sample is 0. 062, the magnitude of the coefficient means that voluntarily choosing the dual audit increases companies' cost of equity by approximately 9. 7%, compared to complying with the mandatory dual audit requirement. This finding is consistent with my expectation in H1 that the cost of equity is lower when companies comply with the mandatory dual audit requirement than when they voluntarily choose the dual audit. The coefficient on $DUAL_{t,i}$ is negative and significant at the 0. 01 level, indicating that companies complying with the mandatory dual audit requirement have a lower cost of equity than those using the single audit in the period of 2007-2009. The coefficient on $POST_{t,i}$ is positive and significant at the 0. 01 level, implying that the average cost of equity in the years 2010-2015 is higher than that in the years 2007-2009.

The results of most controls are in line with prior studies. For example, market risk ($Beta_{t,i}$), financial risk ($DE_{t,i}$), long-term growth ($Growth_{t,i}$), and forecast bias ($Bias_{t,i}$) are positively related to the cost of equity. In addition, cross-listing in Hong Kong has a positive relationship with the cost of equity ($AH_{t,i}$), and this result is consistent with that of Hung et al. (2008) [369]. The cost of equity is lower for companies with higher market-to-book ratio ($MB_{t,i}$) and greater liquidity ($Liq_{t,i}$) and for SOEs ($SOE_{t,i}$). $Size_{t,i}$ and $Std\_Ret_{t,i}$ are statistically significant but with non-predicted signs. According to Mao et al. (2012)[355], this occurs in the Chinese setting when estimating the cost of equity following the commonly used models, which is potentially due to overly strong assumptions about the parameters (e. g. , forecast earnings and expected dividend) in the models.

To address the self-selection issue that A-share companies choose whether to cross-list in Hong Kong, I re-run the regression model [i. e. , Eq. (4-6)] with a restriction of 335 AH sample observations over the whole sample period. In Column (2) of Table 4-9, I observe that the coefficient on $DUAL_{t,i} * POST_{t,i}$ remains positive and significant in the model using this reduced sample (coefficient = 0. 013, t = 3. 285). In addition, I further limit the sample to 268 observations using the dual audit (comprising both observations mandatorily using the dual audit and those voluntarily using the dual audit) and re-estimate Eq. (4-6) with firm fixed effects included. This compares over time a dual-audited firm's observations complying with the mandatory dual audit requirement with its observations voluntarily choosing the dual audit and helps to address the concern that unobserved firm characteristics confound the main results. The significant and positive coefficient on $POST_{t,i}$ in Column (3) of Table 4-9 (coefficient = 0. 011, t = 3. 601) suggests that when holding the firms constant, voluntary dual audit still leads to a higher cost of equity than mandatory dual audit does. Overall, these reduced sample analyses reinforce the conclusion drawn from the full sample analysis that companies have a lower cost of equity when they mandatorily have the dual audit than when they voluntarily use the dual audit.

Table 4-9 Regression Results of Tests of H1

Variable	Dependent Variable: $COE\_GLS_{t,i}$		
	(1)	(2)	(3)
Intercept	-0. 000 (-0. 047)	0. 022 (0. 608)	0. 227 * (1. 948)
$DUAL_{t,i}$	-0. 017 *** (-5. 317)	-0. 021 *** (-4. 774)	
$POST_{t,i}$	0. 007 *** (11. 838)		0. 011 *** (3. 601)
$DUAL_{t,i} * POST_{t,i}$	0. 006 ** (2. 440)	0. 013 *** (3. 285)	

续表

Variable	Dependent Variable: $COE\_GLS_{t,i}$		
	(1)	(2)	(3)
$AH_{t,i}$	0.009*** (3.875)		
$Size_{t,i}$	0.003*** (13.958)	0.004** (2.459)	−0.005 (−1.183)
$Beta_{t,i}$	0.010*** (13.691)	0.009 (1.424)	−0.001 (−0.177)
$MB_{t,i}$	−0.004*** (−47.514)	−0.005*** (−6.556)	−0.005*** (−7.379)
$DE_{t,i}$	0.009*** (9.110)	0.003 (0.980)	0.007* (1.746)
$Std\_Ret_{t,i}$	−0.009** (−2.070)	−0.113*** (−3.824)	−0.003 (−0.124)
$Liq_{t,i}$	−0.202*** (−14.249)	−0.020 (−0.142)	−0.444*** (−3.804)
$Growth_{t,i}$	0.001*** (11.030)	0.003** (2.190)	0.002 (1.503)
$SOE_{t,i}$	−0.005*** (−10.877)	−0.003 (−0.329)	−0.014 (−0.935)
$Disp_{t,i}$	−0.000 (−0.579)	0.005 (1.191)	0.002 (0.814)
$Bias_{t,i}$	0.027*** (3.752)	0.032 (0.516)	−0.014 (−0.302)
$Big4_{t,i}$	−0.001 (−1.262)	−0.004 (−1.318)	−0.007 (−1.052)
Firm Fixed Effects			Yes
N	8647	335	268
Adj. R^2	0.460	0.391	0.799
F	492.904	17.476	19.246

Notes: Column (1) shows the results of Eq. (4−6) for the total sample in Chapter 4; Column (2) shows the results of Eq. (4−6) for the sample of 335 AH firm-year observations; Column (3) shows the results of Eq. (4−6) with firm fixed effects included for the sample of 268 observations using the dual audit; in Column (2), variables $POST_{t,i}$ and $AH_{t,i}$ are omitted owing to collinearity; in Column (3), variables $DUAL_{t,i}$, $DUAL_{t,i}$ * $POST_{t,i}$ and $AH_{t,i}$ are omitted owing to collinearity; ***, ** and * represent significance at the 0.01, 0.05 and 0.10 level, respectively, using two-tailed tests; t-statistics are shown in parentheses; variable definitions and measurement are reported in Table 4−6.

4.3.4.2 Tests of H2, H3 and H4

Columns (1) and (2) of Table 4−10 present the findings of the tests of H2 about whether the lower cost of equity for mandatory dual audit (than that for voluntary dual audit) is conditional on firms' equity financing demand. According to prior literature about financial constraints (Kaplan et al., 1997; Lamont et al., 2001; Whited et al., 2006; Hadlock et al., 2010)[370-373], lower cash on hand along with higher leverage generally implies higher demand for equity financing. Based on this notion, I identify firms whose ratio of cash on hand to total assets is in the lowest tercile and asset-liability ratio is in the highest tercile as firms with higher demand for equity financing, and I identify the remaining firms as those with lower demand for equity financing. ① I then re-estimate Eq. (4-6) in these two subsamples, respectively. In Table 4-10, Column (1) shows that the coefficient on $DUAL_{t,i} * POST_{t,i}$ is positive and significant in the sample with higher equity financing demand (coefficient = 0.011, t = 1.993), whereas Column (2) shows that the coefficient on the same term is insignificant in the sample with lower equity financing demand (coefficient = 0.004, t = 1.480). These results suggest that the effect of mandatory dual audit relative to voluntary dual audit on lowering the cost of equity is greater in firms with higher equity financing demand, consistent with H2.

Columns (3) and (4) of Table 4-10 present the findings of the tests of H3 about whether the lower cost of equity for mandatory dual audit (than that for voluntary dual audit) is conditional on firms' agency costs. Lafond and Roychowdhury (2008)[374] suggest managerial ownership as a good proxy for agency costs. Higher managerial ownership better aligns management's interests with shareholders' interests, which helps to relieve agency problems. To test H3, I divide the sample firms into two groups based on the percentage of managerial ownership: one group with higher agency costs (i. e., with managerial ownership lower than the sample median) and the other group with lower agency costs (i. e., with managerial ownership higher than the sample median). Eq. (4-6) is re-estimated in each of these two groups. As reported in Table 4-10, the positive coefficient on $DUAL_{t,i} * POST_{t,i}$ is significant in the sample with higher agency costs [Column (3), coefficient = 0.008, t = 2.620], whilst it is insignificant in the sample with lower agency costs [Column (4), coefficient = 0.001, t = 0.135]. These findings imply that the effect of mandatory dual audit relative to voluntary dual audit on lowering the

---

① This cut-off is arbitrary but not selective. The results are robust to different cut-offs (e. g., quintiles, quartiles or sample median). See Appendix Ⅰ for the results with other cut-offs.

cost of equity is more pronounced in firms with higher agency costs, thereby supporting H3.

Columns (5) and (6) of Table 4−10 present the findings of the tests of H4 about whether the lower cost of equity for mandatory dual audit (than that for voluntary dual audit) is attenuated by the interim report audit. In particular, I separate the full sample into two subsamples based on whether a sample firm voluntarily has its interim financial statements audited, and I re-estimate Eq. (4−6) in the two subsamples. As shown in Columns (5) and (6) of Table 4−10, the positive coefficient on $DUAL_{t,i} * POST$ is significant at the 0.01 level in the sample with audited interim reports [Column (5), coefficient = 0.038, t = 3.627], and it is also significant (though marginally) in the sample with unaudited interim reports [Column (6), coefficient = 0.004, t = 1.709]. These findings are consistent with H4 and suggest that the advantage of mandatory dual audit over voluntary dual audit in lowering the cost of equity is not mitigated by the voluntary interim report audit. In other words, the role of complying with the mandatory dual audit requirement in reducing agency costs and information asymmetry cannot be fully replaced by different forms of voluntary audits.

Table 4−10 Regression Results of Tests of H2, H3 and H4

Variable	Dependent Variable: $COE\_GLS_{t,i}$					
	Equity Financing Demand		Agency Costs		Interim Report Audit	
	(1) Higher	(2) Lower	(3) Higher	(4) Lower	(5) Yes	(6) No
Intercept	0.023 (1.432)	0.004 (0.698)	−0.008 (−1.025)	0.013* (1.737)	−0.006 (−0.245)	0.001 (0.233)
$DUAL_{t,i}$	−0.039*** (−5.299)	−0.007** (−2.119)	−0.018*** (−4.428)	−0.012* (−1.882)	−0.023 (−1.634)	−0.016*** (−5.033)
$POST_{t,i}$	0.004** (2.120)	0.007*** (12.244)	0.005*** (5.696)	0.008*** (9.799)	0.006*** (2.950)	0.007*** (11.438)
$DUAL_{t,i} * POST_{t,i}$	0.011** (1.993)	0.004 (1.480)	0.008*** (2.620)	0.001 (0.135)	0.038*** (3.627)	0.004* (1.709)
$AH_{t,i}$	0.022*** (4.013)	0.005* (1.813)	0.008** (2.444)	0.011*** (3.240)	0.014 (1.106)	0.009*** (3.696)
$Size_{t,i}$	0.002*** (3.448)	0.003*** (11.992)	0.004*** (10.421)	0.003*** (8.281)	0.003*** (3.024)	0.003*** (13.390)

续表

Variable	Dependent Variable: $COE\_GLS_{t,i}$					
	Equity Financing Demand		Agency Costs		Interim Report Audit	
	(1) Higher	(2) Lower	(3) Higher	(4) Lower	(5) Yes	(6) No
$Beta_{t,i}$	0.026*** (6.074)	0.010*** (12.964)	0.014*** (10.623)	0.008*** (8.936)	0.014*** (4.402)	0.010*** (13.144)
$MB_{t,i}$	-0.004*** (-13.931)	-0.004*** (-45.166)	-0.004*** (-30.316)	-0.004*** (-37.282)	-0.004*** (-11.514)	-0.004*** (-46.049)
$DE_{t,i}$	0.005*** (2.792)	0.016*** (12.153)	0.007*** (6.141)	0.013*** (7.594)	0.014*** (2.877)	0.009*** (9.080)
$Std\_Ret_{t,i}$	-0.026* (-1.823)	-0.008** (-1.963)	-0.004 (-0.612)	-0.013*** (-2.646)	-0.010 (-0.668)	-0.009** (-1.982)
$Liq_{t,i}$	-0.223*** (-4.488)	-0.196*** (-13.488)	-0.271*** (-11.132)	-0.164*** (-9.726)	-0.100* (-1.837)	-0.210*** (-14.250)
$Growth_{t,i}$	0.001*** (3.463)	0.001*** (10.750)	0.001*** (7.242)	0.001*** (8.721)	0.001*** (4.147)	0.001*** (10.115)
$SOE_{t,i}$	-0.007*** (-5.033)	-0.005*** (-10.182)	-0.004*** (-5.115)	-0.004*** (-6.881)	-0.004** (-2.130)	-0.005*** (-10.695)
$Disp_{t,i}$	0.002 (0.899)	-0.001 (-1.286)	0.001 (0.822)	-0.003** (-2.277)	-0.004 (-1.006)	-0.000 (-0.475)
$Bias_{t,i}$	0.040** (2.254)	0.021*** (2.619)	0.025** (2.252)	0.032*** (3.234)	0.070** (2.486)	0.024*** (3.168)
$Big4_{t,i}$	-0.001 (-0.363)	-0.001 (-0.987)	-0.000 (-0.253)	-0.003** (-2.326)	-0.001 (-0.134)	-0.001 (-1.233)
N	1238	7409	4156	4491	469	8178
Adj. R^2	0.428	0.470	0.454	0.471	0.524	0.457
F	62.720	438.576	231.275	267.877	35.368	460.549

Notes: Column (1) [Column (2)] shows the results of Eq. (4-6) for the subsample with higher (lower) demand for equity financing; Column (3) [Column (4)] shows the results of Eq. (4-6) for the subsample with higher (lower) agency costs; Column (5) [Column (6)] shows the results of Eq. (4-6) for the subsample with audited (unaudited) interim financial reports; ***, ** and * represent significance at the 0.01, 0.05 and 0.10 level, respectively, using two-tailed tests; t-statistics are shown in parentheses; variable definitions and measurement are reported in Table 4-6.

4.3.5 Robustness Tests

4.3.5.1 Further Considering Audit Quality

Due to the unobservability of the assurance levels supplied by auditors, precisely measuring audit quality is difficult (DeFond et al., 2014)[96]. Scholars have formulated plenty of proxies for audit quality, but there is still no uniform consensus on a perfect one. Although I control for audit quality with a classical measure reflecting the type of auditors (i. e., $Big4_{t,i}$) in the main tests, whether audit quality actually differs across the mandatory dual audit group and the voluntary dual audit group remains unclear. To address this concern, I further check the discretionary accruals ($|DACC|_{t,i}$, calculated following Kothari et al., 2005)[366], the likelihood of restatements ($Restate_{t,i}$) and the likelihood of modified audit opinions ($MAO_{t,i}$) across these groups. The results in Panel A of Table 4-11 suggest that no significant difference is observed between the mandatory dual audit sample and the voluntary dual audit sample in any of the three aspects ($|DACC|_{t,i}$, $Restate_{t,i}$ and $MAO_{t,i}$). These results help strengthen my argument and findings that with the assurance levels controlled, the difference in the cost of equity between these groups is indeed attributable to whether to comply with the mandatory dual audit requirement or to voluntarily choose the dual audit.

I have already included $Big4_{t,i}$ as an audit quality proxy in the baseline regressions. To further rule out the alternative explanation that the results may capture the effect of audit quality on the cost of equity rather than the direct impact of complying with the mandatory dual audit requirement, I introduce $|DACC|_{t,i}$, $Restate_{t,i}$ and $MAO_{t,i}$ separately into Eq. (4-6) to additionally control for audit quality. Columns (1) to (3) in Panel B of Table 4-11 illustrate the results. The coefficient on $DUAL_{t,i} * POST_{t,i}$ remains positive and significant throughout the three columns. These findings are qualitatively similar to those presented in Table 4-9 and suggest that after further mitigating the confounding effect of audit quality, the results still hold. As for the audit-quality proxies, the coefficient on $|DACC|_{t,i}$ is positive and significant in the model, which is consistent with prior studies suggesting that lower audit quality is associated with a higher cost of equity (Chen et al., 2011; Khurana et al., 2004; Huang et al., 2015)[83, 202, 277].

Subsequently, I take several situations of auditor grade changes and audit system changes into consideration to exclude the possibility of a change in audit assurance. I create an indicator for each of the audit-related change situations: (1) $Chg\_NtB_{t,i}$, which equals 1 if the firm switches from a non-Big 4 auditor to a Big 4 auditor (i. e., an auditor upgrade), and 0 otherwise; (2) $Chg\_BtN_{t,i}$, which equals 1 if the firm switches from a Big 4 auditor to a non-Big 4 auditor (i. e., an auditor downgrade), and 0 otherwise; (3) $Chg\_MtV_{t,i}$, which equals 1 if the firm switches from complying with the mandatory dual audit requirement to voluntarily choosing the dual audit, and 0 otherwise; (4) $Chg\_MtS_{t,i}$, which equals 1 if the firm switches from complying with the mandatory dual audit requirement to using only the single audit, and 0 otherwise; (5) $Chg\_VtS_{t,i}$, which equals 1 if the firm switches from voluntarily choosing the dual audit to using only the single audit, and 0 otherwise. Column (4) in Panel B of Table 4-11 illustrates the results after additionally introducing these five variables as controls. In Column (5) in Panel B of Table 4-11, I further exclude 111 observations that change auditor grade (i. e., $Chg\_NtB_{t,i}=1$ or $Chg\_BtN_{t,i}=1$) or change audit system (i. e., $Chg\_MtV_{t,i}=1$, $Chg\_MtS_{t,i}=1$ or $Chg\_VtS_{t,i}=1$) and re-estimate Eq. (4-6). The results in these two columns are similar to the main findings and reinforce my conclusion that the difference in the cost of equity is driven by whether to comply with the mandatory dual audit requirement or to voluntarily choose the dual audit rather than by possible changes in the assurance levels.

Table 4-11 Results After Further Considering Audit Quality

Panel A: Test of Differences Between Mandatory Dual Audit ($DUAL_{t,i}=1$ and $POST_{t,i}=0$) and Voluntary Dual Audit ($DUAL_{t,i}=1$ and $POST_{t,i}=1$)

Variable	Mean		Test of Differences *t*-stat.
	$DUAL_{t,i}=1$ & $POST_{t,i}=0$ ($N=81$)	$DUAL_{t,i}=1$ & $POST_{t,i}=1$ ($N=187$)	
$\lvert DACC \rvert_{t,i}$	0. 094	0. 099	−0. 266
$Restate_{t,i}$	0. 025	0. 032	−0. 326
$MAO_{t,i}$	0. 000	0. 016	−1. 145

Panel B: Regression Results After Further Controlling for Audit Quality

Variable	Dependent Variable: $COE\_GLS_{t,i}$				
	(1) Controlling for $\lvert DACC \rvert_{t,i}$	(2) Controlling for $Restate_{t,i}$	(3) Controlling for $MAO_{t,i}$	(4) Controlling for Auditor Grade Change and Audit System Change	(5) Excluding Sample with Auditor Grade Change or Audit System Change
Intercept	−0. 000 (−0. 003)	−0. 000 (−0. 051)	−0. 000 (−0. 044)	−0. 000 (−0. 031)	0. 000 (0. 016)
$DUAL_{t,i}$	−0. 017*** (−5. 341)	−0. 017*** (−5. 309)	−0. 017*** (−5. 325)	−0. 016*** (−4. 755)	−0. 017*** (−4. 879)

续表

Panel B: Regression Results After Further Controlling for Audit Quality					
Variable	Dependent Variable: $COE\_GLS_{t,i}$				
	(1) Controlling for $\mid DACC \mid_{t,i}$	(2) Controlling for $Restate_{t,i}$	(3) Controlling for $MAO_{t,i}$	(4) Controlling for Auditor Grade Change and Audit System Change	(5) Excluding Sample with Auditor Grade Change or Audit System Change
$POST_{t,i}$	0. 007 *** (11. 880)	0. 007 *** (11. 813)	0. 007 *** (11. 840)	0. 007 *** (11. 867)	0. 007 *** (11. 965)
$DUAL_{t,i}$ * $POST_{t,i}$	0. 006 ** (2. 509)	0. 006 ** (2. 430)	0. 006 ** (2. 452)	0. 008 *** (3. 045)	0. 009 *** (3. 259)
$AH_{t,i}$	0. 009 *** (3. 870)	0. 009 *** (3. 874)	0. 009 *** (3. 882)	0. 008 *** (3. 129)	0. 008 *** (3. 055)
$Size_{t,i}$	0. 003 *** (13. 915)	0. 003 *** (13. 956)	0. 003 *** (13. 953)	0. 003 *** (13. 936)	0. 003 *** (13. 756)
$Beta_{t,i}$	0. 010 *** (13. 600)	0. 010 *** (13. 694)	0. 010 *** (13. 690)	0. 010 *** (13. 648)	0. 010 *** (13. 512)
$MB_{t,i}$	−0. 004 *** (−47. 486)	−0. 004 *** (−47. 505)	−0. 004 *** (−47. 351)	−0. 004 *** (−47. 478)	−0. 004 *** (−47. 337)
$DE_{t,i}$	0. 008 *** (8. 954)	0. 009 *** (9. 099)	0. 009 *** (9. 117)	0. 008 *** (8. 899)	0. 008 *** (8. 805)
$Std\_Ret_{t,i}$	−0. 008 ** (−2. 033)	−0. 009 ** (−2. 067)	−0. 009 ** (−2. 079)	−0. 009 ** (−2. 125)	−0. 009 ** (−2. 062)
$Liq_{t,i}$	−0. 203 *** (−14. 307)	−0. 202 *** (−14. 251)	−0. 202 *** (−14. 239)	−0. 202 *** (−14. 228)	−0. 200 *** (−14. 088)
$Growth_{t,i}$	0. 001 *** (10. 930)	0. 001 *** (11. 034)	0. 001 *** (11. 018)	0. 001 *** (11. 062)	0. 001 *** (11. 132)
$SOE_{t,i}$	−0. 005 *** (−10. 703)	−0. 005 *** (−10. 880)	−0. 005 *** (−10. 851)	−0. 005 *** (−10. 807)	−0. 005 *** (−10. 905)
$Disp_{t,i}$	−0. 001 (−0. 598)	−0. 001 (−0. 586)	−0. 001 (−0. 597)	−0. 000 (−0. 517)	−0. 000 (−0. 383)
$Bias_{t,i}$	0. 027 *** (3. 706)	0. 027 *** (3. 727)	0. 028 *** (3. 811)	0. 027 *** (3. 709)	0. 026 *** (3. 585)
$Big4_{t,i}$	−0. 001 (−1. 216)	−0. 001 (−1. 252)	−0. 001 (−1. 273)	−0. 001 (−1. 077)	−0. 001 (−0. 778)

续表

Panel B: Regression Results After Further Controlling for Audit Quality					
Variable	Dependent Variable: $COE\_GLS_{t,i}$				
	(1) Controlling for $\lvert DACC \rvert_{t,i}$	(2) Controlling for $Restate_{t,i}$	(3) Controlling for $MAO_{t,i}$	(4) Controlling for Auditor Grade Change and Audit System Change	(5) Excluding Sample with Auditor Grade Change or Audit System Change
$\lvert DACC \rvert_{t,i}$	0.004*** (2.732)				
$Restate_{t,i}$		0.000 (0.375)			
$MAO_{t,i}$			−0.002 (−0.780)		
$Chg\_NtB_{t,i}$				−0.002 (−0.632)	
$Chg\_BtN_{t,i}$				0.002 (0.575)	
$Chg\_MtV_{t,i}$				−0.008** (−2.408)	
$Chg\_MtS_{t,i}$				−0.020 (−1.049)	
$Chg\_VtS_{t,i}$				0.006 (1.034)	
N	8641	8647	8647	8647	8536
Adj. R^2	0.461	0.460	0.460	0.461	0.460
F	462.024	462.060	462.114	370.260	485.796

Notes: In Panel B, Column (1) shows the results after additionally introducing $\lvert DACC \rvert_{t,i}$ as a control variable into Eq. (4−6) [6 observations are dropped from the sample used in the baseline Eq. (4−6) owing to missing data in the estimation of $\lvert DACC \rvert_{t,i}$]; Column (2) [Column (3)] shows the results after additionally introducing $Restate_{t,i}$($MAO_{t,i}$) as a control variable into Eq. (4−6); Column (4) shows the results after additionally introducing $Chg\_NtB_{t,i}$, $Chg\_BtN_{t,i}$, $Chg\_MtV_{t,i}$, $Chg\_MtS_{t,i}$ and $Chg\_VtS_{t,i}$ as control variables into Eq. (4−6); Column (5) shows the results of Eq. (4−6) after dropping 111 observations that change auditor grade[i. e., switch from a non-Big 4 auditor to a Big 4 auditor (an upgrade) or vice versa (a downgrade)] or change audit system (i. e., switch from mandatary dual audit to voluntary dual audit, switch from mandatory dual audit to single audit or switch from voluntary dual audit to single audit) in year t; ***, ** and * represent significance at the 0.01, 0.05 and 0.10 level, respectively, using two-tailed tests; t-statistics are shown in parentheses; variable definitions and measurement are reported in Table 4−6.

4. 3. 5. 2 Considering Convergence of CAS with IFRS

A major confounding factor in my study on the longitudinal comparison between mandatory dual audit and voluntary dual audit is the convergence of the CAS with the IFRS. It may be argued that, rather than an advantage arising from complying with the mandatory dual audit requirement over voluntarily choosing the dual audit, the accounting standards convergence leads to the diminishing value of the dual audit and thereby the difference in the cost of equity between the periods before and after the deregulation.

The sample distribution by year shown in Section 4. 3. 1 has already indicated that the considerable voluntary demand for the dual audit in companies that previously were bound by the mandatory dual audit requirement is unlikely to support regulators' concern about the diminishing value of the dual audit. To further address the alternative explanation of the accounting standards convergence, I construct a convergence index ($CI_{t,i}$) for the dual audit sample, following the previous literature (Gray, 1980; Haverty, 2006; Zhang, 2014) [375-377]. This index has been broadly used to compare net income values reported by the same company adopting different accounting standards at the same time (Weetman et al., 1998; Street et al., 2000) [378, 379]. The index is calculated as follows:

$$CI_{t,i} = 1 - \frac{NetIncome_{A_{t,i}} - NetIncome_{H_{t,i}}}{|NetIncome_{A_{t,i}}|} \tag{4-7}$$

where

$NetIncome_{At,i}$ = the net income reported in company i's A-share financial statements (i. e., under the CAS) in year t.

$NetIncome_{Ht,i}$ = the net income reported in company i's H-share financial statements (i. e., under the IFRS/HKFRS) in year t.

A value of $CI_{t,i}$ lower than 0. 900 suggests that the net income reported under the IFRS/HKFRS is at least 10% less than the net income reported under the CAS for the same company. Otherwise, a value of $CI_{t,i}$ higher than 1. 100 implies that the net income reported under the IFRS/HKFRS is at least 10% greater than the net income reported under the CAS for the same company. Accordingly, for a certain company in a certain year, its A-share and H-share financial statements can be regarded as reaching convergence only when $CI_{t,i}$ lies between 0. 900 and 1. 100 (Zhang, 2014) [377].

I then compare the mean values of $CI_{t,i}$ between the mandatory dual audit sample and the voluntary dual audit sample. The results are shown in Panel A of Table 4-12. The mean $CI_{t,i}$ of the sample for which $DUAL_{t,i}=1$ and $POST_{t,i}=0$ (i. e. , the mandatory dual audit sample) is 0. 980, which is higher than 0. 900 and lower than 1. 100. This result suggests that there was no material difference in the reported CAS net income and the reported IFRS net income on average during the period before 2010. In other words, the statistics show that the CAS had generally reached substantial convergence with the IFRS even before the deregulation of the mandatory dual audit system. The mean $CI_{t,i}$ of the sample for which $DUAL_{t,i}=1$ and $POST_{t,i}=1$ (i. e. , the voluntary dual audit sample) is 0. 922, which also lies in the range of 0. 900 ~ 1. 100 and is not significantly different from the mean value for the mandatory dual audit sample. These findings indicate that the convergence of the CAS with the IFRS exists constantly during the sample period. As I use 2010 as the cut-off point, the constant convergence of accounting standards is unlikely to be an explanation for the difference in the cost of equity between the periods before and after the deregulation.

Subsequently, I introduce $CI_{t,i}$ as an additional control variable into Eq. (4-6) and re-run the model for the dual audit sample. Panel B of Table 4 - 12 demonstrates the results. In Column (1), after further controlling for the convergence of accounting standards ($CI_{t,i}$), the coefficient on $POST_{t,i}$ remains significant and positive, confirming the main findings that voluntarily choosing the dual audit results in a higher cost of equity than complying with the mandatory dual audit requirement. In addition, I further control for firm fixed effects to compare a dual-audited firm to itself over time. Panel B Column (2) of Table 4-12 shows that holding the firms constant, the coefficient on $POST_{t,i}$ remains positive and significant after controlling for accounting standards convergence. This within-firm comparison strengthens my argument about the effect of mandatory dual audit relative to voluntary dual audit on reducing the cost of equity.

Taken together, the findings on the difference in the cost of equity between the periods before and after the deregulation reflect the mechanism by which complying with the mandatory dual audit requirement reduces agency costs and information asymmetry more than voluntarily choosing the dual audit does, rather than the convergence of the CAS with the IFRS.

Table 4-12 Results After Considering Convergence of CAS with IFRS

Panel A: Test of Difference in $CI_{t,i}$ Between Mandatory Dual Audit ($DUAL_{t,i}$ = 1 and $POST_{t,i}$ = 0) and Voluntary Dual Audit ($DUAL_{t,i}$ = 1 and $POST_{t,i}$ = 1)

Variable	Mean		Test of Differences t-stat.
	$DUAL_{t,i}=1$ & $POST_{t,i}=0$ (N=81)	$DUAL_{t,i}=1$ & $POST_{t,i}=1$ (N=187)	
$CI_{t,i}$	0.980	0.922	1.321

Panel B: Regression Results After Additionally Introducing $CI_{t,i}$ as a Control Variable

Variable	Dependent Variable: $COE\_GLS_{t,i}$	
	(1)	(2)
Intercept	-0.001 (-0.014)	0.237** (2.012)
$DUAL_{t,i}$		
$POST_{t,i}$	0.014*** (3.454)	0.011*** (3.602)
$DUAL_{t,i} * POST_{t,i}$		
$AH_{t,i}$		
$Size_{t,i}$	0.003** (1.997)	-0.006 (-1.247)
$Beta_{t,i}$	0.005 (0.713)	-0.001 (-0.157)
$MB_{t,i}$	-0.005*** (-6.281)	-0.005*** (-7.363)
$DE_{t,i}$	-0.002 (-0.415)	0.007* (1.707)
$Std\_Ret_{t,i}$	-0.099*** (-2.859)	-0.003 (-0.113)
$Liq_{t,i}$	-0.060 (-0.372)	-0.447*** (-3.819)
$Growth_{t,i}$	0.003** (2.037)	0.002 (1.568)
$SOE_{t,i}$	-0.001 (-0.068)	-0.014 (-0.942)
$Disp_{t,i}$	0.007 (1.596)	0.002 (0.860)
$Bias_{t,i}$	0.014 (0.203)	-0.010 (-0.222)
$Big4_{t,i}$	-0.005 (-1.338)	-0.007 (-1.011)

续表

Panel B: Regression Results After Additionally Introducing $CI_{t,i}$ as a Control Variable		
Variable	Dependent Variable: $COE\_GLS_{t,i}$	
	(1)	(2)
$CI_{t,i}$	0.006 (1.117)	−0.002 (−0.594)
Firm Fixed Effects		Yes
N	268	268
Adj. R^2	0.358	0.798
F	12.476	18.867

Notes: In Panel B, Column (1) shows the results of Eq. (4−6) for the dual audit sample after additionally introducing $CI_{t,i}$ as a control variable; Column (2) shows the results of Eq. (4−6) for the dual audit sample after additionally introducing $CI_{t,i}$ as a control variable and controlling for firm fixed effects; variables $DUAL_{t,i}$, $DUAL * POST_{t,i}$ and $AH_{t,i}$ are omitted owing to collinearity; ***, ** and * represent significance at the 0.01, 0.05 and 0.10 level, respectively, using two-tailed tests; t-statistics are shown in parentheses; variable definitions and measurement are reported in Table 4−6.

4.3.5.3 Controlling for Differential Impact of Growth

In the GLS model, the industry median ROE is assumed to be the terminal value in the estimation process. This implies that individual companies' net new investments have no incremental profits beyond the forecast horizon (Gebhardt et al., 2001) [2]. This assumption potentially leads to an underestimation of the cost of equity for companies with high growth (Chen et al., 2011) [83]. To deal with this concern, I follow Chen et al. (2011) [83] by interacting $Growth_{t,i}$ with $DUAL_{t,i}$, $POST_{t,i}$ and $DUAL_{t,i} * POST_{t,i}$ separately in Eq. (4−6) to further control for the differential impact of growth on the cost of equity. As shown in Table 4−13, the coefficient on $DUAL_{t,i} * POST_{t,i}$ continues to be positive and significant, whereas all the additionally introduced interaction terms are insignificant. The results of this test indicate that the main findings hold after taking the differential impact of growth into account.

Table 4−13 Regression Results After Controlling for Differential Impact of Growth

Variable	Dependent Variable: $COE\_GLS_{t,i}$
Intercept	−0.000 (−0.013)
$DUAL_{t,i}$	−0.019*** (−5.475)

续表

Variable	Dependent Variable: $COE\_GLS_{t,i}$
$POST_{t,i}$	0.007*** (10.608)
$DUAL_{t,i} * POST_{t,i}$	0.007** (2.380)
$AH_{t,i}$	0.009*** (3.878)
$Size_{t,i}$	0.003*** (13.888)
$Beta_{t,i}$	0.010*** (13.705)
$MB_{t,i}$	−0.004*** (−47.524)
$DE_{t,i}$	0.009*** (9.170)
$Std\_Ret_{t,i}$	−0.009** (−2.081)
$Liq_{t,i}$	−0.202*** (−14.205)
$Growth_{t,i}$	0.001*** (5.321)
$SOE_{t,i}$	−0.005*** (−10.896)
$Disp_{t,i}$	−0.001 (−0.598)
$Bias_{t,i}$	0.027*** (3.751)
$Big4_{t,i}$	−0.001 (−1.310)
$DUAL_{t,i} * Growth_{t,i}$	0.002 (1.543)
$POST_{t,i} * Growth_{t,i}$	−0.000 (−0.622)
$DUAL_{t,i} * POST_{t,i} * Growth_{t,i}$	−0.000 (−0.077)

续表

Variable	Dependent Variable: $COE\_GLS_{t,i}$
N	8647
Adj. R^2	0. 460
F	410. 990

Notes: * * *, * * and * represent significance at the 0. 01, 0. 05 and 0. 10 level, respectively, using two-tailed tests; t-statistics are shown in parentheses; variable definitions and measurement are reported in Table 4-6.

4. 3. 5. 4 Alternative Measurement of Cost of Equity

For robustness check, I separately use $COE\_OJ_{t,i}$, $GLS\_CT_{t,i}$, $GLS\_PEG_{t,i}$ and $GLS\_AVG_{t,i}$ as the dependent variable and re-run Eq. (4-6). The results of these sensitivity tests are presented in Table 4-14. The coefficients on $DUAL_{t,i} * POST_{t,i}$ are positive across all four columns and significant when the cost of equity is estimated by the OJ model [Column (1)] and the PEG model [Column (3)]. The results of these tests with alternative estimations of the cost of equity, although not highly consistent owing to measurement errors, provide some further support for the main findings of this chapter.

Table 4-14 Regression Results of Alternative Cost-of-Equity Measures

Variable	Dependent Variable: $COE\_OJ_{t,i}$ (1)	Dependent Variable: $COE\_CT_{t,i}$ (2)	Dependent Variable: $COE\_PEG_{t,i}$ (3)	Dependent Variable: $COE\_AVG_{t,i}$ (4)
Intercept	0. 070*** (3. 134)	0. 048 (0. 739)	0. 330*** (16. 344)	0. 152*** (5. 606)
$DUAL_{t,i}$	−0. 033** (−1. 981)	−0. 101** (−2. 574)	−0. 025** (−2. 085)	−0. 044** (−2. 166)
$POST_{t,i}$	−0. 017*** (−6. 564)	−0. 074*** (−10. 696)	−0. 038*** (−17. 893)	−0. 034*** (−10. 898)
$DUAL_{t,i} * POST_{t,i}$	0. 029** (2. 082)	0. 013 (0. 410)	0. 019* (1. 934)	0. 024 (1. 408)
$AH_{t,i}$	−0. 013 (−1. 200)	0. 029 (1. 001)	−0. 005 (−0. 527)	−0. 018 (−1. 346)
$Size_{t,i}$	0. 004*** (4. 227)	0. 010*** (3. 556)	−0. 005*** (−5. 082)	0. 002 (1. 518)

续表

Variable	Dependent Variable: $COE\_OJ_{t,i}$ (1)	Dependent Variable: $COE\_CT_{t,i}$ (2)	Dependent Variable: $COE\_PEG_{t,i}$ (3)	Dependent Variable: $COE\_AVG_{t,i}$ (4)
$Beta_{t,i}$	0.002 (0.660)	0.025*** (2.795)	-0.002 (-0.728)	0.002 (0.566)
$MB_{t,i}$	-0.003*** (-8.204)	-0.003*** (-3.288)	-0.004*** (-12.033)	-0.004*** (-8.073)
$DE_{t,i}$	0.032*** (8.224)	-0.003 (-0.234)	0.031*** (8.782)	0.027*** (5.742)
$Std\_Ret_{t,i}$	-0.049*** (-2.843)	-0.197*** (-3.942)	-0.044*** (-2.816)	-0.067*** (-3.201)
$Liq_{t,i}$	-0.576*** (-9.619)	-1.343*** (-7.717)	-0.864*** (-16.059)	-0.720*** (-9.829)
$Growth_{t,i}$	0.007*** (14.193)	0.013*** (8.994)	0.006*** (15.112)	0.011*** (17.580)
$SOE_{t,i}$	-0.005** (-2.422)	-0.054*** (-9.758)	-0.038*** (-22.058)	-0.018*** (-7.942)
$Disp_{t,i}$	-0.007 (-1.613)	-0.008 (-0.727)	0.001 (0.173)	-0.001 (-0.256)
$Bias_{t,i}$	0.208*** (5.731)	-0.727*** (-7.563)	0.350*** (12.093)	0.226*** (4.995)
$Big4_{t,i}$	0.003 (0.839)	-0.021** (-2.070)	-0.010*** (-2.989)	0.000 (0.055)
N	6861	7305	8138	6233
Adj. R^2	0.132	0.062	0.176	0.131
F	70.682	32.963	117.266	63.797

Notes: ***, ** and * represent significance at the 0.01, 0.05 and 0.10 level, respectively, using two-tailed tests; *t*-statistics are shown in parentheses; variable definitions and measurement are reported in Table 4-6.

4.4 Results Discussion

In the tests of hypotheses H1 to H4 in this chapter, the empirical results show that (1) companies have a lower cost of equity when they mandatorily have the dual audit before the deregulation than when they voluntarily use the dual audit after the deregulation. (2) The effect of mandatory dual audit relative to voluntary dual audit on reducing the cost of equity is greater in companies with higher demand for equity financing. (3) The effect of mandatory dual audit relative to voluntary dual audit on reducing the cost of equity is greater in companies with higher agency costs. (4) The effect of mandatory dual audit relative to voluntary dual audit on reducing the cost of equity is not attenuated by other voluntary audit mechanisms, such as the interim report audit. In addition, the main findings are robust after alternative audit-quality measures, convergence of accounting standards, and differential impact of firm growth are controlled and when alternative cost-of-equity measures are used as the dependent variable.

Consistent with the commitment effect of complying with mandatory requirements, these results provide supportive evidence for the idea that the role of complying with the mandatory dual audit requirement in reducing the cost of equity cannot be fully replaced by voluntarily choosing the dual audit. That is to say, in investors' perception, compliance with the mandatory dual audit requirement serves as a mechanism for companies to credibly commit, on an ex-ante basis, to be under the monitoring of two audit firms and disclose two sets of audited financial statements. Such a perceived commitment relieves investors' concerns on management's self-serving behavior. Moreover, the powerful enforcement systems make it costly to breach the mandatory dual audit requirement, thereby ensuring companies' sustainable compliance with this requirement. By contrast, voluntarily choosing the dual audit after the deregulation allows companies to evaluate the possible consequences before making a dual audit decision and thereby is self-serving. Besides, whether the voluntary use of the dual audit system will be sustained in the future is questionable because companies can freely opt out without any threat of punishment from regulators.

Overall, the empirical results suggest that complying with the mandatory dual audit requirement has a higher potential than voluntarily choosing the dual audit in reducing the cost of equity in the Chinese capital market. In other words, the loss of this role of complying with the mandatory dual audit requirement is costly and cannot be fully replaced by voluntarily choosing the dual audit after the deregulation of the mandatory dual audit system.

4. 5 Chapter Summary

Based on a sample of A-share listed companies in China for the period 2007 to 2015, this chapter investigates the economic consequences of the deregulation of the mandatory dual audit system on the capital market by testing the effect of mandatory dual audit before the deregulation relative to voluntary dual audit after the deregulation on reducing the cost of equity. Based on the main arguments, this chapter first develops four hypotheses (H1 to H4). Then, this chapter conducts validation tests among several commonly used cost-of-equity measures, and selects the measure derived from the GLS model as the proxy for the cost of equity in the main tests. Next, this chapter designs the empirical model for hypothesis testing. Through conducting descriptive statistical, univariate, multivariate regression and robustness analyses, the empirical results support all hypotheses in this chapter and are robust to different model specifications. Table 4-15 summarizes the results of hypothesis testing in this chapter.

Table 4-15 Summary of Empirical Findings in Chapter 4

No.	Hypothesis	Empirical Findings
H1	Ceteris paribus, companies have a lower cost of equity when they mandatorily have the dual audit than when they voluntarily use the dual audit.	Supported
H2	Ceteris paribus, the lower cost of equity for mandatory dual audit than voluntary dual audit is more pronounced for companies with higher equity financing demand.	Supported
H3	Ceteris paribus, the lower cost of equity for mandatory dual audit than voluntary dual audit is more pronounced for companies with higher agency costs.	Supported
H4	Ceteris paribus, the lower cost of equity for mandatory dual audit than voluntary dual audit is not attenuated by the interim report audit.	Supported

5 Capital-Market Consequences: Effect of Voluntary Dual Audit on Cost of Equity

Chapter 4 finds that mandatory dual audit before the deregulation has a lower cost of equity than voluntary audit after the deregulation. On the basis of the theoretical framework proposed in Chapter 3, this chapter analyzes the economic consequences of the deregulation of the mandatory dual audit system on the capital market by examining whether voluntary dual audit after the deregulation leads to a lower cost of equity than single audit in the same period.

5. 1 Hypothesis Development

As stated in Section 3. 1, since the deregulation of the mandatory dual audit system, an AH company has been allowed to choose whether to continue with the dual audit (HKEx, 2009)[9]. Accordingly, since 2010, some AH companies have stopped using the dual audit in the form of dismissing their Hong Kong-based auditors. They retain mainland-based auditors to perform the single audit just like the domestic-listed-only companies do. By contrast, other AH companies continue to hire two audit firms from both sides to perform the dual audit.

Melumad and Thoman (1990)[222] and Lennox and Pittman (2011)[223] note that a company can voluntarily incur audit costs to exploit a signaling mechanism in the absence of mandatory audit requirements. The costly decision to have financial accounts audited can send outsiders incremental information regarding a company's risk characteristics over and above the information conveyed by the verified financial statements. That is, a company's willingness to purchase audit services likely signals the company's low-risk type to the market. In addition, the decision to be audited informs outsiders that a company may have very profitable prospects, otherwise the additional audit costs will not be incurred (Kausar et al.,

2016) [344]. Voluntary audit choices also create a separating equilibrium. In such an equilibrium, high-quality companies choose to have audit services, whereas these services are too costly to afford for low-quality companies (Kausar et al., 2016) [344]. Consequently, companies choosing to be audited likely win more preference from investors and raise external equity capital at lower costs than those who decide not to have a voluntary audit. Based on this signaling theory, I argue that after the deregulation of the mandatory dual audit system, voluntarily choosing the dual audit, which is more costly than using only the single audit, potentially conveys incremental information regarding a company's higher quality, lower risk and more profitable prospects beyond the audited financial information (i. e., audit quality). As a result, a positive signal that differentiates companies voluntarily choosing the dual audit from companies using only the single audit can be generated. With this signal, the former are more likely to be preferred by investors and raise external equity financing at lower costs than the latter. That is to say, if voluntarily choosing the dual audit can serve as a positive signal, then I expect to find a lower cost of equity for voluntary dual audit than for single audit after the deregulation. Importantly, I focus on the A-share financial and auditing data of the total sample firms whose A-share financial statements are all audited by mainland-based audit firms. Therefore, the effects of the audited financial information (i. e., audit quality) can be effectively measured and controlled in the empirical process. This practice helps ensure that any difference in the cost of equity between voluntary dual audit and single audit will be attributed to the signaling effect of voluntarily choosing the dual audit rather than a difference in audit quality.

On the basis of the aforementioned arguments, I formulate the fifth hypothesis in this study.

Hypothesis 5: Ceteris paribus, after the deregulation, companies voluntarily using the dual audit have a lower cost of equity than companies using only the single audit.

Firms with greater demand for equity financing usually care more about the cost of equity. They have stronger motivation to win external investors' preference and reduce financing costs. To achieve this purpose, they may incur additional costs to signal themselves. For example, they can choose to use the dual audit to signal their better properties than those using only the single audit and thereby mitigate financing frictions. That is to say, after the deregulation of the mandatory dual audit system, if voluntary dual audit can serve as a signaling mechanism to reduce the cost of equity, firms with a greater equity capital need are more likely to benefit from this effect.

Therefore, I formulate the sixth hypothesis in this study.

Hypothesis 6: Ceteris paribus, the lower cost of equity for voluntary dual audit than single audit is more pronounced for companies with higher equity financing demand.

Jensen and Meckling (1976) [257] suggest that firms have the motivation to voluntarily undertake monitoring expenditure, such as purchasing audit services, to take advantage of the signal and make external investors believe that activities harmful to their interests would be restrained. After the deregulation of the mandatory dual audit system, as a kind of voluntary monitoring expenditure, choosing the dual audit may signal a firm's good quality, such as management integrity, to investors. Thus, voluntary dual audit has the potential to reduce agency conflicts. That is to say, if voluntary dual audit can distinguish firms making such a choice with those not doing so by a positive signal, this beneficial effect can be particularly important to firms with severer agency conflicts.

Therefore, I formulate the seventh hypothesis in this study.

Hypothesis 7: Ceteris paribus, the lower cost of equity for voluntary dual audit than single audit is more pronounced for companies with higher agency costs.

Firms may also seek for alternative forms of voluntary audits, for instance, having the interim reports audited by external auditors (Haw et al., 2008) [341]. The act of purchasing audit services for the interim reports also has the potential to convey incremental information about a company's good properties beyond the audited information. To the extent that companies also voluntarily use the interim report audit to signal their good types, voluntary dual audit may provide less incremental information for investors and thereby have a smaller influence on the cost of equity of these companies. Accordingly, voluntary dual audit (being examined in this study) and the interim report audit (as a common alternative voluntary audit mechanism in China) have the likely similar voluntary nature. They are likely to act as substitutes for each other in sending positive signals.

Therefore, I formulate the eighth hypothesis in this study.

Hypothesis 8: Ceteris paribus, the lower cost of equity for voluntary dual audit than single audit is less pronounced for companies with audited interim reports.

5.2 Research Design

5.2.1 Sample and Data

The sample used in this chapter comprises A-share listed companies in China for the period 2010 to 2015. They are selected on the basis of those used in Chapter 4. In particular, out of the 8647 firm-year observations in Chapter 4, 6963 observations are in the period after the deregulation (i. e., 2010–2015). I further delete the 1684 observations in 2007–2009, and finally leave the 6963 firm-year observations in 2010–2015 for the empirical analyses in this chapter. ① All the financial and auditing data used in this chapter come from the CSMAR and WIND databases. Table 5-1 demonstrates the sample selection process. All continuous variables are winsorized at 0.01 and 0.99 to minimize the impact of outliers. ②

Table 5-1 Sample Selection in Chapter 5

Description	Number of Observations
A-share listed observations with available data on estimating the cost of equity during the period of 2007–2015	11809
Less: observations in the initial public offering year	(1207)
Less: observations that were delisted, terminated, or under special treatment	(218)
Less: observations in financial industry	(313)
Less: observations that are AH companies listing on the A-share market or the H-share market on or after 2010	(63)
Less: observations with missing financial and auditor data	(1361)
Sample used in Chapter 4	8647
Less: observations in 2007–2009	(1684)
Final Sample used in Chapter 5 (2012 firms)	6963

① For consistency, I use the financial data reported in the A-share market for all the sample companies, including AH companies.

② Keeping original values or omitting extreme observations from the sample does not change the results.

5. 2. 2 Empirical Model

To empirically test H5 (and the further hypotheses H6 to H8) about the effect of voluntary dual audit relative to single audit on the cost of equity, I formulate Eq. (5-1) as follows:

$$COE\_GLS_{t,i} = \alpha_0 + \alpha_1 DUAL\_V_{t,i} + \alpha_2 AH_{t,i} + \alpha_3 Size_{t,i} + \alpha_4 Beta_{t,i} + \alpha_5 MB_{t,i} + \alpha_6 DE_{t,i} + \alpha_7 Std\_Ret_{t,i} + \alpha_8 Liq_{t,i} + \alpha_9 Growth_{t,i} + \alpha_{10} SOE_{t,i} + \alpha_{11} Disp_{t,i} + \alpha_{12} Bias_{t,i} + \alpha_{13} Big4_{t,i} + Year\ Fixed\ Effects + Industry\ Fixed\ Effects + \varepsilon_{t,i} \quad (5-1)$$

where the dependent variable ($COE\_GLS_{t,i}$) is the cost of equity based on Eq. (4-1), as discussed in Section 4. 2. 2. The independent variable of interest, $DUAL\_V_{t,i}$, refers to an indicator variable that equals 1 if a company chooses to use the dual audit in year t, and 0 otherwise. Under H5, I expect that the cost of equity of companies voluntarily using the dual audit after the deregulation is lower than that of companies using only the single audit in the same period. Thus, I expect the coefficient on $DUAL\_V_{t,i}$ to be negative in the regression model. I also control for year fixed effects and industry fixed effects in this model. Other variables in Eq. (5-1) are the same as those defined in Eq. (4-6). It is noteworthy again that $Big4_{t,i}$ is included to ensure that any difference in the cost of equity between voluntary dual audit and single audit will not be attributed to the assurance levels provided by auditors (i. e. , audit quality). Variable definitions can be seen in Table 5-2.

Table 5-2 Variable Definitions in Chapter 5

Variable	Description
Variables in Baseline Model[Eq. (5-1)]	
Dependent Variable	
$COE\_GLS_{t,i}$	Cost of equity estimated following Gebhardt et al. (2001) [2].
Independent Variable of Interest	
$DUAL\_V_{t,i}$	1 if the company chooses to use the dual audit, and 0 otherwise.
Control Variables	
$AH_{t,i}$	1 if the company is an AH company, and 0 otherwise.
$Size_{t,i}$	Natural log of total assets.
$Beta_{t,i}$	Unleveraged beta, calculated as the market beta divided by (1 + equity ratio).

续表

Variable	Description
$MB_{t,i}$	The market value of equity divided by the book value of equity.
$DE_{t,i}$	Long-term debt divided by the market value of equity.
$Std\_Ret_{t,i}$	The standard deviation of monthly stock returns in the year.
$Liq_{t,i}$	The sum of daily trading volume divided by the number of trading days in the year.
$Growth_{t,i}$	Average growth in revenues in the prior 3 years.
$SOE_{t,i}$	1 if the company is an SOE, and 0 otherwise.
$Disp_{t,i}$	The standard deviation of analyst forecasts for year *t* EPS divided by mean analyst forecasts for year *t* EPS.
$Bias_{t,i}$	Forecast EPS minus reported EPS divided by stock price at the beginning of the year.
$Big4_{t,i}$	1 if the company engages a Big 4 auditor in year *t*, and 0 otherwise.
Variables in Robustness Tests	
$\|DACC\|_{t,i}$	The absolute value of performance-adjusted discretionary accruals for year *t* (Kothari et al. , 2005) [366].
$Restate_{t,i}$	1 if the company announces at least 1 accounting restatement in the year, and 0 otherwise.
$MAO_{t,i}$	1 if the company receives a modified audit opinion, and 0 otherwise.
$Chg\_NtB_{t,i}$	1 if the company switches from a non-Big 4 to a Big 4 auditor, and 0 otherwise.
$Chg\_BtN_{t,i}$	1 if the company switches from a Big 4 to a non-Big 4 auditor, and 0 otherwise.
$Chg\_MtV_{t,i}$	1 if the company switches from mandatory to voluntary dual audit, and 0 otherwise.
$Chg\_MtS_{t,i}$	1 if the company switches from mandatory dual audit to single audit, and 0 otherwise.
$Chg\_VtS_{t,i}$	1 if the company switches from voluntary dual audit to single audit, and 0 otherwise.
$COE\_OJ_{t,i}$	Cost of equity estimated following Ohlson and Juettner (2005) [24].
$COE\_CT_{t,i}$	Cost of equity estimated following Claus and Thomas (2001) [22].
$COE\_PEG_{t,i}$	Cost of equity estimated following Easton (2004) [23].
$COE\_AVG_{t,i}$	The average of $COE\_GLS_{t,i}$, $COE\_OJ_{t,i}$, $COE\_CT_{t,i}$ and $COE\_PEG_{t,i}$.

5. 3 Empirical Results

5. 3. 1 Sample Distribution

Table 5-3 reports the sample distribution. Panel A of Table 5-3 shows that the sample firms are distributed across 17 different industries. The manufacturing industry has the largest number of observations (4211 observations), followed by the information transmission, software and information technology services industry (429 observations), the wholesale and retail trades industry (400 observations) and the real estate industry (377 observations).

Table 5-3 Panel B shows a description of distribution by year. Column (1) indicates an increasing yearly trend of the total sample after the deregulation, while Column (2) shows that the annual sample size of the AH sample remains relatively stable during this period. Column (3) reports that, after the deregulation, the number of companies voluntarily choosing the dual audit shows a generally declining trend, especially from 2010 to 2011. However, even at the end of the sample period (i. e., 2015), companies voluntarily choosing the dual audit still occupy 63. 6% (28/44) of the AH sample. This implies that most of the companies in the sample previously bound by the mandatory dual audit requirement choose to keep the dual audit after the deregulation. This non-trivial proportion suggests unneglectable voluntary demand for the dual audit after the deregulation. Column (4) presents that the sample size of companies using only the single audit decreases from 2010 to 2011, and then rises year by year afterwards.

Table 5-3 Sample Distribution in Chapter 5

Panel A: Sample Distribution by Industry	
Industry	Number
Agriculture, Forestry, Husbandry and Fishery	106
Construction	196
Culture, Sports and Entertainment	94
Education	3
Electricity, Heat, Gas and Water Production and Supply	283
Health and Social Work	23

续表

Panel A: Sample Distribution by Industry	
Industry	Number
Hotels and Catering Services	38
Information Transmission, Software and Information Technology Services	429
Leasing and Business Services	87
Manufacturing	4211
Mining	244
Miscellaneous	37
Real Estate	377
Scientific Research and Technical Services	39
Transport, Storage and Post	302
Water Conservancy, Environment and Public Facilities Management	94
Wholesale and Retail Trades	400
Total	6963

Panel B: Sample Distribution by Year				
Year	(1) Number of Total Sample	(2) Number of AH sample	(3) Number of Voluntary Dual Audit Sample	(4) Number of Single Audit Sample
2010	916	43	42	874
2011	836	41	30	806
2012	1041	42	30	1011
2013	1208	42	29	1179
2014	1441	42	28	1413
2015	1521	44	28	1493
Total	6963	254	187	6776

Notes: The industry classification is adapted from the "Revised Guidance for Industry Classification of China's Listed Companies" (CSRC, 2012) [367].

5. 3. 2 Descriptive Statistics

The descriptive statistics of the total sample in this chapter are presented in Panel A of Table 5 - 4. The mean (median) cost of equity ($COE\_GLS_{t,i}$) is 6. 4%

(6.3%). Among all the sample firms in this chapter, 2.7% of observations choose to use the dual audit ($DUAL\_V_{t,i}$). As for the control variables, 3.6% of observations refer to AH companies ($AH_{t,i}$). The mean values of $Size_{t,i}$, $Beta_{t,i}$, $MB_{t,i}$, $Growth_{t,i}$ and $DE_{t,i}$, which are quite similar to those reported in Panel A of Table 4-8, imply that the sample firms in the period after the deregulation are large-sized firms in good financial condition and with growth potential. Of the sample firms, 44.9% of observations are SOEs ($SOE_{t,i}$). Similar to those presented in Panel A of Table 4-8, the mean (median) analyst forecast dispersion ($Disp_{t,i}$) is 0.112 (0.070), while the mean (median) analyst forecast bias ($Bias_{t,i}$) is 0.008 (0.005). Big 4 auditors provide audit services for 7.7% of the sample observations ($Big4_{t,i}$).

Table 5-4 Descriptive Statistics and Test of Differences

Panel A: Descriptive Statistics of Total Sample in Chapter 5 (*N*=6963)					
Variable	Mean	Median	Std. Dev.	25%	75%
$COE\_GLS_{t,i}$	0.064	0.063	0.025	0.046	0.081
$DUAL\_V_{t,i}$	0.027	0.000	0.162	0.000	0.000
$AH_{t,i}$	0.036	0.000	0.187	0.000	0.000
$Size_{t,i}$	22.388	22.180	1.279	21.447	23.149
$Beta_{t,i}$	0.478	0.439	0.313	0.260	0.660
$MB_{t,i}$	3.756	2.870	2.925	1.864	4.609
$DE_{t,i}$	0.151	0.031	0.283	0.006	0.149
$Std\_Ret_{t,i}$	0.137	0.121	0.063	0.094	0.161
$Liq_{t,i}$	0.025	0.020	0.018	0.012	0.034
$Growth_{t,i}$	0.972	0.546	1.809	0.190	1.071
$SOE_{t,i}$	0.449	0.000	0.497	0.000	1.000
$Disp_{t,i}$	0.112	0.070	0.233	0.027	0.148
$Bias_{t,i}$	0.008	0.005	0.025	-0.001	0.014
$Big4_{t,i}$	0.077	0.000	0.266	0.000	0.000

续表

Panel B: Test of Differences Between Voluntary Dual Audit ($DUAL\_V_{t,i}=1$) and Single Audit ($DUAL\_V_{t,i}=0$)

Variable	Mean		Test of Differences
	$DUAL\_V_{t,i}=1$ ($N=187$)	$DUAL\_V_{t,i}=0$ ($N=6776$)	t-stat.
$COE\_GLS_{t,i}$	0. 083	0. 064	10. 279 ***
$AH_{t,i}$	1. 000	0. 010	136. 820 ***
$Size_{t,i}$	25. 122	22. 313	31. 685 ***
$Beta_{t,i}$	0. 459	0. 478	-0. 812
$MB_{t,i}$	1. 790	3. 810	-9. 373 ***
$DE_{t,i}$	0. 603	0. 138	22. 975 ***
$Std\_Ret_{t,i}$	0. 112	0. 138	-5. 367 ***
$Liq_{t,i}$	0. 010	0. 026	-11. 511 ***
$Growth_{t,i}$	0. 460	0. 986	-3. 929 ***
$SOE_{t,i}$	0. 968	0. 435	14. 675 ***
$Disp_{t,i}$	0. 070	0. 113	-2. 478 **
$Bias_{t,i}$	0. 006	0. 008	-1. 362
$Big4_{t,i}$	0. 727	0. 059	37. 131 ***

Notes: ***, ** and * represent significance at the 0. 01, 0. 05 and 0. 10 level, respectively, using two-tailed tests; variable definitions and measurement are reported in Table 5-2.

5. 3. 3 Univariate Tests

Panel B of Table 5-4 compares the mean values of the dependent variable and control variables between the companies voluntarily using the dual audit (i. e. , the sample for which $DUAL\_V_{t,i}=1$; $N=187$) and the companies using only the single audit (i. e. , the sample for which $DUAL\_V_{t,i}=0$; $N=6776$). The last column reports the t-statistics in the mean difference test. As shown in the panel, the mean cost of equity ($COE\_GLS_{t,i}$) of the companies voluntarily using the dual audit (0. 083) is significantly higher than that of the companies using only the single audit (0. 064), which is inconsistent with H5. Nevertheless, the companies voluntarily using the dual audit also significantly differ from the companies using only the single audit in several firm-level and analyst-level characteristics. For example, the former have larger size ($Size_{t,i}$), lower market-to-book ratio ($MB_{t,i}$), lower long-term solvency ($DE_{t,i}$), smaller volatility ($Std\_Ret_{t,i}$), lower liquidity ($Liq_{t,i}$), lower long-term growth ($Growth_{t,i}$) and smaller analyst forecast dispersion ($Disp_{t,i}$) and are more likely to be owned by government ($SOE_{t,i}$) and hire Big 4 auditors ($Big4_{t,i}$). I will further verify the results and control for the underlying characteristics in the multivariate regressions in the sections below.

5.3.4 Multivariate Regressions

5.3.4.1 Tests of H5

Table 5-5 presents the findings of the tests of H5 that compares the cost of equity between voluntary dual audit and single audit after the deregulation. All the regression models have statistical significance at the 0.01 level. In Column (1), the sample consists of the total 6963 firm-year observations in the deregulation period. It is unlikely that the test variables suffer from multicollinearity, given that the VIF for each variable is lower than 10 (unreported) (Kennedy, 2003)[368]. The coefficient on $DUAL\_V_{t,i}$ is negative and significant at the 0.01 level (coefficient = −0.007, t = −3.217). This result suggests that after controlling for the underlying determinants[including audit quality ($Big4_{t,i}$)], voluntarily choosing the dual audit is associated with a lower cost of equity than using only the single audit. As for economic significance, given that the mean cost of equity of the total sample is 0.064, the magnitude of the coefficient means that the cost of equity of companies voluntarily choosing the dual audit is about 10.9% lower than that of companies using only the single audit. This finding is consistent with my expectation in H5, which states that companies voluntarily choosing the dual audit after the deregulation have a lower cost of equity than those using only the single audit in the same period.

As for the control variables, market risk ($Beta_{t,i}$), financial risk ($DE_{t,i}$) and long-term growth ($Growth_{t,i}$) are positively related to the cost of equity. The cost of equity is lower for companies with higher market-to-book ratio ($MB_{t,i}$) and greater liquidity ($Liq_{t,i}$) and for SOEs ($SOE_{t,i}$). $Size_{t,i}$ and $Std\_Ret_{t,i}$ are statistically significant with non-predicted signs due to the potential issue of assumptions regarding the parameters in the cost-of-equity estimation model (Mao et al., 2012)[355].

Table 5-5 Regression Results of Tests of H5

Variable	Dependent Variable: $COE\_GLS_{t,i}$	
	(1)	(2)
Intercept	−0. 043 *** (−7. 430)	
$DUAL\_V_{t,i}$	−0. 007 *** (−3. 217)	−0. 006 ** (−2. 225)
$AH_{t,i}$	0. 001 (0. 365)	
$Size_{t,i}$	0. 004 *** (17. 592)	0. 003 * (1. 661)
$Beta_{t,i}$	0. 003 *** (3. 805)	−0. 007 (−1. 068)
$MB_{t,i}$	−0. 004 *** (−42. 310)	−0. 004 *** (−5. 603)
$DE_{t,i}$	0. 010 *** (10. 625)	0. 005 (1. 328)
$Std\_Ret_{t,i}$	−0. 031 *** (−6. 888)	−0. 094 *** (−2. 789)
$Liq_{t,i}$	−0. 074 *** (−4. 904)	−0. 005 (−0. 030)
$Growth_{t,i}$	0. 001 *** (7. 298)	0. 001 (0. 285)
$SOE_{t,i}$	−0. 002 *** (−4. 727)	−0. 000 (−0. 062)
$Disp_{t,i}$	0. 000 (0. 169)	0. 005 (1. 129)
$Bias_{t,i}$	0. 000 (0. 011)	0. 080 (1. 125)
$Big4_{t,i}$	−0. 000 (−0. 380)	−0. 000 (−0. 080)
Year Fixed Effects	Yes	Yes
Industry Fixed Effects	Yes	Yes
N	6963	242
Adj. R^2	0. 604	0. 561
F	313. 550	14. 981

Notes: Column (1) shows the results of Eq. (5-1) for the total sample in Chapter 5; Column (2) shows the results of Eq. (5-1) for the sample of 242 firm-year observations, matched by the PSM method; in Column (2), variable $AH_{t,i}$ is omitted owing to collinearity in the first stage of the PSM procedure; * * *, * * and * represent significance at the 0. 01, 0. 05 and 0. 10 level, respectively, using two-tailed tests; t-statistics are shown in parentheses; variable definitions and measurement are reported in Table 5-2.

My basic assumption is that investors interpret voluntary dual audit as a positive signal and require lower rate of return on companies voluntarily choosing the dual audit than those using only the single audit. However, Panel B of Table 5-4 demonstrates that significant differences exist between these two groups in many characteristics. The multivariate regression above has used these charac-teristics as control variables. To further rule out the possibility that investors make investment decisions based on the differences in firm characteristics instead of the signaling role of voluntary dual audit, I use the propensity score matching (PSM) method. With this method, each sample for which $DUAL\_V_{t,i}=1$ can be matched to its closest match in the sample for which $DUAL\_V_{t,i}=0$ on the dimensions of the control variables. ① I first run the following Logit model[i. e., Eq. (5-2)] using the total sample in this chapter, and predict for each observation the probability of choosing to use the dual audit:

$$DUAL\_V_{t,i}=\alpha_0+\alpha_1 Size_{t,i}+\alpha_2 Beta_{t,i}+\alpha_3 MB_{t,i}+\alpha_4 DE_{t,i}+\alpha_5 Std\_Ret_{t,i}+\alpha_6 Liq_{t,i}+\alpha_7 Growth_{t,i}+\alpha_8 SOE_{t,i}+\alpha_9 Disp_{t,i}+\alpha_{10} Bias_{t,i}+\alpha_{11} Big4_{t,i}+Year\ Fixed\ Effects+Industry\ Fixed\ Effects+\varepsilon_{t,i} \quad (5-2)$$

Panel A of Table 5-6 shows the results of the first stage. Firm size ($Size_{t,i}$), market risk ($Beta_{t,i}$), market-to-book ratio ($MB_{t,i}$), long-term solvency ($DE_{t,i}$), long-term revenue growth ($Growth_{t,i}$), ownership property ($SOE_{t,i}$) and auditor type ($Big4_{t,i}$) are significantly associated with a firm's voluntary dual audit choice. Subsequently, I use the predicted probabilities to perform the without-replacement matching. The caliper in the predicted probabilities between a sample and its matched sample is set to be less than 3% to ensure close matches (Lawrence et al., 2011)[380]. 121 observations voluntarily choosing the dual audit and 121 observations using only the single audit are left after removing the matched pairs that have differences larger than the caliper. Panel B of Table 5-6 reports the descriptive statistics of the matched sample. The last column shows that the differences between the voluntary dual audit sample and the single audit sample become statistically insignificant throughout all the observable dimensions, indicating that the PSM method achieves covariate balance between these two groups, that is, the two samples are tightly matched (Armstrong et al., 2010)[381].

---

① Variable $AH_{t,i}$ is omitted in this process owing to collinearity.

I then use the 242 matched sample observations to re-estimate Eq. (5-1). Column (2) of Table 5-5 demonstrates the results. As reported in this column, I consistently find a negative and significant coefficient on $DUAL\_V_{t,i}$(coefficient = -0.006, t = -2.225), which confirms the robustness of the findings obtained in Column (1) of Table 5-5 and further supports H5. Overall, these findings suggest that voluntary dual audit is associated with a lower cost of equity than single audit after the deregulation.

Table 5-6 Results of Propensity Score Model and Descriptive Statistics of Propensity Score-Matched Sample

Panel A: Results of Propensity Score Model[i. e. , Eq. (5-2)]	
Variable	Dependent Variable: $DUAL\_V_{t,i}$
Intercept	-41.748*** (-12.743)
$Size_{t,i}$	1.481*** (11.307)
$Beta_{t,i}$	0.912* (1.657)
$MB_{t,i}$	0.260*** (3.970)
$DE_{t,i}$	1.159*** (3.751)
$Std\_Ret_{t,i}$	1.518 (0.570)
$Liq_{t,i}$	9.954 (0.768)
$Growth_{t,i}$	-0.886*** (-4.197)
$SOE_{t,i}$	0.991** (2.135)
$Disp_{t,i}$	-0.130 (-0.376)
$Bias_{t,i}$	4.693 (1.029)
$Big4_{t,i}$	2.163*** (8.911)

续表

Panel A: Results of Propensity Score Model[i. e. , Eq. (5-2)]	
Variable	Dependent Variable: $DUAL\_V_{t,i}$
Year Fixed Effects	Yes
Industry Fixed Effects	Yes
N	5613
Pseudo. R^2	0. 593
LR Chi^2	973. 096

Panel B: Descriptive Statistics of Propensity Score-Matched Sample			
Variable	$DUAL\_V_{t,i}=1$ (N=121) Mean Std. Dev	$DUAL\_V_{t,i}=0$ (N=121) Mean Std. Dev	Test of Differences t-stat.
$Size_{t,i}$	24. 755 1. 172	24. 641 1. 254	0. 725
$Beta_{t,i}$	0. 488 0. 282	0. 460 0. 222	0. 869
$MB_{t,i}$	1. 986 2. 288	2. 165 2. 709	-0. 555
$DE_{t,i}$	0. 471 0. 481	0. 489 0. 486	-0. 293
$Std\_Ret_{t,i}$	0. 115 0. 062	0. 113 0. 057	0. 167
$Liq_{t,i}$	0. 012 0. 011	0. 013 0. 014	-0. 426
$Growth_{t,i}$	0. 487 0. 594	0. 498 0. 536	-0. 145
$SOE_{t,i}$	0. 950 0. 218	0. 967 0. 180	-0. 644
$Disp_{t,i}$	0. 083 0. 338	0. 107 0. 279	-0. 603
$Bias_{t,i}$	0. 006 0. 018	0. 005 0. 020	0. 431
$Big4_{t,i}$	0. 628 0. 485	0. 678 0. 469	-0. 808

Notes: * * *, * * and * represent significance at the 0. 01, 0. 05 and 0. 10 level, respectively, using two-tailed tests; t-statistics are shown in parentheses; variable definitions and measurement are reported in Table 5-2.

5. 3. 4. 2 Tests of H6, H7 and H8

Columns (1) and (2) of Table 5-7 present the findings of the tests of H6 about whether the lower cost of equity for voluntary dual audit (than that for single audit after the deregulation) is conditional on firms' equity financing demand. Consistent with the practice in Section 4. 3. 4, firms whose ratio of cash on hand to total assets is in the lowest tercile and asset-liability ratio is in the highest tercile are identified as firms with higher demand for equity financing, whereas the remaining firms are identified as those with lower demand for equity financing. [①] I then re-estimate Eq. (5-1) in these two subsamples, respectively. Column (1) of Table 5-7 shows that the coefficient on $DUAL\_V_{t,i}$ is negative and significant in the sample with higher equity financing demand (coefficient = -0. 018, t = -3. 393), whereas Column (2) of Table 5-7 shows that the coefficient on the same term is insignificant in the sample with lower equity financing demand (coefficient = -0. 003, t = -1. 267). These results suggest that the effect of voluntary dual audit relative to single audit on lowering the cost of equity is greater in firms with higher equity financing demand, consistent with H6.

Columns (3) and (4) of Table 5-7 present the findings of the tests of H7 about whether the lower cost of equity for voluntary dual audit (than that for single audit after the deregulation) is conditional on firms' agency costs. Consistent with the practice in Section 4. 3. 4, firms with managerial ownership lower than the sample median are classified into the group with higher agency costs, whereas firms with managerial ownership higher than the sample median are classified into the group with lower agency costs. Eq. (5-1) is then re-estimated in each of these two groups. As reported in Table 5-7, the negative coefficient on $DUAL\_V_{t,i}$ is significant in the sample with higher agency costs [Column (3), coefficient = -0. 008, t = -2. 507], while it is insignificant in the sample with lower agency costs [Column (4), coefficient = -0. 003, t = -0. 692]. These findings imply that the effect of voluntary dual audit relative to single audit on reducing the cost of equity is more pronounced in firms with higher agency costs, thereby supporting H7.

Columns (5) and (6) of Table 5-7 present the findings of the tests of H8 about whether the lower cost of equity for voluntary dual audit (than that for single audit

---

① This cut-off is arbitrary but not selective. The results are robust to different cut-offs (e. g. , quintiles, quartiles or sample median). See Appendix Ⅰ for the results with other cut-offs.

after the deregulation) is less pronounced in firms with audited interim reports. As shown in Columns (5) and (6) of Table 5-7, the coefficient on $DUAL\_V_{t,i}$ is insignificant in the sample with audited interim reports [Column (5), coefficient = 0.017, t = 1.514] while it becomes negative and significant at the 0.01 level in the sample with unaudited interim reports [Column (6), coefficient = -0.008, t = -3.344]. These findings are consistent with H8 and suggest that the advantage of voluntary dual audit over single audit in reducing the cost of equity is weakened by the interim report audit. That is to say, the role of voluntary dual audit in sending a positive signal to the market can be substituted by alternative voluntary audit mechanisms, such as the interim report audit.

Table 5-7 Regression Results of Tests of H6, H7 and H8

Variable	Dependent Variable: $COE\_GLS_{t,i}$					
	Equity Financing Demand		Agency Costs		Interim Report Audit	
	(1) Higher	(2) Lower	(3) Higher	(4) Lower	(5) Yes	(6) No
Intercept	-0.020 (-1.127)	-0.044*** (-7.035)	-0.033*** (-3.507)	-0.051*** (-6.577)	-0.043 (-1.430)	-0.042*** (-7.074)
$DUAL\_V_{t,i}$	-0.018*** (-3.393)	-0.003 (-1.267)	-0.008** (-2.507)	-0.003 (-0.692)	0.017 (1.514)	-0.008*** (-3.344)
$AH_{t,i}$	0.013*** (2.758)	-0.003 (-1.422)	0.001 (0.289)	0.001 (0.184)	-0.004 (-0.390)	0.001 (0.303)
$Size_{t,i}$	0.004*** (4.786)	0.004*** (16.296)	0.004*** (10.376)	0.005*** (13.874)	0.004*** (3.124)	0.004*** (17.081)
$Beta_{t,i}$	0.005 (1.125)	0.003*** (4.072)	0.003** (2.193)	0.003*** (3.892)	0.007** (2.217)	0.003*** (3.732)
$MB_{t,i}$	-0.004*** (-11.633)	-0.004*** (-40.913)	-0.004*** (-24.522)	-0.004*** (-35.225)	-0.004*** (-9.863)	-0.004*** (-41.097)
$DE_{t,i}$	0.007*** (3.733)	0.014*** (10.802)	0.008*** (6.299)	0.015*** (9.266)	0.015*** (2.994)	0.010*** (10.384)
$Std\_Ret_{t,i}$	-0.074*** (-4.894)	-0.025*** (-5.264)	-0.046*** (-5.656)	-0.023*** (-4.322)	-0.020 (-1.281)	-0.033*** (-7.064)
$Liq_{t,i}$	-0.037 (-0.618)	-0.077*** (-4.992)	-0.075** (-2.554)	-0.072*** (-4.233)	-0.044 (-0.809)	-0.077*** (-4.892)

续表

Variable	Dependent Variable: $COE\_GLS_{t,i}$					
	Equity Financing Demand		Agency Costs		Interim Report Audit	
	(1) Higher	(2) Lower	(3) Higher	(4) Lower	(5) Yes	(6) No
$Growth_{t,i}$	0.000* (1.652)	0.001*** (7.234)	0.001*** (3.740)	0.001*** (6.998)	0.001*** (4.245)	0.001*** (6.460)
$SOE_{t,i}$	−0.003** (−2.453)	−0.002*** (−4.441)	−0.002*** (−3.172)	−0.002*** (−2.642)	−0.002 (−0.921)	−0.002*** (−4.627)
$Disp_{t,i}$	0.002 (1.278)	−0.001 (−0.870)	0.001 (1.071)	−0.002** (−1.992)	−0.004 (−0.960)	0.000 (0.242)
$Bias_{t,i}$	−0.028 (−1.516)	0.009 (1.008)	−0.012 (−0.987)	0.016 (1.595)	0.031 (0.978)	−0.002 (−0.208)
$Big4_{t,i}$	−0.001 (−0.636)	0.000 (0.071)	0.001 (1.201)	−0.004*** (−2.749)	0.011 (1.646)	−0.000 (−0.545)
Year Fixed Effects	Yes	Yes	Yes	Yes	Yes	Yes
Industry Fixed Effects	Yes	Yes	Yes	Yes	Yes	Yes
N	961	6002	3072	3891	335	6628
Adj. R^2	0.596	0.605	0.586	0.619	0.690	0.601
F	43.838	271.689	128.921	187.006	24.989	294.117

Notes: Column (1) [Column (2)] shows the results of Eq. (5-1) for the subsample with higher (lower) demand for equity financing; Column (3) [Column (4)] shows the results of Eq. (5-1) for the subsample with higher (lower) agency costs; Column (5) [Column (6)] shows the results of Eq. (5-1) for the subsample with audited (unaudited) interim financial reports; *** , ** and * represent significance at the 0.01, 0.05 and 0.10 level, respectively, using two-tailed tests; *t*-statistics are shown in parentheses; variable definitions and measurement are reported in Table 5-2.

5.3.5 Robustness Tests

5.3.5.1 Further Considering Audit Quality

While audit quality is controlled in the main tests with a classical measure reflecting the type of auditors (i.e., $Big4_{t,i}$), it is still unclear whether audit quality actually differs across the voluntary dual audit group and the single audit group. To address this concern, similar to the practices in Section 4.3.5, I further check the discretionary accruals ($|DACC|_{t,i}$), the likelihood of restatements ($Restate_{t,i}$) and the likelihood of modified audit opinions ($MAO_{t,i}$) across these groups in the period after the deregulation. The results in Panel A of Table 5 – 8 show that there is no significant difference between the voluntary dual audit sample and the single audit sample in any of the three aspects ($|DACC|_{t,i}$, $Restate_{t,i}$ and $MAO_{t,i}$), suggesting that audit quality does not differ across these groups. These findings help strengthen my argument and findings that with the assurance levels controlled, the difference in the cost of equity between these groups is indeed attributable to whether to voluntarily choose the dual audit or to use only the single audit after the deregulation.

Subsequently, to further rule out the alternative explanation that the main results may capture the effect of audit quality on the cost of equity rather than the direct impact of voluntarily choosing the dual audit, I introduce $|DACC|_{t,i}$, $Restate_{t,i}$ and $MAO_{t,i}$ separately into Eq. (5 – 1) to additionally control for audit quality. Columns (1) to (3) in Panel B of Table 5 – 8 illustrate the results. The coefficient on $DUAL\_V_{t,i}$ remains negative and significant throughout the three columns. These findings are qualitatively similar to those reported in Table 5–5 and suggest that after further mitigating the confounding effect of audit quality, the results continue to hold. Regarding the audit-quality proxies, the coefficient on $|DACC|_{t,i}$ is positive and significant, supporting the argument about a negative relationship between audit quality and the cost of equity (Chen et al., 2011)[83].

Furthermore, I also consider the situations of auditor grade changes and audit system changes (as mentioned in Section 4. 3. 5) to exclude the possibility of a change in audit assurance. Specifically, I introduce the variables of auditor grade changes (i. e., $Chg\_NtB_{t,i}$ and $Chg\_BtN_{t,i}$) and those of audit system changes (i. e., $Chg\_MtV_{t,i}$, $Chg\_MtS_{t,i}$ and $Chg\_VtS_{t,i}$) into Eq. (5 – 1) as additional controls. Column (4) in Panel B of Table 5 – 8 shows the results. Alternatively, I further exclude 97 observations that change auditor grade (i. e., $Chg\_NtB_{t,i} = 1$ or $Chg\_BtN_{t,i} = 1$) or change audit system (i. e., $Chg\_MtV_{t,i} = 1$, $Chg\_MtS_{t,i} = 1$ or $Chg\_VtS_{t,i} = 1$) and re-estimate Eq. (5 – 1). The results of this reduced sample are presented in Column (5) in Panel B of Table 5–8. Combinedly, the results in these two columns are similar to the main findings and reinforce my conclusion that the difference in the cost of equity is driven by whether to voluntarily choose the dual audit or to use only the single audit after the deregulation rather than by possible changes in the assurance levels.

Table 5-8 Results After Further Considering Audit Quality

Panel A: Test of Differences Between Voluntary Dual Audit ($DUAL\_V_{t,i}$ = 1) and Single Audit ($DUAL\_V_{t,i}$ = 0)

Variable	Mean		Test of Differences t-stat.
	$DUAL\_V_{t,i}=1$ (N=187)	$DUAL\_V_{t,i}=0$ (N=6776)	
$\|DACC\|_{t,i}$	0.099	0.110	-0.808
$Restate_{t,i}$	0.032	0.028	0.292
$MAO_{t,i}$	0.016	0.009	0.939

Panel B: Regression Results After Further Controlling for Audit Quality

Variable	Dependent Variable: $COE\_GLS_{t,i}$				
	(1) Controlling for $\|DACC\|_{t,i}$	(2) Controlling for $Restate_{t,i}$	(3) Controlling for $MAO_{t,i}$	(4) Controlling for Auditor Grade Change and Audit System Change	(5) Excluding Sample with Auditor Grade Change or Audit System Change
Intercept	-0.043*** (-7.416)	-0.043*** (-7.430)	-0.043*** (-7.429)	-0.043*** (-7.362)	-0.044*** (-7.502)
$DUAL\_V_{t,i}$	-0.007*** (-3.179)	-0.007*** (-3.217)	-0.007*** (-3.216)	-0.008*** (-2.926)	-0.008*** (-2.914)
$AH_{t,i}$	0.001 (0.367)	0.001 (0.366)	0.001 (0.367)	-0.000 (-0.119)	-0.000 (-0.168)
$Size_{t,i}$	0.004*** (17.614)	0.004*** (17.591)	0.004*** (17.591)	0.004*** (17.482)	0.004*** (17.529)
$Beta_{t,i}$	0.003*** (3.773)	0.003*** (3.804)	0.003*** (3.805)	0.003*** (3.788)	0.003*** (3.780)
$MB_{t,i}$	-0.004*** (-42.319)	-0.004*** (-42.304)	-0.004*** (-42.231)	-0.004*** (-42.266)	-0.004*** (-42.141)
$DE_{t,i}$	0.010*** (10.419)	0.010*** (10.625)	0.010*** (10.626)	0.010*** (10.707)	0.010*** (10.452)
$Std\_Ret_{t,i}$	-0.031*** (-6.881)	-0.031*** (-6.887)	-0.031*** (-6.887)	-0.031*** (-6.915)	-0.030*** (-6.705)
$Liq_{t,i}$	-0.075*** (-4.979)	-0.074*** (-4.901)	-0.074*** (-4.901)	-0.074*** (-4.916)	-0.073*** (-4.806)
$Growth_{t,i}$	0.001*** (7.148)	0.001*** (7.293)	0.001*** (7.296)	0.001*** (7.312)	0.001*** (7.432)

续表

Panel B: Regression Results After Further Controlling for Audit Quality					
Variable	Dependent Variable: $COE\_GLS_{t,i}$				
	(1) Controlling for $\lvert DACC \rvert_{t,i}$	(2) Controlling for $Restate_{t,i}$	(3) Controlling for $MAO_{t,i}$	(4) Controlling for Auditor Grade Change and Audit System Change	(5) Excluding Sample with Auditor Grade Change or Audit System Change
$SOE_{t,i}$	-0. 002*** (-4. 675)	-0. 002*** (-4. 728)	-0. 002*** (-4. 721)	-0. 002*** (-4. 699)	-0. 002*** (-4. 856)
$Disp_{t,i}$	0. 000 (0. 151)	0. 000 (0. 173)	0. 000 (0. 164)	0. 000 (0. 130)	0. 000 (0. 148)
$Bias_{t,i}$	-0. 000 (-0. 030)	0. 000 (0. 013)	0. 000 (0. 027)	0. 000 (0. 035)	-0. 000 (-0. 048)
$Big4_{t,i}$	-0. 000 (-0. 318)	-0. 000 (-0. 382)	-0. 000 (-0. 382)	0. 000 (0. 032)	0. 000 (0. 329)
$\lvert DACC \rvert_{t,i}$	0. 004*** (3. 207)				
$Restate_{t,i}$		-0. 000 (-0. 128)			
$MAO_{t,i}$			-0. 000 (-0. 169)		
$Chg\_NtB_{t,i}$				-0. 004 (-1. 234)	
$Chg\_BtN_{t,i}$				0. 003 (0. 621)	
$Chg\_MtV_{t,i}$				0. 004 (1. 477)	
$Chg\_MtS_{t,i}$				-0. 010 (-0. 613)	
$Chg\_VtS_{t,i}$				0. 005 (1. 063)	
Year Fixed Effects	Yes	Yes	Yes	Yes	Yes
Industry Fixed Effects	Yes	Yes	Yes	Yes	Yes
N	6958	6963	6963	6963	6866

续表

Panel B: Regression Results After Further Controlling for Audit Quality					
Variable	Dependent Variable: $COE\_GLS_{t,i}$				
	(1) Controlling for $\lvert DACC \rvert_{t,i}$	(2) Controlling for $Restate_{t,i}$	(3) Controlling for $MAO_{t,i}$	(4) Controlling for Auditor Grade Change and Audit System Change	(5) Excluding Sample with Auditor Grade Change or Audit System Change
Adj. R^2	0. 604	0. 604	0. 604	0. 604	0. 603
F	313. 131	304. 549	304. 550	273. 517	308. 246

Notes: In Panel B, Column (1) shows the results after additionally introducing $\lvert DACC \rvert_{t,i}$ as a control variable into Eq. (5-1) [5 observations are dropped from the sample used in the baseline Eq. (5-1) owing to missing data in the estimation of $\lvert DACC \rvert_{t,i}$]; Column (2) [Column (3)] shows the results after additionally introducing $Restate_{t,i}$($MAO_{t,i}$) as a control variable into Eq. (5 - 1); Column (4) shows the results after additionally introducing $Chg\_NtB_{t,i}$, $Chg\_BtN_{t,i}$, $Chg\_MtV_{t,i}$, $Chg\_MtS_{t,i}$ and $Chg\_VtS_{t,i}$ as control variables into Eq. (5-1); Column (5) shows the results of Eq. (5-1) after dropping 97 observations that change auditor grade[i. e. , switch from a non-Big 4 auditor to a Big 4 auditor (an upgrade) or vice versa (a downgrade)] or change audit system (i. e. , switch from mandatary dual audit to voluntary dual audit, switch from mandatory dual audit to single audit or switch from voluntary dual audit to single audit) in year t; * * *, * * and * represent significance at the 0. 01, 0. 05 and 0. 10 level, respectively, using two-tailed tests; t-statistics are shown in parentheses; variable definitions and measurement are reported in Table 5-2.

5. 3. 5. 2 Impact Threshold for a Confounding Variable Analysis

Considering the self-selection problem in the horizontal comparison of voluntary dual audit and single audit after the deregulation, I have used the PSM method to match these two groups on a series of observed characteristics (as discussed in Section 5. 3. 4). However, unobserved confounding factors could still be present and drive the main findings in this chapter. To examine this possibility, I take advantage of the impact threshold for a confounding variable (ITCV) analysis following the previous studies (Frank, 2002; Larcker et al. , 2010; Croci et al. , 2015) [382-384] . This approach has become more and more broadly used to address endogeneity issues in empirical research. By definition, the ITCV is the product of the following two partial correlations: the one between the dependent variable and the unobserved variable, and the other between the independent variable of interest and the unobserved variable. Its computation is based on the commonly known notion that the unobserved variable's correlations with the dependent variable and the independent variable of interest jointly determine the bias introduced by this unobserved variable. The extent of the bias in the estimated coefficient on the independent variable of interest increases with the strength of these two correlations. Accordingly, ITCV, which is regarded as the lowest correlation required to overturn a statistically significant result (Larcker et al., 2010)[383], can be a reflection of the extent of the bias. A larger value of ITCV implies a more robust OLS result to unobservable factors (Fu et al., 2012)[385].

I calculate ITCV for variable $DUAL\_V_{t,i}$ in Eq. (5－1) separately in the regression using the total sample of 6963 observations and in the regression using the sample of 242 propensity score-matched observations. Panel A of Table 5－9 demonstrates the baseline results of Eq. (5－1) with impact statistics. The threshold value for $DUAL\_V_{t,i}$ is −0.0154, suggesting that once each of the partial correlation between $COE\_GLS_{t,i}$ and the unobserved variable and the partial correlation between $DUAL\_V_{t,i}$ and the unobserved variable reaches 0.124 ($\sqrt{|-0.0154|}$), the OLS result will be overturned. In the absence of other comparative data, it cannot be determined whether the ITCV is large enough to ensure the robustness of the result. Although the unobserved variable is not available, the impacts of the control variables can be used to judge the robustness. Subsequently, I follow the previous literature and compute the impact of each control variable to benchmark the size of possible correlations involving the unobserved confounding variable. Column (2) in Panel A of Table 5－9 shows the potential impact of the inclusion of each control variable on the coefficient on $DUAL\_V_{t,i}$. Similar to the calculation of the ITCV, the impact of each control variable is the product of the partial correlation between $COE\_GLS_{t,i}$ and the control variable and the partial correlation between $DUAL\_V_{t,i}$ and the control variable. A positive (negative) impact score suggests that including the control variable strengthens (weakens) the significance of the coefficient on $DUAL\_V_{t,i}$. As shown in Column (2), the impact score with the largest magnitude is that of $MB_{t,i}$ ($|-0.0093|$), and is much smaller than the magnitude of the threshold value ($|-0.0154|$). This finding implies that among these control variables, market-to-book ratio ($MB_{t,i}$) has the greatest impact on the coefficient on $DUAL\_V_{t,i}$. An unobserved variable that can overturn the result needs to have a larger impact than $MB_{t,i}$ does; in other words, it needs to be more highly correlated with $COE\_GLS_{t,i}$ and $DUAL\_V_{t,i}$ than $MB_{t,i}$ is. Similarly, Panel B of Table 5－9 shows that the threshold value for $DUAL\_V_{t,i}$ in the regression within the propensity score-matched sample is −0.0193, whose magnitude is larger than the largest impact of the control variables (i. e., −0. 0103, the impact score of $Big4_{t,i}$).

Taken together, as I control for a series of factors that are proved to be powerful controls by the previous cost-of-equity literature, an unobserved confounding variable that can render the coefficients on $DUAL\_V_{t,i}$ statistically insignificant is unlikely to exist. The results of the ITCV analysis suggest that self-selection bias does not seriously affect the stability of the main results in this chapter. The main findings in this chapter are robust.

Table 5-9 Results of Impact Threshold for a Confounding Variable Analysis

Panel A: Results of Eq. (5-1) for Total Sample in Chapter 5 (N=6963), with Impact Statistics		
Variable	Dependent Variable: $COE\_GLS_{t,i}$	
	(1) ITCV	(2) Impact
$DUAL\_V_{t,i}$	−0. 0154	
$AH_{t,i}$		−0. 0003
$Size_{t,i}$		0. 0050
$Beta_{t,i}$		0. 0066
$MB_{t,i}$		−0. 0093
$DE_{t,i}$		0. 0051
$Std\_Ret_{t,i}$		0. 0009
$Liq_{t,i}$		−0. 0012
$Growth_{t,i}$		−0. 0007
$SOE_{t,i}$		0. 0040
$Disp_{t,i}$		0. 0003
$Bias_{t,i}$		−0. 0001
$Big4_{t,i}$		−0. 0002
Panel B: Results of Eq. (5-1) for Propensity Score-Matched Sample (N=242), with Impact Statistics		
Variable	Dependent Variable: $COE\_GLS_{t,i}$	
	(1) ITCV	(2) Impact
$DUAL\_V_{t,i}$	−0. 0193	
$Size_{t,i}$		0. 0063

续表

Panel B: Results of Eq. (5-1) for Propensity Score-Matched Sample (N=242), with Impact Statistics		
Variable	Dependent Variable: $COE\_GLS_{t,i}$	
	(1) ITCV	(2) Impact
$Beta_{t,i}$		0.0015
$MB_{t,i}$		0.0045
$DE_{t,i}$		-0.0023
$Std\_Ret_{t,i}$		0.0002
$Liq_{t,i}$		0.0019
$Growth_{t,i}$		-0.0007
$SOE_{t,i}$		-0.0001
$Disp_{t,i}$		-0.0008
$Bias_{t,i}$		0.0026
$Big4_{t,i}$		-0.0103

Notes: Variable definitions and measurement are reported in Table 5-2.

5.3.5.3 Controlling for Differential Impact of Growth

As mentioned in Section 4.3.5, the assumption in the GLS model possibly leads to an underestimation of the cost of equity for companies with high growth. Accordingly, similar to the practice in that section, I follow Chen et al. (2011) [83] by interacting $Growth_{t,i}$ with $DUAL\_V_{t,i}$ in Eq. (5-1) to further control for the differential impact of growth on the cost of equity. As shown in Table 5-10, the coefficient on $DUAL\_V_{t,i}$ remains negative and significant in this model specification. This result suggests that the main findings hold after taking the differential impact of firm growth into consideration.

Table 5-10 Regression Results after Controlling for Differential Impact of Growth

Variable	Dependent Variable: $COE\_GLS_{t,i}$
Intercept	-0.044*** (-7.446)
$DUAL\_V_{t,i}$	-0.007*** (-2.733)

续表

Variable	Dependent Variable: $COE\_GLS_{t,i}$
$AH_{t,i}$	0. 001 (0. 363)
$Size_{t,i}$	0. 004 * * * (17. 597)
$Beta_{t,i}$	0. 003 * * * (3. 790)
$MB_{t,i}$	−0. 004 * * * (−42. 308)
$DE_{t,i}$	0. 010 * * * (10. 563)
$Std\_Ret_{t,i}$	−0. 031 * * * (−6. 883)
$Liq_{t,i}$	−0. 074 * * * (−4. 884)
$Growth_{t,i}$	0. 001 * * * (7. 312)
$SOE_{t,i}$	−0. 002 * * * (−4. 728)
$Disp_{t,i}$	0. 000 (0. 175)
$Bias_{t,i}$	0. 000 (0. 008)
$Big4_{t,i}$	−0. 000 (−0. 368)
$DUAL\_V_{t,i} * Growth_{t,i}$	−0. 001 (−0. 533)
Year Fixed Effects	Yes
Industry Fixed Effects	Yes
N	6963
Adj. R^2	0. 604
F	304. 568

Notes: * * *, * * and * represent significance at the 0. 01, 0. 05 and 0. 10 level, respectively, using two-tailed tests; t-statistics are shown in parentheses; variable definitions and measurement are reported in Table 5-2.

5. 3. 5. 4 Alternative Measurement of Cost of Equity

Similar to the practice in Section 4. 3. 5, I separately use the four alternative measures of the cost of equity (i. e., $COE\_OJ_{t,i}$, $COE\_CT_{t,i}$, $COE\_PEG_{t,i}$ and $COE\_AVG_{t,i}$) as the dependent variable and re-run Eq. (5-1) for robustness check. Table 5-11 presents the results of these sensitivity tests. The coefficients on $DUAL\_V_{t,i}$ are negative in three of the four columns and significant when the cost of equity is estimated using the CT model[Column (2)] and the average of the four commonly used measures[Column (4)]. The results of these tests with alternative estimations of the cost of equity, although not highly consistent owing to measurement errors, provide some further support for the main findings of this chapter.

Table 5-11 Regression Results of Alternative Cost-of-Equity Measures

Variable	Dependent Variable: $COE\_OJ_{t,i}$ (1)	Dependent Variable: $COE\_CT_{t,i}$ (2)	Dependent Variable: $COE\_PEG_{t,i}$ (3)	Dependent Variable: $COE\_AVG_{t,i}$ (4)
Intercept	-0. 057** (-2. 171)	-0. 303*** (-3. 845)	0. 147*** (6. 951)	-0. 021 (-0. 663)
$DUAL\_V_{t,i}$	-0. 008 (-0. 691)	-0. 094*** (-2. 990)	0. 001 (0. 061)	-0. 024* (-1. 698)
$AH_{t,i}$	-0. 008 (-0. 790)	0. 034 (1. 229)	-0. 006 (-0. 776)	-0. 014 (-1. 139)
$Size_{t,i}$	0. 010*** (8. 892)	0. 020*** (6. 158)	0. 002** (2. 258)	0. 009*** (6. 410)
$Beta_{t,i}$	-0. 014*** (-4. 198)	-0. 013 (-1. 246)	-0. 015*** (-5. 369)	-0. 017*** (-4. 257)
$MB_{t,i}$	-0. 002*** (-4. 664)	-0. 001 (-0. 640)	-0. 002*** (-6. 671)	-0. 002*** (-4. 624)
$DE_{t,i}$	0. 017*** (4. 053)	-0. 051*** (-4. 061)	0. 013*** (3. 906)	0. 008 (1. 563)
$Std\_Ret_{t,i}$	0. 037* (1. 873)	-0. 039 (-0. 654)	-0. 032** (-1. 988)	0. 021 (0. 883)
$Liq_{t,i}$	-0. 140** (-2. 094)	-0. 463** (-2. 268)	-0. 175*** (-3. 227)	-0. 170** (-2. 074)
$Growth_{t,i}$	0. 005*** (9. 460)	0. 007*** (4. 517)	0. 004*** (10. 026)	0. 009*** (12. 679)

续表

Variable	Dependent Variable: $COE\_OJ_{t,i}$ (1)	Dependent Variable: $COE\_CT_{t,i}$ (2)	Dependent Variable: $COE\_PEG_{t,i}$ (3)	Dependent Variable: $COE\_AVG_{t,i}$ (4)
$SOE_{t,i}$	-0.008*** (-3.805)	-0.067*** (-10.978)	-0.034*** (-20.791)	-0.020*** (-8.254)
$Disp_{t,i}$	-0.010** (-2.369)	0.004 (0.388)	-0.004 (-1.201)	-0.003 (-0.579)
$Bias_{t,i}$	0.110*** (2.759)	-0.940*** (-8.358)	0.223*** (7.713)	0.127** (2.518)
$Big4_{t,i}$	0.004 (0.982)	-0.014 (-1.239)	-0.010*** (-3.375)	-0.002 (-0.375)
Year Fixed Effects	Yes	Yes	Yes	Yes
Industry Fixed Effects	Yes	Yes	Yes	Yes
N	5904	6030	6663	5364
Adj. R^2	0.224	0.115	0.316	0.203
F	52.760	24.137	91.382	42.323

Notes: ***, ** and * represent significance at the 0.01, 0.05 and 0.10 level, respectively, using two-tailed tests; t-statistics are shown in parentheses; variable definitions and measurement are reported in Table 5-2.

5.4 Results Discussion

In the tests of hypotheses H5 to H8 in this chapter, the empirical results show that: ① after the deregulation of the mandatory dual audit system, companies voluntarily using the dual audit have a lower cost of equity than companies using only the single audit. ②The effect of voluntary dual audit relative to single audit on reducing the cost of equity is greater in companies with higher demand for equity financing. ③The effect of voluntary dual audit relative to single audit on reducing the cost of equity is greater in companies with higher agency costs. ④The effect of voluntary dual audit relative to single audit on reducing the cost of equity is substitutable by alternative voluntary audit mechanisms, such as the interim report audit. In addition, the main findings are robust after alternative audit-quality measures and differential impact of firm growth are controlled and when alternative cost-of-equity measures are used as the dependent variable. The results are also not seriously affected by self-selection bias.

Consistent with the signaling effect of making voluntary audit choices, these results provide supportive evidence for the idea that after the deregulation of the mandatory dual audit system, voluntarily choosing the dual audit has a higher potential than using only the single audit in reducing the cost of equity. That is to say, voluntarily choosing the dual audit, which incurs higher audit and disclosure costs than using only the single audit, conveys incremental information about a company's good properties over and above the audited financial information. Such properties include higher quality, lower risk and more profitable prospects. Therefore, voluntarily choosing the dual audit generates a positive signal to distinguish companies doing so from those using only the single audit. This signal makes companies that voluntarily choose the dual audit preferred by investors and facilitates them to obtain external equity financing at lower costs.

In summary, the empirical results in this chapter suggest that after the deregulation of the mandatory dual audit system, voluntarily choosing the dual audit provides companies with a positive signal to differentiate themselves from those using only the single audit, and thereby is more contributory to reducing the cost of equity in the Chinese capital market.

5. 5 Chapter Summary

This chapter investigates the economic consequences of the deregulation of the mandatory dual audit system on the capital market by testing the effect of voluntary dual audit after the deregulation relative to single audit in the same period on reducing the cost of equity. This chapter uses a sample of A-share listed companies in China for the period 2010 to 2015, which is selected on the basis of the total sample used in Chapter 4. Based on the main arguments, this chapter first develops four hypotheses (H5 to H8). Next, this chapter follows the practice in Chapter 4 and uses the measure derived from the GLS model as the proxy for the cost of equity in the main tests. Subsequently, this chapter designs the empirical model for hypothesis testing. By conducting descriptive statistical, univariate, multivariate regression and robustness analyses, the empirical results support all hypotheses in this chapter and are robust to different model specifications. Table 5-12 summarizes the results of hypothesis testing in this chapter.

Table 5-12 Summary of Empirical Findings in Chapter 5

No.	Hypothesis	Empirical Findings
H5	Ceteris paribus, companies voluntarily using the dual audit have a lower cost of equity than companies using only the single audit.	Supported
H6	Ceteris paribus, the lower cost of equity for voluntary dual audit than single audit is more pronounced for companies with higher equity financing demand.	Supported
H7	Ceteris paribus, the lower cost of equity for voluntary dual audit than single audit is more pronounced for companies with higher agency costs.	Supported
H8	Ceteris paribus, the lower cost of equity for voluntary dual audit than single audit is less pronounced for companies with audited interim reports.	Supported

6 Audit-Market Consequences: Effect of Canceling Dual Audit on Audit Quality

Chapter 4 and Chapter 5 of this study investigate the economic consequences of the deregulation of the mandatory dual audit system on the capital market. Chapter 4 finds that mandatory dual audit before the deregulation has a lower cost of equity than voluntary audit after the deregulation, while Chapter 5 finds that voluntary dual audit after the deregulation has a lower cost of equity than single audit in the same period. Based on the theoretical framework proposed in Chapter 3, after understanding the economic consequences of the deregulation on the capital market in the previous two chapters, this chapter analyzes the economic consequences of the deregulation on the audit market by comparing canceling the dual audit with keeping the dual audit after the deregulation. In particular, based on a potential positive spillover effect from high- to low-quality auditors through the dual audit process (Ke et al., 2015) [5], this chapter examines whether canceling the dual audit causes a decline in audit quality by foregoing the positive spillover effect from Hong Kong-based auditors.

6.1 Hypothesis Development

Although the abolition of the mandatory dual audit system aims at improving audit efficiency and lowering audit costs of AH companies, this policy change has also raised concerns about possible impairment of these companies' financial reporting quality associated with the single audits performed by their mainland-based auditors. As documented in the *Consultation Conclusions on Acceptance of Mainland Accounting and Auditing Standards and Mainland Audit Firms for Mainland Incorporated Companies Listed in Hong Kong* (HKEx, 2010) [292], there are concerns that mainland-based auditors lack the necessary knowledge and experience of Hong Kong rules and regulations, and thus, the quality of audits performed singly by them might not be guaranteed. In academia, a reasonable explanation for the audit quality decline after companies cancel the dual audit refers to the loss of a potential positive spillover effect from Hong Kong-based auditors. This effect stems from the institutional environment gap, particularly, in the cross-listing setting comprising AH companies (Ke et al., 2015) [5].

The dual audit conducted by a mainland-based audit firm and a Hong Kong-based audit firm complicates the traditional single audit. This audit system can ensure relatively higher audit quality mainly due to an indirect positive spillover effect from Hong Kong-based auditors to mainland-based auditors (Ke et al., 2015) [5]. Specifically, Hong Kong-based auditors are subject to stringent regulatory supervision by Hong Kong regulators (e. g., HKEx, HKICPA, and the Hong Kong Securities and Futures Commission), effective monitoring by market participants (e. g., analysts and institutional investors), active claims against them by investors, and scrutiny by Hong Kong media. Such stringent institutional environment leads to high independence and audit quality of Hong Kong-based auditors. By comparison, mainland-based auditors are exposed to the institutional environment in mainland China, which is not as sound as that in Hong Kong in the abovementioned aspects. (Allen et al., 2005; Pistor et al., 2005; Chen et al., 2013) [386-388]. The lack of demand for high audit quality may discourage mainland-based auditors from dutifully playing the role of quality assurers. The dual audit system can improve this situation. In the dual audit process, as the other set of financial statements (i. e., the H-share financial statements) are signed off by a Hong Kong-based auditor, a mainland-based auditor who conducts the A-share audits of the same company can benefit from an indirect positive spillover effect from the Hong Kong-based auditor. This effect involves an influence that the Hong Kong-based auditor plays an exemplary role by performing the audits with due diligence and an impact that the Hong Kong-based auditor takes the position of monitoring the mainland-based auditor (Lin et al., 2014) [12]. Consequently, a company's audit quality can be ensured. Overall, I expect that the positive spillover effect from Hong Kong-based auditors through the dual audit system contributes to guaranteeing higher audit quality for companies keeping this audit system. In other words, if there exists a positive spillover effect from Hong Kong-based auditors in the dual audit process, I expect to find that the audit quality of companies keeping the dual audit increases with the strength of this effect.

On the basis of the aforementioned arguments, I formulate the ninth hypothesis in this study.

Hypothesis 9: Ceteris paribus, companies keeping the dual audit have higher audit quality when they are exposed to a more positive spillover effect from Hong Kong-based auditors.

As mentioned in Section 3. 1, the official abolition of the mandatory dual audit system in 2010 means that the HKEx has accepted mainland accounting and auditing standards and mainland-based audit firms for mainland incorporated companies listed in Hong Kong (including AH companies). As a result, this policy change has led some AH companies to cancel the dual audit in the form of dismissing their Hong Kong-based auditors while retaining their mainland-based auditors. With this practice, AH companies cease to be a part of the Hong Kong audits. This is likely to forego the positive spillover effect emerging from Hong Kong-based auditors. Hence, it is assumed that the single audits performed by mainland-based auditors may provide lower assurance, resulting in a decrease in AH companies' audit quality (Ke et al. , 2015) [5]. That is to say, if audit quality declines after companies cancel the dual audit, I expect to find that the loss of the positive spillover effect from Hong Kong-based auditors is a main driver of this audit quality decline.

Therefore, I formulate the tenth hypothesis in this study.

Hypothesis 10: Ceteris paribus, the loss of the positive spillover effect due to canceling the dual audit by companies leads to a decline in their audit quality.

6. 2 Research Design

6. 2. 1 Sample and Data

The sample used in this chapter comprises AH-share cross-listed companies in China for the period 2010 to 2015, as a subset of the samples used in the previous two chapters. In the empirical analyses of the previous two chapters, domestic-listed-only A-share companies serve well as a part of the control group because they are unaffected by the policy change and have the same single audit system as the AH companies opting out of the dual audit system do. However, in this chapter, the existence and loss of the potential positive spillover effect from Hong Kong- to mainland-based auditors through the dual audit system, which are stated in detail in Section 6. 1 and explored deeply in the empirical process, are involved in only AH companies. Therefore, I do not incorporate other A-share listed companies into the sample in this chapter. Accordingly, I start the sample selection procedure of this chapter by collecting all AH-share cross-listed firm-year observations between 2010 and 2015 from the CSMAR and WIND databases. This yields an initial sample of 475 firm-year observations. For the estimation of the audit quality change models [i. e., Eqs. (6-3) and (6-5)], I need data from the preceding year, and thus, the data collection for these observations starts from 2009. I then drop 24 observations for companies that were delisted, terminated or under special treatment, given their substantial differences in firm characteristics from other listed companies. Subsequently, I exclude 85 observations in the financial industry because of their non-comparable financial indices with those in other industries. To ensure that all the sample companies go through the policy change, I delete 79 observations of AH companies listing on the A-share market or the H-share market on or after 2010. Finally, after removing 24 observations with missing data, 263 firm-year observations (i. e., 47 firms) are left for the empirical analyses in this chapter. Out of the 263 observations, 192 keep the dual audit system. I use the subsample of 192 observations to examine H9, and the total sample of 263 observations to examine H10. Table 6-1 shows the sample selection process.

It is noteworthy that all variables in Eqs. (6-2) to (6-5) are derived from the A-share financial and auditing data of the sample firms, except for the variable measuring the spillover effect from Hong Kong-based auditors (i. e., $Spillover_{t,i}$), which is calculated using both the A-share and H-share financial data. I winsorize all continuous variables at 0. 01 and 0. 99 to minimize the impact of outliers. ①

Table 6-1 Sample Selection in Chapter 6

Description	Number of Observations
AH-share observations during the period of 2010-2015	475
Less: observations that were delisted, terminated or under special treatment	(24)

① Keeping original values or omitting extreme observations from the sample does not change the results.

续表

Description	Number of Observations
Less: observations in financial industry	(85)
Less: observations that are AH companies listing on the A-share market or the H-share market on or after 2010	(79)
Less: observations with missing financial and auditor data	(24)
Final Sample used in Chapter 6 (47 firms)	263

6.2.2 Measurement of Audit Quality

Following Ke et al. (2015)[5], Carey and Simnett (2006)[160] and DeFond and Park (2001)[389], I use the absolute abnormal working capital accruals in the A-share financial statements ($|AWCA|_{A\text{-}share_{t,i}}$) as a proxy for audit quality. This measure is suggested as a good reflection of management discretion and is powerful in audit quality research (Becker et al., 1998; Ashbaugh et al., 2003)[390, 391]. $AWCA_{t,i}$ is derived from the following model:

$$AWCA_{t,i} = WC_{t,i} - [(WC_{t-1,i}/S_{t-1,i}) \times S_{t,i}] \tag{6-1}$$

where

$WC_{t,i}(WC_{t-1,i})$ = company i's non-cash working capital in year t ($t-1$); it is computed as (current assets−short-term investments) − (current liabilities−short-term debt).

$S_{t,i}(S_{t-1,i})$ = company i's revenue in year t ($t-1$). All variables in Eq. (6-1) are scaled by average total assets (Myers et al., 2003)[151].

6.2.3 Measurement of Spillover Effect from Hong Kong-Based Auditors

Previous studies do not propose any measure for quantifying the potential spillover effect from Hong Kong-based auditors. This study aims to fill this gap via an empirical process. For the same business transaction, a company is not allowed to use different accounting estimates in its A-share and H-share financial statements (CSRC, 2001)[392]. Therefore, a company's A-share financial statements are supported by accounting assumptions that are inseparably connected with the assumptions underpinning its H-share financial statements (Ke et al., 2015)[5]. Meanwhile, given that the A-share and H-share financial statements are compiled based on different accounting standards (i. e., the CAS and IFRS), there is flexibility for a company to choose different accounting policies for different sets of financial statements. However, even if a company has this freedom of choice, it is compulsory for the company to reconcile its A-share and H-share financial statements and to elaborate in its annual reports about the differences in accounting policy. The engaged auditors are required to keep a close eye on whether the reconciliation is authentic and complete. With these constraints, the stricter H-share audits of a company can help prevent earnings management in the company's A-share financial statements, and thereby have a positive spillover effect on the company's A-share audits (Ke et al., 2015)[5]. Accordingly, I shall expect that a closer gap between a company's H-share's absolute abnormal accruals and its A-share's absolute abnormal accruals in the dual audit process represents a larger constraint effect of the H-share audits on the A-share audits. In other words, for a company keeping the dual audit, a shorter distance between the H-share's absolute abnormal accruals audited by the Hong Kong-based auditor and the A-share's absolute abnormal accruals audited by the mainland-based auditor reflects a more effective positive spillover effect from the Hong Kong-based auditor. Subsequently, based on the above explanation about the rationale, I calculate the distance (i. e., the absolute value of the difference) between the H-share's absolute abnormal working capital accruals audited by the Hong Kong-based auditor and the A-share's absolute abnormal working capital accruals audited by the mainland-based auditor (i. e., $\left| |AWCA|_{H\text{-}share_{t,i}} - |AWCA|_{A\text{-}share_{t,i}} \right|$) for a company keeping the dual audit. As it is more intuitive to assume a more positive spillover effect when the value of the relevant variable is larger, I flip the sign of $\left| |AWCA|_{H\text{-}share_{t,i}} - |AWCA|_{A\text{-}share_{t,i}} \right|$ when constructing the variable. Specifically, I define a variable $Spillover_{t,i}$ to equal $-\left| |AWCA|_{H\text{-}share_{t,i}} - |AWCA|_{A\text{-}share_{t,i}} \right|$ when a company keeps the dual audit; otherwise, $Spillover_{t,i}$ equals 0 after a company dismisses the Hong Kong-based auditor (i. e., cancels the dual audit). ① By definition, for a company keeping the dual audit, a larger value of $Spillover_{t,i}$ (i. e., a shorter distance between $|AWCA|_{H\text{-}share_{t,i}}$ and $|AWCA|_{A\text{-}share_{t,i}}$) implies a more positive spillover effect from the Hong

① In the total sample in this chapter, there is no case in which the difference between $|AWCA|_{H\text{-}share_{t,i}}$ and $|AWCA|_{A\text{-}share_{t,i}}$ of the same company keeping the dual audit is exactly 0, whereas the value of $Spillover_{t,i}$ is always 0 after a company cancels the dual audit. Therefore, there is no overlap between the observations for which $Spillover_{t,i} = -\left| |AWCA|_{H\text{-}share_{t,i}} - |AWCA|_{A\text{-}share_{t,i}} \right|$ and the observations for which $Spillover_{t,i} = 0$.

Kong-based auditor.

Since the construction of both $|AWCA|_{A\text{-}share_{t,i}}$ and $Spillover_{t,i}$ includes the A-share's absolute abnormal working capital accruals, some may argue that these two variables actually measure the same object, and thereby are necessarily related to each other. I check the correlation between $|AWCA|_{A\text{-}share_{t,i}}$ and $Spillover_{t,i}$ and the correlation between their change forms (i. e., the difference in values of the two variables between the current year and previous year: $\Delta|AWCA|_{A\text{-}share_{t,i}}$ and $\Delta Spillover_{t,i}$). The untabulated results show that while $|AWCA|_{A\text{-}share_{t,i}}$ ($\Delta|AWCA|_{A\text{-}share_{t,i}}$) is significantly and negatively correlated with $Spillover_{t,i}$ ($\Delta Spillover_{t,i}$), the correlation coefficient between $|AWCA|_{A\text{-}share_{t,i}}$ ($\Delta|AWCA|_{A\text{-}share_{t,i}}$) and $Spillover_{t,i}$ ($\Delta Spillover_{t,i}$) is only −0. 279 (−0. 177). These results imply that $|AWCA|_{A\text{-}share_{t,i}}$ ($\Delta|AWCA|_{A\text{-}share_{t,i}}$) and $Spillover_{t,i}$ ($\Delta Spillover_{t,i}$) separately capture variations in different underlying constructs. It remains unclear whether $Spillover_{t,i}$ ($\Delta Spillover_{t,i}$) has a significant impact on $|AWCA|_{A\text{-}share_{t,i}}$ ($\Delta|AWCA|_{A\text{-}share_{t,i}}$) after controlling for other factors in the models in the following section.

6. 2. 4 Empirical Models

6. 2. 4. 1 Models for Tests of H9

To empirically test H9 about the effect of the existence of the positive spillover effect from Hong Kong-based auditors on the audit quality of companies keeping the dual audit, I estimate the audit quality model [Eq. (6−2)] as follows:

$$\begin{aligned}|AWCA|_{A\text{-}share_{t,i}} = {} & \alpha_0 + \alpha_1 Spillover_{t,i} + \alpha_2 Size_{t,i} + \alpha_3 Lev_{t,i} + \alpha_4 Loss_{t,i} + \alpha_5 CFOTA_{t,i} + \\ & \alpha_6 BM_{t,i} + \alpha_7 Vol_{t,i} + \alpha_8 SOE_{t,i} + \alpha_9 Big4_{t,i} + \alpha_{10} LnFee_{t,i} + \\ & Year\ Fixed\ Effects + Industry\ Fixed\ Effects + \varepsilon \qquad (6-2)\end{aligned}$$

where the dependent variable ($|AWCA|_{A\text{-}share_{t,i}}$) is the A-share audit quality proxy derived from Eq. (6−1). The independent variable of interest is $Spillover_{t,i}$, which is defined in Section 6. 2. 3. By definition, for a company keeping the dual audit, a larger value of $Spillover_{t,i}$ (i. e., a shorter distance between the H-share's absolute abnormal accruals and the A-share's absolute abnormal accruals) implies a more positive spillover effect from its Hong Kong-based auditor. As per H9, I predict that companies exposed to a more positive spillover effect from Hong Kong-based auditors have higher audit quality. Thus, the sign of $Spillover_{t,i}$ is expected to be negative.

Following Ke et al. (2015) [5], I control for several firm-level characteristics. In particular, I control for company size ($Size_{t,i}$), which is measured by the natural log of total assets; leverage ($Lev_{t,i}$), which is measured by total debt divided by total assets; an indicator for profitability ($Loss_{t,i}$), which equals 1 if the company reports a loss during the year, and 0 otherwise; operating cash flows ($CFOTA_{t,i}$), which is measured by operating cash flow divided by lagged total assets; book-to-market ratio ($BM_{t,i}$), which is measured by the book value of equity divided by the market value of equity. I also control for volatility ($Vol_{t,i}$), which is measured by the standard deviation of residuals from the market model. State ownership is controlled ($SOE_{t,i}$), which equals 1 if the company is an SOE, and 0 otherwise. Auditor type is also controlled ($Big4_{t,i}$), which equals 1 if the company engages a Big 4 auditor, and 0 otherwise. Variable $LnFee_{t,i}$ (the natural log of audit fees) is included to control for the effects of audit fees on audit quality. Finally, I also control for year fixed effects and industry fixed effects in this model. Variable definitions can be seen in Table 6-2.

In addition, to deal with omitted variable issues, I use the following audit quality change model[Eq. (6-3)] to test H9. This helps to address omitted variable issues via differencing out time-invariant factors.

$$\Delta\,|AWCA|_{A\text{-}share_{t,i}} = \alpha_0 + \alpha_1 \Delta Spillover_{t,i} + \alpha_2 \Delta Size_{t,i} + \alpha_3 \Delta Lev_{t,i} + \alpha_4 \Delta Loss_{t,i} + \alpha_5 \Delta CFOTA_{t,i} + \alpha_6 \Delta BM_{t,i} + \alpha_7 \Delta Vol_{t,i} + \alpha_8 SOE_{t,i} + \alpha_9 \Delta Big4_{t,i} + \alpha_{10} \Delta LnFee_{t,i} + Year\ Fixed\ Effects + Industry\ Fixed\ Effects + \varepsilon \quad (6\text{-}3)$$

where all the variables beginning with Δ measure the difference in values between the current year and previous year. In line with my prediction in Eq. (6-2), the sign of $\Delta Spillover_{t,i}$ is expected to be negative.

6.2.4.2 Models for Tests of H10

In order to lead to the tests of H10, I start by confirming the audit quality deterioration following companies' cancelation of the dual audit by estimating the audit quality model[Eq. (6-4)] as follows:

$$|AWCA|_{A\text{-}share_{t,i}} = \alpha_0 + \alpha_1 CANCEL_{t,i} + \alpha_2 Spillover_{t,i} + \alpha_3 Size_{t,i} + \alpha_4 Lev_{t,i} + \alpha_5 Loss_{t,i} + \alpha_6 CFOTA_{t,i} + \alpha_7 BM_{t,i} + \alpha_8 Vol_{t,i} + \alpha_9 SOE_{t,i} + \alpha_{10} Big4_{t,i} + \alpha_{11} LnFee_{t,i} + Year\ Fixed\ Effects + Industry\ Fixed\ Effects + \varepsilon \quad (6\text{-}4)$$

where the independent variable of interest is $CANCEL_{t,i}$. $CANCEL_{t,i}$ equals 1 after a company cancels the dual audit, and 0 otherwise. As stated in Section 2.4.1, previous research generally implies that the cancelation of the dual audit system is likely associated with a deterioration in audit quality. Thus, I predict the sign of $CANCEL_{t,i}$ to be positive. Other variables are the same as those defined in Eq. (6-2).

Notably, introducing the interaction term of $CANCEL_{t,i}$ and $Spillover_{t,i}$ into Eq. (6-4) cannot test the impact of the loss of the positive spillover effect on the audit quality decline following companies' cancelation of the dual audit stated by H10. The reason is that variable $Spillover_{t,i}$ only captures the positive spillover effect from Hong Kong-based auditors before companies cancel the dual audit but becomes 0 for companies after the cancelation of the dual audit. Given this variable definition, interacting $CANCEL_{t,i}$ with $Spillover_{t,i}$ is not meaningful, and a level version of the audit quality model is unable to capture the loss of the positive spillover effect. By comparison, it is more appropriate to emphasize changes in positive spillover effect and audit quality in the analysis of H10.

Subsequently, I use the audit quality change model as follows [Eq. (6-5)] to empirically test H10 about the effect of the loss of the positive spillover effect from Hong Kong-based auditors on the audit quality of companies canceling the dual audit:

$$\begin{aligned}\Delta |AWCA|_{A\text{-}share_{t,i}} = {} & \alpha_0+\alpha_1 CANCEL_{t,i}+\alpha_2 \Delta Spillover_{t,i}+\alpha_3 CANCEL_{t,i} * \Delta Spillover_{t,i}+ \\ & \alpha_4 \Delta Size_{t,i}+\alpha_5 \Delta Lev_{t,i}+\alpha_6 \Delta Loss_{t,i}+\alpha_7 \Delta CFOTA_{t,i}+\alpha_8 \Delta BM_{t,i}+ \\ & \alpha_9 \Delta Vol_{t,i}+\alpha_{10} SOE_{t,i}+\alpha_{11} \Delta Big4_{t,i}+\alpha_{12} \Delta LnFee_{t,i}+Year\ Fixed \\ & Effects+Industry\ Fixed\ Effects+\varepsilon \qquad (6\text{-}5)\end{aligned}$$

where all the variables beginning with Δ measure the difference in values between the current year and previous year. The independent variable of interest is the interaction term of $CANCEL_{t,i}$ and $\Delta Spillover_{t,i}$. As defined in Section 6.2.3, $Spillover_{t,i}$ equals $-\left| |AWCA|_{H\text{-}share_{t,i}} - |AWCA|_{A\text{-}share_{t,i}} \right|$ when a company keeps the dual audit, while it equals 0 after a company cancels the dual audit. As defined in this section, $CANCEL_{t,i}$ equals 1 after a company cancels the dual audit, and 0 otherwise. Accordingly, when $CANCEL_{t,i}$ equals 1, $CANCEL_{t,i} * \Delta Spillover_{t,i}$ equals $0-Spillover_{t-1,i}$ in the first year of canceling the dual audit, whereas this interaction term equals 0 afterwards. Thus, the non-0 values of $CANCEL_{t,i} * \Delta Spillover_{t,i}$ reflect the loss of the positive spillover effect from Hong Kong-based auditors. That is to say, this interaction term can capture the loss of the positive spillover effect following companies' cancelation of the dual audit. ① As per H10, I assume that the loss of the positive spillover effect is a predictor of the audit quality decline of companies canceling the dual audit. Hence, I predict the sign of $CANCEL_{t,i}$ * $\Delta Spillover_{t,i}$ to be positive. Other variables are the same as those defined in Eqs. (6-2) to (6-4). In line with my prediction in Eq. (6-4) about the audit quality decline after companies cancel the dual audit, the sign of $CANCEL_{t,i}$ in Eq. (6-5) is expected to be positive. $\Delta Spillover_{t,i}$ in Eq. (6-5) represents the change in the positivity of the spillover effect from Hong Kong-based auditors when $CANCEL_{t,i}$ equals 0, that is, when a company keeps the dual audit. In line with my prediction in Eq. (6-2) about the benefits of the existence of the positive spillover effect for companies' audit quality, the sign of $\Delta Spillover_{t,i}$ is expected to be negative.

Table 6-2 Variable Definitions in Chapter 6

Variable	Description
Variables in Baseline Models[Eq. (6-2) and Eq. (6-5)]	
Dependent Variable	
$\lvert AWCA \rvert_{A\text{-}share\ t,i}$	The absolute value of abnormal working capital accruals in the company's A-share financial statements for year t, estimated from Eq. (6-1).
Independent Variables of Interest	
$Spillover_{t,i}$	The negative value of the absolute difference between $\lvert AWCA \rvert_{H\text{-}share\ t,i}$ and $\lvert AWCA \rvert_{A\text{-}share\ t,i}$ before the company cancels the dual audit, and 0 after the company cancels the dual audit.
$CANCEL_{t,i}$	1 after the company cancels the dual audit, and 0 otherwise.
Control Variables	
$Size_{t,i}$	Natural log of total assets.
$Lev_{t,i}$	Total debt divided by total assets.
$Loss_{t,i}$	1 if the company reports a loss during year t, and 0 otherwise.
$CFOTA_{t,i}$	Operating cash flow divided by lagged total assets.
$BM_{t,i}$	The book value of equity divided by the market value of equity.

① I recognize that the loss of the positive spillover effect from Hong Kong-based auditors occurs only in the first year of a company canceling the dual audit. Thus, I note that by making variable $CANCEL_{t,i}$ equal 1 for all observations after a company cancels the dual audit, I am potentially understating the effect of the loss of this positive spillover when using the interaction term of $CANCEL_{t,i}$ and $\Delta Spillover_{t,i}$ to represent it.

续表

Variable	Description
$Vol_{t,i}$	The standard deviation of residuals from the market model.
$SOE_{t,i}$	1 if the company is an SOE, and 0 otherwise.
$Big4_{t,i}$	1 if the company engages a Big 4 auditor in year t, and 0 otherwise.
$LnFee_{t,i}$	Natural log of audit fees.
Variables in Other Tests	
$\mid AWCA \mid_{H\text{-}share\ t,i}$	The absolute value of abnormal working capital accruals in the company's H-share financial statements for year t[estimated from Eq. (6-1)] before the company cancels the dual audit, and 0 after the company cancels the dual audit.
$Con_{t,i}$	The convergence index in year t[calculated from Eq. (4-7)] before the company cancels the dual audit, and 1.000 after the company cancels the dual audit.
$Rep_{t,i}$	1 if the company engages a mainland-based auditor and a Hong Kong-based auditor from the same brand in year t, and 0 otherwise.
$Spillover\_H_{t,i}$	The negative value of $\mid AWCA \mid_{H\text{-}share\ t,i}$.
$\mid DACC \mid_{A\text{-}share\ t,i}$	The absolute value of performance-adjusted discretionary accruals in the company's A-share financial statements for year t(Kothari et al., 2005)[366].
$Spillover\_D_{t,i}$	The negative value of the absolute difference between $\mid DACC \mid_{H\text{-}share\ t,i}$ and $\mid DACC \mid_{A\text{-}share\ t,i}$ before the company cancels the dual audit, and 0 after the company cancels the dual audit. $\mid DACC \mid_{H\text{-}share\ t,i}$ is the absolute value of performance-adjusted discretionary accruals in the H-share financial statements before the company cancels the dual audit, and 0 after the company cancels the dual audit.

6.3 Empirical Results

6.3.1 Sample Distribution

Table 6-3 reports the sample distribution. Panel A of Table 6-3 shows that the sample firms are distributed across 6 different industries. The manufacturing industry has the largest number of observations (110 observations), followed by the transport, storage and post industry (62 observations) and the mining industry (48 observations).

Table 6-3 Panel B shows a description of distribution by year. Column (1) shows that the annual distribution of AH firm sample rises from 2010 to 2013 and remains steady afterwards. Column (2) indicates that the number of companies canceling the dual audit grows after 2010, especially from 2010 to 2012 by an average of 6 companies per year. Column (3) presents that the number of companies keeping the dual audit first declines by 6 companies (from 37 to 31 companies) and then becomes relatively stable after 2011. At the end of the sample period, 36. 17% (71/263) of the sample firms cancel the dual audit, whereas 63. 83% (192/263) of them keep the dual audit. Overall, these statistics suggest a variation among the sample firms in terms of whether to cancel the dual audit; the cancelation of this audit system has been put into practice in a staggered manner since the deregulation in 2010.

Table 6-3 Sample Distribution in Chapter 6

Panel A: Sample Distribution by Industry	
Industry	Number
Construction	15
Electricity, Heat, Gas and Water Production and Supply	22
Manufacturing	110
Mining	48
Real Estate	6
Transport, Storage and Post	62
Total	263

Panel B: Sample Distribution by Year			
Year	(1) Number of Total Sample	(2) Number of Sample Canceling Dual Audit	(3) Number of Sample Keeping Dual Audit
2010	38	1	37
2011	40	9	31
2012	44	13	31
2013	47	15	32
2014	47	16	31

续表

Panel B: Sample Distribution by Year			
Year	(1) Number of Total Sample	(2) Number of Sample Canceling Dual Audit	(3) Number of Sample Keeping Dual Audit
2015	47	17	30
Total	263	71	192

Notes: The industry classification is adapted from the "Revised Guidance for Industry Classification of China's Listed Companies" (CSRC, 2012) [367].

6.3.2 Descriptive Statistics

Panel A of Table 6-4 reports the descriptive statistics of the total sample in this chapter. The mean (median) value of $|AWCA|_{A\text{-}share\ t,i}$ is 0.039 (0.024). The mean value of $CANCEL_{t,i}$ shows that 27% of the total sample are the observations canceling the dual audit. ① The mean (median) value of $Spillover_{t,i}$ is −0.016 (−0.04). In general, the descriptive statistics of the control variables are similar to those reported by previous studies involving examination on AH companies, such as Ke et al. (2015) [5]. The mean values of $Lev_{t,i}$, $Loss_{t,i}$ and $BM_{t,i}$ are 0.583, 0.091 and 0.751, respectively, suggesting that the sample firms are generally moderately indebted, and they are profitable companies with good growth opportunities. Of the sample firms, 96.2% are SOEs ($SOE_{t,i}$). As for the audit firm characteristics, the results show that Big 4 auditors provide audit service for 65% of the total sample ($Big4_{t,i}$). The mean (median) value of $LnFee_{t,i}$ is 15.793 (15.857), which can be converted to average audit fees of approximately RMB 7.22 million (RMB 7.70 million).

Table 6-4 Panel A also reports the descriptive statistics for the change forms of the main variables in this chapter. The mean (median) value of $\Delta|AWCA|_{A\text{-}share\ t,i}$ is −0.000 (−0.001), suggesting that the audit quality of the sample firms is relatively stable across years. The mean (median) value of $\Delta Spillover_{t,i}$ is 0.002 (0.000). Firm size rises 0.099 units per year on average ($\Delta Size_{t,i}$), while the annual increase in book-to-market ratio averages at about 4.2% ($\Delta BM_{t,i}$). The mean/median values

① By definition, $CANCEL_{t,i}$ is assigned 1 for firm-year observations that not only cancel the dual audit in the current year but also all years afterwards. Therefore, the observations canceling the dual audit refer to the situations after the cancelation of the dual audit by companies.

of all the other control variables do not exceed 0.01 units or fall below -0.01 units, implying that the sample firms witness gradual slow changes in these aspects on an annual basis.

Table 6-4 Descriptive Statistics and Test of Differences

Panel A: Descriptive Statistics of Total Sample in Chapter 6 (N=263)					
Variable	Mean	Median	Std. Dev.	25%	75%
$\mid AWCA \mid_{A\text{-}share\ t,i}$	0.039	0.024	0.043	0.012	0.048
$CANCEL_{t,i}$	0.270	0.000	0.445	0.000	1.000
$Spillover_{t,i}$	-0.016	-0.004	0.029	-0.018	0.000
$Size_{t,i}$	24.784	25.079	1.694	23.910	25.820
$Lev_{t,i}$	0.583	0.598	0.182	0.452	0.730
$Loss_{t,i}$	0.091	0.000	0.289	0.000	0.000
$CFOTA_{t,i}$	0.071	0.073	0.068	0.024	0.122
$BM_{t,i}$	0.751	0.668	0.426	0.432	1.002
$Vol_{t,i}$	0.080	0.070	0.039	0.053	0.099
$SOE_{t,i}$	0.962	1.000	0.192	1.000	1.000
$Big4_{t,i}$	0.650	1.000	0.478	0.000	1.000
$LnFee_{t,i}$	15.793	15.857	1.095	14.914	16.490
$\Delta \mid AWCA \mid_{A\text{-}share\ t,i}$	-0.000	-0.001	0.049	-0.021	0.017
$\Delta Spillover_{t,i}$	0.002	0.000	0.032	-0.005	0.007
$\Delta Size_{t,i}$	0.099	0.084	0.135	0.019	0.148
$\Delta Lev_{t,i}$	0.003	0.004	0.053	-0.024	0.031
$\Delta Loss_{t,i}$	0.004	0.000	0.365	0.000	0.000
$\Delta CFOTA_{t,i}$	-0.005	-0.002	0.061	-0.038	0.028
$\Delta BM_{t,i}$	0.042	0.046	0.296	-0.087	0.226
$\Delta Vol_{t,i}$	0.004	-0.002	0.033	-0.013	0.017
$\Delta Big4_{t,i}$	-0.008	0.000	0.123	0.000	0.000
$\Delta LnFee_{t,i}$	-0.006	0.000	0.339	-0.049	0.058

续表

Panel B: Test of Differences Between Canceling Dual Audit ($CANCEL_{t,i}=1$) and Keeping Dual Audit ($CANCEL_{t,i}=0$)

Variable	Mean		Test of Differences
	$CANCEL_{t,i}=1$ ($N=71$)	$CANCEL_{t,i}=0$ ($N=192$)	t-stat.
$\|AWCA\|_{A\text{-}share\ t,i}$	0. 047	0. 036	1. 873*
$Spillover_{t,i}$	0. 000	−0. 022	5. 900***
$Size_{t,i}$	24. 132	25. 025	−3. 893***
$Lev_{t,i}$	0. 595	0. 578	0. 660
$Loss_{t,i}$	0. 085	0. 094	−0. 230
$CFOTA_{t,i}$	0. 059	0. 075	−1. 748*
$BM_{t,i}$	0. 727	0. 760	−0. 550
$Vol_{t,i}$	0. 082	0. 079	0. 483
$SOE_{t,i}$	0. 944	0. 969	−0. 942
$Big4_{t,i}$	0. 521	0. 698	−2. 695***
$LnFee_{t,i}$	15. 200	16. 012	−5. 650***
$\Delta\|AWCA\|_{A\text{-}share\ t,i}$	0. 006	−0. 003	1. 213
$\Delta Spillover_{t,i}$	0. 007	−0. 000	1. 638
$\Delta Size_{t,i}$	0. 100	0. 099	0. 057
$\Delta Lev_{t,i}$	0. 007	0. 002	0. 651
$\Delta Loss_{t,i}$	0. 000	0. 005	−0. 102
$\Delta CFOTA_{t,i}$	−0. 006	−0. 005	−0. 065
$\Delta BM_{t,i}$	−0. 007	0. 060	−1. 634
$\Delta Vol_{t,i}$	0. 008	0. 002	1. 168
$\Delta Big4_{t,i}$	0. 000	−0. 010	0. 607
$\Delta LnFee_{t,i}$	−0. 013	−0. 004	−0. 206

Notes: ***, ** and * represent significance at the 0. 01, 0. 05 and 0. 10 level, respectively, using two-tailed tests; variable definitions and measurement are reported in Table 6-2.

6.3.3 Univariate Tests

Panel B of Table 6-4 compares the mean values of the level and change forms of the main variables between the observations canceling the dual audit (i. e., the sample for which $CANCEL_{t,i}$ = 1; N = 71) and the observations keeping the dual audit (i. e., the sample for which $CANCEL_{t,i}$ = 0; N = 192). The last column reports the t-statistics in the mean difference test. The mean $|AWCA|_{A\text{-}share\ t,i}$ of the observations canceling the dual audit (0.047) is significantly higher than that of the observations keeping the dual audit (0.036). Furthermore, the mean $\Delta|AWCA|_{A\text{-}share\ t,i}$ of the observations canceling (keeping) the dual audit is 0.006 (−0.003), which suggests that canceling (keeping) the dual audit is associated with a decline (improvement) in audit quality manifested as an average increase (decrease) of 0.006 (0.003) units in the absolute abnormal working capital accruals per year. These preliminary results are consistent with prior indirect evidence implying the negative impact of canceling the dual audit on companies' audit quality. The mean $Spillover_{t,i}$ is −0.022 for the observations keeping the dual audit, which indicates that the average distance between the H-share's absolute abnormal accruals audited by Hong Kong-based auditors and the A-share's absolute abnormal accruals audited by mainland-based auditors is 0.022. The mean value of $\Delta Spillover_{t,i}$ for the observations canceling the dual audit is 0.007, which is slightly higher than the mean $\Delta Spillover_{t,i}$ for those keeping the dual audit (−0.000). In addition, I find that the observations canceling the dual audit have smaller firm size ($Size_{t,i}$) and lower operating cash flows ($CFOTA_{t,i}$), are less likely to engage a Big 4 auditor ($Big4_{t,i}$), and pay lower audit fees ($LnFee_{t,i}$) than the observations keeping the dual audit.

6.3.4 Comparison of Audit Quality Between Hong Kong-Based Auditors and Mainland-Based Auditors

Before testing the main hypotheses, I first compare audit quality between Hong Kong- and mainland-based auditors in the dual audit system. Table 6-5 shows the results. In the dual audit system (i. e., for the group of 192 observations keeping the dual audit), the mean value of the H-share's absolute abnormal working capital accruals audited by Hong Kong-based auditors (i. e., $|AWCA|_{H\text{-}share\ t,i}$) is 0.035, which is lower than the mean value of the A-share's absolute abnormal working capital accruals audited by mainland-based auditors (i. e., $|AWCA|_{A\text{-}share_{t,i}}$) (0. 037). The difference between the mean value of $|AWCA|_{H\text{-}share_{t,i}}$ and that of $|AWCA|_{A\text{-}share_{t,i}}$ is −0. 002 (0. 035−0. 037), which is not significantly different from 0. With these results, I have two preliminary findings. First, the insignificant difference between the mean $|AWCA|_{H\text{-}share_{t,i}}$ and the mean $|AWCA|_{A\text{-}share_{t,i}}$ suggests that the practice of the dual audit follows the rule stipulated in CSRC (2001)[392] by ensuring companies to use accounting estimates with no essential distinctions in their A-share and H-share financial statements for the same accounting event. Second, given that lower absolute abnormal working capital accruals imply higher audit quality, the smaller $|AWCA|_{H\text{-}share_{t,i}}$ (compared to $|AWCA|_{A\text{-}share_{t,i}}$) indicates that Hong Kong-based auditors tend to have a positive spillover effect on mainland-based auditors through the dual audit process.

Table 6-5 Comparison of Audit Quality Between Hong Kong- and Mainland-Based Auditors in Dual Audit System

Variable	Mean	Test of Difference *t*-stat.
$|AWCA|_{H\text{-}share_{t,i}}$	0. 035	−0. 670
$|AWCA|_{A\text{-}share_{t,i}}$	0. 037	

Notes: Variable definitions and measurement are reported in Table 6-2.

6. 3. 5 Multivariate Regressions

6. 3. 5. 1 Tests of H9

Columns (1) and (2) in Panel A of Table 6-6 present the findings of the tests of H9 about the impact of the existence of the positive spillover effect on the audit quality of companies keeping the dual audit. Both the regression models have statistical significance at the 0. 01 level. It is unlikely that the test variables suffer from multicollinearity, given that the VIF for each variable is lower than 10 (unreported) (Kennedy, 2003)[368]. In the level regression shown in Column (1) [i. e., Eq. (6-2)], the coefficient on $Spillover_{t,i}$ is significant and negative at the 0. 05 level (coefficient =−0. 481, t =−2. 524). This result is consistent with H9 and suggests that the audit quality of companies keeping the dual audit is higher when they are subject to a more positive spillover effect from Hong Kong-based auditors. In the change regression shown in Column (2) [i. e., Eq. (6-3)], the coefficient on $\Delta Spillover_{t,i}$ is also significant and negative at the 0.05 level (coefficient = −0.378, t = −2.038). This result suggests a positive impact of an increase in the positivity of the spillover effect from Hong Kong-based auditors on an increase in the audit quality of companies keeping the dual audit, providing additional support for H9.

To further rule out the possibility that the audit quality difference/change I find is due to an auditor upgrade or downgrade (rather than Hong Kong-based auditors' positive spillover effect), I also estimate Eqs. (6−2) and (6−3) by excluding the observations that switch from a non-Big 4 auditor to a Big 4 auditor (i.e., involve an auditor upgrade) or vice versa (i.e., involve an auditor downgrade). The results are demonstrated in Columns (1) and (2) in Panel B of Table 6-6. The coefficients on $Spillover_{t,i}$ in Column (1) and $\Delta Spillover_{t,i}$ in Column (2) continue to be significant and negative in this reduced sample. These results suggest that auditor grade changes are unlikely to explain the main results.

Table 6-6 Regression Results of Tests of H9 and H10

Panel A: Baseline Regression Results					
Variable	Dependent Variable: $\lvert AWCA \rvert_{A\text{-}share\ t,i}$	Dependent Variable: $\Delta \lvert AWCA \rvert_{A\text{-}share\ t,i}$	Dependent Variable: $\lvert AWCA \rvert_{A\text{-}share\ t,i}$		Dependent Variable: $\Delta \lvert AWCA \rvert_{A\text{-}share\ t,i}$
	(1)	(2)	(3)	(4)	(5)
Intercept	0.091 (1.481)	0.021 (1.567)	0.112* (1.968)	0.148 (0.340)	0.002 (0.186)
$Spillover_{t,i}$	−0.481** (−2.524)		−0.466** (−2.420)	−0.397*** (−3.697)	
$\Delta Spillover_{t,i}$		−0.378** (−2.038)			−0.416** (−2.226)
$CANCEL_{t,i}$			0.016** (2.219)	0.037*** (3.004)	0.011** (2.155)
$CANCEL_{t,i}$ * $\Delta Spillover_{t,i}$					0.825** (2.049)
$Size_{t,i}$	−0.007* (−1.941)		−0.006** (−2.224)	−0.006 (−0.368)	
$\Delta Size_{t,i}$		0.044 (1.088)			0.056 (1.674)
$Lev_{t,i}$	−0.004 (−0.211)		0.013 (0.783)	0.053 (1.077)	

续表

Variable	Dependent Variable: $\lvert AWCA \rvert_{A\text{-}share\ t,i}$	Dependent Variable: $\Delta \lvert AWCA \rvert_{A\text{-}share\ t,i}$	Dependent Variable: $\lvert AWCA \rvert_{A\text{-}share\ t,i}$		Dependent Variable: $\Delta \lvert AWCA \rvert_{A\text{-}share\ t,i}$
	(1)	(2)	(3)	(4)	(5)
$\Delta Lev_{t,i}$		−0.081 (−1.190)			−0.065 (−0.640)
$Loss_{t,i}$	−0.010 (−0.833)		−0.001 (−0.059)	0.007 (0.642)	
$\Delta Loss_{t,i}$		0.004 (0.518)			0.011 (1.070)
$CFOTA_{t,i}$	0.115* (1.837)		0.068 (1.208)	0.133** (2.176)	
$\Delta CFOTA_{t,i}$		0.102 (1.405)			0.080 (0.933)
$BM_{t,i}$	0.002 (0.218)		0.004 (0.323)	0.015 (1.069)	
$\Delta BM_{t,i}$		0.018 (1.224)			0.008 (0.576)
$Vol_{t,i}$	0.094 (0.727)		0.113 (0.897)	0.107 (1.018)	
$\Delta Vol_{t,i}$		0.034 (0.269)			0.097 (0.666)
$SOE_{t,i}$	−0.020* (−1.969)	−0.032** (−2.598)	0.002 (0.244)	−0.046 (−1.230)	−0.012 (−1.505)
$Big4_{t,i}$	−0.012* (−1.941)		−0.008 (−1.352)	−0.022 (−0.740)	
$\Delta Big4_{t,i}$		−0.094*** (−2.928)			−0.035 (−0.798)
$LnFee_{t,i}$	0.008* (1.853)		0.002 (0.597)	0.001 (0.138)	
$\Delta LnFee_{t,i}$		0.015 (1.625)			0.000 (0.008)
Year Fixed Effects	Yes	Yes	Yes	Yes	Yes
Industry Fixed Effects	Yes	Yes	Yes		Yes
Firm Fixed Effects				Yes	
N	192	192	263	263	263
Adj. R^2	0.246	0.149	0.176	0.239	0.068

续表

Panel B: Results for Sample Without Auditor Grade Change					
Variable	Dependent Variable: $\vert AWCA \vert_{A\text{-}share\ t,i}$	Dependent Variable: $\Delta \vert AWCA \vert_{A\text{-}share\ t,i}$	Dependent Variable: $\vert AWCA \vert_{A\text{-}share\ t,i}$		Dependent Variable: $\Delta \vert AWCA \vert_{A\text{-}share\ t,i}$
	(1)	(2)	(3)	(4)	(5)
Intercept	0. 085	0. 019	0. 115 **	0. 140	−0. 002
	(1. 600)	(1. 563)	(2. 212)	(0. 327)	(−0. 202)
$Spillover_{t,i}$	−0. 458 **		−0. 444 **	−0. 341 ***	
	(−2. 332)		(−2. 232)	(−3. 235)	
$\Delta Spillover_{t,i}$		−0. 384 **			−0. 396 **
		(−2. 039)			(−2. 105)
$CANCEL_{t,i}$			0. 017 **	0. 034 ***	0. 012 **
			(2. 345)	(2. 814)	(2. 246)
$CANCEL_{t,i}$ * $\Delta Spillover_{t,i}$					0. 795 **
					(2. 092)
$Size_{t,i}$	−0. 006 *		−0. 005 *	−0. 009	
	(−1. 735)		(−1. 988)	(−0. 495)	
$\Delta Size_{t,i}$		0. 036			0. 052
		(0. 846)			(1. 572)
$Lev_{t,i}$	−0. 013		0. 006	0. 020	
	(−0. 640)		(0. 374)	(0. 405)	
$\Delta Lev_{t,i}$		−0. 087			−0. 086
		(−1. 272)			(−0. 868)
$Loss_{t,i}$	−0. 009		−0. 001	0. 007	
	(−0. 836)		(−0. 142)	(0. 628)	
$\Delta Loss_{t,i}$		0. 005			0. 015
		(0. 753)			(1. 512)
$CFOTA_{t,i}$	0. 061		0. 005	0. 062	
	(1. 023)		(0. 100)	(1. 007)	
$\Delta CFOTA_{t,i}$		0. 094			0. 075
		(1. 322)			(0. 886)
$BM_{t,i}$	−0. 005		−0. 001	0. 007	
	(−0. 553)		(−0. 111)	(0. 497)	
$\Delta BM_{t,i}$		0. 016			0. 004
		(1. 134)			(0. 266)

续表

Variable	Dependent Variable: $\mid AWCA \mid_{A\text{-}share\ t,\ i}$	Dependent Variable: $\Delta \mid AWCA \mid_{A\text{-}share\ t,\ i}$	Dependent Variable: $\mid AWCA \mid_{A\text{-}share\ t,\ i}$		Dependent Variable: $\Delta \mid AWCA \mid_{A\text{-}share\ t,\ i}$
	(1)	(2)	(3)	(4)	(5)
$Vol_{t,\ i}$	-0.023 (-0.288)		0.010 (0.095)	0.031 (0.291)	
$\Delta Vol_{t,\ i}$		0.002 (0.013)			0.032 (0.240)
$SOE_{t,\ i}$	-0.019* (-1.954)	-0.030** (-2.615)	0.002 (0.263)	0.019 (0.474)	-0.010 (-1.243)
$Big4_{t,\ i}$	-0.008 (-1.378)		-0.003 (-0.469)	0.035 (1.015)	
$\Delta Big4_{t,\ i}$					
$LnFee_{t,\ i}$	0.007 (1.628)		0.002 (0.433)	0.004 (0.477)	
$\Delta LnFee_{t,\ i}$		0.013 (1.359)			0.001 (0.117)
Year Fixed Effects	Yes	Yes	Yes	Yes	Yes
Industry Fixed Effects	Yes	Yes	Yes		Yes
Firm Fixed Effects				Yes	
N	190	190	259	259	259
Adj. R^2	0.247	0.072	0.174	0.224	0.053

Notes: In both Panels A and B, Column (1) shows the results of Eq. (6-2); Column (2) shows the results of Eq. (6-3); Column (3) shows the results of Eq. (6-4); Column (4) shows the results of Eq. (6-4) with firm fixed effects included; Column (5) shows the results of Eq. (6-5); in Columns (2) and (5) in Panel B, variable $\Delta Big4_{t,\ i}$ is omitted owing to collinearity; ***, ** and * represent significance at the 0.01, 0.05 and 0.10 level, respectively, using two-tailed tests; t-statistics are shown in parentheses; variable definitions and measurement are reported in Table 6-2.

6.3.5.2 Tests of H10

Columns (3) and (4) in Panel A of Table 6-6 report the results for the regressions of the A-share's absolute abnormal working capital accruals on companies' cancelation of the dual audit [i. e., Eq. (6-4)]. In Column (3), the coefficient on $CANCEL_{t,i}$ is significant and positive at the 0.05 level (coefficient = 0.016, t = 2.219), suggesting that companies' audit quality is lower after they cancel the dual audit. This result confirms that canceling the dual audit causes companies' audit quality to deteriorate. In Column (4), I include firm fixed effects, instead of industry fixed effects, in Eq. (6-4) to ensure that I compare over time a company's observations keeping the dual audit with its observations canceling the dual audit. The coefficient on $CANCEL_{t,i}$ remains significant and positive.

Column (5) in Panel A of Table 6-6 presents the findings of the tests of H10 about the impact of the loss of the positive spillover effect on the audit quality of companies canceling the dual audit. The regression model [i. e., Eq. (6-5)] has statistical significance at the 0.01 level. It is unlikely that the test variables suffer from multicollinearity, given that the VIF for each variable is lower than 10 (unreported) (Kennedy, 2003)[368]. As shown in Column (5), the coefficient on $CANCEL_{t,i} * \Delta Spillover_{t,i}$ is significant and positive at the 0.05 level (coefficient = 0.825, t = 2.049). This result indicates that after the cancelation of the dual audit by companies, there is a positive association of a loss of the positive spillover effect from Hong Kong-based auditors with a decrease in audit quality. This finding is consistent with H10 and implies that the removal (by companies' cancelation of the dual audit) of Hong Kong-based auditors' positive spillover effect drives the decline of companies' audit quality. With regard to economic significance, for a 1 standard deviation increase in the difference in values of $Spillover_{t,i}$ between the current year and previous year, the change in the difference in values of $|AWCA|_{A\text{-}share\ t,i}$ between the current year and previous year is 0.539 standard deviation higher after the cancelation of the dual audit than before the cancelation of the dual audit.① In addition, the coefficient on $\Delta Spillover_{t,i}$ ($CANCEL_{t,i}$) is significant and negative (positive), qualitatively similar to the result shown in Column (2) [Column (3)] in Panel A of Table 6-6.

---

① By definition, $\Delta Spillover_{t,i}$ have different interpretations for different situations. When a company keeps the dual audit, it means the change in the positivity of the spillover effect from Hong Kong-based auditors, whereas after a company cancels the dual audit, its means the loss of the positive spillover effect from Hong Kong-based auditors. Therefore, an increase in $\Delta Spillover_{t,i}$ means an increase in the change in the positivity of the spillover effect for situations before the cancelation of the dual audit, while an increase in $\Delta Spillover_{t,i}$ means an increase in the loss of the positive spillover effect for situations after the cancelation of the dual audit.

To further rule out the possibility that the audit quality difference/change I find is due to an auditor upgrade or downgrade (rather than canceling the dual audit and the loss of the positive spillover effect from Hong Kong-based auditors), I also estimate Eqs. (6-4) and (6-5) by excluding the observations that switch from a non-Big 4 auditor to a Big 4 auditor or vice versa. The qualitatively similar results are shown in Columns (3) to (5) in Panel B of Table 6-6, suggesting that auditor grade changes are unlikely to be an alternative explanation of the main results.

6. 3. 6 Robustness Tests

6. 3. 6. 1 Considering Convergence of CAS with IFRS

As mentioned in Section 3. 1, the deregulation of the mandatory dual audit system took place alongside the convergence of the CAS with the IFRS. Hence, it may be argued that the variable I construct (i. e. , $Spillover_{t,i}$) possibly captures the convergence of accounting standards between mainland China and Hong Kong rather than the audit quality-related positive spillover effect in my main argument. To address this concern, I generate a measure to represent the convergence of accounting standards, namely, $Con_{t,i}$, for all the sample firms in this chapter. To assign values to this variable, I first follow the practice in Section 4. 3. 5 about the calculation of a convergence index for companies adopting different accounting standards at the same time. Specifically, I use Eq. (4-7) to compute the convergence index for the sample firms keeping the dual audit. As interpreted in Section 4. 3. 5, the closer the value of this index is to 1. 000, the higher will be the degree of convergence of accounting standards. Accordingly, for a company keeping the dual audit, $Con_{t,i}$ takes the value of the convergence index in year t. Otherwise, after a company cancels the dual audit, $Con_{t,i}$ takes the value of 1. 000.

Subsequently, I re-estimate Eq. (6-2) with the inclusion of $Con_{t,i}$, and re-estimate Eqs. (6-3) and (6-5) with the inclusion of $\Delta Con_{t,i}$. The results shown in Table 6-7 are qualitatively similar to the main results. As reported in Table 6-7, these results minimize the possibility that the convergence of accounting standards refers to an alternative explanation for the main findings.

Table 6-7 Regression Results After Considering Convergence of CAS with IFRS

Variable	Dependent Variable: $\mid AWCA \mid_{A\text{-}share\ t,\ i}$	Dependent Variable: $\Delta \mid AWCA \mid_{A\text{-}share\ t,\ i}$	
	(1)	(2)	(3)
Intercept	0. 105 (1. 494)	0. 021 (1. 544)	0. 003 (0. 281)
$Spillover_{t,\ i}$	-0. 491 * * (-2. 579)		
$\Delta Spillover_{t,\ i}$		-0. 377 * * (-2. 031)	-0. 418 * * (-2. 235)
$CANCEL_{t,\ i}$			0. 012 * * (2. 305)
$CANCEL_{t,\ i} * \Delta Spillover_{t,\ i}$			0. 784 * (1. 966)
$Size_{t,\ i}$	-0. 008 * * (-2. 040)		
$\Delta Size_{t,\ i}$		0. 044 (1. 063)	0. 057 * (1. 685)
$Lev_{t,\ i}$	-0. 004 (-0. 171)		
$\Delta Lev_{t,\ i}$		-0. 083 (-1. 211)	-0. 064 (-0. 631)
$Loss_{t,\ i}$	-0. 008 (-0. 734)		
$\Delta Loss_{t,\ i}$		0. 003 (0. 390)	0. 012 (1. 047)
$CFOTA_{t,\ i}$	0. 119 * (1. 916)		
$\Delta CFOTA_{t,\ i}$		0. 101 (1. 413)	0. 080 (0. 923)
$BM_{t,\ i}$	0. 001 (0. 135)		
$\Delta BM_{t,\ i}$		0. 018 (1. 208)	0. 009 (0. 668)

续表

Variable	Dependent Variable: $\mid AWCA \mid_{A\text{-}share\ t,i}$	Dependent Variable: $\Delta \mid AWCA \mid_{A\text{-}share\ t,i}$	
	(1)	(2)	(3)
$Vol_{t,i}$	0. 087 (0. 674)		
$\Delta Vol_{t,i}$		0. 033 (0. 257)	0. 105 (0. 747)
$SOE_{t,i}$	−0. 020 * * (−2. 017)	−0. 032 * * (−2. 579)	−0. 013 (−1. 635)
$Big4_{t,i}$	−0. 012 * (−1. 902)		
$\Delta Big4_{t,i}$		−0. 094 * * * (−2. 971)	−0. 035 (−0. 788)
$LnFee_{t,i}$	0. 008 * (1. 785)		
$\Delta LnFee_{t,i}$		0. 015 (1. 644)	−0. 000 (−0. 006)
$Con_{t,i}$	−0. 005 (−0. 523)		
$\Delta Con_{t,i}$		0. 005 (0. 432)	−0. 008 (−0. 568)
Year Fixed Effects	Yes	Yes	Yes
Industry Fixed Effects	Yes	Yes	Yes
N	192	192	263
Adj. R^2	0. 243	0. 145	0. 066

Notes: Column (1) shows the results of Eq. (6−2) after additionally introducing $Con_{t,i}$ as a control variable; Column (2) shows the results of Eq. (6−3) after additionally introducing $\Delta Con_{t,i}$ as a control variable; Column (3) shows the results of Eq. (6−5) after additionally introducing $\Delta Con_{t,i}$ as a control variable; * * *, * * and * represent significance at the 0. 01, 0. 05 and 0. 10 level, respectively, using two-tailed tests; t-statistics are shown in parentheses; variable definitions and measurement are reported in Table 6−2.

6. 3. 6. 2 Considering Auditors' Concern on Shared Reputation

Among the observations keeping the dual audit, around 85. 9% (165/192) of them engage a mainland-based auditor and a Hong Kong-based auditor who are member audit firms sharing the same international brand. This case contains 81.2% (134/165) of firms that engage auditors from the same Big 4 brand, and 18.8% (31/165) of firms that engage auditors from the same non-Big 4 brand. Firms that engage a mainland-based non-Big 4 auditor and a Hong Kong-based Big 4 auditor account for 9.4% (18/192). The remaining 4.7% (9/192) of firms engage a mainland-based non-Big 4 auditor and a Hong Kong-based non-Big 4 auditor from different brands. Detailed information about mainland- and Hong Kong-based auditors engaged by the sample firms each year are shown in Appendix Ⅱ. It can be seen from this sample structure that a majority of the sample firms choose two auditors from the same brand when performing the dual audit. Therefore, the higher audit quality when companies keep the dual audit (or before companies cancel the dual audit) is likely to result from the two engaged auditors' concern that the same brand they share would lose reputation if either of the two audits were to fail, rather than from the positive spillover effect from Hong Kong-based auditors.

To rule out this possibility, I generate a dummy variable to represent the shared reputational concern of the two engaged auditors. Specifically, I define $Rep_{t,i}$ to equal 1 when the mainland-based auditor and the Hong Kong-based auditor hired by a company are member firms sharing the same brand (including both the cases of the same Big 4 brand and those of the same non-Big 4 brand), and 0 otherwise. I re-estimate Eq. (6-2) with the inclusion of $Rep_{t,i}$, and re-estimate Eqs. (6-3) and (6-5) with the inclusion of $\Delta Rep_{t,i}$. I find that the results shown in Table 6-8 are consistent with the main results in Table 6-6. These results imply that the main results are not driven by the engaged mainland- and Hong Kong-based auditors' concern regarding potential damage to their shared reputation or by any change in this concern. Furthermore, I re-estimate Eq. (6-5) by removing the cases in which shared reputational concern between the two engaged auditors may exist (i.e., drop the observations for which $Rep_{t,i} = 1$).[①] The inferences drawn from this reduced sample, as shown in Column (4) of Table 6-8, remain unchanged.

① If the observations for which $Rep_{t,i} = 1$ are removed from the sample keeping the dual audit, only 27 observations are left for the estimation of Eqs. (6-2) and (6-3). This too small sample size does not meet the basic requirement of large sample statistical tests (i.e., the sample shall include at least 30 observations). Therefore, I do not re-estimate Eqs. (6-2) and (6-3) within this reduced sample.

Table 6-8 Regression Results After Considering Auditors' Concern on Shared Reputation

Variable	Dependent Variable: $\mid AWCA \mid_{A\text{-}share\ t,i}$	Dependent Variable: $\Delta \mid AWCA \mid_{A\text{-}share\ t,i}$		
	(1)	(2)	(3)	(4)
Intercept	0. 083 (1. 402)	0. 017 (1. 268)	0. 001 (0. 093)	−0. 003 (−0. 097)
$Spillover_{t,i}$	−0. 490 * * (−2. 564)			
$\Delta Spillover_{t,i}$		−0. 397 * * (−2. 127)	−0. 420 * * (−2. 252)	−0. 570 * (−2. 042)
$CANCEL_{t,i}$			0. 013 * * (2. 136)	0. 038 * (1. 741)
$CANCEL_{t,i}$ * $\Delta Spillover_{t,i}$			0. 950 * * (2. 075)	1. 006 * * (2. 175)
$Size_{t,i}$	−0. 008 * (−1. 828)			
$\Delta Size_{t,i}$		0. 040 (1. 050)	0. 054 (1. 669)	0. 058 * (1. 728)
$Lev_{t,i}$	−0. 006 (−0. 285)			
$\Delta Lev_{t,i}$		−0. 095 (−1. 190)	−0. 064 (−0. 628)	−0. 118 (−0. 563)
$Loss_{t,i}$	−0. 009 (−0. 786)			
$\Delta Loss_{t,i}$		0. 002 (0. 331)	0. 011 (1. 036)	0. 015 (0. 642)
$CFOTA_{t,i}$	0. 114 * (1. 874)			
$\Delta CFOTA_{t,i}$		0. 086 (1. 140)	0. 077 (0. 902)	0. 072 (0. 634)
$BM_{t,i}$	0. 001 (0. 148)			
$\Delta BM_{t,i}$		0. 016 (1. 114)	0. 007 (0. 491)	0. 004 (0. 180)
$Vol_{t,i}$	0. 088 (0. 727)			

续表

Variable	Dependent Variable: $\vert AWCA \vert_{A\text{-}share\,t,\,i}$	Dependent Variable: $\Delta \vert AWCA \vert_{A\text{-}share\,t,\,i}$		
	(1)	(2)	(3)	(4)
$\Delta Vol_{t,\,i}$		0. 021 (0. 164)	0. 091 (0. 628)	0. 325 (1. 098)
$SOE_{t,\,i}$	−0. 022 * (−1. 924)	−0. 029 * * (−2. 579)	−0. 011 (−1. 216)	−0. 012 (−0. 809)
$Big4_{t,\,i}$	−0. 015 (−1. 427)			
$\Delta Big4_{t,\,i}$		−0. 097 * * (−2. 651)	−0. 037 (−0. 859)	−0. 015 (−0. 290)
$LnFee_{t,\,i}$	0. 009 (1. 545)			
$\Delta LnFee_{t,\,i}$		0. 011 (1. 238)	−0. 001 (−0. 074)	−0. 047 (−1. 041)
$Rep_{t,\,i}$	0. 006 (0. 349)			
$\Delta Rep_{t,\,i}$		0. 134 * * * (7. 066)	0. 018 (0. 933)	
Year Fixed Effects	Yes	Yes	Yes	Yes
Industry Fixed Effects	Yes	Yes	Yes	Yes
N	192	192	263	98
Adj. R^2	0. 242	0. 189	0. 068	0. 121

Notes: Column (1) shows the results of Eq. (6−2) after additionally introducing $Rep_{t,\,i}$ as a control variable; Column (2) shows the results of Eq. (6−3) after additionally introducing $\Delta Rep_{t,\,i}$ as a control variable; Column (3) shows the results of Eq. (6−5) after additionally introducing $\Delta Rep_{t,\,i}$ as a control variable; Column (4) shows the results of Eq. (6−5) after removing the observations for which $Rep_{t,\,i}=1$; * * *, * * and * represent significance at the 0. 01, 0. 05 and 0. 10 level, respectively, using two-tailed tests; t-statistics are shown in parentheses; variable definitions and measurement are reported in Table 6−2.

6. 3. 6. 3 Impact Threshold for a Confounding Variable Analysis

The deregulation of the mandatory dual audit system brings an endogenous problem that AH companies voluntarily choose whether to cancel the dual audit. Thus, the main findings in this chapter could result from self-selection bias. I have already conducted the analyses of changes in the main tests to eliminate bias induced by time-invariant factors. To further address the concern that unobservable time-varying factors drive the audit quality difference/change I find, I use the ITCV analysis following the practice in Section 5. 3. 5. As interpreted in that section, the ITCV is the product between the partial correlation between the dependent variable and the unobserved variable and the partial correlation between the independent variable of interest and the unobserved variable. A larger ITCV value implies an OLS result that is more robust to unobservable factors (Fu et al. , 2012)[385].

I calculate ITCV for variable $CANCEL_{t,i}$. In Panel A of Table 6 – 9, the threshold value for $CANCEL_{t,i}$ in the level model is 0. 0808. This value implies that the significant OLS result will be turned into an insignificant result once each of the partial correlation between $|AWCA|_{A\text{-}share\,t,i}$ and the unobserved variable and the partial correlation between $CANCEL_{t,i}$ and the unobserved variable reaches 0. 284 ($\sqrt{0.0808}$). Without comparative data, it is difficult to determine whether the ITCV is large enough to ensure the robustness of the result. Similar to the practice in Section 5. 3. 5, I compute the impact of each control variable to benchmark the size of possible correlations involving the unobserved confounding variable. The impact of each control variable is defined as the product of the partial correlation between $|AWCA|_{A\text{-}share\,t,i}$ and that control variable and the partial correlation between $CANCEL_{t,i}$ and that control variable. Column (2) in Panel A of Table 6–9 shows the potential impact of the inclusion of each control variable on the coefficient on $CANCEL_{t,i}$. The ITCV (0. 0808) is larger than the magnitude of impact scores of all control variables except $Spillover_{t,i}$(with an impact score of –0. 0982). This finding means that I need an unobserved variable with a greater impact than $Spillover_{t,i}$ to overturn the results. In Panel B of Table 6–9, the threshold value for $CANCEL_{t,i}$ in the change model is 0. 0367. This value suggests that the significant result will be turned into an insignificant result once each of the partial correlation between $\Delta|AWCA|_{A\text{-}share\,t,i}$ and the unobserved variable and the partial correlation between $CANCEL_{t,i}$ and the unobserved variable reaches 0. 192 ($\sqrt{0.0367}$). Column (2) in Panel B of Table 6 – 9 shows that none of the control variables has an impact stronger than the ITCV (0. 0367).

Accordingly, an unobserved confounding variable that can render the coefficients on $CANCEL_{t,i}$ statistically insignificant is unlikely to exist, given that I control for (1) a strong predictor of audit quality difference and change around the cancelation of the dual audit system and (2) a set of factors proven to have good explanatory power on variation in audit quality by the previous literature. I conclude that the stability of the main results in this chapter is not seriously affected by self-selection bias.

Table 6-9 Results of Impact Threshold for a Confounding Variable Analysis

Panel A: Results of Level Model for Total Sample in Chapter 6 (N=263), with Impact Statistics		
Variable	Dependent Variable: $\mid AWCA \mid_{A\text{-}share\, t,i}$	
	(1) ITCV	(2) Impact
$CANCEL_{t,i}$	0.0808	
$Spillover_{t,i}$		−0.0982
$Size_{t,i}$		−0.0044
$Lev_{t,i}$		0.0155
$Loss_{t,i}$		0.0004
$CFOTA_{t,i}$		−0.0003
$BM_{t,i}$		−0.0001
$Vol_{t,i}$		−0.0035
$SOE_{t,i}$		0.0002
$Big4_{t,i}$		0.0002
$LnFee_{t,i}$		0.0000
Panel B: Results of Change Model for Total Sample in Chapter 6 (N=263), with Impact Statistics		
Variable	Dependent Variable: $\Delta \mid AWCA \mid_{A\text{-}share\, t,i}$	
	(1) ITCV	(2) Impact
$CANCEL_{t,i}$	0.0367	
$\Delta Spillover_{t,i}$		−0.0156
$\Delta Size_{t,i}$		0.0014
$\Delta Lev_{t,i}$		−0.0022
$\Delta Loss_{t,i}$		−0.0018
$\Delta CFOTA_{t,i}$		−0.0023
$\Delta BM_{t,i}$		−0.0051
$\Delta Vol_{t,i}$		0.0038
$SOE_{t,i}$		0.0027
$\Delta Big4_{t,i}$		−0.0033
$\Delta LnFee_{t,i}$		0.0000

Notes: Variable definitions and measurement are reported in Table 6-2.

6.3.6.4 Alternative Measurement of Spillover Effect from Hong Kong-Based Auditors

As mentioned in Section 6.2.3, the construction of $|AWCA|_{A\text{-}share_{t,i}}$ and $Spillover_{t,i}$ both includes the A-share's absolute abnormal working capital accruals. This leads to a concern on potential econometric problems brought by such variable construction. As defined in Table 6-2, $|AWCA|_{H\text{-}share_{t,i}}$ is the absolute value of abnormal working capital accruals in a company's H-share financial statements for year t audited by its Hong Kong-based auditor before the company cancels the dual audit, and 0 after the company cancels the dual audit. Based on the logic upon which $Spillover_{t,i}$ is created, the stricter H-share audits of a company likely have a positive spillover effect on the company's A-share audits by helping prevent earnings management in its A-share financial statements. Therefore, if such a spillover effect exists, I expect that a negative association between $-|AWCA|_{H\text{-}share_{t,i}}$ and $|AWCA|_{A\text{-}share_{t,i}}$ can, to a certain degree, reflect the potential impact of this effect.

Accordingly, to address the aforementioned concern, I define $Spillover\_H_{t,i}$ to equal the negative value of $|AWCA|_{H\text{-}share_{t,i}}$, as an alternative measure to represent the spillover effect from Hong Kong-based auditors at a rougher level. Then, I re-estimate Eq. (6-2) with $Spillover_{t,i}$ replaced by $Spillover\_H_{t,i}$, and re-estimate Eqs. (6-3) and (6-5) with $\Delta Spillover_{t,i}$ replaced by $\Delta Spillover\_H_{t,i}$. The results are shown in Panel A of Table 6-10. The inferences drawn from these results of my attempt to address the potential econometric issue are consistent with those from Table 6-6.

Table 6-10 Regression Results of Alternative Measures

Panel A: Regression Results of Alternative Spillover-Effect Measure			
Variable	Dependent Variable: $\|AWCA\|_{A\text{-}share_{t,i}}$	Dependent Variable: $\Delta\|AWCA\|_{A\text{-}share_{t,i}}$	
	(1)	(2)	(3)
Intercept	0.079 (1.227)	0.013 (1.343)	-0.004 (-0.276)
$Spillover\_H_{t,i}$	-0.462*** (-3.383)		
$\Delta Spillover\_H_{t,i}$		-0.461*** (-3.189)	-0.524*** (-3.553)
$CANCEL_{t,i}$			0.009* (1.762)

续表

Panel A: Regression Results of Alternative Spillover-Effect Measure			
Variable	Dependent Variable: $\mid AWCA \mid_{A\text{-}share\ t,i}$	Dependent Variable: $\Delta \mid AWCA \mid_{A\text{-}share\ t,i}$	
	(1)	(2)	(3)
$CANCEL_{t,i}$ * $\Delta Spillover\_H_{t,i}$			0.761** (2.019)
$Size_{t,i}$	−0.004 (−1.181)		
$\Delta Size_{t,i}$		0.017 (0.507)	0.035 (1.186)
$Lev_{t,i}$	0.000 (0.001)		
$\Delta Lev_{t,i}$		−0.099* (−2.015)	−0.068 (−0.757)
$Loss_{t,i}$	−0.007 (−0.822)		
$\Delta Loss_{t,i}$		0.001 (0.204)	0.009 (0.777)
$CFOTA_{t,i}$	0.069 (1.450)		
$\Delta CFOTA_{t,i}$		0.016 (0.297)	0.019 (0.302)
$BM_{t,i}$	0.005 (0.467)		
$\Delta BM_{t,i}$		0.005 (0.373)	0.001 (0.073)
$Vol_{t,i}$	0.041 (0.350)		
$\Delta Vol_{t,i}$		0.026 (0.210)	0.095 (0.654)
$SOE_{t,i}$	−0.026* (−1.991)	−0.020*** (−2.989)	−0.004 (−0.367)
$Big4_{t,i}$	−0.012 (−1.377)		
$\Delta Big4_{t,i}$		−0.108*** (−7.365)	−0.050 (−1.371)

续表

Panel A: Regression Results of Alternative Spillover-Effect Measure			
Variable	Dependent Variable: $\mid AWCA \mid_{A\text{-}share\ t,i}$	Dependent Variable: $\Delta \mid AWCA \mid_{A\text{-}share\ t,i}$	
	(1)	(2)	(3)
$LnFee_{t,i}$	0.003 (0.631)		
$\Delta LnFee_{t,i}$		0.006 (0.930)	−0.008 (−0.851)
Year Fixed Effects	Yes	Yes	Yes
Industry Fixed Effects	Yes	Yes	Yes
N	192	192	263
Adj. R^2	0.276	0.279	0.177

Panel B: Regression Results of Alternative Audit-Quality Measure			
Variable	Dependent Variable: $\mid DACC \mid_{A\text{-}share\ t,i}$	Dependent Variable: $\Delta \mid DACC \mid_{A\text{-}share\ t,i}$	
	(1)	(2)	(3)
Intercept	−0.046 (−1.063)	0.000 (0.033)	−0.001 (−0.125)
$Spillover\_D_{t,i}$	−0.613*** (−7.859)		
$\Delta Spillover\_D_{t,i}$		−0.499*** (−10.113)	−0.443*** (−7.856)
$CANCEL_{t,i}$			0.005* (1.710)
$CANCEL_{t,i}$ * $\Delta Spillover\_D_{t,i}$			0.270* (1.927)
$Size_{t,i}$	0.000 (0.082)		
$\Delta Size_{t,i}$		−0.023 (−0.830)	0.016 (0.646)
$Lev_{t,i}$	−0.013 (−0.903)		
$\Delta Lev_{t,i}$		0.021 (0.266)	0.016 (0.282)

续表

Panel B: Regression Results of Alternative Audit-Quality Measure			
Variable	Dependent Variable: $\|DACC\|_{A\text{-}share\ t,i}$	Dependent Variable: $\Delta\|DACC\|_{A\text{-}share\ t,i}$	
	(1)	(2)	(3)
$Loss_{t,i}$	0.011 (1.069)		
$\Delta Loss_{t,i}$		0.019* (1.787)	0.017** (2.037)
$CFOTA_{t,i}$	0.068 (0.948)		
$\Delta CFOTA_{t,i}$		0.139* (1.693)	0.139* (1.973)
$BM_{t,i}$	-0.012* (-1.689)		
$\Delta BM_{t,i}$		0.009 (0.705)	-0.010 (-0.805)
$Vol_{t,i}$	0.013 (0.150)		
$\Delta Vol_{t,i}$		0.013 (0.122)	-0.032 (-0.345)
$SOE_{t,i}$	0.012* (1.794)	0.003 (0.550)	0.003 (0.514)
$Big4_{t,i}$	0.002 (0.535)		
$\Delta Big4_{t,i}$		-0.011 (-1.145)	-0.012** (-2.297)
$LnFee_{t,i}$	0.003 (1.149)		
$\Delta LnFee_{t,i}$		-0.018* (-1.685)	-0.018 (-1.586)
Year Fixed Effects	Yes	Yes	Yes
Industry Fixed Effects	Yes	Yes	Yes
N	183	183	253
Adj. R^2	0.481	0.381	0.262

Notes: In Panel A, Column (1) shows the results of Eq. (6-2) with $Spillover_{t,i}$ replaced by $Spillover\_H_{t,i}$; Column (2) shows the results of Eq. (6-3) with $\Delta Spillover_{t,i}$ replaced by $\Delta Spillover\_H_{t,i}$; Column (3) shows the results of Eq. (6-5) with $\Delta Spillover_{t,i}$ replaced by $\Delta Spillover\_H_{t,i}$. In Panel B, Column (1) shows the results of Eq. (6-2) with $|AWCA|_{A\text{-}share\ t,i}$ replaced by $|DACC|_{A\text{-}share\ t,i}$ and $Spillover_{t,i}$ replaced by $Spillover\_D_{t,i}$; Column (2) shows the results of Eq. (6-3) with $\Delta|AWCA|_{A\text{-}share\ t,i}$ replaced by $\Delta|DACC|_{A\text{-}share\ t,i}$ and $\Delta Spillover_{t,i}$ replaced by $\Delta Spillover\_D_{t,i}$; Column (3) shows the results of Eq. (6-5) with $\Delta|AWCA|_{A\text{-}share\ t,i}$ replaced by $\Delta|DACC|_{A\text{-}share\ t,i}$ and $\Delta Spillover_{t,i}$ replaced by $\Delta Spillover\_D_{t,i}$; ***, ** and * represent significance at the 0.01, 0.05 and 0.10 level, respectively, using two-tailed tests; t-statistics are shown in parentheses; variable definitions and measurement are reported in Table 6-2.

6.3.6.5 Alternative Measurement of Audit Quality

For robustness check, I use the absolute value of discretionary accruals in the A-share financial statements ($|DACC|_{A\text{-}share\ t,i}$) as an alternative proxy for audit quality. This measure is calculated as the absolute value of residuals from the modified Jones model adjusted by controlling for operating performance (Kothari et al., 2005)[366]. Correspondingly, a variable, namely, $Spillover\_D_{t,i}$, is constructed to measure the spillover effect from Hong Kong-based auditors. $Spillover\_D_{t,i}$ equals the negative value of the distance between the H-share's absolute discretionary accruals and the A-share's absolute discretionary accruals when a company keeps the dual audit (i.e., $-\left||DACC|_{H\text{-}share\ t,i} - |DACC|_{A\text{-}share\ t,i}\right|$), and 0 after a company cancels the dual audit. I re-estimate Eq. (6-2) with $|AWCA|_{A\text{-}share\ t,i}$ replaced by $|DACC|_{A\text{-}share\ t,i}$ and $Spillover_{t,i}$ replaced by $Spillover\_D_{t,i}$. I re-estimate Eqs. (6-3) and (6-5) with $\Delta|AWCA|_{A\text{-}share\ t,i}$ replaced by $\Delta|DACC|_{A\text{-}share\ t,i}$ and $\Delta Spillover_{t,i}$ replaced by $\Delta Spillover\_D_{t,i}$. The results demonstrated in Panel B of Table 6-10 are similar to those reported in Table 6-6 and suggest that the main inferences continue to hold for the alternative audit-quality measure.

6.4 Results Discussion

In the tests of hypotheses H9 and H10 in this chapter, the empirical results show that: ①auditors' practice of the dual audit abides by the rule stipulated in CSRC (2001)[392] by ensuring that companies use consistent estimates for the same accounting event in their A-share and H-share financial statements. ②On average, Hong Kong-based auditors tend to have a positive spillover effect on mainland-based auditors when performing the dual audit. ③Companies keeping the dual audit have higher audit quality when they are subject to a more positive spillover effect from Hong Kong-based auditors. ④After companies cancel the dual audit, there is a positive association between the loss of the positive spillover effect from Hong Kong-based auditors and the decrease in audit quality. In addition, the main findings are robust after convergence of accounting standards and engaged auditors' shared reputational concern are controlled and when alternative spillover-effect and audit-quality measures are used. The results are also not seriously affected by self-selection bias.

These results are consistent with the inference drawn from the previous studies that canceling the dual audit may lead to an audit quality deterioration. The results support the idea that the existence of a positive spillover effect from Hong Kong-based auditors is beneficial to the audit quality of companies keeping the dual audit, whereas the loss of this positive spillover is primarily responsible for the decline in the audit quality of companies canceling the dual audit. In particular, the abolition of the mandatory dual audit system aims to improve audit efficiency and lower listing costs of AH companies. However, this policy change has been questioned for possibly impairing the audit quality of these companies because it may forego a positive spillover effect from high- to low-quality auditors through the dual audit process. This potential positive spillover effect is suggested to stem from the institutional environment gap faced by mainland- and Hong Kong-based auditors. However, this effect has not yet been measured directly, and it is still unclear whether the audit quality decrease following companies' cancelation of the dual audit is driven by the loss of this effect (if any). To fill these voids, this chapter creates a measure to represent the spillover effect from Hong Kong-based auditors and obtains the aforementioned findings.

Taken together, the empirical results in this chapter suggest that the spillover effect from Hong Kong- to mainland-based auditors through the dual audit process positively influences companies' audit quality when they keep the dual audit. Canceling the dual audit causes audit quality to deteriorate, and the loss of this positive spillover effect from Hong Kong-based auditors is the main driver of this audit quality deterioration. The deregulation of the mandatory dual audit system has an adverse impact on audit quality.

6. 5 Chapter Summary

This chapter investigates the economic consequences of the deregulation of the mandatory dual audit system on the audit market by comparing canceling the dual audit with keeping the dual audit after the deregulation and deeply exploring the role that a positive spillover effect from Hong Kong- to mainland-based auditors plays in audit quality. This chapter uses a sample of AH-share cross-listed companies in China for the period 2010 to 2015, which is a subset of the samples used in Chapter 4 and Chapter 5. Based on the main arguments, this chapter first develops two hypotheses (H9 and H10). Then, this chapter uses the absolute abnormal working capital accruals to measure audit quality in the main tests, and constructs a novel measure to represent the spillover effect from Hong Kong-based auditors. Next, this chapter designs the empirical models for hypothesis testing. Through conducting descriptive statistical, univariate, multivariate regression and robustness analyses, the empirical results support both hypotheses in this chapter and are robust to different model specifications. Table 6-11 summarizes the results of hypothesis testing in this chapter.

Table 6-11 Summary of Empirical Findings in Chapter 6

No.	Hypothesis	Empirical Findings
H9	Ceteris paribus, companies keeping the dual audit have higher audit quality when they are exposed to a more positive spillover effect from Hong Kong-based auditors.	Supported
H10	Ceteris paribus, the loss of the positive spillover effect due to canceling the dual audit by companies leads to a decline in their audit quality.	Supported

7 Conclusions

Through the elaborations and analyses in previous chapters, this study investigates the economic consequences of the deregulation of the mandatory dual audit system on the capital market and audit market. As the last chapter in this study, it summarizes the main conclusions and highlights the contributions of this study. The limitations of the study and possible directions for future research are also specified.

7.1 Main Conclusions

This study is conducted under the institutional background of the deregulation of the mandatory dual audit system for AH companies. This study investigates the economic consequences of this policy change on the capital market and audit market. In particular, this study investigates the impacts of the deregulation on the cost of equity by separately comparing (1) companies that comply with the mandatory dual audit requirement before the deregulation with companies that voluntarily choose the dual audit after the deregulation and (2) companies that voluntarily choose the dual audit after the deregulation with companies that use only the single audit in the same period. In addition, this study investigates the impacts of the deregulation on audit quality by (1) constructing a novel measure of the spillover effect from Hong Kong-based auditors through the dual audit process and (2) comparing companies canceling the dual audit with companies keeping the dual audit after the deregulation. Based on a sample of A-share listed companies in 2007-2015, this study provides new evidence on the economic consequences of the deregulation of the mandatory dual audit system. The main findings are as follows.

First, companies have a lower cost of equity when they mandatorily have the dual audit before the deregulation than when they voluntarily use the dual audit after the deregulation. This study first investigates the economic consequences of the deregulation of the mandatory dual audit system on the capital market by testing the effect of mandatory dual audit before the deregulation relative to voluntary dual audit after the deregulation on reducing the cost of equity. Under the condition that the assurance value of audits is effectively controlled in the empirical process, this study finds that the cost of equity is lower when companies comply with the mandatory dual audit requirement than when they voluntarily choose the dual audit. Furthermore, the effect of mandatory dual audit relative to voluntary dual audit on reducing the cost of equity is greater in companies with higher demand for equity financing and in companies with higher agency costs. The effect of mandatory dual audit relative to voluntary dual audit on reducing the cost of equity is not attenuated by other voluntary audit mechanisms, such as the interim report audit. The main results, which are robust to various model specifications, are unlikely to be attributable to audit assurance levels, accounting standards convergence and differential impact of firm growth.

Second, after the deregulation of the mandatory dual audit system, companies voluntarily using the dual audit have a lower cost of equity than companies using only the single audit. After examining the effect of mandatory dual audit relative to voluntary dual audit on the cost of equity, this study then investigates the economic consequences of the deregulation of the mandatory dual audit system on the capital market by testing the effect of voluntary dual audit after the deregulation relative to single audit in the same period on reducing the cost of equity. Under the condition that the assurance value of audits is effectively controlled in the empirical process, this study finds that the cost of equity is lower for companies voluntarily choosing the dual audit than for companies using only the single audit. Furthermore, the effect of voluntary dual audit relative to single audit on reducing the cost of equity is more pronounced in companies with higher demand for equity financing and in companies with higher agency costs. The effect of voluntary dual audit relative to single audit on reducing the cost of equity is substitutable by alternative voluntary audit mechanisms, such as the interim report audit. The main results, which are robust to various model specifications, are unlikely to be attributed to audit assurance levels, differential impact of firm growth and unobserved confounding factors.

Third, companies keeping the dual audit have higher audit quality when they are subject to a more positive spillover effect from Hong Kong-based auditors, whereas a positive association is observed between the loss of the positive spillover effect from Hong Kong-based auditors and the decrease in companies' audit quality after they cancel the dual audit. After understanding the capital-market consequences of the deregulation of the mandatory dual audit system, this study investigates its economic consequences on the audit market by comparing canceling the dual audit with keeping the dual audit after the deregulation and deeply exploring the role that a positive spillover effect from Hong Kong- to mainland-based auditors through the dual audit process plays in audit quality. To examine these issues, this study creates a novel measure to represent the spillover effect from Hong Kong-based auditors. Briefly, when a company keeps the dual audit, the measure is calculated as the negative value of the absolute difference between the H-share's absolute abnormal working capital accruals (audited by the Hong Kong-based auditor) and the A-share's absolute abnormal working capital accruals (audited by the mainland-based auditor). Otherwise, after the company cancels the dual audit, this measure takes the value of 0. Based on this empirical progress, this study finds that the existence of the positive spillover effect from Hong Kong-based auditors benefits companies' audit quality when they keep the dual audit. This study also finds that canceling the dual audit causes audit quality to deteriorate, and the loss of this positive spillover effect is the main driver of this audit quality deterioration. The main results, which are robust to various model specifications, are unlikely to be attributable to accounting standards convergence, engaged auditors' shared reputational concern and unobserved confounding factors.

Overall, this study completes the planned research tasks and achieves the expected research purposes. This study proposes ten hypotheses, all of which are supported by the empirical results. In terms of the capital-market consequences, the main conclusions suggest that after the deregulation, voluntarily choosing the dual audit helps companies maintain a lower cost of equity than using only the single audit by sending a positive signal to investors. However, voluntarily choosing the dual audit cannot totally make up for the loss of the role that complying with the mandatory dual audit requirement plays in reducing information asymmetry and agency costs. Hence, the cost of equity increases when companies change from mandatory to voluntary dual audit. In terms of the audit-market consequences, the main conclusions suggest that there exists a positive spillover effect from Hong

Kong- to mainland-based auditors in the dual audit process, and the loss of this positive spillover is the main driver of the declining audit quality of companies canceling the dual audit. In a word, the deregulation of the mandatory dual audit system has an adverse impact on both the capital market and audit market in China. This study enriches the literature on the economic consequences of the dual audit system, the determinants of the cost of equity and the determinants of audit quality. This study also serves as an important reference for policy-makers and regulators to re-evaluate the costs and benefits of abolishing the mandatory dual audit system.

7. 2 Policy Implications

First, the findings indicate that the deregulation of the mandatory dual audit system has an adverse impact on both the capital market and audit market. This study provides a new reference for regulators and policy-makers to evaluate the costs and consequences of this policy change. On the one hand, the main findings suggest a significant increase in the cost of equity, which is attributed to the loss of the role that complying with the mandatory dual audit requirement plays in reducing agency conflicts and information asymmetry. On the other hand, the main findings suggest a significant decline in audit quality, which is largely driven by the loss of a positive spillover effect from Hong Kong-based auditors following the cancelation of the dual audit. The main findings of the cost of equity reflect an increase in investors' suspicions after the deregulation of the mandatory dual audit system about companies' self-serving behavior that may harm their interests (Zhang et al., 2022)[393]. The main findings of audit quality confirm practitioners' concern on a likely damage to companies' audit quality when the audits are performed singly by mainland-based auditors (HKEx, 2010; Zhang et al., 2021)[292, 394].

From this perspective, it might not be a wise decision for a company to simply focus on cost-saving and cancel the dual audit. These implications echo the unsmooth implementation of this policy change in practice. As demonstrated in Panel B of Table 4-7 (and Tables 5-3 and 6-3), only 1 company responded to the abolition of the mandatory dual audit system within the year of regulators' official announcement (i. e., 2010). While the proportion of companies canceling the dual audit has grown since then, they comprised only a small part of the total AH sample at the end of my sample period (i. e., 2015) when compared with those keeping the dual audit. In addition, Figure 1-2 shows that approximately 62.39% (68/109) of AH companies kept the dual audit even at the end of 2018. This phenomenon reflects companies' doubt about whether the economic benefits of canceling the dual audit can exceed its costs. Accordingly, the implementation of this policy change is not as successful as regulators originally expected, and retaining only the single audit remains far from becoming a common trend among AH companies.

This study reinforces the benefits of the dual audit regime from the perspectives of the cost of equity and audit quality. Combined with the unsatisfactory implementation process, I wish to call policy-makers and regulators' attention to cautiously reassessing the appropriateness of abolishing the mandatory dual audit system.

The implications for other emerging markets with audit rules and regulations that have not yet been well developed are as follows. Powerful mandatory audit regimes adapted to national conditions may be uneconomical, but not to the extent that they erode the benefits of easing financing frictions and developing a high-quality financial reporting environment.

Second, this study cautions that it could be an arduous long-term task for mainland local audit firms to become genuinely big and strong. A worldwide trend of IFRS adoption (convergence) has lasted for many years. In addition, China's economy develops in a rapid speed along with constant expansion of company scales. In this context, it is inevitable for auditing in China to be in line with the international practices, and the market and regulators increasingly call for bigger and stronger local audit firms. Taking effect in 2007, the new CAS symbolized the convergence of the accounting and auditing work in China with the international practices at the theoretical level. Nonetheless, the convergence in theory is not equal to the convergence in implementation; high auditing standards do not necessarily bring high audit quality. Compared with overseas audit firms, mainland local audit firms generally have a weaker historical root and brand effect. Con-sequently, the latter are usually less sensitive to reputation while more sensitive to audit costs than the former. Correspondingly, the latter often have much smaller business scales and are more likely to loosen quality control requirements on themselves than the former, leading to lower audit quality of mainland local audit firms. To bring up local audit firms with brand reputation, Chinese regulators have taken many measures to support the development of local auditors during these years. Regulators' efforts in encouraging audit firm mergers have raised a few large local audit firms that earn revenue approaching the level of top international audit firms. However, this growth in revenue seems to reflect only the growth in scales of local audit firms. To the extent that audit failure occurs frequently among them, the market performance (or service quality) of local audit firms is not that satisfactory even after mergers. In this study, the main findings which show an audit quality deterioration after companies cancel the dual audit system confirm practitioners' relevant worries. These findings also echo AH companies' low acceptance, in practice, of the single audits performed by mainland auditors. Therefore, although regulators have provided considerable policy support for developing the mainland audit profession, it remains a long way to go for local auditors to possess high quality and completely win trust from the market in the absence of the positive spillover effect from overseas auditors.

To become high-quality alternatives to top international audit firms, mainland local audit firms should learn quality control from them and standardize the self-disciplines of the whole audit profession. They should also attach sufficient importance to implementing the new accounting and auditing standards, developing quality-oriented corporate culture and training staff's professional ethics and practical capability. Moreover, they should optimize merging paths and properly integrate resources after mergers. At the same time, regulators should regulate the self-discipline practices of the audit profession while focus on cultivating the core audit firms to take the lead in building brand. Through this "from point to area" policy, regulators can help promote the overall audit quality of the mainland audit industry.

7.3 Contributions

Compared with the previous literature, this study makes the following contributions.

First, this study theoretically elaborates and empirically verifies that mandatory dual audit and voluntary dual audit reduce the cost of equity to different extents, providing empirical evidence for the economic consequences of the deregulation of the mandatory dual audit system on the capital market. Previous studies focus on the audit-related consequences of the deregulation. These studies only compare companies that have the dual audit with those that do not or companies in the regulated period with those in the period after the deregulation. To the contrary, this study classifies dual audits into mandatory dual audit (before the deregulation) and voluntary dual audit (after the deregulation) and analyzes how both separately affect the cost of equity. The theory of commitment effect of complying with mandatory requirements and the theory of signaling effect of making voluntary choices are used as bases. This study derives the cost-of-equity measure from the GLS model and effectively controls for the effects of the audited financial information in the empirical process. The theoretical elaborations and relevant results suggest that the deregulation of the mandatory dual audit system affects investors' perceptions and decisions. Such effects yield significant economic consequences on the capital market. These results not only enrich the research on the dual audit system and that on the cost of equity, but also enhance understanding of the differential albeit important roles that mandatory and voluntary dual audits separately play in the cost of equity. Furthermore, these results serve as new references for regulators and policy-makers to learn about the influences of the mandatory dual audit system on investor protection. To a certain extent, these results imply why a majority of AH companies persist using the dual audit system even years after the abolition of the mandatory requirement. The results warn regulators to cautiously reassess the costs and consequences of the deregulation of the mandatory dual audit system.

Second, this study verifies that the loss of the positive spillover effect from Hong Kong-based auditors is the main driver of the declining audit quality of companies canceling the dual audit. Although previous studies discuss the audit-related consequences of the deregulation of the dual audit system, they lack thorough analysis and verification of a mechanism that possibly drives the audit quality change under this policy change. This study measures audit quality by abnormal accruals, quantifies the spillover effect and uses the analyses of changes. The findings provide initial evidence confirming that the positive spillover effect from Hong Kong-based auditors helps ensure the higher audit quality of companies keeping the dual audit, whereas the loss of this effect is primarily responsible for the decline in the audit quality of companies canceling the dual audit. Compared with previous studies, the analyses of this study effectively rule out the potential impacts of cross-listing, accounting standards convergence, auditors' shared reputational concern and unobserved confounding factors. These analyses help to reach rigorous and robust conclusions. Extending the research on the dual audit system and that on audit quality, the results of this study contribute to further understanding of the indispensable role played by the positive spillover effect from

Hong Kong-based auditors in the dual audit regime. Furthermore, these results confirm practitioners' concern on the likely damage to audit quality when companies cancel the dual audit and accept the single audits performed by mainland-based auditors. The results caution regulators and mainland local audit firms that becoming truly big and strong is a long and arduous task for local audit firms.

Third, this study develops a measurement method to directly and effectively capture the spillover effect from Hong Kong-based auditors in the dual audit process. Owing to its unobservability, this effect is limited to a description by previous studies, which restricts researchers to deeply exploring the audit-quality issues in the dual audit setting from this perspective. According to relevant rules and previous studies, this study assumes that the stricter H-share audits of a company are likely to have a positive spillover effect on the company's A-share audits by helping prevent earnings management in its A-share financial statements. Accordingly, a closer gap (i. e. , a shorter distance) between a company's H-share and A-share audit quality represents a larger constraint effect of the H-share audits performed by its Hong Kong-based auditor on the A-share audits performed by its mainland-based auditor, that is, a more effective positive spillover effect from the Hong Kong-based auditor. Following this rationale and from the perspective of earnings management, this study creates a proxy for the spillover effect based on the calculation of the distance between the H-share's and A-share's absolute abnormal accruals of a company keeping the dual audit. Compare with previous studies, this study intuitively presents the spillover effect from Hong Kong- to mainland-based auditors through the dual audit system by constructing a novel measure. This study is among the first empirical works on this research topic. It promotes the development of research on the dual audit system and that on audit quality.

7. 4 Limitations and Future Research

While this study obtains important findings and potentially makes incremental contributions to academia and practice, it still has some limitations. I discuss these limitations below and suggest future research directions.

First, while this study demonstrates the adverse consequences of the deregulation of the mandatory dual audit system, it does not investigate the benefits of this policy change. For example, regulators suggest that canceling the mandatory dual audit system can reduce audit costs for AH companies, improve audit efficiency and provide mainland local audit firms with opportunities to go abroad. Audit fees-related outcomes could be the most intuitive consequences of this policy change awaiting further exploration. Although audit report lag is used as a proxy for audit efficiency by several studies, this measure is questioned for involving many confounding factors. Without an available appropriate measure on audit efficiency, it is difficult to examine the consequences from this aspect. Future research could try getting access to cleaner proxies, such as audit hours, and explore whether the deregulation of the mandatory dual audit system contributes to higher audit efficiency. Future research could also investigate whether mainland local audit firms' competitiveness and bargaining power in the A-share and H-share markets significantly increase after the deregulation. Moreover, future research could pay attention to other economic effects of this policy change. For example, whether this policy change further affects companies' real activities, such as investment and performance.

Second, when checking the robustness of the results in Chapter 6, I use only the discretionary accruals as an alternative audit-quality measure. The common practice in audit quality research is to use proxies other than the accrual-related measures used in the main tests for robustness check. However, in Chapter 6, the typical audit-quality proxies, such as the likelihood of modified audit opinions and that of earnings restatements, are inapplicable due to lack of variation in them among the sample firms. Another classical measure, namely, audit fees, is also unlikely to be a proper representative for audit quality in this study. The original intention of regulators abolishing the mandatory dual audit system is to reduce audit fees for AH companies, which implies that audit fees and audit quality are supposed to be considered separately. Furthermore, based on Ke et al. (2015) [5] and the CSRC (2001) [392], the most direct reflection of a positive spillover effect from Hong Kong-based auditors is a constraint on the A-share earnings management, which can be intuitively represented by the accrual-related measures rather than other ones. Therefore, I use the discretionary accruals to check robustness. Future research could try getting access to proxies for audit inputs that are less affected by management (e. g. , audit adjustments) to better capture the quality of the audits and make the empirical analysis more perfect.

Third, this study does not emphasize examining the relations between the audit-market consequences and capital-market consequences. However, this does not mean that these two consequences are completely isolated from each other or this study is not an interconnected whole. In fact, the (negative) relationship of audit quality with the cost of equity has already been supported by a wealth of relevant studies. Accordingly, based on an adverse impact of the deregulation of the mandatory dual audit system on audit quality shown by this study, it can be inferred that this policy change possibly increases the cost of equity through decreasing audit quality. Meanwhile, the capital-market consequences of the deregulation focused on by this study are about how complying with the mandatory dual audit requirement and voluntarily choosing the dual audit separately affect the cost of equity. These effects are tested under the condition that the assurance value of audits (i. e. , audit quality) is effectively controlled in the empirical process. The objective is to find out whether these two acts (i. e. , the act of complying with the mandatory dual audit requirement and that of voluntarily choosing the dual audit) can have incremental effects on the cost of equity beyond the effects of audit quality. Although the relationship of audit quality with the cost of equity can already be inferred from previous studies, future research could examine and confirm this relationship under the dual audit setting.

Finally, for the following reasons, I investigate the economic consequences of the deregulation of the mandatory dual audit system on only the A-share capital market rather than the H-share capital market. ① The mainland China market nowadays has attracted increasing attention from international scholars. I aim to draw conclusions against the background of the mainland China market and generalize my conclusions to offer practical implications to other emerging economies besides the mainland China. ②Companies that cancel the dual audit all dismiss their Hong Kong-based auditors and retain the A-share audits. Thus, using the A-share financial and auditing data of the total sample firms can ensure that the effects of the audited financial information are effectively measured and controlled in the empirical process. ③ Doing so can ensure consistency with the market focused on by the investigation on the audit-market consequences of this policy change. Future research could further investigate the consequences of this policy change on the H-share capital market.

References

[1] SUN S Q. A research on the evolution and economic results of dual system of auditing: based on the angle of opening H-stock auditing market[D]. Nanjing: Nanjing University of Finance & Economics, 2014. (in Chinese)

[2] GEBHARDT W R, LEE C M C, SWAMINATHAN B. Toward an implied cost of capital[J]. Journal of Accounting Research, 2001, 39(1): 135-176.

[3] STULZ R M. Globalization, corporate finance, and the cost of capital[J]. Journal of Applied Corporate Finance, 1999, 12(3): 8-25.

[4] LANG M, RAEDY J S, YETMAN M H. How representative are firms that are cross-listed in the United States? An analysis of accounting quality[J]. Journal of Accounting Research, 2003, 41(2): 363-386.

[5] KE B, LENNOX C S, XIN Q Q. The effect of China's weak institutional environment on the quality of Big 4 audits[J]. The Accounting Review, 2015, 90(4): 1591-1619.

[6] TIAN G L, ZHANG R, SI Y, et al. The impact of cross-listing and dual auditing on domestic audit fees and audit quality: evidence from A and H shares cross-listings in China[J]. Journal of Audit & Economics, 2017, 32(3): 24-34. (in Chinese)

[7] Ministry of Finance of the People's Republic of China (MOF). Responses from the heads of the accounting department of the Ministry of Finance and the accounting department of the China Securities Regulatory Commission to journalists on "pilot work scheme of mainland audit firms engaging in the H-share audits" [EB/OL]. (2009-11-16) [2022-11-19]. http://kjs. mof. gov. cn/zhengcejiedu/200911/t20091116_233218. htm. (in Chinese)

[8] Ministry of Finance of the People's Republic of China (MOF). Interpretation of road map for the continuous and comprehensive convergence of the Chinese Accounting Standards with the International Financial Reporting Standards [EB/OL]. (2010-04-20) [2022-11-19]. http://www. chinaacc. com/new/635_797/2010_4_20_su8818204919024010221160. shtml. (in Chinese)

[9] Hong Kong Exchanges and Clearing Limited (HKEx). Consultation paper on

acceptance of mainland accounting and auditing standards and mainland audit firms for mainland incorporated companies listed in Hong Kong[EB/OL]. (2009-08) [2022-11-19]. https://www.hkex.com.hk/-/media/HKEX-Market/News/Market-Consultations/2006-to-2010/August-2009-Consultation-Paper/Consultation-paper/cp200908_e.pdf.

[10] ZHENG W, LIU J, MA J W. Study on domestic CPA firms to participate in auditing of H-share companies: based on the domestic CPA firms' internationalization strategy and H-share audit market[J]. Auditing Research, 2011 (6): 98-106. (in Chinese)

[11] WENG S C, HUANG J Q. A brief discussion on the opportunities and challenges of local audit firms undertaking H-share audit[J]. China Township Enterprises Accounting, 2012 (4): 177-178. (in Chinese)

[12] LIN C J, LIN H L, YEN A R. Dual audit, audit firm independence, and auditor conservatism[J]. Review of Accounting and Finance, 2014, 13 (1): 65-87.

[13] WANG M X. An assessment of dual audit effect and contagious effect on the audit quality of non-Big N CPA firms for Chinese companies in different markets[D]. Hong Kong: Lingnan University, 2014.

[14] SUN S Q. An analysis on the preliminary effects of the dual-audit system cancellation of H share[J]. Securities & Futures of China, 2013 (4): 25-25. (in Chinese)

[15] WANG B, XIN Q Q. Auditor choice and accruals patterns of cross-listed firms [J]. China Journal of Accounting Research, 2011, 4 (4): 233-251.

[16] ZHONG Z Y, ZHANG J N. Review and prospect of dual audit research[J]. Modern Business Trade Industry, 2019 (30): 111-113. (in Chinese)

[17] MODIGLIANI F, MILLER M H. The cost of capital, corporation finance and the theory of investment [J]. American Economic Review, 1959, 48 (4): 443-453.

[18] SOLOMON E. Leverage and the cost of capital[J]. The Journal of Finance, 1963, 18 (2): 273-279.

[19] SHARPE W F. Capital asset prices: a theory of market equilibrium under conditions of risk[J]. The Journal of Finance, 1964, 19 (3): 425-442.

[20] FELTHAM G A, OHLSON J A. Valuation and clean surplus accounting for operating and financial activities [J]. Contemporary Accounting Research,

1995, 11 (2): 689-731.

[21] GORDON J R, GORDON M J. The finite horizon expected return model[J]. Financial Analysts Journal, 1997, 53 (3): 52-61.

[22] CLAUS J J, THOMAS J K. Equity premia as low as three percent? Evidence from analysts' earnings forecasts for domestic and international stock markets [J].The Journal of Finance, 2001, 56 (5): 1629-1666.

[23] EASTON P D. PE ratios, PEG ratios, and estimating the implied expected rate of return on equity capital[J].The Accounting Review, 2004, 79 (1): 73-95.

[24] OHLSON J A, JUETTNER NAUROTH B E. Expected EPS and EPS growth as determinants of value [J]. Review of Accounting Studies, 2005, 10 (10): 349-365.

[25] LEVITT A. The importance of high quality accounting standards[J].Accounting Horizons, 1998, 12 (1): 79-82.

[26] HAIL L, LEUZ C. Cost of capital and cash flow effects of US cross listings[EB/OL]. (2005-04) [2022-11-19].https://econpapers. repec. org/paper/eclupafin/05-2. htm.

[27] HIMMELBERG C P, HUBBARD R G, LOVE I. Investor protection, ownership, and the cost of capital[EB/OL]. (2004-04) [2022-11-19].https://ssrn. com/abstract=303969.

[28] JIANG F X, ZHI X Q, ZHANG M. Investor protection and cost of equity: A study of Chinese listed companies[J].Management World, 2008 (2): 117-125. (in Chinese)

[29] XIAO M, SHEN Y F. On the cost of equity of cross-listing companies[J]. Journal of Financial Research, 2008 (10): 93-103. (in Chinese)

[30] HONG J, CHEN S H. Ultimate ownership structure, legal system and cost of equity[J].Friends of Accounting, 2016 (2): 36-41. (in Chinese)

[31] XU H P, LV C J. Role of government, ownership property and cost of equity [J].Accounting Research, 2007 (6): 61-67. (in Chinese)

[32] XIAO H, XIA X P. Government intervention, political connections and cost of equity capital[J].Chinese Journal of Management, 2010, 7 (6): 921-929. (in Chinese)

[33] ZHAO F, GAO M H. Can political connections decrease private firms' cost of equity capital[J].Journal of Shanxi Finance and Economics University, 2012, 34 (8): 88-98. (in Chinese)

[34] WANG J Q. Political connections, earnings quality and cost of equity capital [J].Management Review, 2013, 25 (10): 80–90. (in Chinese)

[35] ZOU Y, YANG X W. Political connections, financial ecological environment and cost of equity capital: an analysis based on the data from the year of 2005 to 2012[J]. East China Economic Management, 2014, 28 (10): 98–104. (in Chinese)

[36] BOTOSAN C A. Disclosure level and the cost of equity capital [J]. The Accounting Review, 1997, 72 (3): 323–349.

[37] BOTOSAN C A, PLUMLEE M A. A re-examination of disclosure level and the expected cost of equity capital[J].Journal of Accounting Research, 2002, 40 (1): 21–40.

[38] CAO S J, LIU X, YANG J Y. Audit quality attributes, client size and the cost of equity capital [J]. Journal of Shanxi Finance and Economics University, 2012, 34 (8): 117–124. (in Chinese)

[39] TIAN Y H, LIU J F. An empirical study of cost of capital and capital structure of Chinese listed companies [J]. Journal of Huazhong University of Science and Technology: Nature Science, 2003, 31 (1): 92–94. (in Chinese)

[40] YE K T, LU Z F. An analysis of the determinants of the cost of equity of Chinese listed companies [J]. Management World, 2004 (5): 127–131. (in Chinese)

[41] FAMA E F, FRENCH K R. The cross-section of expected stock returns[J]. The Journal of Finance, 1992, 47 (2): 427–465.

[42] RICHARDSON A J, WELKER M. Social disclosure, financial disclosure and the cost of equity capital[J].Accounting, Organizations and Society, 2001, 26 (7–8): 597–616.

[43] CHEN X, SHAN X. Will debt financing increase the financing cost of listed companies?[J].Economic Research Journal, 1999, 9 (9): 39–46. (in Chinese)

[44] TANG G Z, LIU L. Impact of interest rate regulation on the capital structure of Chinese listed companies [J]. Management World, 2005 (1): 50–58. (in Chinese)

[45] JIN X H. Impact of financial leverage on the cost of equity: based on the capital asset pricing model [J]. Research of Financial & Accounting, 2008 (13): 45–48. (in Chinese)

[46] BERK J B, GREEN R C, NAIK V. Optimal investment, growth options, and

security returns[J].The Journal of Finance, 1999, 54 (5): 1553–1607.

[47] CHENG C S A, COLLINS D, HUANG H H. Shareholder rights, financial disclosure and the cost of equity capital[J].Review of Quantitative Finance and Accounting, 2006, 27 (2): 175–204.

[48] LEI T, ZHOU J N. Equity incentive, executive inner pay gap and the cost of equity capital[J].Journal of Management Science, 2014, 27 (6): 12–26. (in Chinese)

[49] ASHBAUGH H, COLLINS D W, LAFOND R. Corporate governance and the cost of equity capital[EB/OL]. (2004–10–20) [2022–11–19].https://w4. stern. nyu. edu/accounting/docs/speaker_papers/fall2004/Hollis_Ashbaugh_10–20–04–nyu-emory. pdf.

[50] HUANG H H. Shareholder rights and the cost of equity capital[D].Houston: University of Houston, 2005.

[51] MAZZOTTA R, VELTRI S. The relationship between corporate governance and the cost of equity capital: evidence from the Italian stock exchange[J]. Journal of Management & Governance, 2014, 18 (2): 419–448.

[52] JIANG Y. Cost of equity, cost of debt, and corporate covernance: a study on the differences in impact[J].Management World, 2009 (11): 144–155. (in Chinese)

[53] JIANG Y, LU Z F. Corporate governance and the cost of equity capital[J]. The Journal of Quantitative & Technical Economics, 2009 (2): 60–75. (in Chinese)

[54] YAN H H. Research on the relationship between internal governance and cost of capital[J].Public Finance Research, 2011 (6): 54–58. (in Chinese)

[55] LAI Y X, FAN L M. Corporate governance efficiency, investor confidence and cost of equity[J].Communication of Finance and Accounting, 2016 (36): 56–60. (in Chinese)

[56] KE L. Corporate governance, performance persistence and financing cost[J]. Friends of Accounting, 2017 (6): 23–27. (in Chinese)

[57] DIAMOND D W, VERRECCHIA R E. Disclosure, liquidity, and the cost of capital[J].The Journal of Finance, 1991, 46 (4): 1325–1359.

[58] MANGENA M, LI J, TAURINGANA V. Disentangling the effects of corporate disclosure on the cost of equity capital: a study of the role of intellectual capital disclosure[J].Journal of Accounting, Auditing & Finance,

2016, 31 (1) : 3-27.

[59] WANG W, JIANG G F. Information disclosure, transparency and cost of capital[J].Economic Research Journal, 2004 (7) : 107-114. (in Chinese)

[60] ZENG Y, LU Z F. The relationship between disclosure quality and cost of equity capital of listed companies in China[J].Economic Research Journal, 2006, 41 (2) : 69-79. (in Chinese)

[61] SHEN H T, YOU J X, LIU J H. On the environmental inspection for refinancing, environmental disclosure and the cost of equity capital[J].Journal of Financial Research, 2010 (12) : 159-172. (in Chinese)

[62] LI H Y, LIU D. Marketization process, voluntary disclosure and the cost of equity capital[J].Accounting Research, 2016 (1) : 71-78. (in Chinese)

[63] ZHOU H Q, ZHU Y N. Relationship between information disclosure quality and cost of equity capital [J]. Journal of Beijing University of Posts and Telecommunications (Social Sciences Edition) , 2016 (1) : 72-77. (in Chinese)

[64] KIM O. Disagreements among shareholders over a firm's disclosure policy[J]. The Journal of Finance, 1993, 48 (2) : 747-760.

[65] YANG H, YANG S E, ZHANG P. Time trend of the effect the information disclosure quality on the cost of equity capital: an empirical study based on entropy measuring of Chinese listed companies[J].Journal of Shanxi Finance and Economics University, 2012, 34 (12) : 68-82. (in Chinese)

[66] LI S, ZHAO Y, TONG J. Can corporate social responsibility report reduce cost of equity capital? Evidence from Chinese stock market[J]. Accounting Research, 2013 (9) : 64-70. (in Chinese)

[67] CHE P R, TIAN X L. Relationship between information disclosure level of social responsibility and capital cost[J].Journal of Beijing University of Posts and Telecommunications (Social Sciences Edition), 2016 (6): 64 - 73. (in Chinese)

[68] ZHANG Z Y, CHEN H. Corporate social responsibility disclosure and the cost of equity capital: the roles of corporate financial transparency and outside governance environment [J]. Journal of Nanjing University of Finance and Economics, 2017 (1) : 60-71. (in Chinese)

[69] EASLEY D, O'HARA M. Information and the cost of capital[J].The Journal of Finance, 2004, 59 (4) : 1553-1583.

[70] SUIJS J. On the value relevance of asymmetric financial reporting policies[J].

Journal of Accounting Research, 2008, 46 (5): 1297-1321.

[71] LAFOND R, WATTS R L. The information role of conservatism [J]. The Accounting Review, 2008, 83 (2): 447-478.

[72] LARA J M G, OSMA B G, PENALVA F. Conditional conservatism and cost of capital[J].Review of Accounting Studies, 2011, 16 (2): 247-271.

[73] GUAY W R, VERRECCHIA R E. Conservative disclosure [J]. Journal of Financial Reporting, 2018, 3 (1): 73-92.

[74] WANG J, HAO D Y, ZHANG T X. Conservative accounting information, cost of equity capital and company's investment efficiency: empirical evidence from the sample of Chinese A-share stock market[J].Research on Economics and Management, 2013 (2): 52-61. (in Chinese)

[75] LU J, WU M Y, ZHANG C J, et al. Research on accounting conservatism and cost of equity capital: evidence from listed companies in electronic equipment manufacturing industry [J]. Friends of Accounting, 2016 (24): 47 - 51. (in Chinese)

[76] LI Z G, CAO F, ZHAO X B, et al. Institutional investors heterogeneity, accounting conservatism and the cost of equity: evidence from China's listed firms[J].Management Review, 2016, 28 (7): 42-52. (in Chinese)

[77] WANG S N, XU Y F. Financing constraints, accounting conservatism and the cost of equity capital[J].Modern Finance and Economics: Journal of Tianjin University of Finance and Economics, 2016 (11): 64-75. (in Chinese)

[78] MA Z M, YUAN Z H, ZHOU Z Z, et al. Carbon information disclosure, accounting conservatism and cost of capital: a study on A-share listed companies[J].Communication of Finance and Accounting, 2017 (34): 10-14. (in Chinese)

[79] CHOI J H, LEE W J. Association between Big 4 auditor choice and cost of equity capital for multiple-segment firms[J].Accounting & Finance, 2014, 54 (1): 135-163.

[80] HOUQE M N, AHMED K, ZIJL T V. Audit quality, earnings management, and cost of equity capital: evidence from India[J].International Journal of Auditing, 2017, 21 (2): 177-189.

[81] YU L S, WANG Y Y, CHEN Z Y. Do information intermediaries have economic added value? Theoretical and empirical evidence [J]. Management World, 2008 (7): 134-144. (in Chinese)

[82] WANG B, XIN Q Q, YANG D M. Whether auditor reputation influences share pricing: evidence from IPO market in China[J].Accounting Research, 2009(11):73–81. (in Chinese)

[83] CHEN H W, CHEN J Z Y, LOBO G J, et al. Effects of audit quality on earnings management and cost of equity capital: evidence from China[J]. Contemporary Accounting Research, 2011, 28(3):892–925.

[84] LI X Y, ZHAO J T, DUAN Z M. Reasearch on the role of audit quality in stock pricing: based on the analysis of A-share market in our country[J]. Auditing Research, 2017(4):39–47. (in Chinese)

[85] ZHU D, LI Y. Audit quality, media coverage and equity capital cost: empirical evidence from listed companies in China[J].Industrial Economics Research, 2017(6):65–74. (in Chinese)

[86] AMIHUD Y, MENDELSON H. Asset pricing and the bid-ask spread[J]. Journal of Financial Economics, 1986, 17(2):223–249.

[87] JACOBY G, FOWLER D J, GOTTESMAN A A. The capital asset pricing model and the liquidity effect: a theoretical approach[J].Journal of Financial Markets, 2000, 3(1):69–81.

[88] SAAD M, SAMET A. Liquidity and the implied cost of equity capital[J]. Journal of International Financial Markets, Institutions and Money, 2017, 51(s):15–38.

[89] WANG C F, SUN H G, FANG Z M. The experience validation of relationship between cost of capital and asset liquidity [J]. Modern Finance and Economics: Journal of Tianjin University of Finance and Economics, 2012(9):74–83. (in Chinese)

[90] YANG H F. Analysis on cost of equity capital's influencing factors of listed companies[J].Financial Theory & Practice, 2016(8):42–48. (in Chinese)

[91] SHEN Y F, XIAO M, HUANG J J. Investor protection and corporation cost of equity[J].Economic Research Journal, 2005(6):115–124. (in Chinese)

[92] FAMA E F, MACBETH J D. Risk, return, and equilibrium: empirical tests[J]. Journal of Political Economy, 1973, 81(3):607–636.

[93] ROSS S A. The arbitrage theory of capital asset pricing[J].Journal of Economic Theory, 1976, 13(3):341–360.

[94] WANG L L. Real activities earnings management and cost of equity capital[J].Journal of Management Science, 2013, 26(5):87–99. (in Chinese)

[95] WANG P, ZHANG Z Y. Research on the determinants of the cost of equity capital of listed companies[J].Communication of Finance and Accounting, 2014(16):25–30. (in Chinese)

[96] DEFOND M, ZHANG J Y. A review of archival auditing research[J].Journal of Accounting and Economics, 2014, 58(2–3):275–326.

[97] DEANGELO L E. Auditor size and audit quality[J].Journal of Accounting and Economics, 1981a, 3(3):183–199.

[98] WATTS R L, ZIMMERMAN J L. Agency problems, auditing, and the theory of the firm: some evidence[J].The Journal of Law and Economics, 1983, 26(3):613–633.

[99] PALMROSE Z V. Audit fees and auditor size: further evidence[J].Journal of Accounting Research, 1986, 24(1):97–110.

[100] TEOH S H, WONG T J. Perceived auditor quality and the earnings response coefficient[J].The Accounting Review, 1993, 68(2):346–366.

[101] LEE C W J, GU Z Y. Low balling, legal liability and auditor independence [J].The Accounting Review, 1998, 73(4):533–555.

[102] FRANCIS J R. A framework for understanding and researching audit quality [J].Auditing: A Journal of Practice & Theory, 2011, 30(2):125–152.

[103] ZHANG L P, ZHANG D L. On the characteristics of audit quality and the idea of audit quality control[J].Auditing Research, 1997(5):27–28. (in Chinese)

[104] FENG J K. Research on certified public accountant audit quality control theory[M].Beijing: China Financial & Economic Publishing House, 2002. (in Chinese)

[105] DOPUCH N, SIMUNIC D. Competition in auditing: an assessment[C]. Urbana: University of Illinois, 1982.

[106] FIRTH M, SMITH A. Selection of auditor firms by companies in the new issue market[J].Applied Economics, 1992, 24(2):247–255.

[107] DEFOND M L, WONG T J, LI S H. The impact of improved auditor independence on audit market concentration in China[J]. Journal of Accounting and Economics, 1999, 28(3):269–305.

[108] WU S P, LI Q F. Audit quality of international Big 4, domestic Big 10, and domestic non-Big 10: evidence from Chinese listed companies in 2003[J]. Contemporary Finance & Economics, 2006(2):114–118. (in Chinese)

[109] LIN Y J, WANG Z Q. Is audit quality in international Big 4 accounting firms higher?[J]. Journal of Finance and Economics, 2013, 39 (6): 73–83. (in Chinese)

[110] WU H M, WU C X, YANG X Q. Disciplinary risk, auditor size and audit quality: evidence from China audit market[J]. Auditing Research, 2015 (1): 75–83. (in Chinese)

[111] LU J W, SHI X, ZHANG K. Whether large audit firms provide higher-quality audits or are more sensitive to policy? A natural experiment based on the changes of compilation rules for information disclosure[J]. Journal of Audit & Economics, 2017, 32 (4): 16–29. (in Chinese)

[112] WU X L, WANG H D, ZHOU S L. The relation between size of accounting house and auditing quality[J]. Journal of Shanxi Finance and Economics University, 2005, 27 (3): 121–123. (in Chinese)

[113] GUO Z R. International big four accounting firms and high auditing quality: evidence from China's securities market[J]. Auditing Research, 2011 (1): 98–107. (in Chinese)

[114] OWHOSO V E, MESSIER W F, LYNCH J G. Error detection by industry-specialized teams during sequential audit review[J]. Journal of Accounting Research, 2002, 40 (3): 883–900.

[115] KRISHNAN G V. Does Big 6 auditor industry expertise constrain earnings management?[J]. Accounting Horizons, 2003, 17 (s-1): 1–16.

[116] LIU W J, MI L, FU J X. Auditor industry specialization and audit quality: evidence from financial fraud companies[J]. Auditing Research, 2010 (1): 47–54. (in Chinese)

[117] XIE S W, SUN J Q. Institutional environment, audit industry specialization and audit quality: an empirical study [J]. Contemporary Finance & Economics, 2010 (7): 119–127. (in Chinese)

[118] FAN J H, ZHANG Y M, LIU Q L. Internal control, auditor industry expertise, accrual and real earnings management[J]. Accounting Research, 2013 (4): 81–88. (in Chinese)

[119] CAI C, XIAN W D. Study on the correlation between auditor industry specialization and audit quality: evidence from the audit market of the listed companies in China[J]. Accounting Research, 2007 (6): 41–47. (in Chinese)

[120] MUZATKO S R, JOHNSTONE K M, MAYHEW B W, et al. An empirical

investigation of IPO underpricing and the change to the LLP organization of audit firms [J]. Auditing: A Journal of Practice & Theory, 2004, 23 (1): 53-67.

[121] FIRTH M, MO P L L, WONG R M K. Auditors' organizational form, legal liability, and reporting conservatism: evidence from China[J]. Contemporary Accounting Research, 2012, 29 (1): 57-93.

[122] ZHU J D. Research on the internal governance mechanism of accounting firms: based on governance practices from BDO China[J]. Accounting and Economics Research, 2013 (1): 46-54. (in Chinese)

[123] CHEN B. Internal governance of accounting firms, state ownership and audit quality: based on the data of Chinese A-share listed companies from 2008 to 2010[J]. Accounting and Economics Research, 2014, 28 (5): 68-86. (in Chinese)

[124] LIU X J, WANG K T. Did auditors' organizational transformation have an impact on audit quality? [J]. Accounting Research, 2014 (4): 88-94. (in Chinese)

[125] LIU Q L, GUO J X, TANG Y Y. Audit firms' organizational form, legal liability, and audit quality: an individual auditor level analysis[J]. Accounting Research, 2015 (4): 86-94. (in Chinese)

[126] HUANG J C, LIN B, ZHAO J. A study on how accounting firm structural reform influence the audit quality and the relevant mechanism: evidence from market perception [J]. Auditing Research, 2017 (2): 73-79. (in Chinese)

[127] CHOW C W. The demand for external auditing: size, debt and ownership influences[J]. The Accounting Review, 1982, 57 (2): 272-291.

[128] FRANCIS J R, WILSON E R. Auditor changes: a joint test of theories relating to agency costs and auditor differentiation [J]. The Accounting Review, 1988, 63 (4): 663-682.

[129] LENNOX C. Management ownership and audit firm size [J]. Contemporary Accounting Research, 2005a, 22 (1): 205-227.

[130] BLOUIN J, GREIN B M, ROUNTREE B R. An analysis of forced auditor change: the case of former Arthur Andersen clients [J]. The Accounting Review, 2007, 82 (3): 621-650.

[131] FRANCIS J R, RICHARD C, VANSTRAELEN A. Assessing France's joint

audit requirement: are two heads better than one?[J].Auditing: A Journal of Practice & Theory, 2009, 28 (2) : 35–63.

[132] GUEDHAMI O, PITTMAN J A, SAFFAR W. Auditor choice in privatized firms: empirical evidence on the role of state and foreign owners[J].Journal of Accounting and Economics, 2009, 48 (2–3) : 151–171.

[133] WANG Y Y, CHEN H W, YU L S. Agency conflicts and demand for high audit quality: evidence from Chinese listed companies[J].Economic Science, 2006 (2) : 72–82. (in Chinese)

[134] GAO L, ZHANG J. Agency costs, management ownership and audit quality [J].Journal of Finance and Economics, 2011, 37 (1) : 48–58. (in Chinese)

[135] QI L G, HAN C M. A study on customer property differences, audit fees and audit quality: research on risk-based auditing theory[J].Auditing Research, 2016 (2) : 66–73. (in Chinese)

[136] CARCELLO J V, NEAL T L. Audit committee composition and auditor reporting[J].The Accounting Review, 2000, 75 (4) : 453–467.

[137] BEASLEY M S, PETRONI K R. Board independence and audit-firm type [J].Auditing: A Journal of Practice & Theory, 2001, 20 (1) : 97–114.

[138] BEASLEY M S, SALTERIO S E. The relationship between board characteristics and voluntary improvements in audit committee composition and experience [J]. Contemporary Accounting Research, 2001, 18 (4): 539–570.

[139] STEWART J, KENT P. Relation between external audit fees, audit committee characteristics and internal audit [J]. Accounting & Finance, 2006, 46 (3): 387–404.

[140] ENGEL E, HAYES R M, WANG X. Audit committee compensation and the demand for monitoring of the financial reporting process [J]. Journal of Accounting and Economics, 2010, 49 (1–2) : 136–154.

[141] CASSELL C A, GIROUX G A, MYERS L A, et al. The effect of corporate governance on auditor-client realignments[J].Auditing: A Journal of Practice & Theory, 2012, 31 (2) : 167–188.

[142] XIAO Z P. Does corporate governance affect audit quality? Evidence from China's capital market [J]. Management World, 2006 (7): 22 – 33. (in Chinese)

[143] YU Y Y, LIU Q L. Does the system of corporate governance contribute to

improving audit quality? [J]. Auditing Research, 2007 (5): 77 - 83. (in Chinese)

[144] SHEN Y Q, QI W J, ZENG Y. The different effect of auditor tenure on earnings quality: based on different level of corporate[J].Auditing Research, 2009 (2): 50-56. (in Chinese)

[145] PAN Q, WEN Q. Governance structure and audit quality of listed companies: an empirical study on GEM companies [J]. Modern Management Science, 2017 (3): 106-108. (in Chinese)

[146] YE C G, WU J F, TAN Z D. Corporate governance structure, audit fees and audit quality: an empirical analysis based on data of China's listed companies [J]. Contemporary Economic Management, 2015, 37 (5): 18 - 25. (in Chinese)

[147] LOEBBECKE J K, EINING M M, WILLINGHAM J J. Auditors experience with material irregularities-frequency, nature, and detectability[J].Auditing: A Journal of Practice & Theory, 1989, 9 (1): 1-28.

[148] PETTY R, CUGANESAN S. Auditor rotation: framing the debate[J].Australian Accountant, 1996, 66 (5): 40-42.

[149] JOHNSON V E, KHURANA I K, REYNOLDS J K. Audit-firm tenure and the quality of financial reports [J]. Contemporary Accounting Research, 2002, 19 (4): 637-660.

[150] GEIGER M A, RAGHUNANDAN K. Auditor tenure and audit reporting failures[J].Auditing: A Journal of Practice & Theory, 2002, 21 (1): 67-78.

[151] MYERS J N, MYERS L A, OMER T C. Exploring the term of the auditor-client relationship and the quality of earnings: a case for mandatory auditor rotation[J].The Accounting Review, 2003, 78 (3): 779-799.

[152] LITT B, SHARMA D S, SIMPSON T, et al. Audit partner rotation and financial reporting quality[J].Auditing: A Journal of Practice & Theory, 2014, 33 (3): 59-86.

[153] XIA L J, CHEN X Y, FANG Y Q. Audit tenure and audit independence: empirical evidence from China's securities market[J].China Accounting and Finance Review, 2005, 7 (1): 54-101. (in Chinese)

[154] CHEN X Y, XIA L J. Auditor tenure and audit quality: empirical evidence from the Chinese securities market[J]. Accounting Research, 2006 (1): 44-53. (in Chinese)

[155] LIU Q L, TANG J X. Study effect, private relationship, audit tenure and audit quality[J].Auditing Research, 2009(4): 52-64. (in Chinese)

[156] DEANGELO L E. Auditor independence, "low balling", and disclosure regulation[J].Journal of Accounting and Economics, 1981b, 3(2): 113-127.

[157] SHOCKLEY R A. Perceptions of auditors' independence: an empirical analysis[J].The Accounting Review, 1981, 56(4): 785-800.

[158] ARRUNADA B, Cá NDIDO P A. Mandatory rotation of company auditors: a critical examination[J].International Review of Law and Economics, 1997, 17(1): 31-61.

[159] AREL B, BRODY R G, PANY K. Audit firm rotation and audit quality[J]. The CPA Journal, 2005, 75(1): 36-39.

[160] CAREY P, SIMNETT R. Audit partner tenure and audit quality[J].The Accounting Review, 2006, 81(3): 653-676.

[161] YE P, CARSON E, SIMNETT R. Threats to auditor independence: the impact of relationship and economic bonds[J]. Auditing: A Journal of Practice & Theory, 2011, 30(1): 121-148.

[162] LIU Q L. Auditor tenure and audit quality: evidence from China's securities market[J].Auditing Research, 2006(4): 40-49. (in Chinese)

[163] JIANG W, LI B. Tenure and auditor independence: an empirical analysis based on going-concern opinions[J].Journal of Audit & Economics, 2011, 26(2): 47-55. (in Chinese)

[164] LI S F, LIU L, WANG H C. Auditor industry specialization, economic dependence and audit quality: a perspective of auditing tenure[J].Journal of Shanxi Finance and Economics University, 2014, 36(5): 112-124. (in Chinese)

[165] YU Y M, LI L. Theoretical analysis of the relationship between auditor tenure and audit quality[J].Economic Review, 2003(5): 124-128. (in Chinese)

[166] DONG N Y, ZHANG J R. Study on the influence of corporate governance on the relationship between auditor tenure and audit quality[J].Journal of Shanxi Finance and Economics University, 2010, 32(9): 98-107. (in Chinese)

[167] SHEN Y Q, QI W J, ZENG Y. Audit partner tenure, audit firm tenure and audit independence[J].Management Review, 2010, 22(9): 93-99, 104. (in Chinese)

[168] CHOI J H, KIM C S, KIM J B, et al. Audit office size, audit quality, and audit pricing[J]. Auditing: A Journal of Practice & Theory, 2010, 29 (1): 73-97.

[169] KANAGARETNAM K, KRISHNAN G V, LOBO G J. An empirical analysis of auditor independence in the banking industry[J]. The Accounting Review, 2010, 85 (6): 2011-2046.

[170] HOSSAIN S, MONROE G S, WILSON M, et al. The effect of networked clients' economic importance on audit quality [J]. Auditing: A Journal of Practice & Theory, 2016, 35 (4): 79-103.

[171] ZHANG Y Y. Client importance and audit quality, office level evidence from the banking industry: a pitch[J]. Accounting Research Journal, 2017, 30 (2): 147-152.

[172] LU Z F, WANG C F, WU L N. Institutional improvement, client importance of business groups and modified audit opinion[J]. Accounting Research, 2012 (10): 71-78. (in Chinese)

[173] CAO Q, HU N W, WANG L C. Client importance, risk nature and audit quality: evidence from financial restatement[J]. Auditing Research, 2012 (6): 60-70. (in Chinese)

[174] JIA N, LI D. Does the economic dependence on clients impair the audit quality: evidence comes from the Chinese firms listed on the US markets[J]. Auditing Research, 2015 (5): 102-112. (in Chinese)

[175] XIE S W, YANG Q H, LIU R. Client importance and accounting information comparability: empirical evidence from Chinese stock market[J]. Journal of Nanjing Audit University, 2017 (1): 74-84. (in Chinese)

[176] YANG Y M, YANG H Y. Client importance, audit firm reputation and financial restatement[J]. Shandong Social Sciences, 2019 (9): 142-146. (in Chinese)

[177] STICE J D. Using financial and market information to identify pre-engagement factors associated with lawsuits against auditors [J]. The Accounting Review, 1991, 66 (3): 516-533.

[178] BONNER S E, PALMROSE Z V, YOUNG S M. Fraud type and auditor litigation: an analysis of SEC accounting and auditing enforcement releases [J]. The Accounting Review, 1998, 73 (4): 503-532.

[179] ZHANG P. A bargaining model of auditor reporting [J]. Contemporary

Accounting Research, 1999, 16 (1): 167–184.

[180] REYNOLDS J K, FRANCIS J R. Does size matter? The influence of large clients on office-level auditor reporting decisions[J]. Journal of Accounting and Economics, 2000, 30 (3): 375–400.

[181] GAVER J J, PATERSON J S. The influence of large clients on office-level auditor oversight: evidence from the property-casualty insurance industry[J]. Journal of Accounting and Economics, 2007, 43 (2–3): 299–320.

[182] FUNG S Y K, ZHOU G G S, ZHU X X K. Monitor objectivity with important clients: evidence from auditor opinions around the world [J]. Journal of International Business Studies, 2016, 47 (3): 263–294.

[183] FANG J X, HONG J Q, LI R S. Research on determinants of audit quality of Chinese listed companies: findings and implications[J]. Auditing Research, 2004 (6): 35–43. (in Chinese)

[184] YU X M, NIE X J, LIU H. Does client importance affect audit quality? Evidence from Chinese listed companies' 2003–2006 data[J]. Accounting Research, 2008 (10): 66–72. (in Chinese)

[185] CHEN S M, SUN S Y J, WU D H. Client importance, institutional improvements, and audit quality in China: an office and individual auditor level analysis[J]. The Accounting Review, 2010, 85 (1): 127–158.

[186] LIU W J. Auditor industry specialization, client importance, and audit quality [J]. South China Journal of Economics, 2012 (6): 44–57. (in Chinese)

[187] LI M H, LIU X X. On the relationship between client importance and audit quality: moderating effects of corporate governance[J]. Journal of Finance and Economics, 2013, 39 (3): 64–74. (in Chinese)

[188] DOWDELL T D, KRISHNAN J. CAP forum on Enron: former audit firm personnel as CFOs: effect on earnings management[J]. Canadian Accounting Perspectives, 2004, 3 (1): 117–142.

[189] MENON K, WILLIAMS D D. Former audit partners and abnormal accruals [J]. The Accounting Review, 2004, 79 (4): 1095–1118.

[190] LENNOX C. Audit quality and executive officers' affiliations with CPA firms[J]. Journal of Accounting and Economics, 2005b, 39 (2): 201–231.

[191] WU X. Accounting firm combination and quality control: the case of Zhongtianqin[J]. Accounting Research, 2006 (10): 79–85. (in Chinese)

[192] LIU J H. Top management's affiliations with CPA firms, CPA firms tenure

and audit quality[J].Auditing Research, 2011 (2): 63–70. (in Chinese)

[193] LIU J H, ZHANG L Z. Top management's working experience of auditors and relationship on accrual-based and real earnings management[J].Auditing Research, 2014 (4): 104–112. (in Chinese)

[194] CHEN X X, WU X, YANG Y L. Do auditors treat their prospective employers more favorably prior to the revolving-door employment? [J]. Auditing Research, 2015 (1): 84–90. (in Chinese)

[195] WU X, WANG C F, LU Z F. Is it a "misfortune" or a "good fortune" if the independent director and the auditor are colleagues? A study on the effect of the control over the company in independence, competition and cooperation [J].Management World, 2015 (9): 137–146. (in Chinese)

[196] GUAN Y Y, SU L X N, WU D H, et al. Do school ties between auditors and client executives influence audit outcomes? [J]. Journal of Accounting and Economics, 2016, 61 (2–3): 506–525.

[197] HE X J, PITTMAN J A, RUI O M, et al. Do social ties between external auditors and audit committee members affect audit quality? [J]. The Accounting Review, 2017, 92 (5): 61–87.

[198] GEIGER M A, NORTH D S, O'CONNELL B T. The auditor-to-client revolving door and earnings management[J].Journal of Accounting, Auditing & Finance, 2005, 20 (1): 1–26.

[199] GEIGER M A, NORTH D S. Does hiring a new CFO change things? An investigation of changes in discretionary accruals [J]. The Accounting Review, 2006, 81 (4): 781–809.

[200] BABER W R, KRISHNAN J, ZHANG Y Q. Investor perceptions of the earnings quality consequences of hiring an affiliated auditor[J].Review of Accounting Studies, 2014, 19 (1): 69–102.

[201] DENG C, GAO Y Q, YANG W Y. The effect of CFO's prior experience as an auditor, the revolving door phenomenonon and accounting conservatism of listed companies[J]. Collected Essays on Finance and Economics, 2017 (3): 71–80. (in Chinese)

[202] KHURANA I K, RAMAN K K. Litigation risk and the financial reporting credibility of Big 4 versus non-Big 4 audits: evidence from Anglo-American countries[J].The Accounting Review, 2004, 79 (2): 473–495.

[203] HUIJGEN C, LUBBERINK M. Earnings conservatism, litigation and contracting:

the case of cross-listed firms[J].Journal of Business Finance & Accounting, 2005, 32(7-8): 1275-1309.

[204] CHOI J H, KIM J B, LIU X H, et al. Audit pricing, legal liability regimes, and Big 4 premiums: theory and cross-country evidence [J]. Contemporary Accounting Research, 2008, 25(1): 55-99.

[205] FRANCIS J R, WANG D C. The joint effect of investor protection and Big 4 audits on earnings quality around the world[J]. Contemporary Accounting Research, 2008, 25(1): 157-191.

[206] FRANCIS J R, KHURANA I K, MARTIN X, et al. The relative importance of firm incentives versus country factors in the demand for assurance services by private entities[J].Contemporary Accounting Research, 2011, 28(2): 487-516.

[207] WANG M, TAN L S. Cross-listing on A-and H-share markets and auditor conservatism: an empirical study on audit opinion [J]. Finance and Accounting Monthly, 2010(12): 68-70. (in Chinese)

[208] XIN Q Q, WANG B. Cross-listing, Big 4 and earnings quality[J].Economic Science, 2010(4): 96-110. (in Chinese)

[209] FENG Y C, LIANG L X. Litigation risk of listed company, audit fees and non-standard audit opinions: Evidence from Chinese listed companies[J]. Auditing Research, 2010(3): 75-81. (in Chinese)

[210] ZHAI H Y, LIAO H. A research on investment opportunities, audit risk and auditing quality[J].Journal of Audit & Economics, 2011, 26(4): 46-53. (in Chinese)

[211] SONG Y H, XIAO X. Supervision risk, auditor size and audit quality[J]. Auditing Research, 2012(3): 83-89. (in Chinese)

[212] LIU W J. Do CICPA inspections improve audit quality? [J]. Auditing Research, 2016(6): 98-104. (in Chinese)

[213] HUANG Y X, LI C A. Can self-regulation of the CPA profession improve audit quality? Based on the evidence of the CICPA's interview [J]. Accounting Research, 2016(11): 84-91. (in Chinese)

[214] ZHOU L, YAO Y F. Negative press coverage, auditor switching and audit quality[J].Auditing Research, 2015(3): 73-81. (in Chinese)

[215] ZHANG L D, FENG J K, CHEN J M. Media supervision, internal control and audit opinion[J].Auditing Research, 2016(5): 73-81. (in Chinese)

[216] WU W R, LI J J. Research on media coverage and audit quality: evidence from China listed companies[J].Journal of Huazhong Agricultural University

(Social Sciences Edition), 2017 (3): 132–139. (in Chinese)

[217] ROCK E B. Securities regulation as lobster trap: a credible commitment theory of mandatory disclosure [J]. Cardozo Law Review, 2002, 23 (2): 675–704.

[218] STULZ R M. Securities laws, disclosure, and national capital markets in the age of financial globalization [J]. Journal of Accounting Research, 2009, 47 (2): 349–390.

[219] CHENG L, LIAO S, ZHANG H W. The commitment effect versus information effect of disclosure: evidence from smaller reporting companies [J]. The Accounting Review, 2013, 88 (4): 1239–1263.

[220] MONAHAN S J. Discussion of why do managers voluntarily issue cash flow forecasts? [J]. Journal of Accounting Research, 2006, 44 (2): 431–436.

[221] HAIL L. Discussion of consequences and institutional determinants of unregulated corporate financial statements: evidence from embedded value reporting [J]. Journal of Accounting Research, 2011, 49 (2): 573–594.

[222] MELUMAD N D, THOMAN L. On auditors and the courts in an adverse selection setting [J]. Journal of Accounting Research, 1990, 28 (1): 77–120.

[223] LENNOX C S, PITTMAN J A. Voluntary audits versus mandatory audits [J]. The Accounting Review, 2011, 86 (5): 1655–1678.

[224] CLATWORTHY M A, PEEL M J. The impact of voluntary audit and governance characteristics on accounting errors in private companies [J]. Journal of Accounting and Public Policy, 2013, 32 (3): 1–25.

[225] HAY D, CORDERY C. The value of public sector audit: literature and history [J]. Journal of Accounting Literature, 2018, 40 (s): 1–15.

[226] WU X. Auditor independence and audit pricing under duplicate auditing arrangements: evidence from Chinese B-share market [M]. Beijing: China Financial & Economic Publishing House, 2005. (in Chinese)

[227] RATZINGER N V S, AUDOUSSET C S, KETTUNEN J, et al. Joint audit: issues and challenges for researchers and policy-makers [J]. Accounting in Europe, 2013, 10 (2): 175–199.

[228] HOLM C, THINGGAARD F. From joint to single audits: audit quality differences and auditor pairings [J]. Accounting and Business Research, 2018, 48 (3): 321–344.

[229] LIN Q. Big 4 auditors and audit quality: evidence from the perspective of cross-listing [D]. Xiamen: Xiamen University, 2014. (in Chinese)

[230] CHE J X. The influence on cross-listing behavior of listing-corporation to

audit quality: a view of the comparative study between A+H share and A share[D].Changchun: Northeast Normal University, 2014. (in Chinese)

[231] LI S H. An empirical analysis of the net income differences between domestic and overseas audit reports of listed companies[J]. Accounting Research, 1997(12): 18-23. (in Chinese)

[232] CHEN C J, CHEN S M, SU X J. Profitability regulation, earnings management, and modified audit opinions: evidence from China [J]. Auditing: A Journal of Practice & Theory, 2001, 20(2): 9-30.

[233] JIANG Y H. An empirical analysis of the differences between domestic and overseas audits of net income: evidence from the annual report of B-share listed companies in China[J]. Management World, 2002 (7): 121-125. (in Chinese)

[234] LI S, WU X. B-share audit market structure and audit fees after the cease of double auditing policy: an exploratory note[J].Auditing Research, 2009(1): 37-42. (in Chinese)

[235] FANG J X. Study on economic consequences of deregulation in China's audit market: evidence from B-share audit market[J].Journal of Finance and Economics, 2010, 36(7): 71-81. (in Chinese)

[236] ZHANG P. An empirical research on the effect of the abolishment of duplicate auditing institution on B-share companies' governance efficiency [D].Shanghai: Shanghai Jiao Tong University, 2011. (in Chinese)

[237] ZHANG P. Empirical research on the level of earnings management for A-share companies and B-share companies before and after the abolishment of duplicate auditing institution[J]. Science Technology and Engineering, 2012, 20(5): 1100-1104. (in Chinese)

[238] WANG Y H, LIU H L. Research on audit quality after the cancellation of dual audit: based on the data of AB-share listed companies[J]. Productivity Research, 2012(1): 241-242. (in Chinese)

[239] LUO S Q, ZHUO Y. The principle of economics [M]. Beijing: Capital University of Economics and Business Press, 2004. (in Chinese)

[240] LAMBERT R, LEUZ C, VERRECCHIA R E. Accounting information, disclosure, and the cost of capital[J].Journal of Accounting Research, 2007, 45(2): 385-420.

[241] CHEN G M, FIRTH M, GAO D N, et al. Is China's securities regulatory agency a toothless tiger? Evidence from enforcement actions[J]. Journal of Accounting and Public Policy, 2005, 24(6): 451-488.

[242] SHEN H B. Market segmentation, cross-listing and expected cost of capital: evidence from the Ohlson-Juettner model[J].Journal of Financial Research, 2007(2):146–155. (in Chinese)

[243] WANG X Y, YE Z H. Does implementation of new accounting standards reduce the cost of equity capital: evidence from Chinese capital market[J]. China Industrial Economics, 2011(3):119–128. (in Chinese)

[244] CHEN Z H, HUANG Y, WEI K C J. Executive pay disparity and the cost of equity capital[J].Journal of Financial and Quantitative Analysis, 2013, 48(3):849–885.

[245] KONG W C, XUE H. An empirical study on corporate governance, investor protection and cost of equity capital[J].Enterprise Economy, 2005(5):77–79. (in Chinese)

[246] HU L, ZHANG Z H. An empirical study on ownership concentration, ownership property and cost of equity capital[J].Statistics & Decision, 2016(19):162–165. (in Chinese)

[247] XIAO Z P. The effect of ultimate ownership structure on cost of equity capital: empirical evidence from Chinese listed companies[J]. Journal of Management Sciences in China, 2016, 19(1):72–86. (in Chinese)

[248] ZOU Y, WANG P, ZHANG L M. Equity incentive, controlling shareholder and cost of equity capital[J].Economic Management Journal, 2015, 37(6):98–109. (in Chinese)

[249] LI X R, DONG H Y. Executive power, corporate property right and cost of equity capital[J].Economic Science, 2015(4):67–80. (in Chinese)

[250] HANDA P, LINN S C. Arbitrage pricing with estimation risk[J].Journal of Financial and Quantitative Analysis, 1993, 28(1):81–100.

[251] ZHI X Q, HE T R. Information disclosure quality and the cost of equity[J]. China Soft Science, 2010(12):125–131. (in Chinese)

[252] CHAN A L C, LIN S W J, STRONG N. Accounting conservatism and the cost of equity capital: UK evidence[J].Managerial Finance, 2009, 35(4):325–345.

[253] ZHANG C H, WU S X. State ownership, accounting conservatism and cost of equity capital: evidence from China's securities market[J].The Theory and Practice of Finance and Economics, 2012, 33(5):209–215. (in Chinese)

[254] ZHANG S L. Institutional ownership, accounting conservatism and cost of equity: empirical evidence from China's capital market[J]. Economic Survey, 2012(5):117–121. (in Chinese)

[255] LI G, ZHANG W, WANG Y Y. An empirical study of earnings information quality and cost of equity capital[J].Journal of Audit & Economics, 2008, 23 (5): 57-62. (in Chinese)

[256] ZHANG S Y, YANG H Y. Accounting conservatism choices, cost of capital and firm value[J].Macroeconomics, 2014 (1): 97-106. (in Chinese)

[257] JENSEN M C, MECKLING W H. Theory of the firm: managerial behavior, agency costs and ownership structure[J].Journal of Financial Economics, 1976, 3 (4): 305-360.

[258] FRANCIS J R. What do we know about audit quality? [J]. The British Accounting Review, 2004, 36 (4): 345-368.

[259] HE K, MIAO P. The impact of audit quality on firms' cost of equity capital [J].Friends of Accounting, 2012 (24): 66-70. (in Chinese)

[260] LIU W L, RUAN S. Research on the impact of audit quality of audit firms on the cost of equity capital of listed companies[J].Commercial Accounting, 2017 (9): 39-42. (in Chinese)

[261] BRENNAN M J, CHORDIA T, SUBRAHMANYAM A. Alternative factor specifications, security characteristics, and the cross-section of expected stock returns[J].Journal of Financial Economics, 1998, 49 (3): 345-373.

[262] LIPSON M L, MORTAL S. Liquidity and capital structure[J].Journal of Financial Markets, 2009, 12 (4): 611-644.

[263] LU Y J, YE H M. The relationship between investor protection and cost of equity capital[J].Securities Market Herald, 2007 (10): 4-11. (in Chinese)

[264] BLUME M E. Betas and their regression tendencies[J].The Journal of Finance, 1975, 30 (3): 785-795.

[265] SUN K, ZHANG X L. An empirical study on audit firm size and audit quality[J].Journal of Dongbei University of Finance and Economics, 2011 (5): 56-61. (in Chinese)

[266] DEFOND M L. The association between changes in client firm agency costs and auditor switching[J].Auditing, 1992, 11 (1): 16-31.

[267] FIRTH M. The provision of nonaudit services by accounting firms to their audit clients[J].Contemporary Accounting Research, 1997, 14 (2): 1-21.

[268] KHALIL S, MAGNAN M L, COHEN J R. Dual-class shares and audit pricing: evidence from the Canadian markets[J]. Auditing: A Journal of Practice & Theory, 2008, 27 (2): 199-216.

[269] BARTON J. Who cares about auditor reputation?[J].Contemporary Accounting Research, 2005, 22 (3): 549-586.

[270] WANG Q, WONG T J, XIA L J. State ownership, the institutional environment, and auditor choice: evidence from China [J]. Journal of Accounting and Economics, 2008, 46 (1): 112–134.

[271] LIU X L, HAO C, CHU Y P. Research on the corporate governance influence on audit opinion: based on the panel data of China's private listed firms from 2007 to 2011 [J]. Auditing Research, 2012 (5): 51 – 57. (in Chinese)

[272] MAGEE R P, TSENG M C. Audit pricing and independence [J]. The Accounting Review, 1990, 65 (2): 315–336.

[273] ELITZUR R R, FALK H. Auctions for audit services and low-balling [J]. Auditing, 1996, 15 (s): 41–56.

[274] DAVIS L R, SOO B S, TROMPETER G M. Auditor tenure and the ability to meet or beat earnings forecasts [J]. Contemporary Accounting Research, 2009, 26 (2): 517–548.

[275] CHI W C, HUANG H C, LIAO Y C, et al. Mandatory audit partner rotation, audit quality, and market perception: evidence from Taiwan [J]. Contemporary Accounting Research, 2009, 26 (2): 359–391.

[276] WANG J S, CHEN H W. Auditor tenure and audit quality of firms cited for fraudulent financial reporting: based on non-financial data [J]. Journal of Shanxi Finance and Economics University, 2010, 32 (1): 115 – 124. (in Chinese)

[277] HUANG H W, RAGHUNANDAN K, HUANG T C, et al. Fee discounting and audit quality following audit firm and audit partner changes: Chinese evidence[J].The Accounting Review, 2015, 90 (4): 1517–1546.

[278] ZHANG R, TIAN G L, QI B, et al. Audit firm change, initial audit fee discount and audit quality[J].Management Review, 2018, 30 (2): 183–199. (in Chinese)

[279] HAN H L, CHEN H W. A structuralist analysis on the determinants of audit market structure [J]. Journal of Zhejiang University (Humanities and Social Sciences), 2009, 39 (2): 91–102. (in Chinese)

[280] CHI W C, DOUTHETT E B, LISIC L L. Client importance and audit partner independence[J]. Journal of Accounting and Public Policy, 2012, 31 (3): 320–336.

[281] SHARMA V D, SHARMA D S, ANANTHANARAYANAN U. Client importance and earnings management: the moderating role of audit committees[J]. Auditing: A Journal of Practice & Theory, 2011, 30 (3):

125–156.

[282] CRASWELL A, STOKES D J, LAUGHTON J. Auditor independence and fee dependence[J]. Journal of Accounting and Economics, 2002, 33 (2): 253–275.

[283] HOPE O K, LANGLI J C. Auditor independence in a private firm and low litigation risk setting[J].The Accounting Review, 2010, 85 (2): 573–605.

[284] CHUNG H, KALLAPUR S. Client importance, nonaudit services, and abnormal accruals[J].The Accounting Review, 2003, 78 (4): 931–955.

[285] HU N W, CHEN H W. Client importance, audit risk and auditor reporting decision[J].Journal of Central University of Finance & Economics, 2014, 1 (6): 52–59. (in Chinese)

[286] WANG L Y. Corporate governance and financial reporting mechanism: a comparison on A-share/H-share financial statements[J]. Journal of Audit & Economics, 2008, 23 (4): 109–109. (in Chinese)

[287] Ministry of Finance of the People's Republic of China (MOF). Responses from the heads of the accounting department of the Ministry of Finance and the accounting department of the China Securities Regulatory Commission to journalists on the approval of large mainland audit firms to engage in the H-share audits[EB/OL]. (2010–12–10) [2022–11–19].http: //kjs. mof. gov. cn/zhengcejiedu/201101/t20110113_412569. htm. (in Chinese)

[288] Wang J, Tweedie D. Joint statement of the secretary-general of the China Accounting Standards Committee and the chairman of the International Accounting Standards Board[EB/OL]. (2005–11–17) [2022–11–19]. http: //upload. news. esnai. com/news/20051171233629722. pdf.

[289] KUAN I C, NORONHA C. The progress of accounting harmonization in China: a comparison of A-share and H-share financial results[J].Managerial Auditing Journal, 2007, 22 (6): 620–640.

[290] China Accounting Standards Committee (CASC) and Hong Kong Institute of Certified Public Accountants (HKICPA). Joint declaration on the converged China Accounting Standards for Business Enterprises and Hong Kong Financial Reporting Standards[EB/OL]. (2007–12–06) [2022–11–19].http: //app1. hkicpa. org. hk/professionaltechnical/mainland_standards_convergence/accounting/JD_e. pdf.

[291] Ministry of Finance of the People's Republic of China (MOF). Letter from the Ministry of Finance seeking opinions on the road map for the continuous

and comprehensive convergence of the Chinese Accounting Standards with the International Financial Reporting Standards[EB/OL]. (2009-09-02) [2022-11-19]. https://www.chinaacc.com/new/63_64_/2009_9_10_wa2146263817101990022048.shtml. (in Chinese)

[292] Hong Kong Exchanges and Clearing Limited (HKEx). Consultation conclusions on acceptance of mainland accounting and auditing standards and mainland audit firms for mainland incorporated companies listed in Hong Kong[EB/OL]. (2010-12) [2022-11-19]. https://www.hkex.com.hk/-/media/HKEX-Market/News/Market-Consultations/2006-to-2010/August-2009-Consultation-Paper/Conclusions/cp200908cc.pdf.

[293] CHEN D N. Audit foundation[M]. Beijing: China Commercial Publishing House, 1998. (in Chinese)

[294] COASE R H. The nature of the firm[J]. Economica, 1937, 4(16): 386-405.

[295] DEMSETZ H. The exchange and enforcement of property rights[J]. The Journal of Law & Economics, 1964, 7(10): 11-26.

[296] ALCHIAN A A, DEMSETZ H. Production, information costs, and economic organization[J]. American Economic Review, 1972, 62(5): 777-795.

[297] CHEUNG S N S. The contractual nature of the firm[J]. The Journal of Law and Economics, 1983, 26(1): 1-21.

[298] JENSEN M C, MECKLING W H. Specific and general knowledge, and organizational structure[J]. Journal of Applied Corporate Finance, 1995, 8(2): 4-18.

[299] COASE R H. The problem of social cost[J]. The Journal of Law and Economics, 1960, 3(10): 1-44.

[300] ALCHIAN A A. Some economics of property rights[J]. https://www.jstor.org/stable/43206327, 1965, 30(4): 816-829.

[301] SHLEIFER A, VISHNY R W. A survey of corporate governance[J]. The Journal of Finance, 1997, 52(2): 737-783.

[302] PORTA L R, LOPEZ D S F, SHLEIFER A. Corporate ownership around the world[J]. The Journal of Finance, 1999, 54(2): 471-517.

[303] BEAVER W, KETTLER P, SCHOLES M. The association between market determined and accounting determined risk measures[J]. The Accounting Review, 1970, 45(4): 654-682.

[304] FANG J X, HONG J Q. Abnormal audit fees and the shredded audit quality:

evidence from China's public companies [J]. China Accounting Review, 2008, 6 (4): 425–442. (in Chinese)

[305] BARYOSEF S, LIVNAT J. Auditor selection: an incentive-signalling approach[J].Accounting and Business Research, 1984, 14 (56): 301–309.

[306] CHOW C W, KRAMER L, WALLACE W A. The environment of auditing [M].Sarasota: American Accounting Association, 1988.

[307] LYS T, WATTS R L. Lawsuits against auditors[J].Journal of Accounting Research, 1994, 32 (s): 65–93.

[308] DYE R A. Auditing standards, legal liability, and auditor wealth[J].Journal of Political Economy, 1993, 101 (5): 887–914.

[309] MENON K, WILLIAMS D D. The insurance hypothesis and market prices [J].The Accounting Review, 1994, 69 (2): 327–342.

[310] WALLACE W A. The economic role of the audit in free and regulated markets: a look back and a look forward [J]. Research in Accounting Regulation, 2004, 17 (s): 267–298.

[311] WALLACE W A. The economic role of the audit in free and regulated markets[M].Rochester: University of Rochester, 1980.

[312] ZHANG H F. The evolution of western economics of regulation[M].Beijing: Economic Science Press, 2005. (in Chinese)

[313] STIGLER G J, FRIEDLAND C. What can regulators regulate? The case of electricity[J].The Journal of Law and Economics, 1962, 5 (10): 1–16.

[314] VISCUSI W K, HARRINGTON J E, VERNON J M. Economics of regulation and antitrust[M].Cambridge: MIT Press, 2005.

[315] NORTH D C. Institutions, institutional change and economic performance[M]. Cambridge: Cambridge University Press, 1990.

[316] STIGLER G J. The theory of economic regulation[J].The Bell Journal of Economics and Management Science, 1971, 2 (1): 3–21.

[317] YANG J W. Industrial economics [M]. Shanghai: Shanghai Academy of Social Sciences Press, 2008. (in Chinese)

[318] ZHANG Y X. Theory and practice of traceability system for quality and safety of agricultural products[M].Beijing: China Agricultural Science and Technology Press, 2008. (in Chinese)

[319] SILVOSO J A, ANDERSON H A, GRINAKER R L, et al. A statement of basic auditing concepts[J].Studies in Accounting Research, 1973, 6 (47):

14-74.

[320] HU L M. Public goods and the function of government[J].Contemporary Finance & Economics, 2001, 27(6): 26-29. (in Chinese)

[321] BARTON J, WAYMIRE G. Investor protection under unregulated financial reporting[J].Journal of Accounting and Economics, 2004, 38(1): 65-116.

[322] SUNDER S, CYERT R M. Theory of accounting and control[M]. Chula Vista: South-Western College Pub, 1997.

[323] SIMUNIC D A, STEIN M T. Product differentiation in auditing: auditor choice in the market for unseasoned new issues[M]. Vancouver: Canadian Certified General, 1987.

[324] PALMROSE Z V. 1987 competitive manuscript co-winner: an analysis of auditor litigation and audit service quality[J].The Accounting Review, 1988, 63(1): 55-73.

[325] DEFOND M L, SUBRAMANYAM K R. Auditor changes and discretionary accruals[J].Journal of Accounting and Economics, 1998, 25(1): 35-67.

[326] HAY J R, SHLEIFER A, VISHNY R W. Toward a theory of legal reform [J].European Economic Review, 1996, 40(3-5): 559-567.

[327] HAY J R, SHLEIFER A. Private enforcement of public laws: a theory of legal reform[J].American Economic Review, 1998, 88(2): 398-403.

[328] MAHONEY P G. Mandatory disclosure as a solution to agency problems[J]. University of Chicago Law Review, 1995, 62(3): 1047-1112.

[329] LEUZ C, VERRECCHIA R E. The economic consequences of increased disclosure[J].Journal of Accounting Research, 2000, 38(s): 91-124.

[330] BUSHEE B J, LEUZ C. Economic consequences of SEC disclosure regulation: evidence from the OTC bulletin board[J].Journal of Accounting and Economics, 2005, 39(2): 233-264.

[331] BAIMAN S, VERRECCHIA R E. The relation among capital markets, financial disclosure, production efficiency, and insider trading[J].Journal of Accounting Research, 1996, 34(1): 1-22.

[332] VERRECCHIA R E. Disclosure and the cost of capital: a discussion[J]. Journal of Accounting and Economics, 1999, 26(1-3): 271-283.

[333] LANSFORD B, LEV B, TUCKER J W. Causes and consequences of disaggregating earnings guidance [J]. Journal of Business Finance & Accounting, 2013, 40(1-2): 26-54.

[334] HOPE O K, THOMAS W B. Managerial empire building and firm disclosure [J].Journal of Accounting Research, 2008, 46 (3) : 591-626.

[335] LEUZ C, WYSOCKI P D. Economic consequences of financial reporting and disclosure regulation: a review and suggestions for future research[EB/OL]. (2008-03-18) [2022-11-19] .https: //ssrn. com/abstract = 1105398.

[336] AGHION P, HERMALIN B. Legal restrictions on private contracts can enhance efficiency[J].Journal of Law, Economics and Organisations, 1990, 6 (2) : 381-409.

[337] CHEN L R, HAN B. Can mandatory internal control auditing bring higher investment efficiency? Empirical evidence from Chinese A-share main board SOE[J].Commercial Research, 2015 (9) : 83-91. (in Chinese)

[338] SPENCE M. Job market signaling[J].Quarterly Journal of Economics, 1973, 87 (3) : 355-374.

[339] DHARAN B G. Auditing as a signal in small business lending [J]. The Journal of Entrepreneurial Finance, 1992, 2 (1) : 1-11.

[340] ETTREDGE M, SIMON D, SMITH D, et al. Why do companies purchase timely quarterly reviews? [J]. Journal of Accounting and Economics, 1994, 18 (2) : 131-155.

[341] HAW I M, QI D Q, WU W. The economic consequence of voluntary auditing [J]. Journal of Accounting, Auditing & Finance, 2008, 23 (1): 63-93.

[342] COLLIS J. Audit exemption and the demand for voluntary audit: a comparative study of the UK and Denmark [J]. International Journal of Auditing, 2010, 14 (2) : 211-231.

[343] COLLIS J. Determinants of voluntary audit and voluntary full accounts in micro-and non-micro small companies in the UK [J]. Accounting and Business Research, 2012, 42 (4) : 441-468.

[344] KAUSAR A, SHROFF N, WHITE H. Real effects of the audit choice [J]. Journal of Accounting and Economics, 2016, 62 (1) : 157-181.

[345] OJALA H, COLLIS J, KINNUNEN J, et al. The demand for voluntary audit in micro-companies: evidence from Finland [J]. International Journal of Auditing, 2016, 20 (3) : 267-277.

[346] HU X. Demand for audit between companies [J]. Journal of the Graduates Sun Yat-Sen University (Social Sciences), 2007, 28 (3) : 73-86. (in Chinese)

[347] LIU B, WANG X F, HE L, et al. Demand motivation, accounting information quality and economic consequences of voluntary interim report audit: evidence from Chinese listed companies in 2002–2006[J].Economic Science, 2008 (3): 97–108. (in Chinese)

[348] YU S H. Research on motivation and quality of voluntary auditing: evidence from interim reporting in China[M].Dalian: Dalian Publishing House, 2008. (in Chinese)

[349] ZHOU L. Research on motivation of voluntary auditing: based on interim reporting in China[J].China Management Informationization, 2010, 13 (14): 42–45. (in Chinese)

[350] JIAN J H, YANG F. Empirical research on the factors and market reaction of voluntary auditing of the interim reports: based on the listed companies in China[J].Auditing Research, 2012 (2): 90–97. (in Chinese)

[351] HAN D Q, ZHANG Y Z. Analysis of motivation and response of voluntary audit of interim financial report[J].Taxation and Economy, 2013 (6): 55–61. (in Chinese)

[352] CHEN C, LEE E, LOBO G J, et al. Who benefits from IFRS convergence in China? [J]. Journal of Accounting, Auditing & Finance, 2019, 34 (1): 99–124.

[353] CHEN C J P, SRINIDHI B, SU X J. Effect of auditing: evidence from variability of stock returns and trading volume [J]. China Journal of Accounting Research, 2014, 7 (4): 223–245.

[354] BOTOSAN C A, PLUMLEE M A. Assessing alternative proxies for the expected risk premium[J].The Accounting Review, 2005, 80 (1): 21–53.

[355] MAO X S, YE K T, ZHANG D. Measuring and evaluating cost of equity capital: evidence from Chinese stock markets[J].Accounting Research, 2012 (11): 12–22. (in Chinese)

[356] DHALIWAL D, HEITZMAN S, LI O Z. Taxes, leverage, and the cost of equity capital[J].Journal of Accounting Research, 2006, 44 (4): 691–723.

[357] LI Z N, WILSON W M, ZHANG S N. The cost of equity implications of accounting for employee stock options[EB/OL]. (2014-01-14) [2022-11-19].https://ssrn.com/abstract=2378952.

[358] GUO L, TANG L. Cost of capital and liquidity of cross-listed Chinese companies[J].Journal of Knowledge Globalization, 2008, 1 (2): 1–18.

[359] EL GHOUL S, GUEDHAMI O, KWOK C C Y, et al. Does corporate social responsibility affect the cost of capital? [J]. Journal of Banking & Finance, 2011, 35 (9): 2388–2406.

[360] MISHRA D R. The dark side of CEO ability: CEO general managerial skills and cost of equity capital [J]. Journal of Corporate Finance, 2014, 29 (c): 390–409.

[361] LU W B, GUAN F, ZHANG P P, et al. Media coverage, information disclosure environment and equity cost[J]. Accounting Research, 2014 (12): 66–71. (in Chinese)

[362] CHEN S S, LI W Y, WU D L. XBRL, corporate governance and cost of equity: based on the full view of financial information value chain [J]. Accounting Research, 2015 (3): 64–71. (in Chinese)

[363] CAO Y, MYERS L A, TSANG A, et al. Management forecasts and the cost of equity capital: international evidence [J]. Review of Accounting Studies, 2017, 22 (2): 791–838.

[364] HAIL L, LEUZ C. International differences in the cost of equity capital: do legal institutions and securities regulation matter? [J]. Journal of Accounting Research, 2006, 44 (3): 485–531.

[365] REICHELT K J, WANG D C. National and office-specific measures of auditor industry expertise and effects on audit quality [J]. Journal of Accounting Research, 2010, 48 (3): 647–686.

[366] KOTHARI S P, LEONE A J, WASLEY C E. Performance matched discretionary accrual measures [J]. Journal of Accounting and Economics, 2005, 39 (1): 163–197.

[367] China Securities Regulatory Commission (CSRC). Revised guidance for industry classification of listed companies [EB/OL]. (2012-10-26) [2022-11-19]. http://www.csrc.gov.cn/csrc/c101864/c1024632/content.shtml. (in Chinese)

[368] KENNEDY P. A guide to econometrics[M]. Cambridge: MIT Press, 2003.

[369] HUNG M Y, WONG T J, ZHANG T Y. Political relations and overseas stock exchange listing: evidence from Chinese state-owned enterprises [C]. Taiwan: 2008 International Conference on Corporate Governance and Financial Integration,
2008.

[370] KAPLAN S N, ZINGALES L. Do investment-cash flow sensitivities provide useful measures of financing constraints? [J]. Quarterly Journal of Economics, 1997, 112(1): 169–215.

[371] LAMONT O, POLK C, SAAá -REQUEJO J. Financial constraints and stock returns[J].Review of Financial Studies, 2001, 14(2): 529–554.

[372] WHITED T M, WU G J. Financial constraints risk[J].Review of Financial Studies, 2006, 19(2): 531–559.

[373] HADLOCK C J, PIERCE J R. New evidence on measuring financial constraints: moving beyond the KZ index[J].Review of Financial Studies, 2010, 23(5): 1909–1940.

[374] LAFOND R, ROYCHOWDHURY S. Managerial ownership and accounting conservatism[J].Journal of Accounting Research, 2008, 46(1): 101–135.

[375] GRAY S J. The impact of international accounting differences from a security-analysis perspective: some European evidence [J]. Journal of Accounting Research, 1980, 18(1): 64–76.

[376] HAVERTY J L. Are IFRS and US GAAP converging? Some evidence from People's Republic of China companies listed on the New York Stock Exchange[J].Journal of International Accounting, Auditing and Taxation, 2006, 15(1): 48–71.

[377] ZHANG X F. Does the accounting standards convergence enhance the accounting transparency? An empirical study on the A+H share companies [J].Economic Survey, 2014, 31(5): 115–120. (in Chinese)

[378] WEETMAN P, JONES E A E, ADAMS C A, et al. Profit measurement and UK accounting standards: a case of increasing disharmony in relation to US GAAP and IASs[J]. Accounting and Business Research, 1998, 28(3): 189–208.

[379] STREET D L, NICHOLS N B, GRAY S J. Assessing the acceptability of international accounting standards in the US: an empirical study of the materiality of US GAAP reconciliations by non-US companies complying with IASC standards[J].International Journal of Accounting, 2000, 35(1): 27–63.

[380] LAWRENCE A, MINUTTIMEZA M, ZHANG P. Can Big 4 versus non-Big 4 differences in audit-quality proxies be attributed to client characteristics? [J].The Accounting Review, 2011, 86(1): 259–286.

[381] ARMSTRONG C S, JAGOLINZER A D, LARCKER D F. Chief executive officer equity incentives and accounting irregularities[J].Journal of Accounting Research, 2010, 48(2): 225–271.

[382] FRANK K A. Impact of a confounding variable on a regression coefficient [J].Sociological Methods & Research, 2000, 29(2): 147–194.

[383] LARCKER D F, RUSTICUS T O. On the use of instrumental variables in accounting research[J].Journal of Accounting and Economics, 2010, 49(3): 186–205.

[384] CROCI E, PETMEZAS D. Do risk-taking incentives induce CEOs to invest? Evidence from acquisitions[J].Journal of Corporate Finance, 2015, 32(c): 1–23.

[385] FU R H, KRAFT A, ZHANG H. Financial reporting frequency, information asymmetry, and the cost of equity[J].Journal of Accounting and Economics, 2012, 54(2–3): 132–149.

[386] ALLEN F, QIAN J, QIAN M. Law, finance, and economic growth in China [J].Journal of Financial Economics, 2005, 77(1): 57–116.

[387] PISTOR K, XU C G. Governing stock markets in transition economies: lessons from China[J].American Law and Economics Review, 2005, 7(1): 184–210.

[388] CHEN Z H, KE B, YANG Z F. Minority shareholders' control rights and the quality of corporate decisions in weak investor protection countries: a natural experiment from China[J].The Accounting Review, 2013, 88(4): 1211–1238.

[389] DEFOND M L, PARK C W. The reversal of abnormal accruals and the market valuation of earnings surprises[J].The Accounting Review, 2001, 76(3): 375–404.

[390] BECKER C L, DEFOND M L, JIAMBALVO J, et al. The effect of audit quality on earnings management[J].Contemporary Accounting Research, 1998, 15(1): 1–24.

[391] ASHBAUGH H, LAFOND R, MAYHEW B W. Do nonaudit services compromise auditor independence? Further evidence[J].The Accounting Review, 2003, 78(3): 611–639.

[392] China Securities Regulatory Commission (CSRC). Q & A No. 5 on the requirements of the financial statement reconciliation and disclosure for

publicly listed firms that prepare financial statements according to both domestic and foreign generally accepted principles[EB/OL].(2001-11-07)[2022-11-19].http://www.sse.com.cn/services/sselisting/relevantrules/info/c/c_20150912_3985758.shtml. (in Chinese)

[393] ZHANG R, WONG R M K, LO A W Y, et al. Can mandatory dual audit reduce the cost of equity? Evidence from China[J].Accounting and Business Research, 2022, 52(3): 291-320.

[394] ZHANG R, WONG R M K, TIAN G L, et al. Positive spillover effect and audit quality: a study of cancelling China's dual audit system[J].Accounting & Finance, 2021, 61(1): 205-239.

Appendices

Appendix Ⅰ Different Cut-Offs of Equity Financing Demand

Based on the notion that lower cash on hand along with higher leverage generally implies higher demand for equity financing, I identify firms whose ratio of cash on hand to total assets is in the lowest tercile and asset-liability ratio is in the highest tercile as firms with higher demand for equity financing, and I identify the remaining firms as those with lower demand for equity financing in the tests of H2 (see Section 4. 3. 4) and H6 (see Section 5. 3. 4) in the main body of this study.

This appendix shows the results with alternative cut-offs. Specifically, I separately rank the sample firms into five quintiles, four quartiles and above- versus below-median according to their ratio of cash on hand to total assets. Based on the sample firms' asset-liability ratio, I also separately rank them into five quintiles, four quartiles and above- versus below-median. In each division category, I identify firms with ratio of cash on hand to total assets in the bottom quantile and asset-liability ratio in the top quantile as firms with higher equity financing demand; the remaining firms are identified as those with lower equity financing demand.

Then, I re-estimate Eq. (4-6) for each subsample in each category. The results are shown in Panel A of Table A-1 below. Column (1) shows the results within firms with ratio of cash on hand to total assets in the lowest quintile and asset-liability ratio in the highest quintile, and Column (2) shows the results within the remaining firms. Column (3) shows the results within firms with ratio of cash on hand to total assets in the lowest quartile and asset-liability ratio in the highest quartile, and Column (4) shows the results within the remaining firms. Column (5) shows the results within firms with ratio of cash on hand to total assets below the sample median and asset-liability ratio above the sample median, and Column (6) shows the results within the remaining firms. Throughout these division categories, the coefficients on $DUAL_{t,i} * POST_{t,i}$ are consistently significant and positive in firms with higher equity financing demand[i. e. , in Columns (1), (3) and (5)] while insignificant in firms with lower equity financing demand[i. e. , in Columns (2), (4) and (6)].These findings are similar to those reported in Columns (1) and (2) of Table 4-10. Therefore, different cut-offs of firms' equity financing demand do not alter the inferences drawn from the results in the main text.

I also re-estimate Eq. (5-1) for each subsample in each category. The results are shown in Panel B of Table A-1. Similarly, Column (1) shows the results within firms with ratio of cash on hand to total assets in the lowest quintile and asset-liability ratio in the highest quintile, and Column (2) shows the results within the remaining firms. Column (3) shows the results within firms with ratio of cash on hand to total assets in the lowest quartile and asset-liability ratio in the highest quartile, and Column (4) shows the results within the remaining firms. Column (5) shows the results within firms with ratio of cash on hand to total assets below the sample median and asset-liability ratio above the sample median, and Column (6) shows the results within the remaining firms. Throughout these division categories, the coefficients on $DUAL\_V_{t,i}$ are consistently significant and negative at the 0. 01 level in firms with higher equity financing demand[i. e. , in Columns (1), (3) and (5)] while only marginally significant or insignificant in firms with lower equity financing demand[i. e. , in Columns (2), (4) and (6)].These findings are similar to those reported in Columns (1) and (2) of Table 5-7. Thus, the inferences drawn from the results in the main text are robust to different cut-offs of firms' equity financing demand.

Table A-1 Regression Results of Tests of H2 and H6 with Different Cut-Offs of Equity Financing Demand

Panel A: Regression Results of Tests of H2 with Different Cut-Offs of Equity Financing Demand [Eq. (4-6)]						
Variable	Dependent Variable: $COE\_GLS_{t,i}$					
	Equity Financing Demand (Quintile)		Equity Financing Demand (Quartile)		Equity Financing Demand (Median)	
	(1) High	(2) Low	(3) High	(4) Low	(5) High	(6) Low
Intercept	0. 073*** (2. 595)	0. 002 (0. 392)	0. 043* (1. 890)	0. 003 (0. 545)	0. 003 (0. 317)	0. 002 (0. 363)

续表

Panel A: Regression Results of Tests of H2 with Different Cut-Offs of Equity Financing Demand [Eq. (4-6)]

Variable	Dependent Variable: $COE\_GLS_{t,i}$					
	Equity Financing Demand (Quintile)		Equity Financing Demand (Quartile)		Equity Financing Demand (Median)	
	(1) High	(2) Low	(3) High	(4) Low	(5) High	(6) Low
$DUAL_{t,i}$	−0.049*** (−4.209)	−0.009*** (−2.704)	−0.047*** (−4.901)	−0.008** (−2.433)	−0.032*** (−6.046)	−0.003 (−0.878)
$POST_{t,i}$	0.005 (1.632)	0.007*** (12.153)	0.005** (2.288)	0.007*** (12.045)	0.004*** (3.538)	0.008*** (12.360)
$DUAL_{t,i} * POST_{t,i}$	0.014* (1.949)	0.004 (1.363)	0.012* (1.856)	0.004 (1.261)	0.014*** (3.212)	0.001 (0.237)
$AH_{t,i}$	0.037*** (4.410)	0.005** (2.007)	0.032*** (4.476)	0.005* (1.858)	0.018*** (4.765)	0.001 (0.327)
$Size_{t,i}$	0.000 (0.283)	0.003*** (13.049)	0.002 (1.635)	0.003*** (12.680)	0.003*** (6.852)	0.003*** (11.145)
$Beta_{t,i}$	0.040*** (4.745)	0.010*** (13.466)	0.033*** (5.391)	0.010*** (13.273)	0.016*** (7.277)	0.009*** (12.035)
$MB_{t,i}$	−0.005*** (−9.101)	−0.004*** (−46.279)	−0.005*** (−10.876)	−0.004*** (−45.898)	−0.004*** (−22.284)	−0.004*** (−42.094)
$DE_{t,i}$	0.001 (0.223)	0.015*** (13.467)	0.002 (0.712)	0.016*** (13.441)	0.007*** (5.165)	0.015*** (8.219)
$Std\_Ret_{t,i}$	−0.027 (−1.118)	−0.008** (−2.047)	−0.022 (−1.149)	−0.009** (−2.073)	−0.014 (−1.635)	−0.009* (−1.890)
$Liq_{t,i}$	−0.130 (−1.459)	−0.202*** (−14.232)	−0.192*** (−2.850)	−0.199*** (−13.859)	−0.201*** (−6.618)	−0.200*** (−12.718)
$Growth_{t,i}$	0.001* (1.850)	0.001*** (10.707)	0.001*** (3.192)	0.001*** (10.484)	0.001*** (5.620)	0.001*** (9.821)
$SOE_{t,i}$	−0.013*** (−4.699)	−0.005*** (−10.691)	−0.010*** (−4.983)	−0.005*** (−10.314)	−0.004*** (−4.881)	−0.005*** (−9.975)
$Disp_{t,i}$	0.004 (1.440)	−0.001 (−1.290)	0.002 (1.113)	−0.001 (−1.217)	0.001 (0.728)	−0.002* (−1.807)
$Bias_{t,i}$	−0.017 (−0.629)	0.029*** (3.766)	−0.002 (−0.072)	0.029*** (3.708)	0.031** (2.560)	0.025*** (2.701)
$Big4_{t,i}$	0.000 (0.042)	−0.001 (−1.163)	0.001 (0.214)	−0.001 (−1.378)	−0.002 (−1.078)	−0.001 (−0.492)

续表

Panel A: Regression Results of Tests of H2 with Different Cut-Offs of Equity Financing Demand [Eq. (4-6)]

Variable	Dependent Variable: $COE\_GLS_{t,i}$					
	Equity Financing Demand (Quintile)		Equity Financing Demand (Quartile)		Equity Financing Demand (Median)	
	(1) High	(2) Low	(3) High	(4) Low	(5) High	(6) Low
N	469	8178	712	7935	2656	5991
Adj. R^2	0. 428	0. 472	0. 425	0. 472	0. 442	0. 465
F	24. 384	488. 237	36. 002	473. 204	141. 488	347. 689

Panel B: Regression Results of Tests of H6 with Different Cut-Offs of Equity Financing Demand[Eq. (5-1)]

Variable	Dependent Variable: $COE\_GLS_{t,i}$					
	Equity Financing Demand (Quintile)		Equity Financing Demand (Quartile)		Equity Financing Demand (Median)	
	(1) High	(2) Low	(3) High	(4) Low	(5) High	(6) Low
Intercept	0. 013 (0. 423)	−0. 044 * * * (−7. 350)	−0. 013 (−0. 494)	−0. 043 * * * (−7. 204)	−0. 034 * * * (−2. 829)	−0. 046 * * * (−6. 766)
$DUAL\_V_{t,i}$	−0. 024 * * * (−2. 850)	−0. 004 * (−1. 723)	−0. 025 * * * (−3. 409)	−0. 004 (−1. 454)	−0. 012 * * * (−3. 157)	−0. 003 (−0. 976)
$AH_{t,i}$	0. 022 * * * (3. 226)	−0. 003 (−1. 302)	0. 020 * * * (3. 255)	−0. 003 (−1. 545)	0. 009 * * * (2. 843)	−0. 006 * * (−2. 421)
$Size_{t,i}$	0. 003 * * (2. 249)	0. 004 * * * (17. 106)	0. 003 * * * (3. 330)	0. 004 * * * (16. 837)	0. 004 * * * (7. 807)	0. 004 * * * (15. 394)
$Beta_{t,i}$	0. 005 (0. 629)	0. 003 * * * (3. 978)	0. 007 (1. 036)	0. 003 * * * (3. 919)	0. 001 (0. 613)	0. 003 * * * (4. 010)
$MB_{t,i}$	−0. 004 * * * (−8. 438)	−0. 004 * * * (−41. 516)	−0. 004 * * * (−8. 885)	−0. 004 * * * (−41. 386)	−0. 004 * * * (−18. 484)	−0. 004 * * * (−38. 702)
$DE_{t,i}$	0. 005 (1. 626)	0. 013 * * * (11. 983)	0. 005 * * (2. 028)	0. 014 * * * (12. 168)	0. 009 * * * (6. 195)	0. 014 * * * (7. 915)
$Std\_Ret_{t,i}$	−0. 056 * * (−2. 098)	−0. 028 * * * (−6. 189)	−0. 063 * * * (−2. 842)	−0. 027 * * * (−5. 966)	−0. 046 * * * (−4. 756)	−0. 025 * * * (−4. 944)
$Liq_{t,i}$	−0. 006 (−0. 052)	−0. 076 * * * (−5. 050)	−0. 074 (−0. 838)	−0. 074 * * * (−4. 915)	−0. 048 (−1. 341)	−0. 082 * * * (−5. 030)

续表

Panel B: Regression Results of Tests of H6 with Different Cut-Offs of Equity Financing Demand [Eq. (5-1)]						
Variable	Dependent Variable: $COE\_GLS_{t,i}$					
	Equity Financing Demand (Quintile)		Equity Financing Demand (Quartile)		Equity Financing Demand (Median)	
	(1) High	(2) Low	(3) High	(4) Low	(5) High	(6) Low
$Growth_{t,i}$	0.000 (0.676)	0.001*** (7.132)	0.000 (1.293)	0.001*** (7.223)	0.001*** (3.249)	0.001*** (6.728)
$SOE_{t,i}$	−0.008*** (−3.129)	−0.002*** (−4.532)	−0.006*** (−2.892)	−0.002*** (−4.236)	−0.001 (−1.038)	−0.003*** (−5.105)
$Disp_{t,i}$	0.006** (2.309)	−0.001 (−1.133)	0.003 (1.488)	−0.001 (−0.861)	0.001 (0.849)	−0.001 (−0.867)
$Bias_{t,i}$	−0.078*** (−3.053)	0.011 (1.341)	−0.072*** (−3.066)	0.013 (1.527)	−0.010 (−0.744)	0.009 (0.837)
$Big4_{t,i}$	−0.002 (−0.395)	−0.000 (−0.118)	−0.001 (−0.184)	−0.000 (−0.278)	−0.002 (−1.190)	0.000 (0.322)
Year Fixed Effects	Yes	Yes	Yes	Yes	Yes	Yes
Industry Fixed Effects	Yes	Yes	Yes	Yes	Yes	Yes
N	372	6591	549	6414	2060	4903
Adj. R^2	0.600	0.609	0.569	0.609	0.586	0.609
F	19.512	302.536	24.384	295.262	89.329	225.800

Notes: In Panel A (B), Column (1) shows the results of Eq. (4-6) [Eq. (5-1)] for the subsample with ratio of cash on hand to total assets in the lowest quintile and asset-liability ratio in the highest quintile, while Column (2) shows the results of Eq. (4-6) [Eq. (5-1)] for the remaining subsample; Column (3) shows the results of Eq. (4-6) [Eq. (5-1)] for the subsample with ratio of cash on hand to total assets in the lowest quartile and asset-liability ratio in the highest quartile, while Column (4) shows the results of Eq. (4-6) [Eq. (5-1)] for the remaining subsample; Column (5) shows the results of Eq. (4-6) [Eq. (5-1)] for the subsample with ratio of cash on hand to total assets below the sample median and asset-liability ratio above the sample median, while Column (6) shows the results of Eq. (4-6) [Eq. (5-1)] for the remaining subsample; ***, ** and * represent significance at the 0.01, 0.05 and 0.10 level, respectively, using two-tailed tests; *t*-statistics are shown in parentheses; variable definitions and measurement in Panel A (B) are reported in Table 4-6 (Table 5-2).

Appendix Ⅱ　Detailed Auditor Information

The detailed auditor information of the sample firms in Chapter 6 are shown in Table A-2.

Table A-2　Auditor Information of Sample Firms in Chapter 6 (N=263)

A-share Stock Code	H-share Stock Code	Year	Mainland-Based Auditor	Hong Kong-Based Auditor
000063. SZ	0763. HK	2012	Ernst & Young Hua Ming CPAs	Ernst & Young CPAs
000063. SZ	0763. HK	2013	Ernst & Young Hua Ming CPAs	Ernst & Young CPAs
000063. SZ	0763. HK	2014	Ernst & Young Hua Ming CPAs	Ernst & Young CPAs
000063. SZ	0763. HK	2015	Ernst & Young Hua Ming CPAs	Ernst & Young CPAs
000338. SZ	2338. HK	2013	Ernst & Young Hua Ming CPAs	—
000338. SZ	2338. HK	2014	Ernst & Young Hua Ming CPAs	—
000338. SZ	2338. HK	2015	Ernst & Young Hua Ming CPAs	—
000488. SZ	1812. HK	2010	RSM China CPAs	RSM Hong Kong CPAs
000488. SZ	1812. HK	2011	RSM China CPAs	—
000488. SZ	1812. HK	2012	RSM China CPAs	—
000488. SZ	1812. HK	2013	Ruihua CPAs	—
000488. SZ	1812. HK	2014	Ruihua CPAs	—
000488. SZ	1812. HK	2015	Ruihua CPAs	—
000585. SZ	0042. HK	2010	Shenzhen Peng Cheng CPAs	Ting Ho Kwan & Chan CPAs
000585. SZ	0042. HK	2011	Shenzhen Peng Cheng CPAs	Ting Ho Kwan & Chan CPAs
000585. SZ	0042. HK	2012	Crowe Horwath CPAs	—
000585. SZ	0042. HK	2013	Ruihua CPAs	—
000585. SZ	0042. HK	2014	Ruihua CPAs	—
000585. SZ	0042. HK	2015	Ruihua CPAs	—
000756. SZ	0719. HK	2010	ShineWing CPAs	ShineWing Hong Kong CPAs
000756. SZ	0719. HK	2011	ShineWing CPAs	ShineWing Hong Kong CPAs
000756. SZ	0719. HK	2012	ShineWing CPAs	ShineWing Hong Kong CPAs
000756. SZ	0719. HK	2013	ShineWing CPAs	ShineWing Hong Kong CPAs
000756. SZ	0719. HK	2014	ShineWing CPAs	ShineWing Hong Kong CPAs
000756. SZ	0719. HK	2015	ShineWing CPAs	—

续表

A-share Stock Code	H-share Stock Code	Year	Mainland-Based Auditor	Hong Kong-Based Auditor
000898. SZ	0347. HK	2010	RSM China CPAs	RSM Hong Kong CPAs
000898. SZ	0347. HK	2011	RSM China CPAs	RSM Hong Kong CPAs
000898. SZ	0347. HK	2012	RSM China CPAs	—
000898. SZ	0347. HK	2013	Ruihua CPAs	—
000898. SZ	0347. HK	2014	Ruihua CPAs	—
000898. SZ	0347. HK	2015	Ruihua CPAs	—
000921. SZ	0921. HK	2010	BDO Da Hua CPAs	BDO McCabe Lo CPAs
000921. SZ	0921. HK	2011	Crowe Horwath CPAs	BDO McCabe Lo CPAs
000921. SZ	0921. HK	2012	Crowe Horwath CPAs	—
000921. SZ	0921. HK	2013	Ruihua CPAs	—
000921. SZ	0921. HK	2014	Ruihua CPAs	—
000921. SZ	0921. HK	2015	Ruihua CPAs	—
600011. SH	0902. HK	2010	PwC Zhong Tian CPAs	PwC CPAs
600011. SH	0902. HK	2011	PwC Zhong Tian CPAs	PwC CPAs
600011. SH	0902. HK	2012	KPMG Hua Zhen CPAs	KPMG CPAs
600011. SH	0902. HK	2013	KPMG Hua Zhen CPAs	KPMG CPAs
600011. SH	0902. HK	2014	KPMG Hua Zhen CPAs	KPMG CPAs
600011. SH	0902. HK	2015	KPMG Hua Zhen CPAs	KPMG CPAs
600012. SH	0995. HK	2010	PwC Zhong Tian CPAs	PwC CPAs
600012. SH	0995. HK	2011	PwC Zhong Tian CPAs	PwC CPAs
600012. SH	0995. HK	2012	PwC Zhong Tian CPAs	PwC CPAs
600012. SH	0995. HK	2013	PwC Zhong Tian CPAs	PwC CPAs
600012. SH	0995. HK	2014	PwC Zhong Tian CPAs	PwC CPAs
600012. SH	0995. HK	2015	PwC Zhong Tian CPAs	PwC CPAs
600026. SH	1138. HK	2010	Baker Tilly International CPAs	Baker Tilly Hong Kong CPAs
600026. SH	1138. HK	2011	Baker Tilly International CPAs	Baker Tilly Hong Kong CPAs
600026. SH	1138. HK	2012	Baker Tilly International CPAs	Baker Tilly Hong Kong CPAs
600026. SH	1138. HK	2013	Baker Tilly International CPAs	Baker Tilly Hong Kong CPAs
600026. SH	1138. HK	2014	Baker Tilly International CPAs	Baker Tilly Hong Kong CPAs
600026. SH	1138. HK	2015	Baker Tilly International CPAs	Baker Tilly Hong Kong CPAs

续表

A-share Stock Code	H-share Stock Code	Year	Mainland-Based Auditor	Hong Kong-Based Auditor
600027. SH	1071. HK	2010	KPMG Hua Zhen CPAs	KPMG CPAs
600027. SH	1071. HK	2011	KPMG Hua Zhen CPAs	KPMG CPAs
600027. SH	1071. HK	2012	KPMG Hua Zhen CPAs	KPMG CPAs
600027. SH	1071. HK	2013	Deloitte & Touche Hua Yong CPAs	Deloitte & Touche CPAs
600027. SH	1071. HK	2014	Deloitte & Touche Hua Yong CPAs	Deloitte & Touche CPAs
600027. SH	1071. HK	2015	Deloitte & Touche Hua Yong CPAs	Deloitte & Touche CPAs
600028. SH	0386. HK	2010	KPMG Hua Zhen CPAs	KPMG CPAs
600028. SH	0386. HK	2011	KPMG Hua Zhen CPAs	KPMG CPAs
600028. SH	0386. HK	2012	KPMG Hua Zhen CPAs	KPMG CPAs
600028. SH	0386. HK	2013	PwC Zhong Tian CPAs	PwC CPAs
600028. SH	0386. HK	2014	PwC Zhong Tian CPAs	PwC CPAs
600028. SH	0386. HK	2015	PwC Zhong Tian CPAs	PwC CPAs
600029. SH	1055. HK	2010	KPMG Hua Zhen CPAs	KPMG CPAs
600029. SH	1055. HK	2011	KPMG Hua Zhen CPAs	KPMG CPAs
600029. SH	1055. HK	2012	KPMG Hua Zhen CPAs	KPMG CPAs
600029. SH	1055. HK	2013	PwC Zhong Tian CPAs	PwC CPAs
600029. SH	1055. HK	2014	PwC Zhong Tian CPAs	PwC CPAs
600029. SH	1055. HK	2015	PwC Zhong Tian CPAs	PwC CPAs
600115. SH	0670. HK	2010	PwC Zhong Tian CPAs	PwC CPAs
600115. SH	0670. HK	2011	PwC Zhong Tian CPAs	PwC CPAs
600115. SH	0670. HK	2012	PwC Zhong Tian CPAs	PwC CPAs
600115. SH	0670. HK	2013	Ernst & Young Hua Ming CPAs	Ernst & Young CPAs
600115. SH	0670. HK	2014	Ernst & Young Hua Ming CPAs	Ernst & Young CPAs
600115. SH	0670. HK	2015	Ernst & Young Hua Ming CPAs	Ernst & Young CPAs
600188. SH	1171. HK	2010	ShineWing CPAs	Jingdu Tianhua Hong Kong CPAs
600188. SH	1171. HK	2011	ShineWing CPAs	Jingdu Tianhua Hong Kong CPAs
600188. SH	1171. HK	2012	ShineWing CPAs	Grant Thornton Hong Kong CPAs
600188. SH	1171. HK	2013	ShineWing CPAs	Grant Thornton Hong Kong CPAs
600188. SH	1171. HK	2014	ShineWing CPAs	Grant Thornton Hong Kong CPAs
600188. SH	1171. HK	2015	ShineWing CPAs	Grant Thornton Hong Kong CPAs

续表

A-share Stock Code	H-share Stock Code	Year	Mainland-Based Auditor	Hong Kong-Based Auditor
600332. SH	0874. HK	2010	BDO China Shu Lun Pan CPAs	PwC CPAs
600332. SH	0874. HK	2011	PwC Zhong Tian CPAs	—
600332. SH	0874. HK	2012	PwC Zhong Tian CPAs	—
600332. SH	0874. HK	2013	BDO China Shu Lun Pan CPAs	—
600332. SH	0874. HK	2014	BDO China Shu Lun Pan CPAs	—
600332. SH	0874. HK	2015	BDO China Shu Lun Pan CPAs	—
600362. SH	0358. HK	2010	Ernst & Young Hua Ming CPAs	Ernst & Young CPAs
600362. SH	0358. HK	2011	Ernst & Young Hua Ming CPAs	Ernst & Young CPAs
600362. SH	0358. HK	2012	Deloitte & Touche Hua Yong CPAs	Deloitte & Touche CPAs
600362. SH	0358. HK	2013	Deloitte & Touche Hua Yong CPAs	Deloitte & Touche CPAs
600362. SH	0358. HK	2014	Deloitte & Touche Hua Yong CPAs	Deloitte & Touche CPAs
600362. SH	0358. HK	2015	Deloitte & Touche Hua Yong CPAs	Deloitte & Touche CPAs
600377. SH	0177. HK	2010	Deloitte & Touche Hua Yong CPAs	Deloitte & Touche CPAs
600377. SH	0177. HK	2011	Deloitte & Touche Hua Yong CPAs	—
600377. SH	0177. HK	2012	Deloitte & Touche Hua Yong CPAs	—
600377. SH	0177. HK	2013	Deloitte & Touche Hua Yong CPAs	—
600377. SH	0177. HK	2014	Deloitte & Touche Hua Yong CPAs	—
600377. SH	0177. HK	2015	Deloitte & Touche Hua Yong CPAs	—
600548. SH	0548. HK	2010	PwC Zhong Tian CPAs	PwC CPAs
600548. SH	0548. HK	2011	PwC Zhong Tian CPAs	—
600548. SH	0548. HK	2012	PwC Zhong Tian CPAs	—
600548. SH	0548. HK	2013	PwC Zhong Tian CPAs	—
600548. SH	0548. HK	2014	PwC Zhong Tian CPAs	—
600548. SH	0548. HK	2015	PwC Zhong Tian CPAs	—
600585. SH	0914. HK	2010	KPMG Hua Zhen CPAs	KPMG CPAs
600585. SH	0914. HK	2011	KPMG Hua Zhen CPAs	KPMG CPAs
600585. SH	0914. HK	2012	KPMG Hua Zhen CPAs	KPMG CPAs
600585. SH	0914. HK	2013	KPMG Hua Zhen CPAs	KPMG CPAs
600585. SH	0914. HK	2014	KPMG Hua Zhen CPAs	KPMG CPAs
600585. SH	0914. HK	2015	KPMG Hua Zhen CPAs	KPMG CPAs

续表

A-share Stock Code	H-share Stock Code	Year	Mainland-Based Auditor	Hong Kong-Based Auditor
600600. SH	0168. HK	2010	PwC Zhong Tian CPAs	—
600600. SH	0168. HK	2011	PwC Zhong Tian CPAs	—
600600. SH	0168. HK	2012	PwC Zhong Tian CPAs	—
600600. SH	0168. HK	2013	PwC Zhong Tian CPAs	—
600600. SH	0168. HK	2014	PwC Zhong Tian CPAs	—
600600. SH	0168. HK	2015	PwC Zhong Tian CPAs	—
600685. SH	0317. HK	2010	Pan-China CPAs	PwC CPAs
600685. SH	0317. HK	2011	ShineWing CPAs	—
600685. SH	0317. HK	2012	ShineWing CPAs	—
600685. SH	0317. HK	2013	ShineWing CPAs	—
600685. SH	0317. HK	2014	ShineWing CPAs	—
600685. SH	0317. HK	2015	ShineWing CPAs	—
600688. SH	0338. HK	2010	KPMG Hua Zhen CPAs	KPMG CPAs
600688. SH	0338. HK	2011	KPMG Hua Zhen CPAs	KPMG CPAs
600688. SH	0338. HK	2012	KPMG Hua Zhen CPAs	KPMG CPAs
600688. SH	0338. HK	2013	PwC Zhong Tian CPAs	PwC CPAs
600688. SH	0338. HK	2014	PwC Zhong Tian CPAs	PwC CPAs
600688. SH	0338. HK	2015	PwC Zhong Tian CPAs	PwC CPAs
600775. SH	0553. HK	2010	Baker Tilly International CPAs	Baker Tilly Hong Kong CPAs
600775. SH	0553. HK	2011	Baker Tilly International CPAs	Baker Tilly Hong Kong CPAs
600775. SH	0553. HK	2012	Baker Tilly International CPAs	Baker Tilly Hong Kong CPAs
600775. SH	0553. HK	2013	Baker Tilly International CPAs	Baker Tilly Hong Kong CPAs
600775. SH	0553. HK	2014	Baker Tilly International CPAs	Baker Tilly Hong Kong CPAs
600775. SH	0553. HK	2015	Baker Tilly International CPAs	Baker Tilly Hong Kong CPAs
600808. SH	0323. HK	2012	Ernst & Young Hua Ming CPAs	—
600808. SH	0323. HK	2013	Ernst & Young Hua Ming CPAs	—
600808. SH	0323. HK	2014	Ernst & Young Hua Ming CPAs	—
600808. SH	0323. HK	2015	Ernst & Young Hua Ming CPAs	—
600871. SH	1033. HK	2010	KPMG Hua Zhen CPAs	KPMG CPAs
600871. SH	1033. HK	2011	KPMG Hua Zhen CPAs	KPMG CPAs

续表

A-share Stock Code	H-share Stock Code	Year	Mainland-Based Auditor	Hong Kong-Based Auditor
600871. SH	1033. HK	2012	KPMG Hua Zhen CPAs	KPMG CPAs
600871. SH	1033. HK	2013	PwC Zhong Tian CPAs	PwC CPAs
600871. SH	1033. HK	2014	Grant Thornton CPAs	Grant Thornton Hong Kong CPAs
600871. SH	1033. HK	2015	Grant Thornton CPAs	Grant Thornton Hong Kong CPAs
600874. SH	1065. HK	2010	PwC Zhong Tian CPAs	PwC CPAs
600874. SH	1065. HK	2011	PwC Zhong Tian CPAs	PwC CPAs
600874. SH	1065. HK	2012	PwC Zhong Tian CPAs	PwC CPAs
600874. SH	1065. HK	2013	PwC Zhong Tian CPAs	PwC CPAs
600874. SH	1065. HK	2014	PwC Zhong Tian CPAs	PwC CPAs
600874. SH	1065. HK	2015	PwC Zhong Tian CPAs	PwC CPAs
600875. SH	1072. HK	2010	ShineWing CPAs	ShineWing Hong Kong CPAs
600875. SH	1072. HK	2011	ShineWing CPAs	—
600875. SH	1072. HK	2012	ShineWing CPAs	—
600875. SH	1072. HK	2013	ShineWing CPAs	—
600875. SH	1072. HK	2014	ShineWing CPAs	—
600875. SH	1072. HK	2015	ShineWing CPAs	—
600876. SH	1108. HK	2010	Wuyige CPAs	PKF Hong Kong CPAs
600876. SH	1108. HK	2011	Wuyige CPAs	PKF Hong Kong CPAs
600876. SH	1108. HK	2012	Wuyige CPAs	PKF Hong Kong CPAs
600876. SH	1108. HK	2013	Wuyige CPAs	—
600876. SH	1108. HK	2014	Wuyige CPAs	—
600876. SH	1108. HK	2015	Wuyige CPAs	—
601088. SH	1088. HK	2010	KPMG Hua Zhen CPAs	KPMG CPAs
601088. SH	1088. HK	2011	KPMG Hua Zhen CPAs	KPMG CPAs
601088. SH	1088. HK	2012	KPMG Hua Zhen CPAs	KPMG CPAs
601088. SH	1088. HK	2013	Deloitte & Touche Hua Yong CPAs	Deloitte & Touche CPAs
601088. SH	1088. HK	2014	Deloitte & Touche Hua Yong CPAs	Deloitte & Touche CPAs
601088. SH	1088. HK	2015	Deloitte & Touche Hua Yong CPAs	Deloitte & Touche CPAs
601107. SH	0107. HK	2011	ShineWing CPAs	Ernst & Young CPAs
601107. SH	0107. HK	2012	ShineWing CPAs	Ernst & Young CPAs

续表

A-share Stock Code	H-share Stock Code	Year	Mainland-Based Auditor	Hong Kong-Based Auditor
601107. SH	0107. HK	2013	ShineWing CPAs	Ernst & Young CPAs
601107. SH	0107. HK	2014	ShineWing CPAs	Ernst & Young CPAs
601107. SH	0107. HK	2015	ShineWing CPAs	Ernst & Young CPAs
601111. SH	0753. HK	2010	Ernst & Young Hua Ming CPAs	Ernst & Young CPAs
601111. SH	0753. HK	2011	Ernst & Young Hua Ming CPAs	Ernst & Young CPAs
601111. SH	0753. HK	2012	Ernst & Young Hua Ming CPAs	Ernst & Young CPAs
601111. SH	0753. HK	2013	KPMG Hua Zhen CPAs	KPMG CPAs
601111. SH	0753. HK	2014	KPMG Hua Zhen CPAs	KPMG CPAs
601111. SH	0753. HK	2015	KPMG Hua Zhen CPAs	KPMG CPAs
601186. SH	1186. HK	2010	Ernst & Young Hua Ming CPAs	Ernst & Young CPAs
601186. SH	1186. HK	2011	Ernst & Young Hua Ming CPAs	—
601186. SH	1186. HK	2012	Ernst & Young Hua Ming CPAs	—
601186. SH	1186. HK	2013	Ernst & Young Hua Ming CPAs	—
601186. SH	1186. HK	2014	Ernst & Young Hua Ming CPAs	—
601186. SH	1186. HK	2015	Ernst & Young Hua Ming CPAs	—
601333. SH	0525. HK	2012	PwC Zhong Tian CPAs	PwC CPAs
601333. SH	0525. HK	2013	PwC Zhong Tian CPAs	PwC CPAs
601333. SH	0525. HK	2014	PwC Zhong Tian CPAs	PwC CPAs
601333. SH	0525. HK	2015	PwC Zhong Tian CPAs	PwC CPAs
601390. SH	0390. HK	2010	Deloitte & Touche Hua Yong CPAs	Deloitte & Touche CPAs
601390. SH	0390. HK	2011	Deloitte & Touche Hua Yong CPAs	Deloitte & Touche CPAs
601390. SH	0390. HK	2012	Deloitte & Touche Hua Yong CPAs	Deloitte & Touche CPAs
601390. SH	0390. HK	2013	Deloitte & Touche Hua Yong CPAs	Deloitte & Touche CPAs
601390. SH	0390. HK	2014	Deloitte & Touche Hua Yong CPAs	Deloitte & Touche CPAs
601390. SH	0390. HK	2015	Deloitte & Touche Hua Yong CPAs	Deloitte & Touche CPAs
601588. SH	0588. HK	2010	PwC Zhong Tian CPAs	PwC CPAs
601588. SH	0588. HK	2011	PwC Zhong Tian CPAs	PwC CPAs
601588. SH	0588. HK	2012	PwC Zhong Tian CPAs	PwC CPAs
601588. SH	0588. HK	2013	PwC Zhong Tian CPAs	PwC CPAs
601588. SH	0588. HK	2014	PwC Zhong Tian CPAs	PwC CPAs

续表

A-share Stock Code	H-share Stock Code	Year	Mainland-Based Auditor	Hong Kong-Based Auditor
601588. SH	0588. HK	2015	PwC Zhong Tian CPAs	PwC CPAs
601600. SH	2600. HK	2013	Ernst & Young Hua Ming CPAs	Ernst & Young CPAs
601600. SH	2600. HK	2014	Ernst & Young Hua Ming CPAs	Ernst & Young CPAs
601600. SH	2600. HK	2015	Ernst & Young Hua Ming CPAs	Ernst & Young CPAs
601618. SH	1618. HK	2013	PwC Zhong Tian CPAs	PwC CPAs
601618. SH	1618. HK	2014	Deloitte & Touche Hua Yong CPAs	—
601618. SH	1618. HK	2015	Deloitte & Touche Hua Yong CPAs	—
601727. SH	2727. HK	2010	Ernst & Young Hua Ming CPAs	Ernst & Young CPAs
601727. SH	2727. HK	2011	Ernst & Young Hua Ming CPAs	Ernst & Young CPAs
601727. SH	2727. HK	2012	Ernst & Young Hua Ming CPAs	Ernst & Young CPAs
601727. SH	2727. HK	2013	Ernst & Young Hua Ming CPAs	Ernst & Young CPAs
601727. SH	2727. HK	2014	PwC Zhong Tian CPAs	PwC CPAs
601727. SH	2727. HK	2015	PwC Zhong Tian CPAs	PwC CPAs
601766. SH	1766. HK	2010	Ernst & Young Hua Ming CPAs	Ernst & Young CPAs
601766. SH	1766. HK	2011	Ernst & Young Hua Ming CPAs	Ernst & Young CPAs
601766. SH	1766. HK	2012	Ernst & Young Hua Ming CPAs	Ernst & Young CPAs
601766. SH	1766. HK	2013	Ernst & Young Hua Ming CPAs	Ernst & Young CPAs
601766. SH	1766. HK	2014	Deloitte & Touche Hua Yong CPAs	Deloitte & Touche CPAs
601766. SH	1766. HK	2015	Deloitte & Touche Hua Yong CPAs	Deloitte & Touche CPAs
601808. SH	2883. HK	2010	Ernst & Young Hua Ming CPAs	Ernst & Young CPAs
601808. SH	2883. HK	2011	Ernst & Young Hua Ming CPAs	Ernst & Young CPAs
601808. SH	2883. HK	2012	Ernst & Young Hua Ming CPAs	Ernst & Young CPAs
601808. SH	2883. HK	2013	Deloitte & Touche Hua Yong CPAs	Deloitte & Touche CPAs
601808. SH	2883. HK	2014	Deloitte & Touche Hua Yong CPAs	Deloitte & Touche CPAs
601808. SH	2883. HK	2015	Deloitte & Touche Hua Yong CPAs	Deloitte & Touche CPAs
601857. SH	0857. HK	2010	PwC Zhong Tian CPAs	PwC CPAs
601857. SH	0857. HK	2011	PwC Zhong Tian CPAs	PwC CPAs
601857. SH	0857. HK	2012	PwC Zhong Tian CPAs	PwC CPAs
601857. SH	0857. HK	2013	KPMG Hua Zhen CPAs	KPMG CPAs
601857. SH	0857. HK	2014	KPMG Hua Zhen CPAs	KPMG CPAs

续表

A-share Stock Code	H-share Stock Code	Year	Mainland-Based Auditor	Hong Kong-Based Auditor
601857. SH	0857. HK	2015	KPMG Hua Zhen CPAs	KPMG CPAs
601866. SH	2866. HK	2011	Baker Tilly International CPAs	PwC CPAs
601866. SH	2866. HK	2012	Baker Tilly International CPAs	Ernst & Young CPAs
601866. SH	2866. HK	2013	Baker Tilly International CPAs	Ernst & Young CPAs
601866. SH	2866. HK	2014	Baker Tilly International CPAs	Ernst & Young CPAs
601866. SH	2866. HK	2015	Baker Tilly International CPAs	Ernst & Young CPAs
601898. SH	1898. HK	2010	PwC Zhong Tian CPAs	PwC CPAs
601898. SH	1898. HK	2011	PwC Zhong Tian CPAs	PwC CPAs
601898. SH	1898. HK	2012	PwC Zhong Tian CPAs	PwC CPAs
601898. SH	1898. HK	2013	PwC Zhong Tian CPAs	PwC CPAs
601898. SH	1898. HK	2014	PwC Zhong Tian CPAs	PwC CPAs
601898. SH	1898. HK	2015	PwC Zhong Tian CPAs	PwC CPAs
601899. SH	2899. HK	2010	Ernst & Young Hua Ming CPAs	Ernst & Young CPAs
601899. SH	2899. HK	2011	Ernst & Young Hua Ming CPAs	—
601899. SH	2899. HK	2012	Ernst & Young Hua Ming CPAs	—
601899. SH	2899. HK	2013	Ernst & Young Hua Ming CPAs	—
601899. SH	2899. HK	2014	Ernst & Young Hua Ming CPAs	—
601899. SH	2899. HK	2015	Ernst & Young Hua Ming CPAs	—
601919. SH	1919. HK	2010	RSM China CPAs	PwC CPAs
601919. SH	1919. HK	2011	RSM China CPAs	PwC CPAs
601919. SH	1919. HK	2012	RSM China CPAs	PwC CPAs
601919. SH	1919. HK	2013	Ruihua CPAs	PwC CPAs
601919. SH	1919. HK	2014	Ruihua CPAs	PwC CPAs
601919. SH	1919. HK	2015	Ruihua CPAs	PwC CPAs
601991. SH	0991. HK	2012	RSM China CPAs	RSM Hong Kong CPAs
601991. SH	0991. HK	2013	Ruihua CPAs	RSM Hong Kong CPAs
601991. SH	0991. HK	2014	Ruihua CPAs	RSM Hong Kong CPAs
601991. SH	0991. HK	2015	Ruihua CPAs	RSM Hong Kong CPAs

Appendix Ⅲ　Chinese Simplified Version

1　绪论

作为一项在促进会计师事务所增强独立性和积累经验、提高上市公司治理水平和会计信息质量等方面都具有重要作用的审计制度，双重审计制度及其变迁一直是会计与审计领域十分关注的研究话题。本书旨在考察双重审计管制取消对资本市场和审计市场产生的经济后果。本章首先介绍本书的实践背景和理论背景。接下来基于实务现状和现有文献的不足之处，提出本书的研究问题，分析本研究的理论意义和实践意义。最后，本章阐述本书的主要研究内容、研究方法和研究框架。

1.1　研究背景

1.1.1　实践背景

我国境内的 A 股市场和香港的 H 股市场成立于 20 世纪 90 年代初。自 1993 年青岛啤酒（A 股代码：600600. SH；H 股代码：00168. HK）作为第一家 A+H 股公司在 A 股市场和 H 股市场交叉上市起，A+H 股公司的数量逐年增加。截至 2018 年年底，A+H 股公司的数量达到 109 家。本书对收集自国泰安 CSMAR 数据库的数据进行了整理，绘制图 1-1（见英文正文第 1 章图 1-1），显示我国 A+H 股公司 1993—2018 年的数量增长情况。

鉴于 A+H 股公司既在我国内地又在香港上市的特点及其数量逐年增加的趋势，这一类公司常常受到研究制度环境、制度变迁以及相关会计、审计等问题的学者的青睐（如 Ke et al. , 2015；田高良等，2017）。自 H 股市场建立初期开始，我国根据内地和香港两地的上市规则对 A+H 股公司实施双重审计管制。20 世纪 90 年代初，我国企业会计准则（CAS）与国际财务报告准则（IFRS）［或香港财务报告准则（HKFRS）］之间存在很大差异，使得境内和境外投资者各自具有不同的信息需求。另外，境内会计师事务所尚处于发展初期，执业能力较低（财政部，2009a）。在当时的情况下，两地要求 A+H 股公司必须采用双重审计制度，以便提高会计信息的可信度、满足不同投资者的信息需求。具体而言，一家 A+H 股公司需要雇用一家境内会计师事务所，按照《中国注册会计师审计准则》审计其依据 CAS 编制的 A 股财务报表；同时需要雇用一家香港会计师事务所，按照《国际审计准则》或《香港审计准则》审计其依据 IFRS 或 HKFRS 编制的 H 股财务报表，两家事务所各自出具独立的审计报告。

随着 CAS 实现与 IFRS 的实质性趋同和与 HKFRS 的等效、香港审计市场在内地会计师事务所国际化进程中的战略地位日益重要、我国政府对本土会计师事务所做大做强的大力扶持，监管部门认为取消双重审计管制的时机已到。自 2007 年 12 月起，两地签署了一系列政策文件，直至 2010 年 12 月，A+H 股双重审计管制被正式取消。自此，是否继续采用双重审计成为 A+H 股公司的自愿选择（香港联合交易所，2009）。如果某一公司决定不再采用双重审计，则其之后只需雇用一家内地事务所实施单一审计。监管部门之所以决定做出取消双重审计管制的决策，是考虑到双重审计对于 A+H 股公司已无太大必要，并且预期大多数公司会响应这一政策变化，从而解雇各自的香港审计师。然而，事实看来并非如此。

本书对收集自国泰安 CSMAR 数据库的数据进行了整理，绘制图 1-2（见英文正文第 1 章图 1-2），显示 2010—2018 年仍然采用双重审计的公司数量及其在 A+H 股公司中所占比重。在两地宣布正式取消双重审计强制要求的年份（2010 年），仅有 1 家 A+H 股公司响应这一政策变更，放弃了双重审计。此后，尽管继续采用双重审计的公司的比重大体上呈下降趋势，但直至 2018 年，这一比重仍然超过 62%（62. 39%）。图 1-2 表明，即便在管制取消后，大部分 A+H 股公司仍坚持采用双重审计。也就是说，监管部门虽然取消了双重审计管制，但这并不意味着双重审计制度就此消失；这一政策变更的实施并未达到预期效果。

双重审计制度在保持审计师独立性、提升公司治理水平、保证向投资者提供信息的准确完整、帮助本土事务所积累经验等方面功不可没（孙素琴，2014）。此外，即便在管制取消后，大多数 A+H 股公司也依然采用双重审计。

由此可见，双重审计与传统的单一审计相比势必有其内在的合理性，具备重要的学术研究价值。同时，A 股公司（包括 A+H 股公司在内）在其所采用的审计制度方面存在丰富的差异性，为本书研究双重审计管制取消对我国市场产生的经济后果提供了良好的机会和条件。管制取消后，投资者十分关心 A+H 股公司是否变更审计制度、其审计质量是否受到影响等（孙素琴，2014）。对双重审计管制取消的经济后果的深入挖掘，有助于理解双重审计制度对财务报告质量、审计质量、投资者认知和决策等方面的作用，从而为有关部门今后设计、安排审计制度提供有益的参考。

1.1.2 理论背景

学术界关于双重审计制度经济后果的研究从未停歇，学者对这一话题给予了持续关注，并且获得了一些有价值和启发性的发现；关于权益成本及其影响因素的研究不断丰富；关于审计质量及其影响因素的研究也经久不衰。通过梳理现有文献，本书获得如下发现：

第一，现有关于 A+H 股双重审计强制要求及其废除的研究局限于考察与审计相关的后果，如审计质量、审计市场结构、审计费用等。尽管该强制要求已于 2010 年废除，但双重审计制度并没有就此消失，至今仍被大部分 A+H 股公司继续采用。对这一审计制度的进一步探索不仅能够加深对其在投资者保护等方面的作用的了解，而且能够为将来的审计制度安排提供借鉴。由此，双重审计管制取消是否以及在多大程度上会对资本市场产生影响，是学术界和实务界都非常感兴趣的话题。然而，目前关于该政策变更的资本市场后果的证据（如其对权益成本的影响）十分匮乏。

第二，现有的关于 A+H 股双重审计制度的研究大体上认同采用双重审计的 A+H 股公司比未采用双重审计的 A 股公司（包括非交叉上市 A 股公司和部分 A+H 股公司）审计质量更高。根据这一共识，可以推测 A+H 股公司在放弃双重审计后，审计质量很可能会有所下降。然而，以往研究无法排除交叉上市公司与非交叉上市公司之间的系统性差异对结果的影响，将采用双重审计的 A+H 股公司与未采用双重审计的 A 股公司之间的审计质量差异归因于审计制度是缺乏可靠性的。

第三，现有的关于 A+H 股双重审计的研究较为详细地阐释了香港审计师通过双重审计过程可能向内地审计师发挥的积极溢出效应（Ke et al.，2015）。从审计师面临的制度环境的角度出发所论述的这一溢出效应，被认为是双重审计帮助维持较高审计质量的潜在机制。然而，由于这一效应的难以观测性，相关研究仅停留在抽象论述阶段。也就是说，与该效应有关的理论尚未转化为切实可行的实证测度。此外，这一效应的存在（消失）是否以及在多大程度上会影响采用（放弃）双重审计的公司的审计质量，仍然是悬而未决的问题。

第四，现有的关于权益成本的研究提出了多种测度方法、发现了主要影响因素，为本书中与权益成本相关的实证研究设计提供了坚实的基础。与此同时，虽然以往研究证实了独立审计对权益成本具有显著影响，但对于某一特定审计制度的变迁，如双重审计管制的取消是否会引发权益成本的变化，则疏于探索。基于本章 1. 2. 1 节提出的研究问题，本书猜想双重审计管制取消后，投资者可能预期信息风险会增加，进而要求比管制取消前更高的风险补偿（回报率）。然而，以往研究尚未对这一影响我国市场中权益成本的潜在因素给予足够的关注。

第五，现有的关于审计质量的文献提出了多种测度方法、发现了主要影响因素，为本书中与审计质量相关的实证研究设计提供了有价值的借鉴。与此同时，具体到本书将要研究的审计质量问题，以往关于审计质量的研究虽然从制度环境的角度阐释了双重审计帮助维持较高审计质量的潜在机制，却忽视了相关的实证工作，这一机制是否存在以及如何对审计质量产生影响，尚未得到有效的分析与验证。

1. 2　研究问题与研究意义

1. 2. 1　研究问题

基于本章 1. 1 节的分析，H 股市场是我国内地企业赴境外融资和发展的重要渠道，A+H 股交叉上市公司数量在逐年增长，针对此类公司的双重审计管制虽已取消，但采用双重审计的公司占比依然很大。管制取消后，投资者对于 A+H 股公司的审计制度变更、审计质量变化等问题十分关注。另外，学术界对于双重审计制度及其变迁的研究从未停歇。对双重审计管制取消的经济后果进行全面、深入的考察，有助于加深人们对双重审计制度所产生的各方面影响的认识和理解，为后续的审计制度安排提供有价值的参考。然而，现有文献局限于研究双重审计管制取消产生的审计方面的后果，并没有对该政策变更产生的其他经济后果（如其对我国资本市场的影响）给予充分的关注。此外，针对其审计市场后果的研究也没有从实证角度深入探析双重审计帮助维持较高审计质量的潜在机制（或者说，导致公司放弃双重审计后审计质量下降的主要原因）。基于以往文献的这些不足之处，本书将考察双重审计管制取消的资本市场后果和审计市场后果，具体而言，本书主要研究以下三个问题。

第一，关于双重审计管制取消的资本市场后果，公司在管制取消前强制接受双重审计时是否比其在管制取消后自愿采用双重审计时拥有更低的权益成本？

如本章1.1.2节所述，现有文献局限于研究双重审计管制取消带来的审计方面的后果，那么，这一政策变更是否会对资本市场产生影响（如引起权益成本的变化）？另外，以往关于双重审计的研究基本上都是通过比较分析不同时段（管制取消前时段与管制取消后时段）或不同审计制度（双重审计与单一审计）得出结论，鲜有研究考虑将双重审计的公司进一步区分为在管制取消前强制接受双重审计的公司和在管制取消后自愿采用双重审计的公司，并在二者之间，或在后者与同一时期内仅接受单一审计的公司之间进行比较分析。也就是说，管制阶段的双重审计与管制取消后的双重审计是否对权益成本具有不同的影响？根据Rock（2002）、Stulz（2009）、Cheng等（2013）的研究，公司对某一具备强有力执行机制的强制要求的遵循，会被投资者视为一项在事前做出的难以逆转的承诺，从而减轻投资者对于管理层可能做出损害股东利益的自利行为的怀疑。因此，这种由于遵循强制要求而产生的遵循效应，能够降低投资者与管理层之间的代理成本和信息不对称程度，进而降低权益成本（Monahan，2006；Hail，2011）。基于这一理论，公司对双重审计强制要求的遵循，可能被投资者视为公司在事前就承诺将接受境内外两家会计师事务所的监督、披露两套经审计的财务报表，从而缓解投资者对管理层自利行为的疑虑；另外，相关部门的有力执行，特别是香港市场上较为完善的执法和监管体系，为双重审计强制要求的有效实施保驾护航，使受到这一要求约束的公司面临高昂的违规成本，从而确保它们能够持续遵循该要求。与之相反，在管制取消后继续采用双重审计，是公司做出的一种事后的自利性质的选择，因为它允许公司在做出双重审计决策前预估这一选择可能带来的后果；另外，即便公司选择采用双重审计，投资者也很难确定这一选择在未来是否具有持续性，因为公司可以在免于受到监管部门惩罚的情况下自行决定放弃双重审计。因此，本书预期，因遵循双重审计强制要求而产生的遵循效应在降低权益成本方面的作用，可能不会被自愿做出的双重审计选择完全取代。基于这一预期，本书首先通过分析公司在管制取消前遵循双重审计强制要求时是否比它们在管制取消后自愿采用双重审计时拥有更低的权益成本，来考察双重审计管制取消的资本市场后果。

第二，关于双重审计管制取消的资本市场后果，管制取消后，自愿采用双重审计的公司是否比仅接受单一审计的公司拥有更低的权益成本？

在考察了强制双重审计（相对于自愿双重审计）对权益成本的影响后，本书接下来分析自愿双重审计（相对于单一审计）对权益成本的影响。根据 Melumad 和 Thoman（1990）、Lennox 和 Pittman（2011）的研究，即便不存在强制审计要求，一家公司也可能自愿购买审计服务，以利用其中的信号机制。基于这一信号理论，自愿采用双重审计比仅接受单一审计需要支付更高的审计与披露成本，能够向投资者显示关于公司优良特质（如高质量、低风险、好前景等）的增量信息。因此，自愿采用双重审计的行为可能向市场传递积极的信号，将做出这一选择的公司与仅接受单一审计的公司区别开来，使得投资者更青睐前者，从而以更低的报酬率为前者提供资金。因此，双重审计管制取消后，本书预期，自愿采用双重审计比仅接受单一审计更可能有效降低权益成本。基于这一预期，本书接下来通过分析管制取消后选择采用双重审计的公司是否比同时期仅接受单一审计的公司的权益成本更低，来考察双重审计管制取消的资本市场后果。

第三，关于双重审计管制取消的审计市场后果，公司放弃双重审计后的审计质量下降是否主要是由来自香港审计师的积极溢出效应的丧失所导致的？

在了解了双重审计管制取消对资本市场产生的经济后果之后，本书接下来考察该政策变更对审计市场产生的经济后果，主要关注放弃双重审计的公司及其与保留双重审计的公司之间的比较分析。如本章 1.1.2 节所述，现有文献大体上认为未采用双重审计的公司比采用双重审计的公司审计质量更低，据此可以推测，放弃双重审计之后，公司的审计质量很可能会下降。根据 Ke 等（2015）的论述，香港审计师可能通过双重审计过程对内地审计师发挥一种积极的溢出效应，上述审计质量的下降或许能够归因于这一积极溢出效应的丧失。具体而言，香港的制度环境比内地更为完善，这使得香港审计师比内地审计师拥有更高的独立性和审计质量。另外，根据相关规章制度，一家公司的 A 股财务报表和 H 股财务报表应当具备实质上的一致性。基于上述现状和要求，在双重审计过程中，一家公司的香港审计师可能会对其内地审计师发挥一种间接的、积极的溢出效应。简而言之，香港审计师审计工作过程更为规范、审计结果更为严谨，会对该公司的内地审计师产生潜在的牵制和监督作用，使得后者不敢在审计质量上有所懈怠，由此保证采用双重审计的公司拥有较高的审计质量。而公司放弃双重审计则会阻碍这一来自香港审计师的积极溢出效应，从而很可能损害审计质量。尽管上述关于这一潜在溢出效应的阐释具有理论上的合理性，但与之相关的分析与验证尚不充分。例如，如何在实证中测度该效应？进一步地，对于保留双重审计的公司来讲，来自香港审计师的溢出效应越积极，公司的审计质量就会越高吗？另外，这一积极溢出效应的丧失是否是导致放弃双重审计的公司审计质量下降的主要原因？基于这些悬而未决的问题，本书通过构建用于衡量来自香港审计师的溢出效应的全新变量，并通过深入探析这一效应的丧失在审计质量下降中所扮演的角色，来考察双重审计管制取消的审计市场后果。

1.2.2 研究意义

1.2.2.1 理论意义

第一，本书丰富了双重审计制度的相关文献。以往研究多局限于关注双重审计管制取消对于审计领域的影响，本书关注该政策变化的资本市场后果，并分别考虑强制双重审计与自愿双重审计的影响，弥补了前人研究的不足。通过考察该政策变化对权益成本的影响，本书有助于更为全面地了解双重审计管制取消的经济后果，丰富了双重审计相关研究的研究视角和研究内容。相关结论表明，除了影响审计市场之外，双重审计管制取消也会影响投资者的认知和决策，进而在我国资本市场上产生显著的经济后果。

第二，本书拓展了权益成本的相关研究。尽管以往研究发现财务报表审计有助于降低公司的权益成本，但是学者们往往将审计的价值归结为它为会计信息可信度提供独立鉴证的能力（如，Clatworthy et al.，2013；DeFond et al.，2014；Hay et al.，2018）；鲜有文献关注在不考虑审计师提供的鉴证水平的情况下，公司所采用的审计制度的差异是否会影响权益成本。本书在实证过程中有效控制了审计的鉴证价值，在此前提下，通过比较管制取消前的强制双重审计与管制取消后的自愿双重审计，以及比较后者与同期的单一审计，发现了强制双重审计与自愿双重审计对权益成本不同程度的抑制作用，拓展了我国资本市场上权益成本的影响因素体系。

第三，本书扩充了审计质量的相关研究。对于一种可能由高质量审计师（香港审计师）对低质量审计师（内地审计师）发挥的积极溢出效应，以往研究仅限于抽象描述，缺乏具体、有效的测度和检验。本书基于相关规章制度和前人论述，建立了对来自香港审计师的溢出效应的测度方法，填补了相关研究在实证工作方面的缺失。接下来，本书基于这一变量进行实证检验，证实了来自香港审计师的积极溢出效应的存在（丧失）对保留（放弃）双重审计的公司的审计质量的显著影响，丰富了我国现实背景下审计质量的影响因素体系。

1.2.2.2 实践意义

第一，本书为监管部门审慎评价双重审计管制取消所带来的成本与后果提供了新的参考。总体而言，本书的结论体现出这一政策变更的一些消极影响，如权益成本增加、审计质量降低。前者反映出在双重审计管制取消后，投资者对于公司管理层可能做出损害股东利益的自利行为的疑虑增加；后者则证实了实务界对于公司解雇香港审计师后审计质量可能下降的担忧。基于这些发现，放弃双重审计难以在不增加投资者怀疑或不牺牲审计质量的前提下帮助公司节约审计成本。本书研究结论在一定程度上解释为何很少有 A+H 股公司响应有关部门对取消双重审计的号召，提醒监管部门审慎评估这一政策变更的价值。

第二，本书的研究结论可以提醒监管部门和会计师事务所注意，实现内地本土事务所真正做大做强是一项漫长而艰巨的任务。改革开放以来，我国经济飞速发展，企业规模不断扩大。在这一背景下，市场和监管部门对内地事务所做大做强的呼声日益增高。近几年，我国政府和注册会计师协会为扶持大规模会计师事务所的发展做出了诸多努力（如促进事务所合并、改制），以期培育本土事务所的自有品牌和声誉。目前，许多大型本土事务所的业务收入已同一些国际顶尖会计师事务所相当接近。然而，这一现状仅是本土事务所“做大”的体现；换句话说，业务收入的增长主要是事务所合并的结果，合并后事务所的业绩表现并不尽如人意。例如，近些年频繁出现的审计失败为本土事务所打上了“低质”“大而不强”等标签。与这些现实情况相呼应，本书的结论显示，公司在放弃双重审计后 A 股审计质量显著下降，并且这一审计质量下降主要是由来自香港审计师的积极溢出效应的丧失所导致的。由此可见，尽管有关部门为内地审计行业的发展提供了许多政策支持，然而想要使本土会计师事务所真正成为国际顶尖会计师事务所的优质替代品，仍有相当长的路要走。

1.3 研究内容、方法与框架

1.3.1 研究内容

围绕研究问题和研究目标，本书展开以下研究。第 1 章为绪论，介绍了本书的研究背景、研究问题、研究意义，阐述了本书的研究内容、方法和框架。第 2 章为文献综述，从双重审计的经济后果、权益成本的影响因素、审计质量的影响因素等方面回顾了现有文献，分析了文献的不足之处，挖掘了相关研究对本研究的启示。第 3 章为制度背景与理论分析，介绍了 A+H 股双重审计制度变迁的相关背景，阐述了本研究所基于的主要理论，并在此基础上提出了本书的理论框架。第 4、第 5、第 6 章为双重审计管制取消的资本市场后果与审计市场后果的理论分析与实证检验。第 7 章为结论与展望，总结了本书的研究结论，探讨了政策启示，着重论述了本研究的创新点，最后指出本研究的不足之处和未来的研究方向。

1.3.2 研究方法

本书采用理论分析和实证分析相结合的研究方法。具体来讲，第 2 章基于理论分析回顾了与双重审计、权益成本、审计质量相关的文献，讨论了现有研究的局限性。第 3 章基于理论分析阐述了本书的制度背景、理论基础，并构建了本书的理论框架。基于理论框架，第 4、第 5、第 6 章提出了研究假设，并基于实证分析进行了假设检验。最后，第 7 章对实证结果进行了理论分析和讨论，继而总结了本书的创新点和不足之处。实证研究过程主要采用了描述性统计分析、组间差异分析（均值 T 检验）、多元回归分析［普通最小二乘（OLS）模型、Logit 模型］、倾向得分匹配法（PSM）、变化分析、混杂变量影响阈值分析（ITCV）等多种方法。关于主要实证方法的简要介绍请参阅英文正文第 1 章 1.3.2 节。

1.3.3 研究框架

请参见英文正文第 1 章图 1-3。

2 文献综述

围绕上一章提出和概括的本书的研究问题和研究内容，本章主要从双重审计的含义与经济后果、权益成本的含义与影响因素、审计质量的含义与影响因素等方面回顾了相关文献。最后，本章对文献进行述评，指出现有研究的不足和对本书的启示。

2.1 双重审计

2.1.1 双重审计的定义

双重审计是指一家公司同时雇用两家会计师事务所进行审计，这两家事务所对各自的审计范围分别出具审计报告的审计制度（Holm et al.，2018），本书研究的是针对我国 A+H 股公司实施的双重审计制度。具体而言，一家 A+H 股公司雇用一家内地会计师事务所，根据《中国注册会计师审计准则》审计该公司按照 CAS 编制的 A 股财务报表；同时雇用一家香港会计师事务所，根据《国际审计准则》或《香港审计准则》审计该公司按照 IFRS 或 HKFRS 编制的 H 股财务报表。内地审计师和香港审计师分别对该公司的 A 股财务报表和 H 股财务报表出具审计报告。这便是所谓的 A+H 股双重审计制度（Wang et al.，2011）。

2.1.2 双重审计的经济后果

双重审计制度及其变迁一直受到学术界的关注。一些学者通过理论分析和定性分析，探讨了双重审计管制取消的潜在影响，指出有关部门废除双重审计强制要求并鼓励内地本土事务所从事 H 股公司审计业务的做法，既为本土事务所发展壮大创造了机会，也为其带来了挑战（郑伟等，2011；翁射超等，

2012）。其他学者则从实证角度考察了双重审计强制要求及其废除在审计领域造成的影响。其中，一些研究通过在 A 股上市公司之间（包括非交叉上市 A 股公司和 A+H 股公司）进行比较，发现双重审计有助于维持较高的审计质量（Lin et al.，2014；Wang，2014；Ke et al.，2015；田高良等，2017）；也有学者进一步探讨了不同类型的会计师事务所在双重审计过程中的动机差异（Wang et al.，2011）。另一些研究则关注双重审计管制取消对内地审计市场结构和审计费用的影响（孙素琴，2013）。双重审计管制取消并不等于双重审计制度的消失。钟子英和张俊倪（2019）指出，对双重审计制度全面、深入的探究有助于理解该制度对企业、审计市场、资本市场等的作用，为我国今后的审计制度安排提供有价值的参考。

关于我国其他领域所采用（过）的双重审计制度的文献回顾请参阅英文正文第 2 章 2.1.2.2 节。

2.2 权益成本

2.2.1 权益成本的定义

权益成本是指企业为获得股东投资而支付的代价，从股东的角度讲，它是股东要求的必要收益率（罗守权、卓岩，2014）。权益成本作为反映投资者对其投资风险的预期和评估的主要指标，几十年来一直受到学术界的广泛关注。在实证研究中，权益成本的衡量方法也多种多样，如 GLS 模型（Gebhardt et al.，2001）、CT 模型（Claus et al.，2001）、OJ 模型（Ohlson et al.，2005）、PEG 模型（Easton，2004）、CAPM 模型（Sharpe，1964）等。

2.2.2 权益成本的影响因素

以往研究发现，权益成本主要受制度环境、政府干预、公司规模、财务风险、账面市值比率、公司治理、信息披露、会计稳健性、审计质量、流动性、市场风险等因素的影响。越完善、严苛的制度环境越有助于降低权益成本（Levit，1998；Hail et al.，2003；Himmelberg et al.，2004；姜付秀等，2008；肖珉、沈艺峰，2008；洪洁、陈少华，2016）。政府干预通常有助于降低权益成本，但其影响会随着一些条件的变化而变化，如在不同的所有权性质（徐浩萍等，2007）、政治关联程度（肖浩、夏新平，2010；赵峰、高明华，2012）、盈余管理水平（王俊秋，2013）、金融生态环境（邹颖、杨晓玮，2014）下，政府干预对权益成本的影响不尽相同。以往文献有关公司规模对权益成本影响的研究结论并不一致，一些研究认为二者之间存在负向关系（Botosan，1997；Botosan & Plumlee，2002；曹书军等，2012），另一些研究结论则恰恰相反（田映华、刘江帆，2003；叶康涛、陆正飞，2004）。财务杠杆也被认为是影响权益成本的一个重要因素，但以往研究的结论不尽相同（Modigliani & Muler，1958；Fama & French，1992；Richardson & Welker，2001；陈晓、单鑫，1999；田映华、刘江帆，2003；唐国正、刘力，2005；金鲜花，2008）。账面市值比率也会对权益成本产生显著影响，一些观点认为这种影响是正向的（Fama & French，1992；Berk et al.，1999；Cheng et al.，2006；雷霆、周嘉南，2014），另一些则认为是负向的（叶康涛、陆正飞，2004）。对于公司治理的作用，以往研究大体上认为完善的公司治理机制有助于降低权益成本（Ashbaugh et al.，2004；Huang，2005；Cheng et al.，2006；Mazzotta & Veltri，2014；蒋琰，2009；蒋琰、陆正飞，2009；闫华红，2011；赖泳杏、范利民，2016；柯丽，2017）。现有文献发现信息披露也会影响权益成本，大多数研究支持信息披露质量的提高对权益成本具有抑制作用（Diamond & Verrecchia，1991；Richardson & Welker，2001；Cheng et al.，2006；Mangena et al.，2016；汪炜、蒋高峰，2004；曾颖、陆正飞，2006；沈洪涛等，2010；李慧云、刘镝，2016；周慧琴、朱亚娜，2016），也有一部分学者认为二者呈正相关或无关（Kim，1993；Botosan & Plumlee，2002；杨红等，2012；李姝等，2013；车培荣、田雪力，2016；张正勇、陈虹，2017）。关于会计稳健性，以往研究基本认同会计稳健性越高越有助于抑制权益成本的上升（Easley & O'Hara，2004；Lafond & Watts，2008；Suijs，2008；Lara et al.，2011；Guay & Verrecchia，2018；王静等，2013；陆杰等，2016；李争光等，2016；王生年、徐亚飞，2016；马忠民等，2017）。现有文献还发现，审计质量越高，越有助于降低权益成本（Choi & Lee，2014；Houqe et al.，2017；于李胜等，2008；王兵等，2009；Chen et al.，2011；李心愉等，2017；朱丹、李琰，2017）。流动性是影响权益成本的另一个重要因素，大多数研究认为权益成本随着流动性的提高而降低（Amihud & Mendelson，1986；Jacoby et al.，2000；Saad & Samet，2017；王春峰等，2012；杨华峰，2016），也有研究得出相反的结论（沈艺峰等，2005）。另外，市场风险也会显著影响权益成本（Sharpe，1964；Fama & MacBeth，1973；Ross，1976），然而具体到我国市场，关于该因素影响的研究结论并不一致（沈艺峰等，2005；王亮亮，2013；汪平、张孜瑶，2014）。

总之，作为企业在融资活动中最为关心的指标之一，权益成本与资本市场中的许多参与者都息息相关。以往关于权益成本影响因素的文献十分丰富。具体到本书的研究情境，笔者预计，在双重审计管制取消后，投资者可能预期信息风险会增加，进而要求比管制取消前更高的风险补偿（收益率）。然而，现有研究对双重审计管制取消的这一潜在经济后果（或者说，这一可能影响我国市场中权益成本的因素）尚未给予足够的关注。

2.3 审计质量

2.3.1 审计质量的定义

独立审计作为一项缓解信息不对称、降低代理冲突、保护外部投资者的重要治理机制，其质量一直是会计和审计研究的核心（DeFond & Zhang，2014）。DeAngelo（1981a）提出，审计质量是指注册会计师发现并报告客户会计信息中所含重大错报的联合概率，受到注册会计师的独立性和专业胜任能力的共同作用；注册会计师发现错报的可能性取决于其专业胜任能力，如判断应实施哪些审计程序、如何选取样本范围等，而是否愿意报告已发现的错报则取决于注册会计师独立于审计客户的程度。此后，一些学者虽然从不同的角度定义了审计质量（Watts & Zimmerman，1983；Palmrose，1986；Teoh & Wong，1993；Lee & Gu，1998；Francis，2011；DeFond & Zhang，2014；张龙平、张敦力，1997；冯均科，2002），但基本强调审计质量依赖于注册会计师的独立性和专业胜任能力。关于审计质量的衡量，前人提出了多种方法和指标，如盈余质量、财务重述、审计意见、审计费用等（DeFond & Zhang，2014）。

2.3.2 审计质量的影响因素

以往研究发现，审计质量主要受会计师事务所规模、审计师行业专长、会计师事务所内部治理、审计客户代理冲突、审计客户公司治理、审计师任期、客户重要性、审计师与客户私人关系、外部环境等因素的影响。以往研究大多认为事务所规模越大，审计质量越高（DeAngelo，1981a；Dopuch &

Simunic, 1982; Firth & Smith, 1992; DeFond et al., 1999; 吴水澎、李奇凤, 2006; 林永坚、王志强, 2013; 吴昊旻等, 2015; 路军伟等, 2017), 也有学者持有不同的观点(武晓玲等, 2005; 郭照蕊, 2011)。现有文献大体上支持审计师行业专长对审计质量具有积极影响(Owhoso et al., 2002; Krishnan, 2003; 刘文军等, 2010; 谢盛纹、孙俊奇, 2010; 范经华等, 2013), 也有研究基于中国背景得出相反的结论(蔡春、鲜文铎, 2007)。事务所内部治理(如组织形式)也是影响审计质量的一个重要因素(Muzatko et al., 2004; Firth et al., 2012; 朱建弟, 2013; 陈波, 2014; 刘行健、王开田, 2014; 刘启亮等, 2015; 黄敬昌等, 2017)。审计客户方面, 代理冲突越严重, 客户对于高质量审计的需求越强烈(Chow, 1982; Francis & Wilson, 1988; Lennox, 2005a; Blouin et al., 2007; Francis et al., 2009; Guedhami et al., 2009; 王艳艳等, 2006; 高雷、张杰, 2011; 齐鲁光、韩传模, 2016); 客户的公司治理越完善, 其对审计质量的要求越高(Carcello & Neal, 2000; Beasley & Petroni, 2001; Beasley & Salterio, 2001; Stewart & Kent, 2006; Engel et al., 2010; Cassell et al., 2012; 肖作平, 2006; 余宇莹、刘启亮, 2007; 沈玉清等, 2009; 潘琦、温权, 2017), 而叶陈刚等(2015)则持相反观点。审计师与客户之间的关系也会对审计质量产生显著影响, 例如, 一些文献发现较长的审计师任期有助于审计质量的提升(Loebbecke et al., 1989; Petty & Cuganesan, 1996; Geiger & Raghunandan, 2002; Johnson et al., 2002; Myers et al., 2003; Litt et al., 2014; 夏立军等, 2005; 陈信元、夏立军, 2006; 刘启亮、唐建新, 2009), 而另一些则认为较长的审计师任期会损害审计质量(DeAngelo, 1981b; Shockley, 1981; Arrunada & Cándido, 1997; Arel et al., 2005; Carey et al. Simnett, 2006; Ye et al., 2011; 刘启亮, 2006; 江伟、李斌, 2011; 李思飞等, 2014), 还有一些研究得出混合的结论(余玉苗、李琳, 2003; 董南雁、张俊瑞, 2010; 沈玉清等, 2010); 一些学者发现客户重要性越高, 审计质量越低(DeAngelo, 1981b; Choi et al., 2010; Kanagaretnam et al., 2010; Hossain et al., 2016; Zhang, 2017; 陆正飞等, 2012; 曹强等, 2012; 贾楠、李丹, 2015; 谢盛纹等, 2017; 杨永淼、杨慧燕, 2019), 而另一些则有不同的看法(Stice, 1991; Bonner et al., 1998; Zhang, 1999; Reynolds & Francis, 2000; Gaver & Paterson, 2007; Chen et al., 2010; Fung et al., 2016; 方军雄等, 2004; 喻小明等, 2008; 刘文军, 2012; 李明辉、刘笑霞, 2013); 此外, 审计师与客户的私人关系

（如雇佣关系、校友关系等）也会影响审计质量，大多数相关研究认为这种私人关系会损害审计质量（Dowdell & Krishnan，2004；Menon & Williams，2004；Lennox，2005b；Guan et al.，2016；He et al.，2017；吴溪，2006；刘继红，2011；刘继红、章丽珠，2014；陈旭霞等，2015；吴溪等，2015），而也有一些学者得出不同的结论（Geiger et al.，2005；Geiger & North，2006；Baber et al.，2014；邓川等，2017）。以往文献发现审计质量还会受到外部环境因素的影响，如制度环境（Lang et al.，2003；Khurana & Raman，2004；Huijgen & Lubberink，2005；Choi et al.，2008；Francis & Wang，2008；Francis et al.，2011；王猛、谭丽莎，2010；辛清泉、王兵，2010；Ke et al.，2015；田高良等，2017）、诉讼风险（冯延超、梁莱歆，2010；翟华云、廖洪，2011）、监管风险（宋衍蘅、肖星，2012；刘文军，2016；黄益雄、李长爱，2016）、媒体监督（周兰、耀友福，2015；张丽达等，2016；吴伟荣、李晶晶，2017）等。

总之，审计质量一直是会计和审计研究领域中的热门话题，现存有大量关于其影响因素的研究，且相关研究仍在不断丰富。具体到本书的研究情境，以往文献从审计师面临的制度环境的角度提出了双重审计帮助维持较高审计质量的潜在机制。然而，目前对这一机制的探索仍停留于文字描述阶段，尚未有研究深入实证过程进行分析与验证。

2.4 文献述评与研究启示

2.4.1 文献述评

本章 2.1 节主要从定义和经济后果两方面回顾了双重审计相关文献。首先，关于 B 股上市公司曾遵循的双重审计强制要求及其废除的研究出现较早，相关文献研究了包括审计师选择、审计费用、审计质量、市场反应、公司治理等在内的多种经济后果。由于 B 股公司仅在境内上市，且近年来有向 A 股合并的趋势，其与 A+H 股公司所面临的制度环境存在较大差异，因而与 B 股双重审计制度变迁相关的研究结论并不一定适用于 A+H 股。其次，具体到本书关注的 A+H 股双重审计强制要求及其取消，以往研究多关注与审计相关的问题（如审计质量、审计费用和审计市场结构等），而忽视了双重审计管制取消可能对资本市场带来的影响。再次，现有关于 A+H 股双重审计制度的研究结论基本上认同未采用双重审计的 A 股公司比采用双重审计的 A+H 股公司的审计质量更低。据此，可以推测 A+H 股公司的审计质量可能在其放弃双重审计后有所下降。然而，仅仅基于对存在实质性差异的样本的比较分析，很难确定采用双重审计的 A+H 股公司与其他 A 股公司之间的审计质量差异究竟是由是否交叉上市引起的，还是由公司所采用审计制度的差异导致的。最后，Ke 等（2015）阐释了香港审计师通过双重审计过程可能向内地审计师发挥的积极溢出效应。这一解释有助于从审计师面临的制度环境的角度了解双重审计帮助维持较高审计质量的潜在机制。然而，Ke 等（2015）仅从理论上论述了这一可能的积极溢出效应，换句话说，这一效应尚未得到直接、有效的实证测度。此外，这一效应的存在（消失）是否以及在多大程度上会影响采用（放弃）双重审计的公司的审计质量，依然是未知数。

本章 2. 2 节主要从定义和影响因素两方面回顾了权益成本相关文献。关于这一主题的研究已进行了数十年，相关成果十分丰富。根据以往文献，权益成本主要受制度环境、政府干预、公司规模、财务风险、账面市值比率、公司治理、信息披露、会计稳健性、审计质量、流动性、市场风险等因素的影响。以往的理论观点与实证发现为本书与权益成本相关的实证研究模型设计奠定了坚实的基础。与此同时，现有文献中存在如下与本书密切相关的问题：尽管学术界普遍认同并证实了独立审计会影响权益成本，但对于某一特定审计制度的变迁（如，双重审计管制取消）是否会导致权益成本的变化，相关证据目前仍然较为匮乏。

本章 2. 3 节主要从定义和影响因素两方面回顾了审计质量相关文献。关于审计质量的研究已开展了近四十年，形成了大量研究成果。根据以往文献，审计质量的影响因素主要有会计师事务所规模、审计师行业专长、会计师事务所内部治理、审计客户代理冲突、审计客户公司治理、审计师任期、客户重要性、审计师与客户私人关系、外部环境等。以往的理论分析和经验证据为本书与审计质量相关的实证研究模型设计提供了有益的借鉴。与此同时，现有文献中存在如下与本书密切相关的问题：尽管前人从制度环境出发阐述了双重审计帮助维持较高审计质量的潜在机制，但尚未有研究从实证角度将这一抽象机制进行具体量化，而审计质量是否以及在多大程度上会受到这一机制的存在与消失的影响，也尚未得到证实。

2. 4. 2 研究启示

现有文献为本书的研究主题提供了充实的理论依据和经验证据，以及如下研究启示：

首先，尽管A+H股双重审计管制已被取消，但双重审计制度却远未消失，学术界也持续关注这一审计制度及其变迁过程。然而，现有文献局限于考察双重审计管制取消在审计领域的影响，那么，这一政策变更是否会产生其他的经济后果？例如，双重审计管制取消是否会作用于权益成本，从而对资本市场产生影响？除此之外，现有研究通常根据样本所处的时段（管制取消前时段和取消后时段）或所采用的审计制度（双重审计制度和单一审计制度）进行比较分析，那么，如果将双重审计公司进一步划分为在管制取消前强制接受双重审计的公司和在管制取消后自愿采用双重审计的公司，然后在二者之间进行比较，会有怎样的发现？在管制取消后，将自愿采用双重审计的公司与仅接受单一审计的公司进行比较，又会有怎样的发现？换句话说，强制双重审计与自愿双重审计是否会对权益成本产生不同的影响？

其次，关于双重审计管制取消对审计领域产生的经济后果，现有结论基本上反映出不采用双重审计的公司的审计质量低于采用双重审计的公司，据此推测，公司在放弃双重审计之后，审计质量很可能受损。尽管前人从制度环境的角度论述了双重审计帮助维持较高审计质量的潜在机制（香港审计师通过双重审计过程可能向内地审计师发挥的积极溢出效应），然而仍有一些问题留待解决。例如，如何有效地测度这一机制？来自香港审计师的溢出效应越积极，保留双重审计的公司的审计质量是否会越高？放弃双重审计的公司的审计质量下降，是否主要是由这一溢出效应的丧失所导致的？

为回答以上问题，本书将深入考察双重审计管制取消对资本市场和审计市场产生的经济后果。具体而言，本书将通过对管制取消前遵循双重审计强制要求的公司与管制取消后自愿采用双重审计的公司的比较分析，以及对后者与同一时段内仅接受单一审计的公司的比较分析，考察双重审计管制取消对权益成本的影响。另外，本书将通过构建衡量来自香港审计师的溢出效应的新变量，以及对放弃双重审计的公司与保留双重审计的公司之间的比较分析，考察双重审计管制取消对审计质量的影响。

3 制度背景与理论分析

本章首先根据 A+H 股双重审计制度的变迁过程详细介绍本书的制度背景，然后阐述支撑本研究的主要理论，最后基于相关理论以及对双重审计管制取消的资本市场后果和审计市场后果的理论分析，提出本书的理论框架。本书后续三个章节将依据该理论框架展开详细的理论与实证分析。

3.1 制度背景

1993 年，第一家 A+H 股公司——青岛啤酒股份有限公司——在 A 股市场和 H 股市场交叉上市，就此拉开此类公司发展的序幕。在当时，一方面，CAS 与 IFRS 之间存在很大差异；另一方面，境内会计师事务所尚处于发展初期，执业能力较低。为了保护投资者利益，两地上市规则要求 A+H 股公司必须采用双重审计制度。具体而言，一家 A+H 股公司应当雇用一家内地会计师事务所依据《中国注册会计师审计准则》审计该公司按 CAS 编制的 A 股财务报表，并出具审计报告；该公司还应当雇用一家香港会计师事务所以《国际审计准则》或《香港审计准则》为依据审计其按 IFRS 或 HKFRS 编制的 H 股财务报表，并出具审计报告（Wang，2008）。

境内外在会计、审计准则方面一度存在的较大差异是导致双重审计强制要求产生的重要原因之一。由于这些差异，一家 A+H 股公司根据不同会计准则编制并接受审计的两套报表中的会计信息也会存在较大不同；此外，准则方面的差异也会使得境内外投资者对 A+H 股公司的财务报告具有不同的信息需求。例如，一些境外投资者可能只会采纳根据 IFRS 或 HKFRS 编制、经过香港会计师事务所鉴证的会计信息。因此，为满足境内外投资者差异化的信息需求，A+H 股公司需要实施双重审计。

双重审计强制要求产生的另一个主要原因是监管者对内地审计行业的大

力扶植。设立于香港的会计师事务所大多历史悠久、经验丰富、声望较高，而与之相比，内地本土会计师事务所长期存在执业质量低下、审计经验（尤其是国际审计经验）缺乏等问题。为改善本土事务所所处的不利地位，监管部门要求包括 A+H 股公司在内的一部分公司同时雇用一家内地事务所和一家香港事务所实施审计，以期前者可以向后者学习与借鉴技术、管理等方面的成熟经验。然而，实际操作过程中，要求公司实施双重审计并未达到监管部门预期的理想效果，甚至在一定程度上使得内地事务所的处境更加艰难——内地事务所的很多业务被香港事务所抢走，依然难以赢得市场的重视和信任。

双重审计强制要求的实施有助于提高会计信息的可信度、满足不同投资者的信息需求。然而，与此同时，该制度的实施也增加了公司的审计和披露成本（财政部，2010b），阻碍了内地事务所的国际化进程。随着经济全球化以及我国加入世界贸易组织，2006 年 2 月 15 日，财政部在充分借鉴国际会计准则的基础上颁布了新的企业会计准则（包括 1 项基本会计准则与 38 项具体会计准则）。新准则中的绝大部分会计政策和会计处理均与国际准则保持一致；新准则的颁布与实施标志着 CAS 与 IFRS 的实质性趋同、与 HKFRS 的等效。2006 年 5 月 12 日，中国会计准则委员会与香港会计师公会在香港召开内地与香港会计准则趋同会议，并签署《中国会计准则委员会与中国香港会计师公会联合声明》，指出会计准则国际趋同是适应经济全球化发展趋势的必然要求，内地与香港近年来在会计准则国际趋同方面均取得了实质性进展，内地企业会计准则的发布与实施和香港的会计准则实现了实质性趋同，双方未来的合作与努力方向是响应国际会计准则理事会制定一套全球通行的高质量的会计准则的号召。在这样的背景下，双重审计强制要求赖以存在的准则差异日益缩小，监管部门也开始考虑是否还有必要要求 A+H 股公司分别按照境内外会计准则编制财务报表并雇用两家会计师事务所实施审计。自 2007 年起，两地有关部门采取了一系列行动，旨在废除双重审计强制要求、推动境内符合资格的会计师事务所直接从事 H 股审计。2007 年 12 月，两地签署内地与香港会计审计准则等效联合声明，双方已与两地监管机构协商并达成共识，在准则等效声明签署后，立即开展工作，尽快研究解决两地在对方上市的企业以其当地的会计准则编制并由当地具备资格的会计师事务所按照当地审计准则审计财务报表的相关问题，以期早日获得对方上市地监管机构的接纳（中国证券监督管理委员会、香港联合交易所，2007）。2009 年 8 月，两地签署《关于内地与香港在对方上市的公司可选择以本地会计准则编制并由本地会计师事务所审计财务报表的建议架构》，确立了力争从 2010 年 1 月 1 日起由内地会计师事务所从事 H 股审计（包括定期审计和 IPO 审计）的工作目标（香港联合交易所，2009）。2010 年 12 月，证监会与香港联合交易所举行会议，决定相互认可彼此当前执行的会计审计准则，两地就落实两地在对方上市的公司可选择以本地会计准则编制财务报表并由本地会计师事务所按照本地审计准则进行审计的事宜达成共识，香港联合交易所接受 A+H 股公司仅采用内地的会计审计准则以及聘用内地会计师事务所。以此为标志，境内 12 家符合资格的会计师事务所获准自 2010 年以后的会计年度期间，可以采用《中国注册会计师审计准则》为 A+H 股上市公司提供单独的审计服务，A+H 股的双重审计管制被正式取消（香港联合交易所，2010）。

然而，相关规定并不妨碍香港会计师事务所继续为 A+H 股客户提供服务，也不要求决定取消双重审计的公司在同一时间取消。自两地有关部门达成共识后，是否继续采用双重审计制度成为 A+H 股公司的自愿选择，取决于市场力量，并成为上市公司与会计师事务所之间的商业决定（香港联合交易所，2009）。在这一背景下，自双重审计管制取消至今，一些 A+H 股公司先后响应这一政策变更，解雇境外审计师，仅接受境内单一审计；另一些公司则依然采用双重审计。根据后文第 4 章 4.3.1 节、第 5 章 5.3.1 节和第 6 章 6.3.1 节的样本按年度分布概况，双重审计管制取消后，之前受到该管制约束的样本在是否放弃双重审计方面存在明显的差异性，而其中大多数（超过六成）仍然保留了这一审计制度。这表明，即便相关的强制要求已经取消，市场上仍然存在着不可忽视的对于双重审计的自发需求，没有如监管部门所料出现绝大多数公司响应该政策变更、放弃双重审计的情况。由此看来，监管部门对于双重审计价值下跌、失去存在必要性的考虑并未得到实践印证。

3.2 理论基础

3.2.1 公司审计需求相关理论

公司对外部独立审计产生自发需求的经济根源是产权安排，随着公司所有权和经营权的分离，为缓解信息不对称、降低代理成本，独立审计作为市场选择的必然结果应运而生。现有关于公司自愿审计需求的理论解释主要包括代理理论、信息（信号）理论和保险理论。审计需求的代理理论认为，公司雇用注册会计师实施独立审计的动机是缓解投资者与管理层之间的代理冲突（Jensen & Meckling，1976）。审计需求的信息（信号）理论认为，公司雇用注册会计师实施独立审计的动机是向投资者传递积极信号、提高财务信息质量、降低投资者与管理层之间的信息不对称程度（Melumad & Thoman，1990；Beaver et al.，1970）。审计需求的保险理论认为，公司雇用注册会计师实施独立审计的动机是发挥其风险转移的价值（Chow et al.，1988）。这三大理论虽然各自有别，但并非完全割裂，而是相互联系、共同作用于公司的自愿审计选择。由于市场上存在信息不对称，投资者与管理层各自的利益出发点也不一致，客观上期望由专业化的第三方实施独立审计，承担信息风险的减少者和保险人的角色，提高财务信息质量，降低信息不对称程度，缓解代理冲突，进而提高投资者信心，减轻企业的融资难度，促进资源的优化配置。

3.2.2 政府管制审计相关理论

基于管制经济学，政府对市场进行管制的理论解释主要包括公共利益理论、管制俘获理论和经济监管理论。公共利益理论认为，政府管制是一种弥补市场失灵的手段（张红凤，2005）。管制俘获理论认为，监管机构随着时间推移会逐渐被管制对象支配，变得更加迁就管制对象的利益而非保护公共利益（North，1990）。经济监管理论认为，政府实施管制是为了帮助利益集团实现收入最大化（Stigler，1971）。政府对审计市场的管制更符合公共利益理论。审计市场既存在信息不对称，符合信用品的特征，又存在外部性，具备公共物品的特性。在这样的市场上，仅通过市场机制无法实现资源的最优配置，从而会出现市场失灵。例如，由于审计服务的外部性，当公司内部人完全出于对自身成本收益（而非社会福利）的考虑时，为了节约成本，可能会选择低质低价的审计服务；而投资者等利益相关者处于信息劣势，无法准确判断审计质量的高低，这就为公司选择低质低价的审计服务提供了便利，同时也降低了会计师事务所保持独立性、提高审计质量的动力。面对市场失灵，政府这只“有形的手”就有必要出面进行管制，如完善法律体系、制定各项规章制度、建立相应的监管机构等，以便明确审计服务需求方和提供方的职责，规范各方的行为，弥补市场失灵，维护注册会计师的独立性和审计质量，努力确保向财务信息使用者提供可靠的信息，促进审计市场乃至整个资本市场的健康、持续发展。

3.2.3 审计师提供高质量相关理论

如前文所述，公司的利益相关者对独立审计存在多方面的需求，然而如果供给方不能超然独立地提供满足客户要求的高质量审计服务（如审计师不仅不能缓解信息不对称，反而使其愈加严重，无法向投资者提供与决策相关的增量信息），那么审计需求也就无从谈起。因此，在审计市场产生和发展的过程中，会计师事务所也有动机保持独立性、提供优质的审计服务；其动机主要来自两个方面——法律机制和声誉机制——的作用。一方面，根据深口袋理论，会计师事务所拥有一定的财产，具备赔偿能力；通过支付审计费用，投资者和管理层将一部分风险转嫁给了会计师事务所。在法律机制的作用下，一旦发生审计失败，会计师事务所将承担较高的诉讼风险和诉讼成本，因而其有动机为避免受到这样的惩罚而保持独立、勤勉尽责、提供较高的审计质量（Palmrose，1988；DeFond & Subramanyam，1988）。另一方面，会计师事务所出于对自身品牌和声誉的维护，也有动机保持独立性和服务质量。良好的声誉需要长期的积累，建立在大量而频繁的业务之上，可以为事务所带来诸多收益，如投资者信任度的提高、市场份额的扩大、收入的增加、长远的发展等。然而，如果发生审计失败，事务所花费较长时间建立起来的声誉就可能毁于一旦，导致其竞争力下降、市场份额减少。因此，在声誉机制的作用下，为了建立良好声誉、获取长远利益、防止因声誉受损而受到市场惩罚，事务所有动机保持独立性、提供高质量的审计服务（DeAngelo，1981a；Simunic & Stein，1987）。

3.2.4 公司遵循强制要求相关理论

在不完美的资本市场中，投资者通常比筹资者的力量薄弱得多，特别是中小投资者，一旦被筹资者欺骗，通过法律途径维权往往非常艰难，因此，仅依靠法院等执法机制难以有效阻止欺诈等损害投资者利益的行为（Hay et al.，1996；Hay & Shleifer，1998）。在这种情况下，由监管部门制定和实施的强制政策或要求，或许更能有效发挥缓解代理冲突的作用（Mahoney，1995）。

Rock（2002）和 Stulz（2009）认为，投资者对于公司管理层存在损害股东利益的自利行为的疑虑，会因公司遵循一项配备了有力执行机制的强制要求而减轻，因为投资者会将这一遵循行为视为公司在事前做出的可信承诺。

以强制披露为例，Cheng 等（2013）指出，在投资者看来，公司遵循某一强制披露要求，意味着在事前就确定了该公司会披露特定信息。此外，监管部门强有力的执行体系使得违反该强制要求的代价高昂，从而提高了这种事前承诺的可信度（Leuz & Verrecchia，2000）。相比之下，自愿披露特定信息允许管理层在决定是否披露之前预估可能出现的后果，是一种事后的、自利的行为（Bushee & Leuz，2005）。此外，自愿披露缺乏持续性（具有不确定性），因为公司可以在免受监管机构约束或惩罚的前提下自由选择是否披露信息。因此，Cheng 等（2013）认为，相比自愿披露，强制披露更能有效降低代理成本和信息不对称。Cheng 等（2013）的实证分析结论显示，从强制披露转变为自愿披露的公司的市场流动性降低，他们将这一发现归因于与遵循强制披露要求相关的遵循效应的消失。

Hail（2011）提出，能够被投资者视为具有遵循效应的信息披露需要具备以下三个特征：①公司事先不知道披露该信息可能产生的后果；②披露该信息需要花费较大的代价；③市场对不同披露水平的反应存在差异性。据此，遵循强制披露要求可以作为公司在事前向投资者做出可信承诺的一种机制，发挥遵循效应。例如，Rock（2002）介绍了美国证券交易委员会发布的信息披露条例，这一条例的实施有监管机构强有力的执行体系作保障，确保了高昂的违规成本。由此，公司在该条例约束下进行的强制信息披露就发挥了遵循效应，成为投资者眼中的事前可信承诺，有效缓解了代理冲突。此外，该条例还统一了披露信息的格式和数量，不断调整企业的报告义务，这些也有助于解决代理问题。

具有遵循效应的信息披露还可以缓解信息不对称（Stulz，2009），从而降低权益成本，提高市场流动性。例如，Diamond 和 Verrecchia（1991）发现，公司遵循的信息披露要求越高，越有助于降低知情投资者与不知情投资者之间的信息不对称。由此，投资者相对更加确信，在信息披露水平较高的公司中，证券交易将以更加公平的价格进行，从而引起这类公司的市场流动性增加。管理层和做市商之间的信息不对称也可以通过公司遵循更高的信息披露要求来缓解，借助这一机制，市场流动性不足能够得到改善（Baiman & Verrecchia，1996；Verrecchia，1999）。

Lansford 等（2013）认为，业绩指引更像是一种事前（而非事后）的选择，因而自愿披露也可能发挥向投资者做出（明确的或隐含的）承诺的遵循效应（Monahan，2006）。然而，以往研究指出，自愿披露在发挥遵循效应方面难以完全取代强制披露（Rock，2002；Stulz，2009）。这是因为，在缺乏强制要求约束的情况下，公司管理层从事后机会主义行为中谋取的潜在利益很可能吞没其对于声誉受损的担忧，也就是说，仅依靠声誉约束不足以确保管理层信守提供更高披露水平的承诺。据此，自愿披露在发挥遵循效应、降低信息不对称方面不如强制披露有效，因而其对权益成本的抑制作用也弱于后者（Monahan，2006；Hail，2011）。此外，从动态来看，当信息披露由强制要求变为自愿选择时，代理问题可能更加严重。Hope 和 Thomas（2008）发现，当美国的会计准则不再强制跨国公司披露其在各个地区内的详细收益后，这类公司往往会减少披露这类信息，以便于管理层打造帝国、攫取私利。这表明，管理层可能利用强制披露管制放松的机会，做出投机取巧的行为，如策略性地披露或隐瞒信息。他们为了获取私利，很可能以牺牲股东利益为代价，从而导致管理层与股东之间的代理冲突加剧。

总而言之，公司遵循强制要求时会产生一种遵循效应，即在投资者看来，这一遵循行为相当于是公司在事前做出的、难以逆转的可信承诺，降低了投资者对于管理层机会主义的怀疑。这种遵循效应有助于缓解代理冲突和信息不对称，目前已被许多研究证实（Rock，2002；Monahan，2006；Stulz，2009；Hail，2011；Cheng et al.，2013）。

Leuz 和 Wysocki（2008）认为，公司对强制要求的遵循能够发挥降低代理成本和信息不对称的作用，而这种作用并不局限于与信息披露相关的制度，其他领域也发现了支持性的证据（Aghion & Hermalin，1990）。在审计领域中，陈丽蓉和韩彬（2015）发现，与自愿性内部控制审计相比，强制性内部控制审计能够显著提高国有企业的投资效率。他们将这一发现解释为，遵循强制性内部控制审计要求不仅剥夺了管理层选择是否进行内部控制审计的自由，对管理层发挥了约束作用，而且还被投资者视为一种事前承诺，缓解了信息不对称。

3.3 理论框架

在前文介绍了制度背景和主要理论后，本节为本书接下来将要考察的双重审计管制取消的经济后果构建理论框架。本书的理论框架图请参见英文正文第 3 章图 3-1。

首先，基于遵循效应理论，本书通过检验管制取消前的强制双重审计是否会比管制取消后的自愿双重审计带来更低的权益成本，分析双重审计管制取消的资本市场后果。如本章3.1节所述，管制取消后，一些A+H股公司不再采用双重审计，解雇了境外审计师，仅接受境内单一审计；另一些公司则仍然保留双重审计。为考察双重审计管制取消的资本市场后果，本书首先关注管制取消前强制接受双重审计的公司与管制取消后自愿采用双重审计的公司之间的比较分析。如本章3.2.4节所述，公司对某一具备强有力执行机制的强制要求的遵循，会被投资者视为一项在事前做出的、难以逆转的承诺。由此，这种遵循行为能够减轻投资者对于公司管理层可能做出损害股东利益的自利行为的怀疑，产生遵循效应（Rock，2002；Stulz，2009；Cheng et al.，2013），进而降低投资者与管理层之间的代理成本和信息不对称程度，最终达到降低权益成本的效果（Monahan，2006；Hail，2011）。基于这一理论，本书认为，在投资者看来，一家公司对于双重审计强制要求的遵循，意味着在事前就确定了该公司会接受境内外两家会计师事务所的监督、披露两套经审计的财务报表，从而可能减轻投资者对管理层自利行为的疑虑。与之相反，在管制取消后做出的自愿双重审计选择，允许一家公司在决策前预估这一选择可能带来的后果，因而是一种事后的、自利性质的选择。另外，相关部门的有力执行，特别是香港市场上较为完善的执法和监管体系（Ke et al.，2015），为双重审计强制要求的有效实施提供了保障，使受到这一要求约束的公司面临高昂的违规成本，从而确保它们对该要求的持续遵循。相比之下，对于管制取消后自愿采用双重审计的公司，投资者难以确定它们在将来是否会坚持这一选择，因为这些公司能够自行决定放弃双重审计而免于受到来自监管部门的约束和惩罚。因此，本书认为，自愿做出的双重审计选择，可能无法完全取代因遵循双重审计强制要求而产生的遵循效应在缓解信息不对称、降低代理成本方面的重要作用。因此，当公司由强制双重审计转变为自愿双重审计后，其权益成本可能增加。换句话说，公司在强制接受双重审计时的权益成本可能低于其在自愿采用双重审计时的权益成本。

接下来，在考察了强制双重审计（相对于自愿双重审计）对权益成本的影响后，基于信号效应理论，本书通过检验管制取消后的自愿双重审计是否会比单一审计带来更低的权益成本，继续分析双重审计管制取消的资本市场后果。也就是说，本书接下来关注管制取消后自愿采用双重审计的公司与同一时期未采用双重审计（仅接受单一审计）的公司之间的比较分析。根据信号理论，优质公司有动机向投资者传递体现自身优势的信号，以便与劣质公司区别开来。为实现这一目的，优质公司通常会采取一些需要支付额外成本的措施（Melumad & Thoman，1990；Spence，1973）。Jensen 和 Meckling（1976）指出，为使投资者相信那些可能损害他们利益的机会主义行为受到了严格限制，管理层有动机列支用于监督自身的支出，设置契约性质的保证，如雇用独立第三方对管理层编制的财务报表实施外部审计。Melumad 和 Thoman（1990）指出，公司会通过雇用审计师来向掌握较少信息的利益相关者传递私有信息；在 Melumad 和 Thoman（1990）构建的模型中，审计选择是自愿性质的，并且创造出一个只有优质公司才能选择接受审计（购买审计服务对于劣质公司来说因代价较高而难以效仿）的分离均衡状态。由于购买审计服务需要付出一定的代价，只有预期所产生的盈利足以负担这项支出的优质公司才有能力做出这种选择，这就为劣质公司设置了较难逾越的模仿障碍，将自愿接受独立审计的优质公司与后者区分开来。因此，无论所购买的审计服务能够发挥多大的鉴证作用，雇用外部审计师这一行为本身就可以被视为一个积极的信号，向投资者传递关于公司优良特质的重要信息，如管理层正直诚信、公司风险较低、前景较好等，从而有助于优质公司获得投资者的青睐（BarYosef & Livnat，1984）。自愿审计选择的这种信号效应已被国内外许多研究证实（Lennox & Pittman，2011；Dharan，1992；Ettredge et al.，1994；Haw et al.，2008；Collis，2010；Collis，2012；Kausar et al.，2016；Ojala et al.，2016；胡晓，2007；刘斌等，2008；喻少华，2008；周莉，2010；简建辉、杨帆，2012；韩道琴、章亚洲，2013）。基于这一信号理论，本书认为，双重审计管制取消后，相比仅接受单一审计，公司做出自愿的双重审计选择需要花费更大的代价，这一选择可能承载着关于公司优良特质（如低风险、好前景等）的信息。这些信息是区别于审计的鉴证作用的增量信息，可能向市场传递积极的信号，将选择双重审计的公司与仅接受单一审计的公司区别开来。因此，本书认为，相比仅接受单一审计的公司，自愿采用双重审计的公司更可能受到投资者青睐、以较低的权益成本获得资金。也就是说，双重审计管制取消后，自愿采用双重审计的公司可能比仅接受单一审计的公司拥有更低的权益成本。

最后，在明确了双重审计管制取消对资本市场产生的经济后果之后，本书通过对管制取消后放弃双重审计的公司与保留双重审计的公司的比较分析，考察双重审计管制取消的审计市场后果；进一步讲，基于在双重审计过程中，高质量审计师可能向低质量审计师发挥的积极溢出效应，本书检验公司放弃双重审计后的审计质量下降是否主要是由来自香港审计师的积极溢出效应的丧失所导致的。与单一审计相比，双重审计的审计过程更为复杂化。一家公司的财务报表不应存在由于舞弊或错误导致的重大错报，该公司雇用的两家会计师事务所各自得出的审计结论应当保持一致。否则，如果出现矛盾结果，其中任何一方出具的审计报告的可信度都可能受到监管机构和投资者的质疑，从而导致声誉受损（辛清泉、王兵，2010）。此外，不一致的结论还可能成为财务信息使用者提起诉讼的把柄，在一定程度上增加了审计师的诉讼风险和诉讼成本。因此，在双重审计过程中，虽然两家事务所不直接复核对方的工作，但二者均能感受到来自对方的同业压力（Wang，2014）。具体到 A+H 股的双重审计制度，香港审计师可能通过双重审计过程对内地审计师发挥一种积极的溢出效应，而这一积极溢出效应的丧失或许能够解释公司放弃双重审计后的审计质量下降；换句话说，这一积极溢出效应被认为是双重审计帮助维持较高审计质量的潜在机制（Ke et al.，2015）。具体而言，香港的制度环境在法规执行、投资者保护、媒体监督等许多方面都比内地更为严苛。较为完善的制度环境使得香港审计师比内地审计师的独立性和审计质量更高。此外，根据 A+H 股的相关规定，一家公司的 A 股财务报表和 H 股财务报表尽管基于不同的会计、审计准则进行编制和审计，但二者之间不应当存在实质性的差异。这意味着，在双重审计过程中，香港审计师通过签署其中一套财务报表（H 股财务报表），可能会对同一公司的内地审计师产生一种间接的、积极的溢出效应：由于香港审计师在审计工作和审计结果等方面比内地审计师更加规范与严谨，并且会对内地审计师形成潜在的牵制与监督，在诸如此类的同业压力的作用下，内地审计师不敢在审计质量上有所懈怠（Lin et al.，2014）。这种由香港审计师向内地审计师发挥的积极溢出效应，有助于保留双重审计的公司维持较高的审计质量。然而，放弃双重审计使得这一来自香港审计师的溢出效应不复存在，当公司的审计业务仅由内地审计师负责时，审计质量很可能降低。因此，本书认为，公司放弃双重审计后，来自香港审计师的积极溢出效应随之消失，从而可能导致审计质量下降。

需要说明的是，本书考察的双重审计管制取消的资本市场后果与审计市场后果并不是两个完全割裂的经济后果，相反，二者之间关系密切，使本研究形成了一个具有内在联系的统一整体。如英文正文第 2 章 2.2.2.2 节所述，以往研究证实了审计质量与权益成本之间存在负相关关系，即提高审计质量有助于降低权益成本。据此，鉴于审计质量与权益成本之间的关系已经可以从大量文献的一致结论中获知，双重审计管制取消的资本市场后果与审计市场后果之间的关系并不作为本书考察的重点。更确切地讲，为增强本研究对学术领域的潜在贡献，本书对资本市场后果的分析重点在于，厘清遵循双重审计强制要求和自愿采用双重审计分别是否以及在多大程度上会影响权益成本；这些潜在影响（如有）不考虑审计师所提供的鉴证水平，也就是说，是区别于已审财务报表（审计质量）之外的增量影响。与此同时，本书对审计市场后果的分析重点在于，建立关于香港审计师通过双重审计过程可能发挥的积极溢出效应的测度方法，并检验这一积极溢出效应的消失是否是导致放弃双重审计的公司审计质量下降的主要原因。

4 资本市场后果：强制双重审计对权益成本的影响研究

基于上一章提出的理论框架，本章通过检验管制取消前的强制双重审计是否会比管制取消后的自愿双重审计拥有更低的权益成本，分析双重审计管制取消的资本市场后果。

4.1 假设提出

本书认为，与管制取消后公司对双重审计的自愿选择相比，管制取消前公司对双重审计强制要求的遵循更能够缓解信息不对称、降低代理成本。根据 Rock（2002）、Stulz（2009）、Cheng 等（2013）的研究，公司对某一具备强有力执行机制的强制要求的遵循，会被投资者视为一项在事前做出的难以逆转的承诺，从而减轻投资者对公司管理层可能做出损害股东利益的自利行为的怀疑，产生遵循效应。基于这一理论，本书认为，在投资者看来，一家公司遵循双重审计强制要求，意味着在事前就确定了该公司会接受境内外两家会计师事务所的监督并披露两套经审计的财务报表，从而有助于缓解投资者与管理层之间的代理冲突和信息不对称。根据 Hail（2011）提出的能够发挥遵循效应的行为的三个特征（见第 3 章 3. 2. 4 节），首先，管制取消前，遵循双重审计强制要求的公司无权自行决定是否采用双重审计，因此，公司管理层无法事先估计实施双重审计可能带来的后果。而管制取消后，仅根据公司对双重审计的自愿选择，投资者难以在事前确定公司是否会接受境内外两家会计师事务所的监督并披露两套经审计的财务报表；相反，公司可以事先对双重审计可能给自身带来的成本与收益进行预期，并基于这一预期选择是否保留双重审计。其次，双重审计为公司带来了较高的审计和披露成本，此外，当双重审计作为一项强制要求时，两地市场（特别是香港市场）上各部门的有力执行使受到这一要求约束的公司还面临高昂的违规成本。相比之下，当公司能够自由选择是否采用双重审计时，投资者很难确定它们在将来是否会坚持这一选择，因为它们可以自行决定放弃双重审计而不再需要承担违规成本。最后，公司是否遵循双重审计强制要求会引发不同的市场反应（方军雄，2010）。综上，当公司遵循双重审计强制要求时，事先不知道可能出现的结果、需要支付较高的成本、不同的做法会引发不同的市场反应。因此，本书认为，公司对双重审计强制要求的遵循符合 Hail（2011）提出的三个特征，能够发挥遵循效应，在缓解投资者对管理层机会主义行为的疑虑、降低代理成本和信息不对称程度方面可能比自愿做出的双重审计选择更胜一筹。

此外，公司遵循双重审计强制要求还有助于强化两家受雇审计师的监督作用。具体而言，当雇用境内外两家会计师事务所实施审计是公司应当遵循的事前要求时，两家审计师能够对公司管理层的决策和实施过程共同发挥事前的监督和约束作用。相比之下，当双重审计变为自愿性质的选择时，审计师的监督作用很可能被削弱，因为只有在公司预期接受两家审计师监督的利大于弊时，才有可能在事后做出采用双重审计的选择。从这一角度讲，相比自愿双重审计，强制双重审计可能会对管理层机会主义形成更加有力的威慑。

基于以上论述，双重审计管制取消会导致与遵循双重审计强制要求相关的遵循效应的丧失，如果该效应丧失的代价无法被自愿采用双重审计完全弥补，那么本书预期，管制取消后的自愿双重审计将会比管制取消前的强制双重审计拥有更高的权益成本。

值得一提的是，本书关注的是 A 股市场的财务和审计数据，而所有样本公司的 A 股财务报表在样本期间内都接受了内地审计师审计，这就便于本书在实证分析中对经过审计的财务信息的影响进行分离、量化和控制。这一做法有助于将结果中混淆的审计质量对权益成本的作用分离出来，从而尽可能地保证本章的主要实证发现反映的是与遵循双重审计强制要求这一行为本身有关的遵循效应。

基于此，本书提出假设 H1 如下：

H1：在其他条件不变的情况下，公司强制接受双重审计时的权益成本比自愿采用双重审计时的权益成本更低。

接下来，在本章主要论点的逻辑线上，本书进一步考虑权益融资需求、代理成本和其他自愿审计形式的调节作用。

首先，希望权益成本降低的公司往往对权益资本具有很强的依赖性

（Chen et al.，2019）。因此，如果遵循双重审计强制要求能够发挥遵循效应、降低权益成本，那么这一作用可能对于权益融资需求高的公司尤其重要。换句话说，伴随着双重审计管制的取消，失去遵循双重审计强制要求在降低权益成本方面的作用，可能会使权益融资需求高的公司付出更大的代价。

基于此，本书提出假设 H2 如下：

H2：在其他条件不变的情况下，在权益融资需求更高的公司中，强制接受双重审计（相比自愿采用双重审计）对权益成本的抑制作用更为显著。

其次，如果公司对双重审计强制要求的遵循能够发挥遵循效应，缓解投资者对管理层机会主义行为的疑虑、降低代理成本，那么这一作用可能对代理冲突较为严重的公司更有价值。换句话说，伴随着双重审计管制的取消，失去遵循双重审计强制要求在降低代理成本方面的作用，可能会使代理冲突严重的公司付出更大的代价。

基于此，本书提出假设 H3 如下：

H3：在其他条件不变的情况下，在代理成本更高的公司中，强制接受双重审计（相比自愿采用双重审计）对权益成本的抑制作用更为显著。

最后，公司也可以购买其他审计服务以降低信息风险，如雇用审计师对其中期报表进行审计（Haw et al.，2008）。然而，本书认为，作为一项事后的、自利的选择，中期报表审计难以完全取代遵循双重审计强制要求在发挥遵循效应、降低权益成本方面的作用。

基于此，本书提出假设 H4 如下：

H4：在其他条件不变的情况下，强制接受双重审计（相比自愿采用双重审计）对权益成本的抑制作用不会被自愿采用中期报表审计削弱。

4.2 研究设计

4.2.1 样本与数据

本章实证分析选用 2007—2015 年我国 A 股上市公司的数据。由于新的 CAS 自 2007 年生效，本书将 2007 年作为样本期间的起点，尽可能降低会计准则对本研究的混杂影响。此外，由于本研究围绕的双重审计管制取消发生在 2010 年，如果样本期间涵盖的管制取消后的年份过多，可能会加剧政策变化前后期间长度的不平衡性、混入更多其他因素的影响，因此，本书选择

2015 年作为样本期间的终点。

另一点需要说明的是，虽然本书关注的政策变化（即双重审计管制取消）影响的主要是 A+H 股公司，但是本书认为，在实证分析中有必要将仅在内地上市的 A 股公司也包含在本章的总样本中。一方面，近年来，我国内地市场吸引了越来越多国际学者的关注，通过在主要分析中将样本范围扩大到整个 A 股（而非局限于 A+H 股），本书试图以我国内地市场为背景得出结论，并期望为其他新兴经济体提供实践启示。因此，本书认为，将视野扩展到整个内地市场，以其他 A 股公司作为比较基准，有助于突出本书的研究贡献，使本研究更具有普遍意义。另一方面，从实证角度讲，将仅在内地上市的 A 股公司纳入样本范围也是适当的，因为它们不受双重审计管制取消的影响，而且与放弃双重审计的 A+H 股公司一样，仅接受境内单一审计，适合成为控制组的一部分。

具体选样过程请参见英文正文第 4 章 4. 2. 1 节和表 4-1。

4. 2. 2　权益成本的测度

第 2 章 2. 2. 1 节提到，现有文献提出了多种测度权益成本的方法。Chen 等（2011）指出，GLS 模型（Gebhardt et al. , 2001）比较适合于中国资本市场。与 Chen 等（2011）的看法相一致，本研究经过一系列测试发现，在我国资本市场上，GLS 模型相比其他常用的权益成本测算模型具有更好的表现力和可靠性。基于此，本章主要利用基于 GLS 模型估算的权益成本指标进行实证分析。对于常用的权益成本测算模型的介绍，以及测试、选择适用于本书的模型的详细过程，请参见英文正文第 4 章 4. 2. 2 节。

4. 2. 3　实证模型

实证模型请参见英文正文第 4 章 4. 2. 3 节等式（4-6）；变量定义请参见表 4-6。

需要说明的是，双重差分法不适用于检验本章的研究问题，所以等式（4-6）并非一个双重差分模型。假设本章采用双重差分模型进行实证分析，模型中的 *Treat* 变量为 1（0）应表示从强制双重审计到自愿双重审计的样本组（从强制双重审计到强制双重审计的样本组）。而实际上，在双重审计管制取消前（后），不存在自愿采用双重审计（强制接受双重审计）的公司，因而强制双重审计与自愿双重审计之间的比较实质上是只存在于管制取消前的情形和只存在于管制取消后的情形之间的纵向比较。据此，等式（4-6）中的变量 $DUAL_{t,i}$ 不同于双重差分模型中的 *Treat* 变量。更确切地说，$DUAL_{t,i}$ 为1表示所有实施双重审计的情况（既包括强制双重审计，也包括自愿双重审计）。当 $POST_{t,i}$ 为0（1）时，$DUAL_{t,i}$ 为1表示强制接受双重审计（自愿采用双重审计）的公司。在等式（4-6）中，本书重点关注交互项 $DUAL_{t,i} \times POST_{t,i}$，它的系数反映了相比于强制双重审计，自愿双重审计对权益成本的增量影响。

4.3 实证分析

4.3.1 样本分布概况

结果显示，在双重审计管制取消后，大多数曾经受到该管制约束的公司认为依然有必要实施双重审计，因而继续采用这一审计制度；市场上对双重审计的自发需求占有不可忽视的比重，与监管部门认为的自会计准则趋同以来双重审计价值锐减的看法相悖。详细的样本分布概况请参见英文正文第4章4.3.1节和表4-7。

4.3.2 描述性统计

请参见英文正文第4章4.3.2节和表4-8 Panel A。

4.3.3 组间差异分析

结果显示，管制取消前强制接受双重审计的样本的权益成本比管制取消后自愿采用双重审计的样本的权益成本显著更低，初步支持了假设H1。详细结果请参见英文正文第4章4.3.3节和表4-8 Panel B。

4.3.4 多元回归分析

4.3.4.1 对假设H1的检验

英文正文表4-9报告了对假设H1的检验结果。本书首先在全样本中进行回归，结果如表4-9第（1）列所示，$DUAL_{t,i} \times POST_{t,i}$ 的回归系数为正，且在0.05的水平上统计显著，表明在控制了包括审计质量（$Big4_{t,i}$）在内的一系列潜在影响因素后，公司在管制取消后自愿采用双重审计时的权益成本比公司在管制取消前强制接受双重审计时的权益成本高出 0.006（9.7%），支持了假设 H1。其次，为解决与交叉上市相关的自选择问题，本书在 A+H 股样本中进行回归，如表 4-9 第（2）列所示，$DUAL_{t,i} \times POST_{t,i}$的回归系数依然显著为正。最后，为排除不可观测的公司特征对实证结果的影响，本书在所有实施双重审计的样本中进行回归，并引入公司固定效应，如表 4-9 第（3）列所示，$POST_{t,i}$的回归系数显著为正，依然支持假设 H1。以上结果及详细分析请参见英文正文第 4 章 4.3.4.1 节和表 4-9。

4.3.4.2 假设 H2~H4 的检验

对于假设 H2~H4，本书采用分组回归的方式进行检验。英文正文表 4-10 第（1）（2）列报告了对假设 H2 的检验结果，$DUAL_{t,i} \times POST_{t,i}$的回归系数在权益融资需求高的样本中显著为正，而在权益融资需求低的样本中不显著，支持了假设 H2。表 4-10 第（3）（4）列报告了对假设 H3 的检验结果，$DUAL_{t,i} \times POST_{t,i}$的回归系数在代理成本高的样本中显著为正，而在代理成本低的样本中不显著，支持了假设 H3。表 4-10 第（5）（6）列报告了对假设 H4 的检验结果，$DUAL_{t,i} \times POST_{t,i}$的回归系数在中期报表经过审计的样本和中期报表未经审计的样本中均显著为正，支持了假设 H4。以上结果及详细分析请参见英文正文第 4 章 4.3.4.2 节和表 4-10。

4.3.5 稳健性检验

稳健性检验排除了以下几种其他可能的解释。

4.3.5.1 进一步排除审计质量的影响

现有文献构建了许多用于测度审计质量的指标，但由于审计师提供的鉴证水平具有不可观测性，如何精确衡量审计质量一直是学术界面临的一个难题（DeFond & Zhang，2014）。本章虽然已经在主要分析中引入变量 $Big4_{t,i}$作为代理变量控制审计质量，但是尚不清楚强制双重审计样本与自愿双重审计样本的审计质量究竟是否存在差异。对此，本章进一步探究发现，两组样本在其他常用的审计质量指标方面（如可操纵性应计、财务重述、审计意见）不存在显著差异。接下来，为进一步分离和控制审计质量对权益成本的影响，本书将上述常用的审计质量指标作为控制变量引入等式（4-6）进行回归，主要结论依然成立。此外，本书还考虑了可能引起审计师鉴证水平发生变化的情形（如公司更换不同水准的审计师或采用不同的审计制度），在排除了这些因素的影响后，结果依然是稳健的。以上结果及详细分析请参见英文正文第 4 章 4. 3. 5. 1 节和表 4-11。

4. 3. 5. 2 会计准则国际趋同

在本章对强制双重审计和自愿双重审计的纵向比较分析中，会计准则国际趋同作为一个主要的混淆因素，可能对结果造成影响。具体而言，本书发现管制取消前的双重审计比管制取消后的双重审计拥有更低的权益成本，这一发现可能反映的不是与遵循双重审计强制要求相关的遵循效应的丧失，而是由会计准则逐步趋同引起的双重审计价值下降。本章 4. 3. 1 节的样本按年度分布概况显示，管制取消后，大部分之前受到双重审计管制约束的样本仍然继续采用双重审计，这一现状并未支持监管部门对于双重审计价值锐减的看法。本书借鉴以往研究，计算会计准则趋同指数，发现强制双重审计样本与自愿双重审计样本的会计准则趋同指数不存在显著差异，CAS 与 IFRS 的实质性趋同在 2007 年就已实现，并且在样本期间内持续。接下来，为排除会计准则国际趋同的影响，本书将会计准则趋同指数作为控制变量引入等式（4-6)进行回归，主要结论依然成立。以上结果及详细分析请参见英文正文第 4 章 4. 3. 5. 2 节和表 4-12。

4. 3. 5. 3 成长性的差异

Chen 等（2011）指出，用 GLS 模型估计权益成本时，将行业中位数设为预计净资产收益率终值的做法，可能低估具有高成长性的公司的权益成本。本章的描述性统计结果也反映出不同样本组之间的预期增长率存在较大差异。由此，为控制成长性差异的潜在影响，本书借鉴 Chen 等（2011）的做法，将 $Growth_{t,i}$ 与 $DUAL_{t,i}$，$POST_{t,i}$，$DUAL_{t,i} \times POST_{t,i}$ 的交乘项引入等式（4-6），回归结果依然是稳健的。详细内容请参见英文正文第 4 章 4. 3. 5. 3 节和表 4-13。

4. 3. 5. 4 权益成本的其他测度

此外，本章还利用其他常用模型（如英文正文第 4 章 4. 2. 2 节所示）测算出来的权益成本指标进行稳健性检验。详细内容请参见英文正文第 4 章 4. 3. 5. 4 节和表 4-14。

4.4 结果讨论

本章对假设 H1～H4 进行检验，得出以下实证结果：①公司在管制取消前强制接受双重审计时的权益成本低于在管制取消后自愿采用双重审计时的权益成本；②强制接受双重审计（相比自愿采用双重审计）对权益成本的抑制作用在股权融资需求更高的公司中更为显著；③强制接受双重审计（相比自愿采用双重审计）对权益成本的抑制作用在代理成本更高的公司中更为显著；④强制接受双重审计（相比自愿采用双重审计）对权益成本的抑制作用没有被其他自愿审计机制（如，中期报表审计）削弱。此外，在控制了其他审计质量指标、会计准则国际趋同、公司成长性差异的影响后，以及在采用其他方法估计权益成本时，主要结果依然是稳健的。

与因遵循强制要求而产生的遵循效应相一致，以上结果证实了本章的观点，即自愿采用双重审计无法完全取代遵循双重审计强制要求在降低权益成本方面的作用。也就是说，一家公司对双重审计强制要求的遵循，会被投资者视为该公司在事前做出的一种可信承诺——承诺接受境内外两家会计师事务所的监督并披露两套经审计的财务报表，从而缓解了投资者对管理层自利行为的疑虑；此外，双重审计强制要求的实施伴随着有关部门强有力的执行机制，使受到这一要求约束的公司面临高昂的违规成本，从而保证这些公司能够持续地遵循该要求。相比之下，管制取消后，对双重审计的自愿选择允许公司在做出决策之前预估这一选择的后果，是一种事后的、自利性质的选择；此外，即便一家公司选择采用双重审计，该公司也可以在免于受到监管部门约束和惩罚的情况下自行决定放弃双重审计，导致投资者难以确定这一选择是否具有持续性。

总而言之，本章的实证结果表明，在我国资本市场上，遵循双重审计强制要求比自愿采用双重审计更有助于维持较低的权益成本。换句话说，在双重审计管制取消后，公司无法再通过遵循双重审计强制要求来抑制权益成本的上升，即便公司选择继续采用双重审计，也难以完全弥补这一作用的丧失。对本章所有假设检验情况的汇总参见英文正文中的表 4-15。

5　资本市场后果：自愿双重审计对权益成本的影响研究

上一章发现双重审计管制取消前的强制双重审计比管制取消后的自愿双重审计拥有更低的权益成本。基于第 3 章提出的理论框架，本章通过检验管制取消后的自愿双重审计是否会比单一审计拥有更低的权益成本，继续分析双重审计管制取消的资本市场后果。

5.1　假设提出

如第 3 章 3.1 节所述，双重审计管制取消后，监管部门允许 A+H 股公司自行决定继续采用或放弃双重审计。自 2010 年起，一些 A+H 股公司放弃了双重审计，转而与仅在内地上市的 A 股公司一样，仅雇用一家境内会计师事务所实施单一审计；另一些 A+H 股公司则仍然坚持双重审计。

Melumad 和 Thoman（1990）、Lennox 和 Pittman（2011）指出，即便不存在强制性的审计要求，公司也可能自愿购买审计服务，以发挥其中的信号作用。购买审计服务需要付出一定的成本，做出这一选择能够向外界传递区别于经审计的财务信息的增量信息，体现公司的风险特征（公司愿意接受审计，可能表明其风险较低）。此外，自愿购买审计服务还可以向投资者显示公司面临的良好前景，因为通常来讲，只有在预期未来所产生的盈利足以负担某项额外的支出时，公司才有可能列支该笔支出（Kausar et al.，2016）。自愿审计还能够创造出一个只有优质公司才能选择接受审计（对于劣质公司来说，购买审计服务代价较高，难以效仿）的分离均衡状态（Kausar et al.，2016）。因此，与其他公司相比，自愿购买审计服务的公司更可能受到投资者的青睐，从而以较低的成本获得权益融资。基于这一信号理论，本书认为，双重审计管制取消后，自愿采用双重审计比仅接受单一审计需要付出更高的审计与披露成本，可以向投资者显示与公司潜在的优良特质有关的信息，如质量较高、风险较低、前景较好等。这些区别于经审计的财务信息的增量信息，可能向市场传递积极的信号，将自愿采用双重审计的公司与仅接受单一审计的公司区别开来。综上，本书认为，相比仅接受单一审计的公司，自愿采用双重审计的公司更可能受到投资者青睐、以较低的权益成本获得资金。也就是说，如果自愿的双重审计选择能够发挥信号作用，本书预期，双重审计管制取消后，自愿采用双重审计的公司比仅接受单一审计的公司的权益成本更低。

值得一提的是，本书关注的是 A 股市场的财务和审计数据，而所有样本公司的 A 股财务报表在样本期间内都接受了内地审计师审计，这就便于本书在实证分析中对经过审计的财务信息的影响进行分离、量化和控制。这一做法有助于将结果中混淆的审计质量对权益成本的作用分离出来，从而尽可能地保证本章的主要实证发现反映的是与自愿采用双重审计这一行为本身有关的信号效应。

基于此，本书提出假设 H5 如下：

H5：在其他条件不变的情况下，管制取消后，自愿采用双重审计的公司比仅接受单一审计的公司的权益成本更低。

接下来，在本章主要论点的逻辑线上，本书进一步考虑权益融资需求、代理成本和其他自愿审计形式的调节作用。

首先，较为依赖权益融资的公司往往更加关注权益成本。因此，双重审计管制取消后，如果自愿采用双重审计能够发挥信号效应、降低权益成本，那么这一作用可能对权益融资需求高的公司尤其重要。

基于此，本书提出假设 H6 如下：

H6：在其他条件不变的情况下，在权益融资需求更高的公司中，自愿采用双重审计（相比仅接受单一审计）对权益成本的抑制作用更为显著。

其次，Jensen 和 Meckling（1976）指出，公司管理层有动机自愿购买审计服务，以发出信号使投资者相信，那些可能损害投资者利益的机会主义行为已经受到限制。双重审计管制取消后，如果对双重审计的自愿选择能够向投资者显示公司包括管理层正直诚信在内的优良特质，那么这一信号作用可能对代理冲突较为严重的公司更有价值。

基于此，本书提出假设 H7 如下：

H7：在其他条件不变的情况下，在代理成本更高的公司中，自愿采用双重审计（相比仅接受单一审计）对权益成本的抑制作用更为显著。

最后，公司也可能购买其他审计服务，如雇用审计师审计其中期报表。中期报表审计作为一种自愿审计选择，也可能向市场发出显示公司优良特质的积极信号。如果中期报表审计也能够发挥信号作用，那么自愿采用双重审计向投资者传递的增量信息可能会因此减少。也就是说，中期报表审计可能在一定程度上取代自愿采用双重审计在发挥信号效应、降低权益成本方面的作用。

基于此，本书提出假设 H8 如下：

H8：在其他条件不变的情况下，在中期报表经过审计的公司中，自愿采用双重审计（相比仅接受单一审计）对权益成本的抑制作用显著减弱。

5.2 研究设计

5.2.1 样本与数据

本章的实证分析选用 2010—2015 年我国 A 股上市公司的数据。本书以上一章总样本为基础，经过进一步筛选，得到本章的总样本。具体选样过程请参见英文正文第 5 章 5.2.1 节和表 5-1。

5.2.2 实证模型

本章的实证模型请参见英文正文第 5 章 5.2.2 节等式（5-1）。在等式（5-1）中，因变量为基于 GLS 模型估算的权益成本指标，对 GLS 模型的介绍参见英文正文第 4 章 4.2.2 节和等式（4-1）；本书重点关注变量 $DUAL\_V_{t,i}$（虚拟变量，为 1 表示公司自愿采用双重审计，否则为 0），该变量的系数反映了双重审计管制取消后，相对于单一审计，自愿双重审计对权益成本的影响。其他变量的定义参见英文正文表 5-2。

5.3 实证分析

5.3.1 样本分布概况

结果显示，在双重审计管制取消后，大多数曾经受到该管制约束的公司依然继续采用双重审计，市场上存在着不可忽视的自发需求。详细的样本分布概况参见英文正文第 5 章 5. 3. 1 节和表 5–3。

5. 3. 2 描述性统计

参见英文正文第 5 章 5. 3. 2 节和表 5–4 Panel A。

5. 3. 3 组间差异分析

结果显示，管制取消后自愿采用双重审计的样本与仅接受单一审计的样本在许多方面都存在显著差异。详细结果参见英文正文第 5 章 5. 3. 3 节和表 5–4 Panel B。

5. 3. 4 多元回归分析

5. 3. 4. 1 对假设 H5 的检验

表 5–5 报告了对假设 H5 的检验结果。本书首先在全样本中进行回归，结果如表 5–5 第（1）列所示，$DUAL_V_{t,i}$的回归系数为负，且在 0. 01 的水平上统计显著，表明在控制了包括审计质量（$Big4_{t,i}$）在内的一系列潜在影响因素后，管制取消后自愿采用双重审计的公司，比仅接受单一审计公司的权益成本低 0. 007（10. 9%），支持了假设 H5。

接下来，本书进一步采用倾向得分匹配法（PSM）排除公司特征差异对结果的潜在影响，基于等式（5–2）预测样本选择双重审计的概率，并据此进行配对，最终得到 242 个配对样本。然后在这些配对样本中进行回归，如表 5–5 第（2）列所示，$DUAL_V_{t,i}$的回归系数依然显著为负，进一步支持了假设 H5。

以上结果及详细分析参见英文正文第 5 章 5. 3. 4. 1 节和表 5–5、表5–6。

5. 3. 4. 2 假设 H6～H8 的检验

对于假设 H6～H8，本书采用分组回归的方式进行检验。英文正文表 5–7 第（1）（2）列报告了对假设 H6 的检验结果，$DUAL_V_{t,i}$的回归系数在权益融资需求高的样本中显著为负，而在权益融资需求低的样本中不显著，支持了假设 H6。表 5–7 第（3）（4）列报告了对假设 H7 的检验结果，$DUAL_V_{t,i}$的回归系数在代理成本高的样本中显著为负，而在代理成本低的样本中不显著，支持了假设 H7。表 5–7 第（5）（6）列报告了对假设 H8 的检验结果，$DUAL_V_{t,i}$的回归系数在中期报表经过审计的样本中不显著，而在中期报表未经审计的样本中显著为负，支持了假设 H8。以上结果及详细分析参见英文正文第 5 章 5. 3. 4. 2 节和表 5-7。

5. 3. 5 稳健性检验

稳健性检验排除了以下几种其他可能的解释。

5. 3. 5. 1 进一步排除审计质量的影响

本章虽然已经在上述主要分析中引入变量 $Big4_{t,i}$作为代理变量控制审计质量，但是尚不清楚自愿双重审计样本与单一审计样本的审计质量究竟是否存在差异。对此，本章进一步探究发现，两组样本的其他常用审计质量指标（如可操纵性应计、财务重述、审计意见）没有显著差异。接下来，为进一步分离和控制审计质量的影响，本书将上述常用的审计质量指标作为控制变量引入等式（5-1）进行回归，结果依然是稳健的。此外，本书还考虑了可能引起审计师鉴证水平发生变化的情形（如公司采用不同的审计制度或更换不同水准的审计师），在排除了这些因素的影响后，主要结论依然成立。以上结果及详细分析参见英文正文第 5 章 5. 3. 5. 1 节和表 5-8。

5. 3. 5. 2 排除不可观测因素的影响

在双重审计管制取消后自愿双重审计与单一审计的比较分析中，可能存在自选择问题。考虑到这一问题，本章的主要分析已采用 PSM 方法排除了可观测因素对结果的影响。为进一步排除不可观测因素可能导致的内生性，本章采用混杂变量影响阈值分析（ITCV）进行处理。分析发现，自选择偏差对本章的主要结论不存在严重影响。详细内容参见英文正文第 5 章 5. 3. 5. 2 节和表 5-9。

5. 3. 5. 3 成长性的差异

用 GLS 模型估计权益成本时，具有高成长性的公司的权益成本可能会被低估（Chen et al.，2011）。本章的描述性统计结果也反映出不同样本组之间的预期增长率存在较大差异。为控制成长性差异的潜在影响，本书借鉴 Chen 等（2011）的做法，将 $Growth_{t,i}$与 $DUAL_V_{t,i}$的交乘项引入等式（5-1）进行回归，主要结论依然成立。详细内容参见英文正文第 5 章 5. 3. 5. 3 节和表5-10。

5.3.5.4 权益成本的其他测度

另外，本章还利用其他常用模型（如英文正文第4章4.2.2节所示）测算出来的权益成本指标进行稳健性检验。详细内容参见英文正文第5章5.3.5.4节和表5-11。

5.4 结果讨论

本章对假设H5~H8进行检验，得出以下实证结果：①在双重审计管制取消后，自愿采用双重审计的公司的权益成本低于仅接受单一审计的公司的权益成本；②自愿采用双重审计（相比仅接受单一审计）对权益成本的抑制作用在股权融资需求更高的公司中更为显著；③自愿采用双重审计（相比仅接受单一审计）对权益成本的抑制作用在代理成本更高的公司中更为显著；④自愿采用双重审计（相比仅接受单一审计）对权益成本的抑制作用会被其他自愿审计机制（如中期报表审计）削弱。此外，在控制了其他审计质量指标、公司成长性差异、不可观测因素的影响后，以及在采用其他方法估计权益成本时，主要结果依然是稳健的。

与因做出自愿审计选择而产生的信号效应相一致，以上结果证实了本章的观点，即双重审计管制取消后，自愿采用双重审计在降低权益成本方面比仅接受单一审计更胜一筹。也就是说，管制取消后，对双重审计的自愿选择比仅接受单一审计需要付出更高的审计与披露成本，能够向市场传递区别于已审财务信息的关于公司优良特质的增量信息，发出积极的信号，将自愿采用双重审计的公司与仅接受单一审计的公司区别开来，使投资者愿意以更低的回报率为前者提供资金。

总而言之，本章的实证结果表明，在我国资本市场上，双重审计管制取消后，自愿采用双重审计比仅接受单一审计更有助于降低权益成本。对本章所有假设检验情况的汇总，参见英文正文中的表5-12。

6 审计市场后果：放弃双重审计对审计质量的影响研究

本书第 4 章、第 5 章探究了双重审计管制取消的资本市场后果。第 4 章发现管制取消前的强制双重审计比管制取消后的自愿双重审计拥有更低的权益成本，而第 5 章发现在管制取消后，自愿双重审计比单一审计拥有更低的权益成本。基于第 3 章提出的理论框架，在厘清了双重审计管制取消的资本市场后果之后，接下来，本章通过比较放弃双重审计和保留双重审计，分析双重审计管制取消的审计市场后果。具体而言，基于在双重审计过程中，高质量审计师可能向低质量审计师发挥积极溢出效应（Ke et al.，2015），本章检验公司放弃双重审计后的审计质量下降是否主要是由来自香港审计师的积极溢出效应的丧失所导致的。

6.1 假设提出

虽然有关部门取消双重审计管制旨在提高审计效率、降低公司上市成本，但这一政策变更也引起了实务界与理论界对审计质量的担忧。例如，《有关接受在香港上市的内地注册成立公司采用内地的会计及审计准则以及聘用内地会计师事务所的咨询总结》指出，许多受咨询人士对内地会计师事务所的服务质量存在较大疑虑，担心它们缺乏对香港市场规章制度的了解和必需的知识、技能、经验；公司放弃双重审计，仅接受境内单一审计，恐怕难以保证较高的会计信息质量（香港联合交易所，2010）。在学术界，以往研究提到，香港审计师可能通过双重审计过程对内地审计师发挥一种积极的溢出效应，这种效应源于境内外审计师所处的制度环境的差异（Ke et al.，2015）；而这一积极溢出效应的丧失，或许是导致公司放弃双重审计后审计质量受损的主要原因。

与单一审计相比，包含一家内地会计师事务所和一家香港会计师事务所在内的双重审计过程更为复杂，主要借助由香港审计师对内地审计师发挥的一种间接的、积极的溢出效应，来帮助维持较高的审计质量（Ke et al.，2015）。具体而言，在香港市场上，审计师受到各大监管机构（如香港证券与期货事务监察委员会、香港联合交易所、香港会计师公会、廉政公署等）的严格监管；分析师较为专业，机构投资者众多，能够有效发挥监督作用；投资者保护水平高，中小投资者维权意识强、维权态度积极；政府干预程度低，较少损害审计师的独立性；媒体监督的力度也比较强。这样严苛的制度环境促使香港审计师保持较高的独立性和审计质量。而内地市场在这些方面较之香港市场则相对较弱，整体上缺乏对高质量审计的需求，这样的制度环境不利于内地审计师提高独立性和审计质量。而双重审计制度有助于改善这一状况。具体来讲，根据 A+H 股的相关规定，一家公司的 A 股和 H 股财务报表尽管基于不同的会计、审计准则进行编制和审计，但二者之间不应当存在实质性的差异。这意味着，在双重审计过程中，香港审计师通过签署其中一套财务报表（H 股财务报表），可能会对同一公司的内地审计师产生一种间接的、积极的溢出效应。例如，香港审计师在审计工作和审计结果等方面比内地审计师更加规范、严谨，并且会对内地审计师形成潜在的牵制与监督；在这些同业压力的作用下，内地审计师也不敢在审计质量上有所懈怠（Lin et al.，2014），从而有助于保留双重审计的公司拥有较高的审计质量。综上，本书认为，来自香港审计师的积极溢出效应，可能是双重审计制度帮助维持较高审计质量的重要内在机制。换句话说，如果在双重审计过程中切实存在这种积极溢出效应，那么本书预期，保留双重审计的公司的审计质量会随着该效应的增强而提高。

基于此，本书提出假设 H9 如下：

H9：在其他条件不变的情况下，来自香港审计师的溢出效应越积极，保留双重审计的公司的审计质量越高。

然而，放弃双重审计会阻碍来自香港审计师的溢出效应，当公司的审计业务仅由内地审计师负责时，审计质量很可能降低。据此，本书认为，公司放弃双重审计之后，来自香港审计师的积极溢出效应随之消失，从而可能导致审计质量下降。

基于此，本书提出假设 H10 如下：

H10：在其他条件不变的情况下，来自香港审计师的积极溢出效应的丧失，导致放弃双重审计的公司的审计质量下降。

6.2 研究设计

6.2.1 样本与数据

本章实证分析选用2010—2015年我国A+H股上市公司的数据。本章的总样本可以视为前两章样本的子集。在前两章的实证分析中，仅在内地上市的A股公司适合作为基组的一部分，因为它们既不受双重审计管制取消这一政策变更的影响，又与放弃双重审计的A+H股公司一样仅接受境内单一审计。而本章关注的重点是来自香港审计师的积极溢出效应的存在与消失；这一效应的变化，所涉及的主要是A+H股公司。基于此，本章的实证分析未将其他A股公司纳入样本范围。

具体选样过程参见英文正文第6章6.2.1节和表6-1。

6.2.2 审计质量的测度

借鉴Ke等（2015）、Carey和Simnett（2006）、DeFond和Park（2001）的做法，本章利用A股报表异常营运资本应计项目的绝对值衡量审计质量，进行主要分析。该指标能够有效反映管理层自由裁量权，适合用于审计质量研究（Becker et al.，1998；Ashbaugh et al.，2003）。该指标的测度方法参见英文正文第6章6.2.2节和等式（6-1）。

6.2.3 来自香港审计师的溢出效应的测度

现有文献中缺乏对香港审计师可能发挥的溢出效应的测度，对此，本书尝试建立新的测度方法。根据相关规定，虽然公司的A股和H股财务报表分别依据不同的会计准则编制，但对于同一交易事项，一家公司不允许在其两套财务报表中采用不同的会计估计（中国证券监督管理委员会，2001）。由此，一家公司在编制A股和H股财务报表时，既要保证两套财务报表所基于的会计假设的一致性，又在会计政策的选择方面具有一定的灵活性。这种灵活性意味着，公司必须在年度报告中解释和调整两套财务报表之间的差异，与此同时，受雇审计师也应当密切关注公司年报中披露的差异调整是否真实、完整。基于以上限制，由香港审计师负责的、更为严格的H股报表审计，可

能能够抑制同一公司 A 股财务报表中的盈余管理，从而对该公司由内地审计师负责的 A 股报表审计产生积极的溢出效应（Ke et al.，2015）。据此，本书认为，一家公司的 A 股审计质量与 H 股审计质量之间的差距越小，反映出香港审计师负责的 H 股报表审计对内地审计师负责的 A 股报表审计的约束作用越强，也就是说，来自香港审计师的溢出效应越积极。基于以上论述，对于保留双重审计的公司，本书首先计算其经内地审计师审计的 A 股报表异常营运资本应计项目绝对值（$|AWCA|_{A\text{-}share_{t,i}}$），以及其经香港审计师审计的 H 股报表异常营运资本应计项目绝对值（$|AWCA|_{H\text{-}share_{t,i}}$），然后取二者之差的绝对值（$\left||AWCA|_{H\text{-}share_{t,i}}-|AWCA|_{A\text{-}share_{t,i}}\right|$），以此衡量保留双重审计的公司 A 股审计质量与 H 股审计质量之间的差距。考虑到以变量越大的值对应越积极的溢出效应显得更为直观，本书进一步取上述差值绝对值的负值（$-\left||AWCA|_{H\text{-}share_{t,i}}-|AWCA|_{A\text{-}share_{t,i}}\right|$），构建测度来自香港审计师的溢出效应的变量。具体而言，本书定义变量 $Spillover_{t,i}$，当公司保留双重审计时，$Spillover_{t,i}$ 等于 $-\left||AWCA|_{H\text{-}share_{t,i}}-|AWCA|_{A\text{-}share_{t,i}}\right|$；当公司放弃双重审计后，$Spillover_{t,i}$ 等于 0。根据这一定义，对于一家保留双重审计的公司而言，$Spillover_{t,i}$ 值越大，表示来自香港审计师的溢出效应越积极。

6.2.4 实证模型

检验假设 H9 的实证模型参见英文正文第 6 章 6.2.4.1 节等式（6-2）（水平模型）、等式（6-3）（变化模型）。在等式（6-2）中，本书重点关注变量 $Spillover_{t,i}$，该变量的系数反映了来自香港审计师的溢出效应对保留双重审计的公司的审计质量的影响；在等式（6-3）中，本书重点关注变量 $\Delta Spillover_{t,i}$（等于 $Spillover_{t,i}$ 与 $Spillover_{t-1,i}$ 之差），该变量的系数反映了来自香港审计师的溢出效应的变化对保留双重审计的公司的审计质量变化的影响。其他变量的定义参见表 6-2。

为引出检验假设 H10 的实证模型，本书首先检验放弃双重审计的公司是否确实比保留双重审计的公司审计质量更低，以便为基于前人发现做出的推测（公司在放弃双重审计之后，审计质量很可能下降）提供直接的证据。有关实证模型参见英文正文第 6 章 6.2.4.2 节等式（6-4）（水平模型）。在等式（6-4）中，本书重点关注变量 $CANCEL_{t,i}$（虚拟变量，在公司放弃双重审计后为 1，否则为 0），该变量的系数反映了相比保留双重审计，放弃双重审计对审计质量的影响。其他变量的定义参见表 6-2。

需要说明的是，即便对等式（6-4）引入 $CANCEL_{t,i}$ 和 $Spillover_{t,i}$ 的交互项，也无法检验来自香港审计师的积极溢出效应的丧失如何影响公司在放弃双重审计之后的审计质量下降（假设 H10）。这是因为，变量 $Spillover_{t,i}$ 只能测度在公司放弃双重审计之前来自香港审计师的积极溢出效应；当公司放弃双重审计之后，$Spillover_{t,i}$ 的值全部为 0。根据这一变量定义，将 $CANCEL_{t,i}$ 与 $Spillover_{t,i}$ 交乘缺乏实证意义，因而如果仅依靠对审计质量的水平分析，难以反映来自香港审计师的积极溢出效应的丧失有何影响。相比之下，假设 H10 更适合利用变化分析进行检验。

基于此，本章引出检验假设 H10 的实证模型，参见英文正文第 6 章 6.2.4.2 节和等式（6-5）（变化模型）。在等式（6-5）中，本书重点关注交互项 $CANCEL_{t,i} \times \Delta Spillover_{t,i}$。根据定义，变量 $CANCEL_{t,i}$ 在公司放弃双重审计后等于 1，否则等于 0；变量 $Spillover_{t,i}$ 在公司保留双重审计时等于 $-\left| |AWCA|_{H\text{-}share\,t,i} - |AWCA|_{A\text{-}share\,t,i} \right|$，在公司放弃双重审计后等于 0。据此，当 $CANCEL_{t,i}$ 等于 1 时，在公司放弃双重审计的当年，交互项 $CANCEL_{t,i} \times \Delta Spillover_{t,i}$ 等于 $0-Spillover_{t-1,i}$，而其后几年，交互项 $CANCEL_{t,i} \times \Delta Spillover_{t,i}$ 等于 0。由此，交互项 $CANCEL_{t,i} \times \Delta Spillover_{t,i}$ 的非零取值就反映了来自香港审计师的积极溢出效应的丧失。也就是说，该交互项能够有效捕捉到这一溢出效应的丧失。其他变量的定义参见表 6-2。

6.3 实证分析

6.3.1 样本分布概况

结果显示，样本公司在是否放弃双重审计方面存在明显的差异性，自 2010 年起，少数公司先后放弃了双重审计。详细的样本分布概况参见英文正文第 6 章 6.3.1 节和表 6-3。

6.3.2 描述性统计

参见英文正文第 6 章 6.3.2 节和表 6-4 Panel A。

6.3.3 组间差异分析

结果显示，放弃双重审计的样本比保留双重审计的样本审计质量显著更低，与前人得出的间接证据（未采用双重审计的 A 股公司的审计质量低于采用双重审计的 A+H 股公司）相互印证。详细结果参见英文正文第 6 章 6. 3. 3 节和表 6-4 Panel B。

6. 3. 4 香港审计师与内地审计师审计质量的比较

在用多元回归分析检验假设之前，本书首先比较参与双重审计的香港审计师与内地审计师之间的审计质量。结果显示，双重审计的具体实践大体上符合相关规定，确保公司在其 A 股和 H 股财务报表中对同一事项所用的会计估计不存在实质性差异；总体来看，在双重审计过程中，香港审计师对内地审计师具有一定的积极溢出效应。详细的结果及分析参见英文正文第 6 章 6. 3. 4 节和表 6-5。

6. 3. 5 多元回归分析

6. 3. 5. 1 对假设 H9 的检验

英文正文表 6-6 报告了对假设 H9 的检验结果。本书首先在保留双重审计的样本中对等式（6-2）进行回归，结果如表 6-6 Panel A 第（1）列所示，$Spillover_{t,i}$的回归系数为负，且在 0. 05 的水平上统计显著，表明来自香港审计师的溢出效应越积极，保留双重审计的公司的异常应计项目绝对值越小，即，审计质量越高，支持了假设 H9。其次，本书在保留双重审计的样本中对等式（6-3）进行回归，表 6-6 Panel A 第（2）列显示，$\Delta Spillover_{t,i}$的回归系数为负，且在 0. 05 的水平上统计显著，表明来自香港审计师的积极溢出效应的增强对保留双重审计的公司审计质量的提升具有正向影响，进一步支持了假设 H9。此外，在排除了公司更换不同水准的审计师对结果的潜在影响后，主要结论依然成立。以上结果及详细分析请参见英文正文第 6 章 6. 3. 5. 1 节和表 6-6。

6. 3. 5. 2 假设 H10 的检验

表 6-6 还报告了对假设 H10 的检验结果。本书首先在全样本中对等式（6-4）进行回归，结果如表 6-6 Panel A 第（3）列所示，$CANCEL_{t,i}$的回归系数为正，且在 0. 05 的水平上统计显著，表明放弃双重审计的样本的审计质量低于保留双重审计的样本。这一结果证实了放弃双重审计会损害审计质量。另外，本书还对等式（6-4）引入公司固定效应，以实现在公司内部的比较、排除公司特征对结果的影响，表 6-6 Panel A 第（4）列显示，$CANCEL_{t,i}$的回

归系数依然显著为正。

接下来，本书在全样本中对等式（6-5）进行回归，结果如表 6-6 Panel A 第（5）列所示，$CANCEL_{t,i} \times \Delta Spillover_{t,i}$的回归系数为正，且在 0.05 的水平上统计显著，表明公司放弃双重审计后，来自香港审计师的积极溢出效应的丧失与审计质量的下降之间存在显著的正向关系，支持了假设 H10。这一结果证实，放弃双重审计使公司失去了来自香港审计师的积极溢出效应，该效应的丧失是导致公司放弃双重审计后审计质量下降的主要原因。

此外，在排除了公司更换不同水准的审计师对结果的潜在影响后，主要结论依然成立。

以上结果及详细分析参见英文正文第 6 章 6.3.5.2 节和表 6-6。

6.3.6 稳健性检验

稳健性检验排除了以下几种其他可能的解释。

6.3.6.1 会计准则国际趋同

如第 3 章 3.1 节所述，双重审计管制取消伴随着会计准则国际趋同。因此，本书构建的变量（$Spillover_{t,i}$）可能测度的是会计准则国际趋同，而非与审计师相关的溢出效应。为排除这一可能的解释，本章基于第 4 章 4.3.5.2 节的做法，对所有保留双重审计的样本，计算其会计准则趋同指数，然后定义变量 $Con_{t,i}$（该变量在公司保留双重审计时等于对应的会计准则趋同指数的值，在公司放弃双重审计后等于 0）。接下来，本书将 $Con_{t,i}$（$\Delta Con_{t,i}$）作为控制变量引入等式（6-2）［等式（6-3）和等式（6-5）］进行回归，主要结论依然成立。以上结果及详细分析请参见英文正文第 6 章 6.3.6.1 节和表 6-7。

6.3.6.2 审计师共享同一品牌

据本书统计，在保留双重审计的样本中，一家公司的内地审计师和香港审计师属于同一国际品牌的情况占绝大多数。因此，公司保留双重审计时较高的审计质量，可能是两家审计师维护共享品牌声誉的结果，而非来自香港审计师的积极溢出效应的产物。为排除这一可能性，本书定义表示审计师共享同一品牌的变量，将其水平形式（变化形式）作为控制变量引入等式（6-2）［等式（6-3）和等式（6-5）］进行回归，结果依然是稳健的。详细内容请参见英文正文第 6 章 6.3.6.2 节和表 6-8。

6.3.6.3 排除不可观测因素的影响

考虑到在双重审计管制取消后，公司可以自行决定保留或放弃双重审计，本章的主要发现很可能受到自选择问题的影响。为解决这一内生性问题，本章采用混杂变量影响阈值分析（ITCV）进行处理。分析发现，自选择偏差对本章的主要结论不存在严重影响。详细内容参见英文正文第 6 章 6.3.6.3 节和表 6-9。

6.3.6.4 溢出效应的其他测度

在本章的主要分析中，审计质量的测度变量和溢出效应的测度变量中均涉及 A 股报表异常营运资本应计项目，将二者分别作为因变量和自变量放入同一等式进行回归，可能存在一定的计量问题。对此，本书基于 H 股报表异常营运资本应计项目绝对值，构建变量 $Spillover\_H_{t,i}$（该变量在公司保留双重审计时等于 H 股报表异常营运资本应计项目绝对值的负值，在公司放弃双重审计后等于 0），较为粗略地衡量来自香港审计师的溢出效应，然后将 $Spillover\_H_{t,i}$（$\Delta Spillover\_H_{t,i}$）代替 $Spillover_{t,i}$（$\Delta Spillover_{t,i}$）放入等式（6-2）［等式（6-3）和等式（6-5）］进行回归，所得结论与主要分析中的一致。详细内容参见英文正文第 6 章 6.3.6.4 节和表 6-10 Panel A。

6.3.6.5 审计质量的其他测度

本章还利用 A 股报表可操纵性应计项目的绝对值衡量审计质量，进行稳健性检验。详细内容请参见英文正文第 6 章 6.3.6.5 节和表 6-10 Panel B。

6.4 结果讨论

本章对假设 H9、H10 进行检验，得出以下实证结果：①双重审计的具体实践大体上符合相关规定，确保公司在其 A 股和 H 股财务报表中对同一事项所用的会计估计不存在实质性差异；②总体来看，在双重审计过程中，香港审计师对内地审计师具有一定的积极溢出效应；③来自香港审计师的溢出效应越积极，保留双重审计的公司的审计质量越高；④公司放弃双重审计后，来自香港审计师的积极溢出效应的丧失与审计质量的下降之间存在显著的正向关系。此外，在控制了会计准则国际趋同、审计师共享同一品牌、不可观测因素的影响后，以及在采用其他指标衡量溢出效应、审计质量时，主要结果依然是稳健的。

与基于以往研究做出的推测（公司放弃双重审计后，审计质量会有所下降）相一致，以上结果证实了在双重审计过程中，香港审计师对内地审计师产生了积极的溢出效应，这一溢出效应使保留双重审计的公司拥有较高的审计质量，而该效应的丧失是导致放弃双重审计的公司审计质量下降的主要原因。具体而言，虽然有关部门取消双重审计管制是出于提高审计效率、降低公司上市成本等考虑，但这一政策变更也被质疑可能引起审计质量下降：公司放弃双重审计可能阻碍高质量的香港审计师向低质量的内地审计师发挥积极的溢出效应。然而，由于这一溢出效应不能被直接观察到，以往研究仅停留在论述层面，忽视了相关的实证工作。为弥补前人研究的不足，本章建立了直接、有效的测度方法，衡量来自香港审计师的溢出效应，然后通过严谨的实证分析，获得了上述发现。

总而言之，本章的实证发现表明，双重审计过程中切实存在来自香港审计师的积极溢出效应，这一溢出效应是双重审计制度帮助维持较高审计质量的重要内在机制；公司的审计质量在其放弃双重审计后有所下降，而该溢出效应的丧失是导致审计质量下降的主要原因。也就是说，双重审计管制取消对审计质量产生了消极的影响。对本章所有假设检验情况的汇总，参见英文正文中的表 6-11。

7 结论与展望

通过上述各章节的理论分析与实证检验，本书考察了双重审计管制取消对资本市场和审计市场产生的经济后果。作为研究内容的最后一部分，本章总结主要研究结论，阐明本研究的创新点，提出政策启示，最后指出本书的局限性和今后的研究方向。

7.1 研究结论

A+H 股双重审计管制虽然已被监管部门取消，但自该管制取消以来，大部分 A+H 股公司依然同时雇用境内外两家会计师事务所实施审计。双重审计有助于保持审计师独立性、提升公司治理水平、保证投资者获取准确完整的会计信息、帮助本土会计师事务所积累经验，投资者十分关心双重审计管制的取消会给我国市场造成哪些影响。此外，双重审计制度及其变迁也引发了学术界广泛而持续的关注。本书通过理论分析和实证检验，探究了双重审计管制取消对资本市场和审计市场可能产生的经济后果。研究发现，在资本市场上，公司在管制取消前强制接受双重审计时的权益成本低于公司在管制取消后自愿采用双重审计时的权益成本；管制取消后，自愿采用双重审计的公司的权益成本低于仅接受单一审计的公司的权益成本；此外，强制双重审计和自愿双重审计对权益成本的抑制作用在股权融资需求更强、代理成本更高的公司中更为显著；强制双重审计对权益成本的抑制作用未被其他自愿审计形式削弱，而自愿双重审计对权益成本的抑制作用则会被其他自愿审计形式替代。另外，在审计市场上，来自香港审计师的溢出效应越积极，保留双重审计的公司审计质量越高；公司放弃双重审计后，这一积极溢出效应的丧失与审计质量的下降之间存在显著的正向关系。总体来说，本书研究主要发现，双重审计管制取消对我国资本市场和审计市场均产生了消极影响。

7.2 政策启示

第一，监管部门应当审慎评价双重审计管制取消所带来的成本与后果。总体而言，本书的结论体现出这一政策变更产生的一些消极影响，如导致权益成本增加、审计质量降低。前者反映出在双重审计管制取消后，投资者对于公司管理层可能做出损害股东利益的自利行为的疑虑增加；后者则证实了实务界对审计质量可能因公司放弃双重审计而受损的疑虑。基于此，放弃双重审计难以在不增加投资者怀疑或不牺牲审计质量的前提下帮助公司节约审计成本。在 A+H 股市场，放弃双重审计尚未形成主要趋势，本研究在一定程度上反映出大多数公司在管制取消多年后依旧坚持双重审计的缘由，提醒监管部门审慎评估这一政策变更的适当性。

第二，实现本土会计师事务所真正做大做强是一项漫长而艰巨的任务。近年来，政府和市场对内地会计师事务所做大做强的呼声日益增高，有关部门为扶持大规模会计师事务所的发展做出了诸多努力。但就目前看来，本土事务所的业绩表现并不尽如人意。与这一现实相呼应，本书的结论显示，公司在放弃双重审计后 A 股审计质量显著下降，并且这一审计质量下降主要是由来自香港审计师的积极溢出效应的丧失所导致的。由此可见，尽管监管部门为内地审计行业的发展提供了许多政策支持，然而想要使本土事务所真正具备能够取代国际顶尖事务所的质量和水准，依然任重而道远。

7.3 主要创新点

相比于以往文献，本研究主要有如下三个创新点。

第一，本书理论解释并实证检验了强制双重审计和自愿双重审计能够不同程度地降低权益成本，为双重审计管制取消的资本市场后果提供了经验证据。以往研究局限于考察双重审计管制取消的审计后果，且多在双重审计管制取消前时段和取消后时段之间，或在双重审计公司和单一审计公司之间进行比较分析。本书则关注这一政策变更可能对资本市场造成的影响，并且将双重审计区分为强制双重审计和自愿双重审计两种形式，基于遵循效应理论和信号效应理论，分别分析二者对于权益成本的影响机制。基于 GLS 模型测算权益成本指标，并在实证分析中有效控制已审财务信息的影响，本书发现，公司在管制取消前强制接受双重审计时的权益成本比在管制取消后自愿采用双重审计时的权益成本要低，而管制取消后自愿采用双重审计的公司的权益成本比仅接受单一审计的公司的权益成本要低。本书的理论分析和相关研究结论表明，双重审计管制取消影响了投资者的认知和决策，进而对资本市场产生了实质性的经济后果，拓展了关于双重审计的研究和权益成本的文献，还有助于理解公司对双重审计强制要求的遵循和对双重审计的自愿选择分别对权益成本所起的作用。

第二，本书深入揭示了香港审计师对内地审计师的积极溢出效应的丧失，是导致公司放弃双重审计后审计质量下降的主要内在机制。以往研究虽然探讨了双重审计管制取消的审计后果，但欠缺对该政策变更中驱动审计质量发生变化的内在机制的分析与验证。本书提供新的经验证据，以异常应计项目衡量审计质量，测度来自香港审计师的溢出效应，采用变化分析的方法，证实了来自香港审计师的积极溢出效应有助于保留双重审计的公司维持较高的审计质量，且这一积极溢出效应的丧失是公司放弃双重审计后审计质量受损的主要原因。相比前人研究，本书的分析有效排除了交叉上市、会计准则国际趋同、审计师共享同一品牌等因素以及不可观测因素的潜在影响，得出了严谨而稳健的结论。研究结论丰富了双重审计的相关研究和审计质量的相关文献，有助于理解来自香港审计师的积极溢出效应在双重审计制度中所扮演的至关重要的角色。

第三，本书建立了一套直接、有效的测度方法，度量双重审计过程中来自香港审计师的溢出效应。由于这一溢出效应的不可观测性，现有文献对此多限于文字论述，限制了学者们从这一角度出发深入探究双重审计背景下的审计质量问题。结合前人论述和相关规定，本书认为，由香港审计师负责的、更为严格的 H 股报表审计能够抑制一家公司 A 股报表中的盈余管理，从而对该公司由内地审计师负责的 A 股报表审计产生积极的溢出效应；一家保留双重审计的公司的 A 股与 H 股审计质量之间的差距越小，反映出 H 股报表审计对 A 股报表审计的约束作用越强，即来自香港审计师的溢出效应越积极。基于此，本书从盈余管理的角度，以异常应计项目衡量审计质量，在计算保留双重审计的公司 A 股和 H 股报表异常应计项目绝对值之间距离的基础上，形成来自香港审计师的溢出效应的代理变量。相比以往研究，本书通过构建新的变量，直观地呈现了香港审计师通过双重审计过程对内地审计师发挥的溢出效应，填补了现有研究在实证工作方面的缺失，有助于推动双重审计相关文献和审计质量相关研究的发展。

7.4 局限性与研究展望

尽管本研究获得了一些重要的研究成果，具有一定的学术贡献和实践意义，但仍存在一些不足之处。例如，本书未考虑双重审计管制取消的积极影响，未检验双重审计管制取消的审计市场后果与资本市场后果之间的关系，未考察双重审计管制取消对 H 股市场可能产生的经济后果等。期待未来的研究能够从这些角度进行进一步的探索和挖掘。

后　记

本书基于我的博士学位论文修改完善而成，也是我主持的国家自然科学基金青年项目和西北大学国家社科基金项目孵化计划的阶段性成果。本书从选题、初稿、修改、定稿到出版都离不开贵人相助，在此谨向他们表达最诚挚的谢意。

感谢我的两位导师，西安交通大学田高良教授和香港城市大学黄敏刚副教授，引领我走上学术道路，为我指明前进方向，谆谆教诲助我成长。

感谢我的工作单位西北大学及所在经济管理学院的各位领导和老师，为本书的出版和本人的科研工作提供大力支持与无私帮助。

感谢来自西安交通大学、西北工业大学、香港城市大学、岭南大学等高校管理学院和商学院的各位专家学者，提出宝贵意见与建议，使本书的水平得到极大提升。

感谢同门兄弟姐妹们的鼓励和启发，感谢家人和朋友的理解与陪伴，为本人工作的顺利开展提供莫大助力。